D1759195

CONCEIVING THE EMBRYO

Conceiving the Embryo

Ethics, Law and Practice
in Human Embryology

Editor

DONALD EVANS

Director, Centre for Philosophy and Health Care
University of Wales, Swansea
Swansea, Wales

Assistant Editor

NEIL PICKERING

Centre for Philosophy and Health Care
University of Wales, Swansea
Swansea, Wales

Martinus Nijhoff Publishers

The Hague / London / Boston

Library of Congress Cataloging-in-Publication Data

ISBN 90-411-0208-6
ISBN 90-411-0209-4 (Set)

Published by Kluwer Law International,
P.O. Box 85889, 2508 CN The Hague, The Netherlands.

Sold and distributed in the U.S.A. and Canada
by Kluwer Law International,
675 Massachusetts Avenue, Cambridge, MA 02139, U.S.A.

In all other countries, sold and distributed
by Kluwer Law International,
P.O. Box 85889, 2508 CN The Hague, The Netherlands.

Printed on acid-free paper

All Rights Reserved
© 1996 Kluwer Law International
Kluwer Law International incorporates the publishing programmes of
Graham & Trotman Ltd, Kluwer Law and Taxation Publishers,
and Martinus Nijhoff Publishers.

No part of the material protected by this copyright notice may be reproduced or
utilized in any form or by any means, electronic or mechanical,
including photocopying, recording, or by any information storage and
retrieval system, without written permission from the copyright owner.

Printed in the Netherlands

To the memory of Patrick Steptoe

Clinician and pioneer of IVF services

CONTENTS

ACKNOWLEGEMENTS

Most of the chapters in this volume and in its companion volume *Creating the Child* were written in the course of a concerted action, executed from 1992-1995 and financed by the European Commission BIOMED I project, entitled *Fertility, infertility and the human embryo: the ethics, law and practice of assisted procreation* and an extension to that action involving East and Central European scholars financed by the PECO funds of the European Commission.

I was privileged to coordinate this action and wish to record my thanks to all the scholars who participated in it, not all of whom are represented on the pages of these volumes. Those whose writings appear here gained much from discussion with those who have not contributed chapters but who attended research conferences and gave generously of their time and expertise.

Some additional chapters have been provided by scholars who were consulted during the concerted action and others who learned of it and offered assistance in providing complementary material.

The action was coordinated from the Centre for Philosophy and Health Care at the University of Wales Swansea from which the impetus for the study originated. This was in no small part due to the collaboration between the Centre in its early days and Dr. Patrick Steptoe the pioneer of IVF treatment. As a clinician he was always concerned about the ethical dimensions of his practice and sought advice from a wide range of people outside medicine. He discussed his worries with staff and students at the Centre in the mid nineteen eighties and in so doing stimulated interest in this novel and challenging area of clinical practice. The two volumes are dedicated to his memory.

Thanks are due to the administrative staff of the Centre, Mrs. Anne Edwards and Miss Gwyneth Abbott, who worked extremely hard to conquer the daunting challenges presented by the coordination of the work of over fifty researchers in some twenty countries.

Some of the material presented in this volume has appeared in some form elsewhere and thanks are due to the following for permission to republish:

Literatura Medica Publishers Ltd for permission to republish parts of 'A müvi abortusz a bioetika szemszögéböl' (Artificial abortion in the light of bioethics) in József Kovács' paper 'The idea of brain-birth in connection with the moral status of the embryo and the foetus'.

The *Journal of Medical Ethics* for permission to reprint Donald Evans' paper 'Procuring gametes for research and therapy' which appeared originally as a guest editorial *Journal of Medical Ethics* 21, October 1995, pp.1-4.

xii

I should like to acknowledge the support of the University of Wales Swansea which has enabled both the coordination of the concerted action and the editing of this volume and its companion. The process of editing would have been impossible without the dedication of my able Assistant Editor, Neil Pickering. Finally thanks are due to my wife Ann who has seen much less of me during the past three years than either of us would have chosen and without whose understanding these books would never have materialised.

Donald Evans
Swansea, January 1996

CONTRIBUTORS

Stephen Beasley, Community Pharmacist, R.A. Hopkins Ltd., 152 Sundon Park Road, Luton, Beds LU3 3AH, England.

Judge Christian Byk, Associate Professor of Law, University of Poitiers, France.

Panagiota Dalla-Vorgia, Department of Hygiene and Epidemiology, University of Athens Medical School, Greece.

Prof. Dr. Drs. h.c. Erwin Deutsch, Faculty of Law, University of Göttingen, Germany.

Donald Evans, Centre for Philosophy and Health Care, University of Wales, Swansea, Singleton Park, Swansea, Wales.

Martyn Evans, Centre for Philosophy and Health Care, University of Wales, Swansea, Singleton Park, Swansea, Wales.

Simon Fishel, NURTURE, Department of Obstetrics and Gynaecology, University Hospital, Queen's Medical Centre, Nottingham, England.

Søren Holm, Department of Medical Philosophy and Clinical Theory, University of Copenhagen, Blegdamsvej 3, DK-2200 N, Copenhagen, Denmark.

Arlene Judith Klotzko, J.D., Research Fellow in Medical Law and Ethics, The London Hospital Medical College, England, Research Fellow, The Center for Bioethics and Health Law, Utrecht University, The Netherlands.

Dr. József Kovács, Semmelweis University of Medicine, Institute of Behavioural Sciences, Department of Bioethics, Budapest POB 370, H-1445, Hungary.

Wiesław Lang, Faculty of Law and Administration, Nicolas Copernicus University, Toruń, Poland.

Jaime Vidal Martínez, Profesor Titular de Derecho Civil, Departmento de Derecho Civil, Universitat de València, Spain.

Alex Mauron, Fondation Louis Jeantet de Médecine, C.P. 277, CH-1211 Genève 17, Switzerland.

Maurizio Mori, Politeia. Centro per la formazione in politica ed etica, Milano, Italy. Editor *Bioetica. Rivista Interdisciplinare.*

Associate Professor of Law Linda Nielsen, Dr. juris, Faculty of Law, The University of Copenhagen, Denmark. Member of the Danish Council of Ethics.

Vassil Prodanov, Institute of Philosophical Research, Sofia 1000, Patriarch Evtimii 6, Bulgaria

Alicja Przyłuska-Fiszer, Zakład Historii Medycyny i Filozofii, Akademia Medyczna, ul. Złota 7, 00-019 Warszawa, Poland.

Knut W. Ruyter, Center for Medical Ethics, University of Oslo, Norway.

Judit Sándor J.D. LLM, Central European University, Budapest College, Hungary.

Zbigniew Szawarski, Centre for Philosophy and Health Care, University of Wales Swansea, Singleton Park, Swansea, Wales.

Jean-Marie Thévoz, Fondation Louis Jeantet de Médecine, C.P. 277, CH-1211 Genève 17, Switzerland.

Prof. dr hab. Eleonora Zielińska, Faculty of Law and Administration, Warsaw University, Poland.

LIST OF FIGURES

Introduction

1. CONCEIVING THE EMBRYO

Donald Evans
Centre for Philosophy and Health Care
University of Wales, Swansea
Singleton Park
Swansea
Wales

It might be thought a rare thing when philosophical questions have a direct bearing upon practical issues. Certainly the development of analytic philosophy during the second half of the twentieth century has apparently laid aside an interest in what might be called the big questions of nature and the world, questions with which philosophers from the time of Plato and before were very much engaged. Whether this impression is accurate or not is not a matter of concern here; suffice it to note that it is at least an understandable one. Recent developments in biology and especially in human embryology have provoked questions about the character of human life which are intimately bound up with important desires and life-plans which people have. Planning and securing one's own biological offspring are taking on new and challenging dimensions which offer both hope to many who are naturally denied the possibility of becoming parents of their own genetic heirs, and threats to long established conceptions of mankind's role in the bringing to be of new generations. At the heart of the weighty problems which confront practitioners and patients alike in the field of assisted procreation and human embryo research is the issue of the status of the human embryo.

How should the human embryo properly be conceived? If this is asked as a moral question then before we shall be able to begin to formulate an answer we shall be forced utter those selfsame words as a philosophical question. How can we know how to deal with the human embryo until we first know what it is that we are dealing with? How can we determine the ways people should be enabled to conceive human embryos, whether by use of donated gametes, surrogate wombs, technical procedures or commercial transactions before we are clear about what the implications of all these means are for the life which they facilitate or in which they intervene? If Philosophy is capable of anything then it should be capable of clarifying issues of a conceptual (*sic*) sort, that is, of helping us to get clear about what we mean when we talk of human embryos or anything else. If Philosophy can come up with some answers which are incontrovertible then such activity might make it possible for us to answer many of the questions about what we ought or ought not to do and about what we ought or ought not to allow other people to do with human embryos. But can Philosophy help us in this way? If so how far can it go? If not then how shall we decide what should or should

3

D. Evans (ed.), Conceiving the Embryo, 3–10.
© 1996 *Kluwer Law International. Printed in the Netherlands.*

not be done with human embryos?

These are among the central questions which are raised in this collection of essays. Most of them were written in the course of a coordinated research action funded by the European Commission over a period of three years from 1992-1995. The project involved philosophers, social scientists, lawyers and scientists from a large number of countries in Western, Central and Eastern Europe. These scholars set out to compare the various cultural and social contexts in which talk of the human embryo occurs, the variety of practices involving human embryos in European countries and the philosophical significance of these practices for determining the status of the human embryo, and the variety of legislation and regulation which exists in Europe governing uses of human embryos. Finally in light of the fruits of this research the group were concerned to ask whether there should be public control of activities involving the human embryo and whether it would be possible and desirable for these to be harmonised throughout European countries.

Biological facts concerning the human embryo have come to light during the past twenty years or so (indeed new facts are emerging almost by the month) which force us to reconsider at least the assumptions which many of us might have made about the earliest stages of the development of human lives. It is now possible to describe the very earliest stages of the development of human lives in detail which hitherto has been unimaginable.[1] These details have had a profound impact on the way in which some observers view the human embryo but have left others unmoved. The nature of these changes or the resolution with which prior views are maintained is of interest to philosophical enquiry. What is the status of such knowledge and how is it related to the moral issues of human embryo research and manipulation? For example, in much philosophical talk about persons various criteria are called for to determine whether an entity is a person or not and most notable amongst them are rationality and sentience.[2] Without a developed nervous system no living entity can satisfy either of these criteria. Thus the definitive account of early embryological development of the human being which is now possible *vis-a-vis* the development of the central nervous system appears unquestionably to rule out the possibility that the very early embryo is a person, and this, it might be thought, has considerable importance in determining what can or cannot be done to such entities.[3] It would appear then that there is a direct relationship between the biological facts and the moral possibilities. But things are not always as they appear to be and here we must look carefully at the nature of the argument employed by the proponent of the non-person or pre-person account of the early embryo.

There are numbers of ways in which philosophical argumentation proceeds which are illustrated in the essays which follow. Perhaps the line of argument most threatening to the position which accords the early embryo the moral status of a person from the 'moment' of fertilisation is that which endeavours to demonstrate that one of the biological facts recently brought to light dictates that we no longer regard the early embryo as *a* human life at all and that to maintain such a perception would be to fly in the face of logic. Of course people cannot be forced to think rationally and they might in fact persist in their earlier view but that would have been shown to be a confused view and one not worthy of defence - and certainly not one on which regulation of the treatment of human embryos should be based. This argument does not simply deny to the early embryo a quality without which it could not be described as a *human* being - the kind of argument referred to above. Rather it denies to the early embryo the possibility of being regarded as *a* life at all and only consequently as being a life of a certain sort, that is a human life. The embryological fact appealed to in such arguments concerns the individuation of the embryo.[4] Biology claims to have shown that at the four cell stage in a normal fertilised ovum each cell is both pluripotential (has the capability itself of developing into a complete embryo) and totipotential (has the capability of becoming either embryonic or placental tissue). It has also shown that at such a stage with some fertilised ova there is no potential for development into an embryo and that with others there is a possibility of splitting and the production of monozygotic twins.[5] Each of these possibilities places a question mark over the description of the early embryo as *a* life. This is not to question that it is alive or that it is human, any more than one questions this in the case of one of my blood cells. It is to question that the cell mass constitutes a life in its own right and that therefore any moral rights attach to it or that its existence imposes any moral obligations on others. The confusion between biological individuality and human individuation is exploited by those who argue that the biological development of the early embryo into the foetus into the person demonstrates that throughout we are involved with a human life.[6] The strongest interpretation of the label *undifferentiated cell* would commit us to the view that biology has already done enough to establish this position.[7] Others might favour a weaker interpretation by resisting the notion of a stochastic (random) development of embryo into foetus and holding out the possibility that there may yet be more information to be yielded by biological investigation which would demonstrate that there are determining factors built into the early cells which dictate the possibility of twinning thus enabling us to talk of two human lives at the earliest stage.[8] The notion of an undifferentiated cell employed here would simply be that there is no difference between the cells as far as is currently known - leaving open the possibility of revision in the light of later biological discovery. With respect to the fertilised cell destined for non-development into a foetus, for example one which would become a hydatidiform mole, it could be claimed that the nature of the tissue ruled it out of consideration as a human being by its not constituting a genuine human genotype.[9]

Proponents of the strong view described above might describe proponents of the weaker view as clutching at straws in order to preserve a deep-going conception of the nature of human life. Whilst this is a possibility in given cases it cannot be demonstrated that it must be so. Indeed there are many kinds of influences which not only determine which conclusions we are reluctant to draw whatever the arguments presented to us but also, more importantly, determine what considerations weigh heavily with us in argumentation. That is, whether a consideration counts as a good reason for drawing a given conclusion may vary from person to person within limits.[10] These limits may be imposed by a variety of cultural or social settings which together identify people and mark out the limits of rationality.[11] Indeed the variety of discourses in which the notion of the embryo figures may embody cultural and social determinants which may be restricted more or less to identifiable geographical and historical settings: for example the language of biology, as we have seen, crosses such boundaries setting up as it were a new cultural context which might sit more uncomfortably in some of these settings than others. The interests of various social groups in addition to scientists might produce similar tensions.[12] This casts doubt on the authority of biological description as being definitive in discussions of the status of the early human embryo and leaves room for radical moral disagreement. Lest it be thought that philosophical reflection might come to the rescue here it should be pointed out that such disagreement is characteristic of that mode of reflection too. Thus, it might be felt that any attempt to provide a definitive account of the human embryo is inevitably destined to come to grief.[13]

So much for the moment for questions about the early human embryo. Even at later stages of development after individuation (which it is generally agreed occurs at about the fourteenth day of gestation) there is room for disagreement about what moral status the human embryo or foetus should be accorded. One approach which has occupied philosophers concerns the potential of the embryo after individuation - having now got over the problems associated with the potentiality for twinning which applied during the first fourteen days. Whether or not we regard the individuated embryo as a human being with all the attendant rights to life of human beings or not it cannot be denied that given that it has the potential for developing into what is indisputably a human person imposes certain limits upon what we should or should not do with it or to it. For example, deliberate injury of the early foetus which leads to a distorted development and the production of a crippled life would at the very least call for a moral justification.[14] This reveals that there is at least some moral considerability attaching to the foetus in terms of its potential. But how much weight such potentiality should be given is a matter of dispute. Certainly the legal status of the foetus in all countries in Europe is not that of a human being[15] and this might suggest to us that it has not been thought generally that potential for development into a human being carries with it the moral force which full personhood carries. However there may be a significant gap between moral and legal status so that the legal analysis offers us supporting but not conclusive evidence for the moral conclusion.

The main problem with the potentiality argument concerns the retrospective and prospective limits of the notion of potential, that is how far back and how far forward potential should be identified and respected.[16] For example was the sperm which played a part in my generation potentially me? Was it also potentially a multiplicity of other people who never materialised (because my father happened not to have had relations with different women from my mother)? Do all sperm have the potential to become people (given that they outnumber the oocytes in the world by a factor of millions in any given week)? Or again does the fact that I am potentially dust justify someone's treating me like dirt? Extreme forms of the potentiality argument will run into all kinds of difficulties associated with these questions. They will have serious implications for the possibility of contraception, abortion and the limitation rather than the promotion of the world's population. For many the consequences of the strict argument from potential will constitute a *reductio ad absurdam* of the position. But we have to be careful not to discard the important implications of potentiality with the ridiculous and the presentation of some *via media* might enable us to avoid this mistake and accord *prima facie* rights to human embryos.[17] Such an account as that suggested in this volume provides us with a view of the developing moral considerability of the human foetus, itself a view espoused by numerous philosophers.[18]

None of the arguments so far referred to will satisfy all enquirers into the status of the human embryo for the reasons alluded to. This seems to leave us in a state of some uncertainty about the matter. We may try to resolve this uncertainty by means of a casuistic approach favoured in much debate in philosophical theology. Here the disputant moves by analogy from an agreed case of relative certainty to other cases of less certainty and searches for similarities to help resolve doubt about the latter cases. But one might then be left with simply an unreasonable doubt - that is a doubt of the form 'It cannot be conclusively proved that the embryo is not a person so we cannot know whether it is so'. That is, because absolute certainty is unrealisable it would be unreasonable and indefensible to proceed with a given course of action which might involve the destruction of an embryo. But we rarely enjoy absolute certainty about anything in this world and human action is judged morally in the light of this fact. A person is judged for his actions on the basis of what it is reasonable to believe is the case in any given situation not on the basis of what is absolutely and demonstrably certain. The tradition of tutiorism in moral theology is also based on this understanding. It might be suggested that where there is any element of uncertainty about so serious a matter as to whether a life is a human life then we ought to act with supreme caution in how we treat it, and most certainly where we plan to do it harm or even extinguish it. Such a tutioristic course is taken in much debate in philosophical theology about whether the embryo is a person. But it is a misuse of this approach to argue that given the lack of absolute certainty we ought to err, if at all, in the direction of caution and ban all destruction of human embryos whatever the circumstances. This is because the doubt in question can be regarded as unreasonable.[19] Once this is conceded however it does not follow that human embryos should be capriciously destroyed. All that has been conceded is that it is not always wrong to destroy human embryos but this is far from saying that it is always right to do so. Which circumstances determine whether and when it is right have yet to be worked out. That is, though we may not wish to accord full personhood to the embryo or foetus we may yet have certain moral responsibilities to it.[20]

Given that the possibility of reaching consensus on the moral status of the embryo is in practical terms well nigh impossible given the very different frameworks we have identified in terms of which the embryo is conceived, what are we to recommend in terms of regulating practice involving the embryo and human embryo research? Perhaps the first question to ask is whether any regulation is required and if so on what grounds. It is clear that there is great scope for commercial exploitation of human embryo research and embryo manipulation for their application in assisted procreation though it is doubtful whether there is much scope for such research in the search for basic knowledge much of which can be gleaned in other ways without sacrificing human embryos.[21] However given the character of the anxiety experienced by sub-fertile couples through their frustated desire to parent their own biological children - an anxiety which is ripe for exploitation - and the natural inquisitiveness of the scientific mind it can be reasonably expected that in the absence of regulation procedures will be carried out on human embryos and foetuses, and such early developmental forms of human lives will be subjected to forms of commercial exploitation which would cause offence to the vast majority of citizens of the countries represented in the research action of which the chapters in this volume form a part. Which procedures and forms these would be are best identified by examining the consensus which already exists in legislative control of embryo research and the use of embryos in practice in European countries. Current consensus proscribes, for example, the commercialisation of gametes and zygotes, the cloning of embryos and the blending of animals and human beings.[22] The sources of the consensus are to be found in shared values throughout the European countries but the manner in which those values are cashed out in reality varies according to various historical, social and cultural factors.[23] For example the protection of the value of human life can be seen in both the ban on embryo research in Germany and the freedom to research on embryos subject to certain conditions in the United Kingdom. In the former case it might be argued that the dignity of human life is sacrificed by the deliberate destruction of such life in however early a form whatever the incidental gains whereas in the latter case the fruit of the research is thought to enhance the possible quality of life of future children and of the parents who would otherwise be denied the supposed human right of founding a family.

There is, however, considerable variety in actual and planned legislation in European countries concerning human embryo research. For example compare those countries whose only protection of the early stages of human life is essentially enshrined in abortion law[24] with those which have adopted specific and detailed legislation relating to the new reproductive techniques such as France.[25] Perhaps the starkest contrast is that referred to above between the German ban on destructive research[26] and the more liberal control of the practice in the United Kingdom.[27] The lack of harmonisation of law and regulation on the use of human embryos will present problems for practitioners. For instance the provision of assisted conception services anywhere in the world can but be enhanced by the results of embryo research, as has already been established. Indeed without such research, technologies such as *in vitro* fertilisation would not be with us. Such techniques are constantly being refined by continued research. It would be irresponsible of any practitioner to operate in deliberate ignorance of and without reference to the latest research. This places practitioners in countries subject to a total ban on embryo research in a morally compromised position. Such bans are also prone to drive such research underground where it escapes the scrutiny of public control.[28]

There is therefore a good case to be made for public control of the use of embryos which would win support from a wide base. The conditions such legislation would need to satisfy would be that it be minimal and that it not be the expression of one particular moral view at the expense of ignoring others discernible amongst considerable sections of the populace.[29] If such general bans were restricted to a minimum sufficient to protect the basic sensibilities regarding the dignity of human life then national differences could be reflected in a system of correlative controls of a regulative kind - such as are found in the United Kingdom where a regulatory body oversees and controls the use of human embryos by a licensing system.[30] Such control could be variable from country to country and would have the advantage of flexibility which legislation lacks by being free to respond to changes in public opinion either in the direction of more conservative or more liberal controls as they occur. Bodies of this kind would be well placed to respond not only to changes in public opinion but also to address practical and ethical issues which arise in practice involving the use of human gametes and zygotes.[31]

Notes

(All references are to authors' works in this volume.)

1. See Fishel, S., pp.13-25.

2. See for example Mori, M., p.154 and pp.158-60; Kovács, J., p.222 and pp.228-231; and Beasley, S., p.91 and pp.102-108.

3. See Kovács, J., pp.231-242.

4. See especially Evans, D., pp.33-35, Mauron, A., pp.55-74, and Evans, M., pp.75-84.

5. See Fishel, S., pp.14-21.

6. See Mauron, A., pp.55-60 and pp.64-65, and Mori, M., pp.153-158.

7. See Evans, D., pp.34-35 and Beasley, S., pp.96-98.

8. See Evans, M., pp.82.

9. See Beasley, S., pp.94.

10. See Evans, D., pp.27-40.

11. See for example Prodanov, V., pp.135-147, for a discussion of cultural considerations and Beasley, S., pp.89-118, for a discussion of the important social consideration of religious commitment.

12. For a discussion of the influence of the interests of the scientific community and other groups on the concept of the human embryo see Szawarski, Z., pp.119-131.

13. See Thévoz, J.-M., pp.47-53.

14. See Beasley, S., pp.105-106.

15. See Lang, W., pp.249-266.

16. See Kovács, J., pp.226-227.

17. See Holm, S., pp.193-217.

18. See Przyłuska-Fiszer, A., pp.165-171.

19. See Ruyter, K., pp.181-184 and Beasley, S., pp.113-114.

20. See for example Mori, M., pp.160-161 and Ruyter, K., pp.176-177.

21. See Mauron, A., pp.283-294.

22. See, for example, Deutsch, E., p.345, Martínez, J.V., p.348.

23. See Nielsen, L., pp.331-333.

24. See Sándor, J., pp.269-274 on the Hungarian legal system and Zielińska, E., pp.277-279 on the Polish system of law governing the human embryo.

25. See Byk, C., pp.339-341.

26. See Deutsch, E., pp.343-346.

27. See Klotzko, A.J., pp.303-312.

28. For a discussion of these points see Mauron, A., p.293.

29. See Evans, D., pp.41-44 and Nielsen, L., p.334.

30. See Klotzko, A.J., pp.306-312.

31. See Evans, D., pp.315-321.

PART ONE

Biological Facts and Moral Values

2. ASSISTED CONCEPTION IN THE HUMAN - THE EMBRYOLOGICAL VIEW

Simon Fishel
NURTURE
Department of Obstetrics and Gynaecology
University Hospital
Queen's Medical Centre
Nottingham, England

1. Introduction

This paper will deal with the embryological and scientific aspects of assisted conception, the clinical aspects having been dealt with elsewhere.[1] However, on one clinical aspect it is important to reiterate that all patients undergoing *in vitro* fertilisation (IVF - this will be used as the generic term throughout this text for all aspects of assisted reproduction technologies requiring conception *in vitro*) require drugs to regulate the menstrual cycle and augment follicular growth. Various concoctions of drugs are administered to stimulate the development of multiple follicles. This became an essential feature of IVF technology since the early observations demonstrating the increasing incidence of pregnancy from 10% to 30% when one embryo versus three embryos, respectively, were transferred to the womb.[2] This led to the first ethical decision; the administration of follicular stimulants to normo-ovulatory women who, under normal circumstances, would not require any form of ovarian stimulation. The production of multiple follicles resulted in the retrieval of multiple oocytes, the conception of numerous embryos and the requirement for cryopreservation to eliminate wastage.

The human oocyte when it is ovulated/recovered from the follicle is surrounded by a specialised layer of cells - the corona radiata - encompassed within large numbers of specialised granulosa cells maintained in a sticky glycocalyx matrix called the oocyte-cumulus complex (OCC). During conventional fertilisation, either *in vitro* or *in vivo*, the fertilising spermatozoon will penetrate through the OCC matrix, between the specialised corona radiata cells to bind to the outer egg shell (zona pellucida) to achieve fertilisation. *In vitro*, however, if it is necessary to observe the oocyte directly, or to manipulate the oocyte, for example, for microinjection technology, then it is necessary to denude the oocyte of its attendant cells. At this stage the oocyte may be in one of three morphological states, (i) the germinal vesicle (GV) - the immature oocyte - (ii) metaphase I or (iii) metaphase II (fully mature oocyte), in which it has completed

13

D. Evans (ed.), Conceiving the Embryo, 13–26.
© 1996 *Kluwer Law International. Printed in the Netherlands.*

meiosis. It is this metaphase II oocyte that is able to achieve fertilisation. However, as is now well established, although the OCC looks mature and healthy, no more than 80 % will contain a fertilisable (i.e. metaphase II) oocyte: not all OCC can be classified as potentially fertile without direct observation of the oocyte per se.

2. Fertilisation

For conventional IVF all gamete/embryo culture may be carried out in a very simple salt solution with an added protein source - either human female serum, human serum albumin or a serum substitute. Spermatozoa are obtained by masturbation, or direct epididymal aspiration; and there are a few reports of successfully using testicular sperm for cases of microinjection. The spermatozoa need to be removed from the seminal plasma by repeated centrifugation and washing and suspended in the culture medium at a particular concentration depending upon the percentage morphology of the sample. It is now known that poor sperm morphology can decrease the incidence of fertilisation. In certain circumstances this can be compensated for by increasing the concentration of motile sperm in the insemination medium. The OCC is transferred to the sperm suspension and incubated under precise ambient conditions at 37°C.

Approximately 14-20 hours later the oocyte is observed for fertilisation. At this time, the OCC has been digested by the spermatozoa, leaving the specialised corona radiata cells around the oocyte (figure 2.1). This is carefully removed mechanically by aspiration through a Pasteur pipette. The denuded oocyte is then examined for the presence of pronuclei (individual nuclear membranes surrounding one complement of female chromosomes and the other complement of male chromosomes) (figure 2.2). Although it is impossible to evaluate the chromosome and genetic status of the zygote (fertilised oocyte) at this stage, the normality of fertilisation per se must be assessed. For example, if two sperm enter the oocyte simultaneously there will be three sets of chromosomes (3 pronuclei) - two male, one female. Similarly, if the oocyte, at the moment of fertilisation, fails to extrude half of its own complement of chromosomes (a second polar body) there will also be three sets of chromosomes, one male and two female. In other cases there may be four pronuclei which could be two sets of female and two sets of male chromosomes or, as a result of three sperm fertilising, three sets of male chromosomes and one set of female chromosomes. In any event, more than two sets of chromosomes (i.e. two pronuclei) would result in an abnormality. The three pronucleate zygote is not an uncommon phenomenon after conception either in vitro or in vivo; and none of these abnormalities is peculiar to conception in vitro. It can be said that one of the advantages of in vitro fertilisation is that abnormalities of fertilisation can be observed and isolated at that stage, whereas after conception in vivo miscarriage or termination would result.

Apart from penetration of the oocyte by the sperm, the oocyte itself may be 'activated' generating its own pronucleus with a haploid (half) set of chromosomes. This situation, i.e. parthenogenesis, can arise in vivo as well as in vitro.

These states of abnormality of fertilisation all generate morphologically normal cleaving embryos (figure 2.3), and experiments in mice have shown that considerable postimplantation development can be obtained from embryos containing only female chromosomes (parthenogenomes or gynogenomes) or with only male chromosomes (androgenomes).[3]

In vivo, there is a common situation called the hydatidiform mole which results in abnormal implantation and placental growth - there are no foetal parts - which can be invasive and dangerous requiring the tissue to be removed surgically. This sort of implantation is a result of two sperm penetrating the oocyte to produce a tripronucleate zygote from which the female chromosomes become extruded generating a diploid set of male only chromosomes. As two sperm have penetrated it could be a diploid male zygote containing XX, XY or YY sex chromosomes. Morphologically normal cleaving embryos result, and if the YY condition arises the embryos will die before implantation. If the XY or XX situation arises, the hydatidiform mole may result.

One other possible scenario from the three pronucleate zygote is a triploid (three sets of chromosomes) foetus - if the female complement of chromosomes was not extruded which results in a whole series of enigmatic abnormalities requiring termination, or the delivery of a foetus non-compatible with life. These examples of abnormal fertilisation, which clearly produce no morphological identification at cleavage (figure 2.3) represent an example of the inconclusive nature of the early product of human conception *in vitro*.

3. Cleavage

In conventional IVF the embryo, approximately 24 hours after fertilisation has been confirmed, is between the two to six-cell stage, depending upon individual cell programme events, and it is at this point in development that transfer to the womb occurs.[4]

Under current *in vitro* culture conditions, the human embryo will cleave for the following six days, before hatching from the zona pellucida and implantation. There are a number of interesting biological events associated with cleavage. The term 'cleavage' rather than 'growth', is used to illustrate the division of the single-celled oocyte into more than 100 cells at the blastocyst stage, without any increase in mass. Up to the blastocyst stage the cells (blastomeres) are cleaving off from the parent cell and each subsequent daughter cell is smaller than its predecessor; hence the term 'cleavage'. It is only after the embryo hatches from its zona pellucida and starts to attach and to implant in the endometrium of the womb that true growth occurs.

During cleavage the first stages of molecular, biochemical and morphological differentiation take place. Initially, each blastomere is totally independent of the other, with full potential to develop on to an individual foetus. For example, up to the four-cell stage - approximately 48 hours after conception - each individual cell is totipotent, i.e. segregated from each other they still could develop on to produce four fully developed babies, identical quads. For the first two cleavage divisions at least, the embryo depends upon the maternal genome, via messages already laid down in the ooplasm before ovulation. The paternal genome - now actually the embryonic genome as it is fused with the maternal genome - becomes functional from the four to eight-cell stage onwards. It is at a similar time that the first biochemical signs of differentiation are occurring. It is known, for example, that during this early cleavage period there are both epigenetic and genetic factors regulating the early differentiative events. For example, should the embryo be prevented from undergoing cytokineses (i.e. cell division) for a few cell divisions, but nuclear division (karyokinesis) continues; a nuclear 'clock' instructs the two-cell embryo to behave as if it were a blastocyst. The morphological event of this phenomenon is the formation of a blastocoelic cavity residing in a two-cell embryo. An example of epigenetic development is the need for one of the blastomeres, at the eight-cell stage, to be totally shielded from the external environment and encased on the inside of the embryo. It is this inside blastomere which is the precursor to the cells eventually generating the embryo proper, whereas the remaining outside cells are the progenitors of the placenta.

An embryo which contains cells at different developmental stages is still viable. Blastomeres which are mosaic - with differing genetic make-up from that of other blastomeres of the same embryo - can generate progeny of varying types. Depending on whether and how the blastomeres inter-relate, situations may arise from the normal, to abnormal or non-viable depending upon the final blastomere 'mix'. Such permutations become fixed only during cleavage - many days after conception.

The events of fertilisation and cleavage demonstrate a variety of abnormal situations - not peculiar to *in vitro* conception, but common in the *in vivo* situation - which demonstrate no fixed genetic or chromosome identity or activity arising at the time of fertilisation or, moreover, even after the fusion of the two sets of chromosomes or beyond into the early cleavage stages.

4. Hatching and Implantation

At approximately 6-7 days after conception, the human blastocyst will begin to expand and contract, but overall increasing in volume and, after thinning of the zona pellucida at a focal point, gradually extruding out of a breach in that region (figure 2.4). This process, known as hatching, occurs around day seven after conception and the hatched blastocyst consists primarily of two fundamental cell types: the majority of cells destined to become placental tissue, primarily regulated by paternal genes, and a small ball of cells, termed the 'inner cell mass', making up a small fraction of the cellular tissue, and which eventually differentiate into the mesoderm, endoderm, and ectoderm tissues. These are the precursors to organogenesis and full foetal development, and primarily under maternal genetic control. The fully expanded blastocyst, once detached from the zona pellucida, marks the beginning of growth as defined by increasing cell mass (figure 2.5). At this stage, i.e. implantation, early embryonic growth is rapid. By the fourteenth day after conception, the primitive streak is formed and fuses, thereby

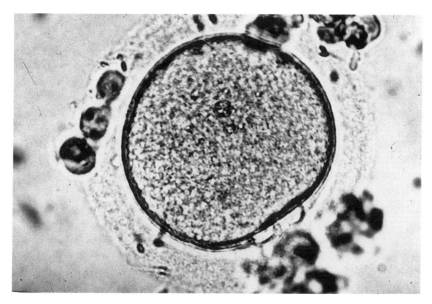

Fig. 2.1: The denuded oocyte, after removal of the oocyte cumulus complex (OCC).

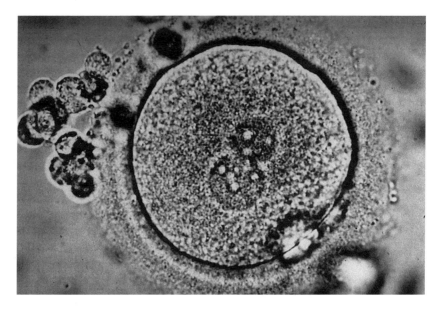

Fig. 2.2: The oocyte with male and female pronuclei.

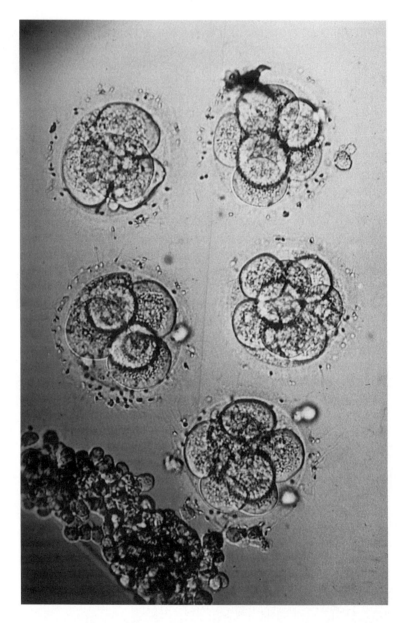

Fig. 2.3: Five human embryos, 2-3 days after conception *in vitro*. Two embryos have three sets of chromosomes (triploid), two have one set each (haploid) and one has the normal two sets of chomosomes (diploid). Morphologically they are indistinguishable.

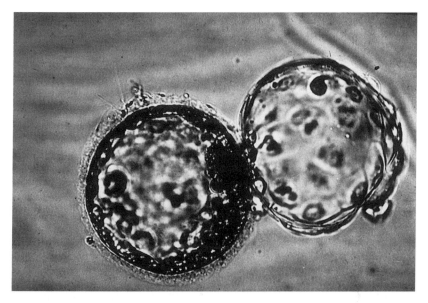

Fig. 2.4: Hatching of the human blastocyst from the *zona pellucida* at approximately 132 hours post conception *in vitro*.

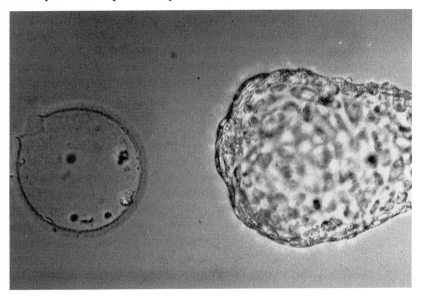

Fig. 2.5: Human blastocyst after complete hatching, approximately 155 hours post conception *in vitro*.

Simon Fishel

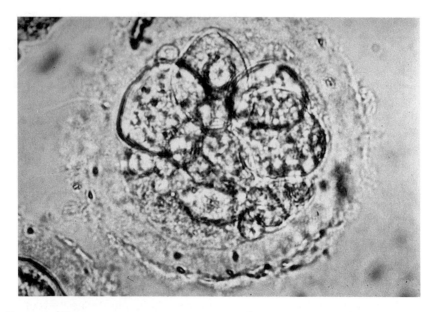

Fig. 2.6: Human embryo after cryopreservation at 7 cells. A healthy child was delivered although three sevenths of the blastomeres degenerated during the freeze thaw process.

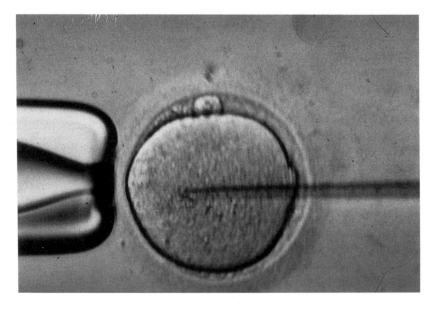

Fig. 2.7: Intracytoplasmic sperm injection.

preventing any further cleavage - i.e. to identical twins. This is the stage at which the embryo can develop (if destined to do so) into a single entity.

5. Cryopreservation

All stages from the fertilised zygote (two pronucleate) stage to the blastocyst stage can be cryopreserved, with up to 10-15% chance of producing viable offspring. The unfertilised oocyte cannot be frozen as a result of deleterious effects on the chromosomes at that particular stage. Currently, in the UK, the Human Fertilisation and Embryology Authority (HFEA) has a legal storage limit of five years.[5] For many who have a number of embryos in storage and have had successful treatment, especially if it has been a multiple pregnancy resulting in twins or triplets, the necessity to use the remaining embryos within a four-year period after delivery is an agonising decision. As there is no biological evidence for increasing anomalies or decreasing success rates, should cryopreservation be extended? This author believes the time limit of five years should be reconsidered.

Cryopreservation has proven some of the interesting embryological phenomena discussed above. For example, the freeze-thaw cycle is known to produce lysis of some blastomeres (lysis being the destruction of the cell membranes and leakage of their contents). However, should 50% or more of the blastomeres survive, this is still compatible with normal development to full term and beyond (figure 2.6).

6. Fertilisation Failure and Micro-Assisted Fertilisation

Those men unable to achieve conception despite IVF technologies can be broadly divided into two large subgroups: those with compromised seminal quality such that conventional IVF treatment is inappropriate, and men who have had conventional IVF but failed to achieve fertilisation. The biochemistry of fertilisation is complex and requires a series of interactions between the egg investments - the zona pellucida and the egg plasma membrane or *oolema* - and the membranes of the spermatozoon; in addition, fertilisation requires the correct motility of the sperm tail. There is a series of distinct interactions during this phase and should a defect exist in one part of the many biochemical processes fertilisation will not result. This is quite common in the group of patients who have apparently no observable defect in spermatogenesis and have undergone IVF only to find fertilisation repeatedly fails. For the group of men who are unable to attempt conventional IVF, this can range from a dysfunction in the shape of the sperm to a defect(s) in the actual production of spermatozoon so that very few are actually ejaculated. This rather simplistic view of the two groups of male infertility fails to reflect the actual dimension of the problem, and to do so properly is beyond the scope of this paper. However, it is now appreciated that male-factor infertility is probably the largest single cause of infertility amongst couples. This has made the introduction of techniques to overcome problems with conceiving *in vitro* one of the most important and fundamental aspects of assisted reproduction technology.

Although there have been techniques developed in recent years which require micromanipulation technology, since 1992 one technique alone has become the treatment of choice in all factors of male infertility.[6] This procedure, known as intracytoplasmic sperm injection (ICSI), is still in its early stages, although more than 600 babies have been delivered following its use to date. The process involves the use of microscopic micro-needles; one for holding the egg in position, and the other for collecting a single spermatozoon and injecting it into the cytoplasm of the oocyte (figure 2.7). This process can achieve a high incidence of fertilisation and viable offspring using severely compromised sperm, for example those which are immotile or abnormally shaped. From the available data to date there is no indication that the health of the offspring is compromised. Further paediatric follow-up investigations are required, but the technique has been readily adopted world-wide.

At NURTURE (Nottingham University Research and Treatment Unit in Reproduction) further research is being conducted on a new technology called Computer Image Sperm Selection (CISS). This process relies on the use of computer technology for assessing sperm motility. A computer is used to observe sperm activity in real time and, using a VDU, the sperm in the field of view of the microscope are colour-coded according to their own individual movement and characteristics. The computer, fed with the information pertaining to different motility characteristics, will colour-code differently those sperm in a potentially more fertile phase. A micro-needle can then be used to aspirate those individual sperms, thereby selecting the potentially more fertile sperm using computer imaging. This sperm can then be injected into the oocyte in the hope of increasing the incidence of fertilisation.[7] Although this technology has been used clinically and viable offspring have been produced, it is still very much in the research phase.

7. Embryo Biopsy

The use of microinjection technology in combination with molecular biological techniques has introduced a new dimension to assisted reproduction technology (ART). Previously, ART was solely concerned with the infertile couple. Using molecular biology and microinjection, it is now possible to isolate a single cell of a four-cell embryo (or two cells from an eight-cell embryo) and evaluate it for the presence of genetic and chromosome disorders in high-risk patients. The removal of a cell from an embryo does not inhibit the further developmental potential of the embryo because of the relatively immature differentiative events occurring at that stage (see above). Pre-conception diagnosis, using the polar body of the unfertilised oocyte, has been attempted, but due to the diffficulties of extrapolating from the polar body to the oocyte (as a result of the complexities of meiosis) this has been difficult (Verlinsky and Kuliev, 1994).[8] Once single cells are available embryos can be screened for single gene defects and sex chromosomes, for example for sex-linked disorders. This technology has been used to scan oocytes and embryos for cystic fibrosis, Duchenne muscular dystrophy, Tay-Sachs disease, Haemophilia A, al-antitrypsin, Retinitis pigmentosa and others. A number of children free of the particular disease have been delivered to families who otherwise had a high chance of bearing an afflicted child or who already had affected offspring. The opportunity for pre-implantation termination as opposed to amniocentesis and termination of a foetus at 20 weeks is far more preferable and ethical to many families in the high risk group.

Microinjection technology can also be used to perform corrective intervention procedures ('zygote/embryo surgery')! For example, the condition of three pronuclei described earlier could be corrected by using a microinjection needle to remove one of the pronuclei thus restoring the zygote to a normal diploid state. This will prevent wastage of embryos, and might also provide the only opportunity for a couple whose sole product of fertilisation is the abnormal zygote. Currently, this procedure is not possible in the UK because of the *Human Fertilisation and Embryology Act (1990)*, although research in other countries indicates that such a procedure would be a feasible scenario for multi-pronucleate zygotes.

8. The Use of Embryonic Cells

The dividing embryo contains all the stem cells for organogenesis and normal development. As described earlier, even at the blastocyst and early implantation stage, the stem cells for all body tissues are being formed. In the UK permissible research before fourteen days would allow the extraction of precursor cells from post-implantation tissue for potential use in re-colonising a host (child or adult) afflicted with a disorder affecting his/her own stem cells. Although the initial research in this field is encouraging, little progress has been made and it could be a research area of considerable activity in the future. This approach - cell therapy - may be preferable to gene therapy as using whole cells to correct degenerative disorders would be less of a risk to the genetic pool than the introduction of copies of a normal gene into the nucleus of a fertilised or unfertilised egg. However, the latter - gene therapy - is a possibility which is under current intensive research investigation.

9. Donor Placenta

There is the potential to help patients who habitually miscarry with micromanipulation technology. For example, a patient who habitually miscarries, and therefore is childless although not technically infertile, would produce a blastocyst. Blastocysts, consisting of the inner-cell mass and the trophectoderm (precursor placental tissue), donated from a fertile patient would be utilised. Using micromanipulation, the inner-cell mass of the donor blastocysts would be removed and discarded leaving the trophoblastic vesicle.

At this stage the inner-cell mass of the patient with habitual miscarriage is transferred to the trophoblastic vesicle of the donor generating an inner-cell mass (precursor foetus) from the patient surrounded by the trophoblast of the donor. This reconstituted blastocyst is transferred back to the patient and implantation and normal gestation can occur. Although the placenta will be that derived from the donor, the child delivered will be the child of the habitual miscarrier. This technology could be utilised for patients who have a certain form of trophoblastic disease and, because of placental dysfunction, always abort a healthy foetus. However, the *Human Fertilisation Embryology Act (1990)* which specifically forbids the transfer to the womb of an embryo resulting from a genetic mix, prevents this technology being utilised in the UK.

10. Ovarian tissue, Oocytes From Abortuses

The reason why ovarian tissue and the use of oocytes from abortuses has become an issue is the extremely large number of oocytes that one can obtain from foetal material. The foetal ovary consists of somewhere in the region of 4 million oocytes which decline in number to approximately 2 million at birth. By the time the female reaches puberty the actual number of oocytes for potential conception range from a few thousand to a few hundred thousand. Hence, the foetal ovary would be a rich source of oocytes for research and donation. However, it is the opinion of this author, along with other scientists, that research should be done initially on adult ovarian tissue to establish the procedures for maturing oocytes *in vitro*, and studying oocyte cryopreservation, before the need to re-discuss the use of aborted ovarian tissue. Studies of cryopreservation are essential. It is not possible, consistently and successfully, to freeze the mature human oocyte (metaphase II) without considerable chromosome damage. The mature oocyte holds its chromosomes in a sensitive condition during the 'metaphase', or replicative, period of the cell-division cycle. (This is in contradistinction to the immature oocyte which holds its chromosomes in a different and less sensitive condition during the non-replicating 'interphase' period.) Hence, the successful combination of cyropreservation of immature oocytes and oocyte maturation *in vitro* would have enormous potential benefit to many fertile as well as infertile women. An example of the former groups are those women requiring chemo- or radio-therapy, rendering further use of their own oocytes hazardous. Some recent studies indicate that further research will not only achieve this on a routine basis, but also that mature, metaphase II oocytes may be rendered viable for successful cryopreservation.

In one specific area of ovarian tissue research it is likely that only foetal tissue will be effective. This is in the area of grafting. Owing to the problems of tissue matching, it is unlikely that ovarian tissue from one adult will ever be successfully grafted to ovarian tissue from another. The current evidence that foetal tissue is less immunogenic and therefore more readily accepted offers one single benefit for couples with ovarian dysfunction; for example, to young girls who, because of various disorders, have inactive ovaries, and to adults for a variety of different reasons. By grafting ovarian tissue they may be able to resume a normal life with regular menstrual cycles, to ovulate and even to gestate and deliver their own children, albeit that the oocytes themselves will be of different genetic origin. Should this become acceptable practice, which would be acceptable to most women in such a condition and prove to be of great benefit to their mental health, then it might be necessary to resort to foetal ovarian tissue.

Two of the major issues surrounding the use of foetal tissue relate to consent and the so-called 'yuk' factor. The problem of consent is not unique, and is met frequently with organ donation in children unable to give consent. There is the philosophical question of the status of ovarian tissue or the oocyte per se. For example, is the oocyte a cell like any other and, by the same token, the ovary an organ like any other; or do they have some other different status? Perhaps a century or two ago, when it was believed that the heart contained the very soul of the individual, the thought of doing a heart transplant (soul transfer) would be philosophically unpalatable and immoral!

The use of oocytes from abortuses presents more of a disgust factor than a rational biological concern. For example, the simple phrase 'your mother was a dead foetus' generates a completely different perception and psychological impact than some other more sensitive and less emotive interpretation.

Notes

1. Cf. Parsons, John, 'Assisted conception: the state of the art' in Evans, Donald, and Pickering, Neil, (eds), *Creating the Child* Dordrecht, Martinus Nijhoff Publishers, 1996, pp.15-27; and Di Renzo, G.C., Cosmi, E.V. and Caserta, G., 'Control of human reproduction: a clinical perspective on bioethical problems' in *ibid.* pp.29-45.

2. Cf. Fishel, S.B., Edwards, R.G. and Purdy, J.M., '*In vitro* fertilisation of human oocytes: factors associated with embryonic development *in vitro*. Replacement of embryos and pregnancy' in Beier, H.M. and Lindner, H.R. (eds), *Fertilisation of the Human Egg In Vitro, Biological Basis and Clinical Application* Berlin, Springer-Verlag, 1983, pp.251-270; and Edwards, R.G., Fishel, S.B., Cohen, J., Fehilly, C. and Purdy, J.M., 'Factors influencing the success of *in vitro* fertilisation for alleviating human infertility' *Journal of In Vitro Fertilisation and Embryo Transfer* 1, 1984, pp.1-23.

3. Cf. Surani, M.A.H. and Barton, S.C. 'Development of gynogenetic eggs in the mouse: implications for parthogenetic embryos' *Science* 222, 1983, p.1034; and Surani. M.A.H., Barton, S.C. and Norris, M.L., 'Development of reconstituted mouse eggs suggests imprinting of the genome during gametogenesis' *Nature* 308, 1984, p.548.

4. Cf. Parsons, *op.cit.*

5. Human Fertilisation and Embryology Act 1990, Section 14 (4).

6. Cf. Palermo. G., Joris. H., Devroey, P. and Van Steirteghem, A.C., 'Pregnancies after intracytoplasmic sperm injection of single spermatozoon into an oocyte' *Lancet* 34, 1992, pp.17-18; Fishel, S.B., Timson, J., Lisi, F., Jacobson, M., Rinaldi, L. and Gobetz, L., 'Micro-assisted (MAF) fertilisation in patients who have

failed subzonal insemination (SUZI)' *Human Reproduction* 9, 1994, pp.501-505; Fishel, S.B., Green, S., Dowell, K. Thornton, S., McDermott, H., Lisi, F., Rinaldi, L., Jacobson, M. and Gobetz, L., 'Fifty-nine cases of extreme male factor infertility - immotile sperm, Kartagener syndrome, globozoospermia, spermatogenic arrest, testicular sperm - treated by SUZI/ICSI' *Human Reproduction* 9 (Supplement 3), 1994, p.5; and Fishel, S.B., Lisi, F., Rinaldi, L., Green, S., Hunter, A., Dowell, K. and Thornton, S., 'Systematic examination of immobilizing spermatozoa before intracytoplasmic sperm injection in the human' *Human Reproduction* 10, 1995, pp.497-500.

7. Green. S., Fishel, S.B., Hall, J.A, Hunter, A., Fleming, S., Hobson, G., Dowell, K., Thornton, S. and Klentzeris, L., 'Computer Image Sperm Selection (CISS) as a novel approach to sub-zonal insemination in the human' *Human Reproduction* 10, 1995, pp.1430-1434.

8. Verlinsky, Y. and Kuliev, A., 'Human preimplantation diagnosis: needs, efficiency and efficacy of genetic and chromosomal analysis' in Fishel, S. (ed.), *Baillière's Clinical Obstetrics and Gynaecology Vol. 8, No. 1: Micromanipulation Techniques* Baillière Tindall, London, 1994, pp.177-196.

3. PRO-ATTITUDES TO PRE-EMBRYOS

Donald Evans
Centre for Philosophy and Health Care
University of Wales, Swansea
Singleton Park
Swansea
Wales

1. Introduction

Recent discoveries in human biology have altered some people's account of the status of the human embryo. However the complex relationship between biological facts and descriptions of the embryo and foetus is difficult to unravel. The prospects of eradicating differences of description of the human embryo by means of philosophical reflection may well be qualified by the selfsame considerations which characterise this relationship. If this turns out to be the case then it will have important repercussions on the enterprise of harmonising public regulation of embryo research and assisted conception services across cultural and societal boundaries.

My purpose in this paper is to rehearse some arguments for construing the pre-embryo in particular ways in order to see just how protagonists handle and weigh the various matters which are canvassed as reasons for opting for one view rather than another. In particular I shall try to track the career of certain biological considerations in these arguments and see why they might be construed as crucial, considerable or irrelevant by the disputing parties. It might well turn out that the deed will count for more than the word in getting clear about the status of the pre-embryo. That is, it might well be that it is by discovering what I am prepared to do with the pre-embryo that I determine what I consider its status to be as opposed to trying to get clear about the matter in order to decide what I shall do. Insofar as this is so then it will be *pro-attitudes* to pre-embryos which are crucial to answering the question rather than rational reflection on the facts.

The paper will consider the character of *pro-attitudes* which will be seen to provide impeccable though not conclusive reasons for various descriptions of the embryo. Historical disagreements between the ovist and spermatozoist preformation theorists will be used to illustrate the point. I shall develop the analysis by asking whether there may not be ultimate stopping places for such disagreement in primitive human reactions to the human form. My claim will be that the disagreement is ideological in kind and that there is no terminus to disagreement to be found in human nature as such. Then might not philosophical reflection enable us to resolve disagreement of this kind? I shall

27

D. Evans (ed.), Conceiving the Embryo, 27–46.
© 1996 *Donald Evans. Printed in the Netherlands.*

attempt to demonstrate that this is not possible for such reflection is itself characterised by similar problems.

In the face of the logical impasse in coming to agreement on the status of the embryo I shall ask whether any legislation or regulation of uses of the human embryo is proper. Using Stephen Lukes' arguments concerning human rights as a model I argue for a minimalist programme of regulation. This practical closure is justified in the most general terms of the protection of respect for human life which should appeal to the vast majority of those who nevertheless cannot of necessity be brought to agreement on the status of the human embryo.

2. An Independent Example

To set down the role of *pro-attitudes* in determining the parameters of descriptions of empirical data let us consider a clinical example removed from the context of embryo research *viz.* a psychoanalytic reading of the data provided by Shakespeare about the character of Hamlet.

It has been suggested that the ideal description of a situation must satisfy, amongst other things, the criterion of comrehensiveness. That is, it must take account of all the relevant features of the case. Thus the behaviour of Hamlet is described by Ernest Jones in terms of the Oedipus Complex as this description comfortably accommodates the data provided by the play.[1] On this view Hamlet's delay in avenging the death of his father assumes centre stage and is given considerable weight. There are two ways of combatting this description of Hamlet's behaviour. The first involves disputing the comprehensiveness of the description and the second involves disputing the weighting which is given to any feature or set of features in the description. In each of these modes of criticism one may find difficulty in agreeing that no distortion occurs in either accommodating all the data or in the arrangement of the data. Such difficulties are usually rooted in the world view which the disputant brings to the data, and the example is a case in point.

For example, with respect to the criterion of comprehensiveness it has been observed that one crucial datum missed by Jones is Hamlet's eloquent avowal of love for his father in the play.[2] Whether it is crucial or not is an issue which it might not be easy to settle. For example, it has been argued that the omission need not be fatal to the Jones's description but that, nevertheless it is. Weitz devises an accommodation which, he alleges, satisfies the criterion of comprehensiveness, but only at the price of distorting the facts of the play.

Jones explains Hamlet's delay in psychoanalytic terms. The concept of the Oedipus Complex, which he uses as an explanatory tool, is derived from a general psychological theory about the behaviour of human beings. Hamlet detests Claudius but cannot bring himself to kill him because Claudius represents those deepest repressed wishes in himself, *viz.* his infantile wish to commit incest with his mother and kill his father:

The call of duty to kill his stepfather cannot be obeyed because it links itself with the unconscious call of his nature to kill his mother's husband, whether this is the first or the second; the absolute 'repression' of the former impulse involves the inner prohibition of the latter also.[3]

Jones shows that this explanation comfortably accommodates a wide range of data of the play - Hamlet's taunts, inaction, lethargy, distractions, depressions, bad dreams, weariness and near madness. Weitz notes his silence on the eloquent avowals of love for his father in the play. The omission is not necessarily fatal, however, for such avowals could be part of a Freudian explanation as being precisely what one would expect from someone with repressed hatred. But, Weitz claims, such an account distorts this datum of the text in that it amounts to a denial of it.

Whether we agree that such a distortion is involved will depend on the ideological framework in which the matters are entertained - the *pro-attitudes* we bring to the reading. These may take the form of a formal theory such as Freudianism or of a more diffuse collection of beliefs, values and expectations. Thus those unsympathetic with Freudianism will be likely to see Weitz's case as conclusive. But what of those whose sympathies lie with the Freudian outlook? It is not at all clear that they will agree that Hamlet's love for his father is an incontrovertible datum of the text, as Weitz claims. What is an incontrovertible datum is that Hamlet eloquently avows love for his father. For the Freudian there is much evidence in the text for a denial of Hamlet's love, and it is bound up with his relationship with his mother, and with her husband, and with Hamlet's general pattern of behaviour.

It might be countered that such evidence is theory-laden, it does not come to us naked and innocent. That most readers of the play would be largely unfamiliar with Freudian theory might suggest to them that their views of matters in the play are free from theoretical bias in a way in which Jones's is not. However, though they may have nothing like the tight theoretical framework Jones employs they nevertheless have expectations and opinions of people's behaviour drawn from their experience of understanding people in ordinary life. In terms of these they construe the data which appear in the drama. I am not holding any brief for the Freudian account here but simply pointing out that what constitutes a distortion of data may be as much a matter of dispute as the reading of the play itself. Where a reading is out of line with the general expectations and opinions of a commentator it may be thought to constitute a contrived accommodation of data. But such expectations and opinions may vary. For some readers matters of sex may be far more significant than for others and reading a drama from the aspect of the sexual will be natural for them, whereas for others it will not. Which reading will weigh with us, and this involves the business of which will seem to us to be natural as opposed to contrived, will depend on such interests and may make the Freudian reading more or less acceptable.

3. The Logical Geography of Pro-Attitudes

Nowell-Smith[4] invented the term *pro-attitude* to describe the logical relation which holds between the reasons one might give for choosing something and the choosing. For example, if I claimed to enjoy ice skating the question 'Why do you go ice skating?' would be redundant. There is a logical relationship between enjoying something and choosing it. This relation is not so tight as to make the claim and the decision to do otherwise contradictory. There may be overriding considerations - I might have a broken leg. But in the absence of such considerations the claim and the failure to choose to skate would come into an unacceptable tension. Thus the claim is an impeccable explanation of the choice. It is also an impeccable reason for choosing to skate. However, impeccable reasons need not be conclusive reasons.[5]

Nowell-Smith asserts that there is no limit to the possible objects of *pro-attitudes*.[6] He also points out that it is artificial to distinguish choosing from doing. Though sometimes I may decide to do something and later execute the action, I can only choose it by doing it. All sorts of things may impede the execution of a decision but choosing has more the character of a performative.[7]

4. Pro-Attitudes and Pre-Embryos

If we employ these two ideas together then we may move the moral argument one stage from where the originator of the term *pro-attitude* actually employed his creation. That is, we may move it back to the level of description. How we are prepared to act towards the embryo demonstrates our choice of how we shall describe it. That choice is impeccably explained by the *pro-attitudes* we hold towards the description of the embryo. In turn these *pro-attitudes* provide impeccable reasons for our describing the embryo as we do. This is not to provide a moral justification for so describing it for, as Nowell-Smith points out, one may have a pro-attitude providing a logically complete reason for morally reprehensible conduct as when one tortures the cat because one enjoys it.[8]

However the matter is somewhat more complex when we apply the notion of *pro-attitude* to descriptions of fact. It is precisely this complexity which, I contend, marks off the possibility of radical moral disagreement on the question of the status of the embryo - that is, disagreement which is not resolvable by an appeal to reason. The parameters of what it is reasonable, and even moral, to do are fixed in part by the descriptions we choose. That is, the identity of subsequent acts is determined by our descriptions of the facts in question. Whether we describe the early embryo as a human soul, a human life, human life, or a mass of undifferentiated cells will set down a variety of possibilities of what we would be doing if we experimented on such an embryo to destruction. How we see and describe the embryo will be determined by a whole variety of interests, convictions and preferences. This set of features may be loosely called an ideology but it need not take the form of a tight theory or even of a coherent and comprehensive world-view. One may, for example, take the view that life is a gift from God and that man is mysteriously made in God's image - a belief that is not necessarily threatened nor undermined by the most detailed description of biological events during reproduction. No amount of embryological investigation could conceivably crack what is held to be an awesome mystery - for by their nature genuine mysteries are not simply states of ignorance. The description of this mystery is an expression of the awe in which the very fact of human life is held. Such life is not a manufactured commodity but rather a divine gift. Armed with this committment a person may well, when faced with the question of the status of the early embryo for the first time, choose to describe it as a human soul. If challenged for a reason he might respond that human life is a mystery, a divine gift. This is an impeccable reason for the description insofar as it renders otiose a further question, *viz.* So why do you describe the early embryo as a human soul?

But we must remember that on Nowell-Smith's account *pro-attitudes* do not provide conclusive reasons for the *pro-attitude* may not be shared by some others. For them the world is not as it has been described by this particular believer. They too may be believers yet not cash that out by means of such a description. Indeed many in the Judaeo-Christian tradition have, through the centuries, not so described the early embryo. Such views might also be tempered by other interests and convictions such as that man's intellect should be employed to further understanding and that being in God's image commits man to creative endeavour in God's world. On this view the so-called mystery of life is seen as a state of ignorance, much of which has already been dispelled, awaiting resolution with many other one-time mysteries such as the mystery of flight - mysteries which must surrender to the inquisitiveness of the human mind. Given such a context the information provided by the microscope and embryology of the earliest stages of human life may explain the choice of the most radical description of the early embryo as a mass of undifferentiated cells. Certainly for many with no religious conviction and with a profound faith in science and its progress, together with a burden for the suffering of infertile couples, the thirst for knowledge would pitch them towards such a choice of description.

It might seem that this must be a rationalisation of subsequent destructive research on embryos, a thinking backwards from practice to description. This would be a mistake. There may be bad faith, of course, but there need not be. How one is prepared to act towards the embryo may demonstrate how one conceives of it. Such a conception may even come as a surprise. How one then goes on to describe one's actions confirms this. Thus one need not have to find a justification for taking human lives for the advance of knowledge when one engages in destructive experimentation on early embryos. One may hope that such a price would be too high for any embryologist to be willing to pay. Certainly we know of some who in the name of research have thought human lives worth sacrificing. To tar embryologists with the same brush as the perpretrators of crimes upon humanity in the Nazi death camps would be to ignore the difference in their descriptions of what they were doing. Of course, it remains open to the holder of the conservative view canvassed above to make such an accusation but this vital difference has to be accounted for. The German camp doctors knew that they were sacrificing people for their so-called research, albeit people they despised. The embryologist experimenting on the pre-embryo rejects such a description as do many who support and admire his work. Here we have a moral disagreement about what it is that is being done, a disagreement at the level of the facts, not a disagreement about purported justifications of actions whose descriptions are agreed.

Nowell-Smith includes a whole range of terms under the heading of *pro-attitude* and offers them only as samples. They include *accept* and *approve of*. These are sufficient for our purposes though we could add to them without doing violence to his account. Con-attitudes such as *reject* and *disapprove of* would cover the non-recognition of rival descriptions.

5. An Example From the History of Human Embryology

Such boundaries of description can be identified in the emergence of rival descriptions of the early stages of reproduction through the centuries. Thus, for example, the emergence of preformation theories of the early foetus can be understood in the light of prevailing theological considerations and the dispute between ovists and spermatozoists never called the preformationism into question. Indeed we shall see that such a background of investigation even determined, in some cases, what the investigators claimed to see.

During the so-called 'embryological revolution' of the seventeenth century the spermatozoists and ovists disputed the relative significance of the sperm and ovum in reproduction. Each thought that the preformed human life was in the preferred gamete and that the corresponding dormant partner gamete either sparked off the growth of the preformed embryo (the role of the sperm in the ovist account) or provided the necessary context for the growth of the preformed embryo (the role of the ovum in the spermatozoist account). What was never disputed between the parties was that the preformed foetus was present somewhere before fertilisation. Some even claimed to have demonstrated the veracity of their account by having observed such a form in sperm by means of the new technology of the microscope. They may not have been perverse in their claims. One's expectations can play a major role in what one claims to observe. However, though one's theoretical framework may produce a certain configuration in the data perceived it is stretching the bounds of credulity to think of the visual discovery of miniature foetuses in sperm or ova facilitated by preformation theories. Indeed the later sophistication of the very technology which was supposed to facilitate such a revelation itself enables us to reject the claim with total confidence.

Brockliss[9] has made a very good case for saying that both the emergence of preformationism and its demise were not evidentially based but, rather, ideologically determined. His argument runs thus: The rise of Cartesian mechanism caused the emergence of the theory. No satisfactory account of changes in state could be given in mechanical terms. As a result it was natural to assume that the foetus was preformed before conception. This tied in with the Cartesian theology that God, in one act of creation, had brought a world to be which did not require constant creative acts on his part. Thus all preformed foetuses were created from the beginning of time.[10] This was clearly not evidentially based. No counter evidence was responsible for the demise of preformation accounts either.[11] Monsters, the traits of the dormant partner and so on were accounted for by various means leaving preformationism intact. That is, nothing could count properly as counter evidence for the theory was never based on evidence in the first place - it had more the character of a dogma in the light of which observational data were construed. It was the advent of Newtonianism, with its different epistemological implications, which heralded the fall of preformationism, not crucial counter evidence.

Insofar as Brockliss is correct then it may be said that it was *pro-attitudes* to pre-embryos which determined how they were to be described. Relations between the human form of the homonculus in either the sperm or ovum was internally related to its status as a human life. We shall have more to say of the attraction in regarding the human form as playing a crucial role in the resolution of disagreement over the status of the human embryo a little later. First let us look a little more closely at the general relation that may be said to hold between *pro-attitudes* and facts about the pre-embryo which have recently been uncovered.

6. Pro-Attitudes and Biological Facts

Here I wish to test the view that there may be certain very basic biological considerations which play a crucial role in settling disputes about the status of the human embryo. That is, certain facts demand that we opt for one description rather than another. On such an account loyalty to some descriptions, though demanded by ideological considerations, would then be seen to be maintained only at the expense of being confused or mistaken. If such a view stands then *pro-attitudes* themselves will be seen to be subject to the test of fact and disagreements arising out of variations between them would be resolvable, given good will and a concern for the truth. I propose to test the view by putting forward the strongest philosophical case I can produce for not regarding the early conceptus as a human being[12], a case based on a crucial purported biological fact which has come to light only in recent advances in human embryology.

We are told that up to the four cell stage of cleavage of the early embryo all the cells are totipotential.[13] That is, as far as we know, there is no discrimination between cells which will later form the placenta and those which will form the foetus. We also know that these cells are pluri-potential. That is, if one of them is separated from the rest, given the right conditions, it too will begin to divide and result in a further embryo which is identical to that which develops from the parent mass of cells. In nature something akin to this occurs occasionally when two primitive streaks develop from one mass of cells and monozygotic twins are produced. What bearing do these facts have upon the descriptions which we choose for the conceptus at this early stage?

The group of cells is sometimes described as an undifferentiated mass. This description is designed to highlight the independence of each cell from the rest save for the fact of their being aggregated together. Separation of one of these from the rest appears to do no harm to those which remain. Neither does it appear to be necessarily harmed itself. The group made up of the four cells does not constitute an organism for there appears to be no functional relation between its parts. Even when cell changes other than cleavage begin to occur this is still the case. This begins to occur before the appearance of the primitive streak but even now the morula is still capable of developing into two organisms at the primitive streak stage. The appearance of the primitive streak marks the end of this possibility.

It seems to me that there are two different senses attaching to the notion of undifferentiation as it may be applied to such cell masses. One I shall call the weak sense and the other the strong sense. The weak sense denotes simply that *so far as we know* there is no difference between the cells and there is no functional relation between them. The strong sense denotes that it follows *from what we already know* that, of their nature, the cells are identical and independent of each other - this is demonstrated by their toti-potentiality and their pluri-potentiality. Theoretically, a number of divisions may be made of an early conceptus producing a multiplicity of different embryos, foetuses and, eventually, people. They would be genetically identical but they would be different people, as are monozygotic twins.

What then might be the significance of this strong sense of undifferentiation? One necessary condition of identifying *a* human life is individuation. An individual mass of cells alone does not constitute an individual life, even though those cells may be human and alive. (Consider, for example, a blood sample.) In an important sense this individuality must persist through time and structural change. I am the same individual human being who was married to Ann on August 1st, 1961, being the son of Aubrey and Mary Evans of Brynmill, Swansea. No cell in my body remains from that day and in some senses I am a very different person. Nevertheless I am the same individual human being. I have no reason to doubt that I developed from an early conceptus. I know also that my twin developed from an early conceptus, though a different one for we are not monozygotic twins. But what if we had been? We would have developed from the same early conceptus. The crucial change, when the one conceptus became two, would be in a different category from all the cellular changes which have occurred in me. That change would not have occurred in me, or in my life, in any sense. Neither would it have occurred in my twin brother's life. It is also very odd to think of all my cellular changes and all those of my brother as being changes in some original life from which we sprang. That would be a third human life. I suspect that no-one would wish to claim that that was a life sacrificed for the lives of my brother and myself. Thus the facts of toti-potentiality and pluri-potentiality of the cells of the early conceptus are obstacles to our identifying that conceptus as *a* human life. Whilst I may retrospectively link a given human life with an early conceptus I cannot know that any early conceptus will become only one life - or even a life at all as it might develop into a hydatidiform mole or, given that it contains too many chromosomes it must perish. Thus, my argument runs, the very early conceptus, that is the conceptus which is made up of a mass of cells each of which is pluri-potential and toti-potential, cannot be properly called *a* human life and that this is not simply because of our current state of ignorance about the nature of the early embryo.

This argument seems to demand, in the name of logic, that reasonable people agree with its conclusion. Disagreement, it seems, can only be at pain of confusion. But is all as it in fact seems? Would an appeal to the mystery of human life here simply be a refusal to face the uncomfortable facts which recently have been uncovered? A philosophical case can be made which suggests that such a refusal is not a counsel of ignorance so much as an expression of religious wonder at the fact of human life. On this account the inexplicability of factors in the origin of a human life is an important feature of a due respect for that life. In this way the activity of philosophical reflection on the nature of the religious promises a resolution of the apparent clash between the purported biological facts and absolute respect for the fertilised ovum.

7. Pro-Attitudes, Religious Wonder and Philosophy

In order to develop the philosophical case let us turn to the work of Wittgenstein as an example of a philosopher who reflected on the sense of the religious and who related it to the idea of wonder.[14]

Churchill shows how Wittgenstein's account of religious awareness is tied up with his insistence throughout his philosophy that justification has to come to an end, which in turn is related to his interest in the stopping places of human reactions and very general facts of nature. This is the point where he asserts that explanation comes to an end and the business of Philosophy is description. Thus to describe a mathematical rule like addition is all that one can do, there is no justifying such a rule as being correct. This is simply what *adding* comes to. Though particular additions are justified in terms of this rule the rule itself cannot stand in need of justification. It is the ground or the boundary of reason giving. In *On Certainty*[15] he describes a number of disparate commitments that do not rest upon reasons but which form the boundaries of doubt and reason. To question these is not therefore to exhibit caution but rather to be in confusion. Yet the temptation recurs to endeavour to press beyond these stopping places to press for explanation of why we think as we do rather than rest with the description of what it is to think. Churchill points out that Wittgenstein sees this temptation as symptomatic of modern, scientific thought. He writes:

Twentieth century thought, he claims, has substituted the endless quest for explanation in terms of reasons for a willingness to stop when we have a solution. The demand for explanation is a recursive demand, by always seeking a justification that shows why this way is the way, and it functions to block another attitude towards the practice - a wonder or astonishment that it does go this way -

happens to go this way - rather than another.[16]

This is a block to wonder and awe of human life as it is. In the case of the human embryo it may seem that pressing for explanations of the process of reproduction back to the morula and earliest conceptus undermines the sense of wonder of human life. It might then appear that this sense of wonder depends on a certain degree of ignorance. In a way it does, though it would be better to think of wondering at nature as a different form of attention, yet one that is more difficult to attain once explanation has been effected. Churchill helps us with the analogy of Mark Twain's boyhood wonder at the variegated textures and colours on the surface of the Mississippi which was destroyed by his training as a steamboat pilot.

> The unsignifying glory of the River, its aesthetic beauty, was lost to him forever, and in its place he saw a system of signs, signals of clear passage, shallow water, cross currents, underwater snags.[17]

One might be tempted to think that this philosophical analysis of the religious sense at least should settle any dispute between religious believers about the status of the human embryo. Yet, once again, we have to note that the divide between philosophers about what counts as an acceptable account of the religious is as profound as the differences between views of the status of the foetus, as Churchill eloquently points out. This divide is again determined by *pro-attitudes* to certain kinds of philosophical activity. Many religious believers see their religious beliefs as involving truth claims and as having explanatory force. Others, in the Wittgenstein mould, may consider that they have missed the point of religion. Yet others, as indeed Churchill intimates, would want to say that there is more than one sort of religion.[18] Philosophy, it seems, is in no position to adjudicate. Thus it leaves us with the kind of rival descriptions of the early embryo we rehearsed above. *Pro-attitudes* make their presence felt in philosophical reflection too.

  The fine detail of the empirical description of the early conceptus might well be regarded as a threat to the possibility of the sense of wonder at the gift of human life. Things suddenly seem more mundane than they did and human life a poorer thing for it. Such a reaction is not inevitable, however. Indeed one may even come to a wonder at the way things are, by realising that one came to be oneself as one of no less than a myriad of random possibilities. Or, given a certain religious perspective on the case discussed above, one might stand in awe of what one may call the mystery of two or more lives being embodied as one at a certain stage of development. 'Our lives are in the hand of God and if this is how He sees fit to develop them then so be it, thanks be to God' may be a religious response to the facts cited. Critics will retort that the power of God cannot be expressed in defying logic, or what makes sense, and such an account will not impress them. The believer in question may refuse to accept the puzzle as it is presented, however, and feel obliged to question the strong sense of 'undifferentiation' employed in setting it up. He may feel that there is no onus on him to provide any explanation. He is willing to live with the wonder at what cannot be understood. In other words, it is his commitment to a certain description of the early conceptus which dictates what counts as an explanation.

Having determined that neither biological facts, as such, nor an appeal to the religious, mark a necessary stopping place for disagreement over the status of the embryo, we must ask whether there are any other promising candidates for the role? There are some which deserve our attention as they offer the only limits to possible *pro-attitudes*, as defined by Nowell-Smith. As *pro-attitudes* have been shown to lie at the root of radical disagreements over the description of the human embryo such candidates offer great promise of a resolution of such disagreement. I have in mind primitive reactions which have been thought to be preconditions of the language we have - in particular, in the case of the human embryo, primitive reactions to the human form.

8. Pro-Attitudes and Primitive Reactions

We may stress the importance of the human form in descriptions of the embryo by a consideration of very general *pro-attitudes* which relate to our concept of persons and to the development of language. This group of *pro-attitudes* may be thought to offer the best chance of providing a resolution to disagreement about the status of the human embryo. Here one would be locating pro- and con-attitudes in features other than beliefs and interests such as those cited earlier. Some of them may be at a more primitive level and consequently be seen as pre-linguistic and near universal insofar as they appear to demand certain descriptions. I have in mind here certain reactions which Wittgenstein included in the group of facts about the natural history of man, reactions without which language as we have it would have been impossible. Insofar as such reactions play such a role we may well have come up against the only limits Nowell-Smith concedes pro- and con-attitudes may be subject to, *viz*. the logical limits of language itself.[19] Whether this however has the consequence of guaranteeing uniformity of description is a possibility we shall canvass.

These reactions are not learned. In connection with descriptions of the developing life of a human embryo one of these may be especially significant. Wittgenstein writes:

> Our attitude to what is alive and to what is dead, is not the same. All our reactions are different. - If anyone says: "That cannot simply come from the fact that a living thing moves about in such-and-such a way and a dead one not", then I want to intimate to him that this is a case of the transition from 'quantity to quality'.[20]

He further elaborates on the notion of such reactions where he discusses the contrast between living and inanimate things:

> What gives us *so much as the idea* that living beings, things, can feel?

Is it that my education has led me to it by drawing my attention to feelings in myself? ... - I do not transfer my idea to stones, plants, etc.[21]

Such reactions are not learned and are not extended to all living things, e.g. plants. One reacts in this way only to those living things which resemble human beings in their behaviour: "Only of what behaves like a human being can one say that it *has* pains".[22] Such reactions together form what Wittgenstein calls an attitude. For example, when speaking of the mechanical behaviour of a friend he shows that it makes no sense to think of the friend as a machine: "My attitude towards him is an attitude towards a soul. I am not of the *opinion* that he has a soul".[23]

One of these unlearned, primitive reactions is to tend and treat the part that hurts when someone else is in pain. Of this reaction he asks:

But what is the word 'primitive' meant to say here? Presumably that this sort of behaviour is pre-linguistic: that a language-game is based on it, that it is a prototype of a way of thinking and not the result of thought.[24]

So then reactions to other human beings as human beings precede, indeed make possible, our language about human beings and thus the possibility of holding opinions about them, gaining knowledge of them and so on.

Being sure that someone is in pain, doubting whether he is, and so on, are so many natural, instinctive, kinds of behaviour towards other human beings, and our language is merely an auxiliary to, and further extension of, this relation. Our language-game is an extension of primitive behaviour.[25]

The central focus of all these reactions and the general attitude to living souls is the human body: "The human body is the best picture of the human soul".[26] So it is, on his account, that the language of persons is rooted in very general shared reactions. These reactions are not eccentric though they need not be universal. Occasional individuals may be cut off from them and consequently possibly cut off from whole areas of human discourse and understanding. Some of these deficits may have considerable moral significance. Nevertheless for those who are able to talk of human beings as living souls the relation between bodily appearances and behaviours on the one hand and concepts on the other is internal. One cannot separate one's concept of a human being from the appearances and behaviours which draw from us such reactions. As Wittgenstein puts it: "My relation to the appearances here is part of my concept".[27]

The interesting question which now arises concerns the question of the appropriateness or otherwise of reactions. Surely, it may be countered, one can have inappropriate reactions to things. This, of course is true. No individual reaction, in itself, confers a particular identity on that which provokes the reaction. If I react to a wax dummy in Madame Tussaud's, as many have to the policeman of whom directions have often been asked, my reaction is akin to my reaction to a human being though, in fact, I am not reacting to a human being at all but merely to something which has the appearance of a human being. In one sense then my reaction is both appropriate and inappropriate. It is appropriate that I do not react to the object as to a marauding lion, if it is a living creature at all then it is a man and not a lion, but I am deceived into taking it for a man. Even this is not something about which, in my reacting, I have an opinion, though if challenged about the number of people in the room I might well voice the opinion that there is x + the individual I have addressed as the policeman. There is then some sense in asking whether certain attitudes or reactions are appropriate or not. But this is not so of the attitudes with which Wittgenstein is interested. They are shared reactions on a very general scale, a scale so general that they may even be described as being part of the natural history of man, not of a particular man. Thus he says:

> Our interest certainly includes the correspondence between concepts and very general facts of nature. (Such facts as mostly do not strike us because of their generality.) ... if anyone believes that certain concepts are absolutely the correct ones, and that having different ones would mean not realizing something that we realise - then let him imagine certain very general facts of nature to be different from what we are used to, and the formation of concepts different from the usual ones will become intelligible to him.[28]

So it is not a question of whether our concept of a human being is correct. That is not a question which it makes sense to ask. It is not the language which is correct or incorrect but what is said in the language. Thus to assert that a given human being is reckless, brave, stubborn, diseased, dying and so on is to claim that something is true. The concept of a human being makes no claim.

Now where does all this leave us with respect to the status of the human embryo? Even at its earliest stage the fertilised ovum is alive and it is human. It therefore constitutes human life. Yet there is no way in which the uninformed viewer could react to it as to a human being. It would not be recognisable as such - and this not because it has been deformed or disfigured by an accident, as might be the case with a person whose gross deformities may call from us an inappropriate reaction in failing to recognise the crushed and mutilated form as a human being. The normal early conceptus is not at all deformed. But neither does it resemble a human being. Some measure of the importance of this appearance in our attitude towards the conceptus may be embodied in the declaration of a clinician who preferred to perform abortions by means of crushing the cranium of a foetus rather than injecting Potassuim Chloride into the foetus to produce cardiac arrest because he did not have to see what he was doing in the former procedure. It is hard to resist the idea that the visible and moving foetus which has human parts down to the last digit is anything other than a human being. We have already noted the power of this reaction to the human form in our observations about the preformation theories of the Seventeenth Century.

But what of the absence of the human form in the conceptus? Is this crucial in fixing our description of the conceptus as a living soul? Well it need not be. But some other generally shared reaction would be required to compensate. Maybe we could find a consensus of reaction to the information that the living cell produced by fertilisation was the product of a human sperm and a human oocyte. Such a consensus is, however, lacking. To regard the early conceptus simply as a mass of undifferentiated cells cannot be shown to be an inappropriate reaction. Then neither can the vision of it as a human being be discounted as inappropriate. However in each case we might feel that it is not a primitive reaction which underlies the vision but a set of general expectations and values which we have earlier identified as determining possible *pro-attitudes* which will be derived from ways of living. The primitive reaction account will assume more force in later phases of gestation where upholders of the human being status view of the foetus will consider a demand for reasons for their view to be as besides the point as is the demand that I have reasons for reacting to the lady in the ticket booth at Madame Tussaud's as a human being.

Yet even here philosophical reflection on the nature of concept formation cannot be decisive in settling what amounts to a moral dispute about the human conceptus. This is because philosophical disagreement is characterised by the same kind of irresolvability as it is being used to resolve. Not all philosophers are impressed with the account of concept formation presented by Wittgenstein. Many assert that concepts are criterial entities. That is, we learn a concept by identifying the criteria which have to be satisfied in order for something to be properly labelled with that concept. Thus we may demand that a human being be sentient, self-conscious, have the ability to value its own existence and so on. There is a considerable literature disputing which of these criteria are necessary.[29] All of this literature disputes the view of Wittgenstein that I am not of the opinion that a given individual is a human being. The *pro-attitudes* which set the parameters of this philosophical dispute lie in different accounts of where the philosophers attention should be focussed. I can see no more prospect of settling this kind of dispute than that of the status of the human embryo.

What then are we to say in the face of this impasse? Does it matter whether we reflect upon the status of the embryo or not? Is philosophical deliberation a waste of time? There is a robust answer to the latter question, *viz.* that the questions are there and, what's more, they are important. If it is true that the unexamined life is not worth living then surely questions about the very nature of human life cannot be evaded. It would be intellectually dishonest to refuse to face them. In any case, it is certainly false to imagine that it follows from the observation that philosophical reflection on these matters may not bring about agreement that either it will never bring about agreement or that having failed to bring about agreement nothing will have been achieved by the reflection. Sometimes inconsistencies in thought or incoherences will be uncovered which will produce agreement. Sometimes new orientations of data will appeal to disputants and new perceptions will result. It should always be the case that a clearer appreciation of opposing viewpoints results even though they may not be convincing. All of these are worthy gains. Nevertheless we have to ask what happens to the task of harmonising regulations governing research on human embryos and their use in therapeutic contexts given that no agreement on the status of the embryo can be guaranteed, and further whether such a task is a proper one to attempt.

9. A Practical Closure

We may find help in answering these questions by considering another area where philosophical agreement has proved impossible but where there is a moral imperative to take action. It is the area of human rights. In an impressively eloquent paper Stephen Lukes[30] has shown that the philosophical dispute about the nature of human rights is dogged by the problem of the philosophical ideologies from which the disputants proceed. It is not as though these ideologies could be dispensed with and the discussion begin from square one. The ideological framework is essential both to the identification of the problem at hand and to the determination of proposed solutions to it. It is this framework, in the case of each disputant, which enables any assessment of possibilities, weighing of considerations and so on. Having identified five distinct ideological stances Lukes shows that all but one preclude the possibility of establishing any agreed human rights either for theoretical or practical reasons. Egalitarianism remains as the only perspective from which they may reasonably be identified. What therefore should be done? Should hands be held up in despair of finding a solution? He thinks that the idea of human rights is an essential weapon in the fight against gross injustices currently suffered in our world and that a practical closure to the debate about their existence and identity should be effected, despite philosophical criticisms which may be made against any specific account of them.

He therefore proposes a minimalist approach which involves making a list of human rights which will be as reasonably *short* and *abstract* as possible.[31] Only such a list will stand any hope of being adopted and maintained. However current evils demand that this much be done. But these two features of the list will lead to problems. Some will feel that they do not cover enough, some will feel that their being made concrete will cause radical disagreement. Yet always such disputes will occur in the context of concern for the interests of all concerned. It will act as a brake to extremes and gross violations, it will serve as a modest (and thus not authoritarian) programme.

We have noted a similar theoretical and practical impasse in agreeing on a description of the human embryo. Nevertheless there is a practical call for some measure of agreement. The best chances of achieving some kind of agreement on the regulation of practice and research employing human embryos are to be found in a minimalist programme of legislation. The rationale for this minimalist programme, in line with the Lukes strategy, is to establish the widest range of support and respect for the regulation. The larger the number of specific restrictions the greater the possibility will be of disagreement between large groups of practitioners, users of assisted conception services and interested parties. Those regulations will also need to be of the most basic kind for this same reason.

There is an additional reason for the legislation to cover only the most basic concerns. This latter gets to the heart of the minimalist programme. The whole point of adopting any programme of legislation is to protect the general public from excesses of practitioners and researchers who may, given unlimited freedom, so act as to threaten fundamental respect for human life as such. Such excesses would parallel the gross abuses of human beings which encourage a minimalist programme of human rights in the Lukes model. Though we could never hope for universal agreement on what people should not ever be allowed to do under any circumstances, as there may always be some for whom there is no limit to what is possible for certain reasons - such as the perpetrators of torture - we can identify certain general parameters of behaviour which would be offensive to the vast majority of citizens and call into question anything which could be called a respect for human life. Thus, for example, the use of human embryos in transgenic experimentation and possibly trade in human embryos would be good candidates for the most basic prohibitions, though, no doubt, there may be some individuals who would be interested to pursue either or each of these activities for one reason or another.

Of course there will be disagreement as to what constitutes the most basic considerations. For example, it may be said, there can be no more basic protection of the respect for human life than to prohibit killing human beings. The common law already recognises this limit to human behaviour and clinicians and researchers are subject to its sanctions. But in the context of assisted procreation and embryo experimentation what is precisely at stake in the disagreement between the pro-life groups and their opponents is whether the prohibition is properly applicable to human embryos. Those who are willing to engage in the practices cannot be properly described as being willing to kill people to achieve their ends. Killing people would be a description which they could not accept as covering their practice. Thus the basic limit of prohibiting killing would not be so precise as to constitute a ban on assisted conception techniques, embryo experimentation or even abortion.

If the limits are so few and so general one may wonder whether they are at all useful. I have no doubt that they may be useful, indeed I firmly believe that they are necessary. The justification for enacting such legislation lies in the gains secured by it. Such gains may be best guaranteed by the prohibition of all types of uses of embryos by all but a circumscribed group of qualified personnel. Such control would be possible by the enforcement of regulation by means of licensing such as has been adopted in the United Kingdom. The gains would include the provision of: a) reassurance to the general public that such activities are controlled and are not engaged in by irresponsible practitioners; b) mechanisms for relating developments in such practices to the sensibilities of the population at large; c) checks and balances guaranteeing the possibility of evaluation and review of the activities.

Law by its very nature is permissive. That is, apart from those activities it proscribes other activities are allowed but not directed. Any set of laws governing the provision of assisted conception services and embryo research would allow such activities to be performed by authorised personnel but would not place any obligation upon any persons to so act. This would therefore allow a wide range of opinion about what is and what is not acceptable behaviour with respect to the human embryo to be respected in that no practitioner would be obliged to engage in activities in this field which constituted an offence to his or her conscience. Some individuals would be restricted in what they may wish to do, or even in what they feel they ought to do insofar that they may think that the prohibitions restrict their ability to provide the best quality of health care to others. The laws would not be unique in this regard. For example, the Abortion Act in English Law prohibits abortions at certain stages of gestation and in most circumstances. Individual clinicians may feel that a given patient would be benefited by receiving such a service. They are not the arbiters of what is proper behaviour in such contexts however though they may be best placed to know what the clinical outcomes of such intervention or lack of it might be.

That such general legislation may be justified is one matter. However we have to face the possibility that some jurisdictions will not be content to rest at the level of basic prohibitions and will determine that far more conservative practice be adopted than that which is permitted in a neighbouring jurisdiction. This will lead to problems of movement of citizens between jurisdictions to seek in another place what is illegal in their own state. It is not the purpose of this paper to attend to these inter-jurisdictional problems. What is true, however, is that the reasons for recommending a minimalist programme of legislation within a community apply equally to the wider ranges of moral disagreement which may be found across national boundaries. If member states of the European Union adopt a minimalist programme which preserves a fundamental respect for human life as it is perceived by all but a very small proportion of their citizens it will leave room for practitioners who morally disapprove of the application of research and therapeutic techniques to refrain from their use. The system of regulation by licence would also allow for more specific restrictions to be applied but be open to more frequent review and modification in the light of both perceived needs and demands from the population in question and of the perceptions and practices of neighbouring countries. A flexible system of regulation of this sort would allow moves in either the direction of more liberal or more conservative control depending on the social and clinical outcomes of practice and the results of research.

Such a system of control is embodied in the United Kingdom legislation enacted in November 1990. This legislation has set a small number of absolute prohibitions on researchers' and practitioners' uses of embryos. It has also set up a regulatory authority to oversee the implementation of licensing and maintainence of good practice. That body can proscribe further activities as it sees fit. It endeavours to keep in touch with public opinion as to what should or should not be allowed and can change its regulations accordingly. Unfortunately this mechanism is not left to perform its work unfettered. For example, on the 7th of January 1994 it produced a consultation document to be widely disseminated in order to test public opinion on the delicate matter of the use of donated ovarian tissue in embryo research and assisted conception. However before the results of this consultation could be known legislation was laid before Parliament to outlaw the use of foetal ovarian tissue due to a heated but brief reaction to the request by a researcher for guidance on experimental work involving the harvesting and use of foetal oocytes. Hastily drafted laws are often not good laws, and laws, once *in situ* are notoriously difficult to amend.   To anticipate how people will feel generally when such possibilities have been mulled over and discussed is unwise. The use of the regulatory body as a holding exercise to better assess the issues seems greatly to be preferred. Such a policy would also allow for greater conferral between neighbouring states and, in the long run, avoid the kinds of dislocation currently experienced in the regulation of research and practice in the European Union without compromising sensibilities of sovereignty of the respective states.

  However, the emergence of the United Kingdom legislation does mirror the central conceptual observation made earlier in this paper. A Committee of Enquiry was set up under the chairmanship of Mary Warnock, a philosopher, to look into and make recommendations concerning legislation in the field of human fertilisation and embryology. That Committee had a membership drawn from a wide range of interested parties and accepted evidence from whomsoever was willing to make representations to it. The result was that a number of conflicting moral views were expressed. The Committee was unable to reconcile these, though in retrospect Mary Warnock speculated that maybe it was the hope of the Government that "the cool and reasonable voice of Philosophy would reconcile the irreconcilable, and find a compromise where none can exist".[32] She admits that the Committee failed to reconcile various rival values such as the absolute sanctity of human life from its earliest stages on the one hand and the importance of progress in medicine on the other. She asserts that the Committee demonstrated this impossibility. In fact it did not quite do that, though it certainly illustrated it. I have tried to provide a demonstration of the matter in this paper. I think it right however that, whether by force of circumstances, as in the case of the Committee, or by a recognition of the conceptual impossibility, that Philosophy be not trusted with the task of providing a resolution of the question of the status of the human embryo on which to base legislation. The question of the status of the human embryo was not discussed as such by the Committee and its recommendations were not based explicitly on any attempted compromise view of its status. I once thought this a fundamental weakness of the Report but now see it as a helpful, if fortuitous, omission. The Committee was in no doubt, however, of the need for legislation. Mary Warnock's expression of this need, an expression with which I wholeheartedly concur, matches the sentiments of Lukes when faced with the impossibility of resolving the question of identifying human rights in the face of obscene possibilities of the abuse of human beings. She writes:

  ... we were conscious of an increasing sense of urgency that controls should be introduced where none exist, and that the law should be brought up to date so that society may be protected from its real and very proper fear of a rudderless voyage into unknown and threatening seas.[33]

Notes

1. Jones, Ernest, *Hamlet and Oedipus* New York, W.W.Norton, 1949.

2. Weitz, Morris, *Hamlet and the Philosophy of Literary Criticism* Chicago, University of Chicago Press, 1964, pp.23ff.

3. *Ibid.*, p.90.

4. I borrow the term from P.H.Nowell-Smith's *Ethics* Harmondsworth, Penguin, 1954, pp.111-121. My employment of the expression is only loosely related to his but bears enough resemblance for it to be useful.

5. *Ibid.*, pp.113-114.

6. *Ibid.*, p.115.

7. *Ibid.*, p.101.

8. *Ibid.*, p.115.

9. Brockliss, L.W.B., 'The embryological revolution in the France of Louis XIV: the dominance of ideology' in Dunstan, G.R. (ed.), *The Human Embryo* Exeter, University of Exeter Press, 1990, pp.158-186.

10. *Ibid.*, p.172.

11. *Ibid.*, pp.175ff.

12. The case is mine though similar cases have been made by others - e.g. Helga Kuhse and Peter Singer in 'Individuals, humans and persons: the issue of moral status' in Singer, P., Kuhse, H., Buckle, S., Dawson, K. and Kasimba, P. (eds), *Embryo Experimentation* Cambridge, Cambridge University Press, 1990, pp.65-75.

13. See, Fishel, Simon, 'Assisted conception in the human: the embryological view' in this volume.

14. I am indebted to John Churchill for a stimulating account of Wittgenstein's work in this area presented in a paper entitled 'Wonder and the end of explanation: Wittgenstein and religious sensibility' *Philosophical Investigations* 17 (2), 1994, pp.388-416.

15. Wittgenstein, Ludwig, (trans. Paul, Denis, and Anscombe, G.E.M.) Anscombe, G.E.M. and von Wright, G.H. (eds), *On Certainty* Oxford, Basil Blackwell, 1969.

16. *Ibid.*, p.405.

17. *Ibid.*, p.411.

18. *Ibid.*, p.391.

19. *Ibid.*, p.115.

20. Wittgenstein, Ludwig, (Trans. Anscombe, G.E.M.), *Philosophical Investigations* Oxford, Basil Blackwell, 1953, para. 284.

21. *Ibid.*, para 283.

22. *Ibid.*

23. *Ibid.*, Part 2: iv.

24. Wittgenstein, Ludwig, (Trans. Anscombe, G.E.M.) Anscombe, G.E.M. and von Wright, G.H. (eds), *Zettel* Oxford, Basil Blackwell, 1967, para. 541.

25. *Ibid.*, para 545.

26. Wittgenstein (1953), *op.cit.*, Part 2: iv.

27. Wittgenstein (1967), *op.cit.*, para. 543.

28. Wittgenstein (1953), *op.cit.*, Part 2: xii.

29. See, for example, Harris, John, *The Value of Life* London, Routledge and Kegan Paul, 1985 and Lockwood, Michael, 'When does a life begin?' in Lockwood, Michael, (ed.), *Moral Dilemmas in Modern Medicine* Oxford, Oxford University Press, 1985, pp.9-31.

30. Lukes, Stephen, 'Five fables about human rights' in Shute, Stephen and Hurley, Susan (eds), *On Human Rights* New York, Basic Books, 1993, pp.19-40.

31. *Ibid.*, p.38.

32. Warnock, Mary, *A Question of Life* Oxford, Basil Blackwell, 1985, p.99.

33. *Ibid.*, p.100.

4. THE STATUS OF THE EMBRYO - MORE PLACE FOR MORAL INTUITIONS

Jean-Marie Thévoz
Fondation Louis Jeantet de Médecine
C.P. 277, CH-1211 Genève 17
Switzerland

1. Introduction

Many scholars, trying to define a moral status for the embryo, often look toward a definition of the human person, in order to see if the human embryo is sufficiently like persons and might receive the same consideration and protection as people who are already born.

My purpose in this paper is to propose some arguments to show that there is no way to establish a status of the embryo based on a definition of the embryo as being or not being a person. Moreover, I will argue against any attempts to define persons. If personhood is really what we value the most, something so special that we ought to respect it, it cannot be defined without disfigurement. Every time someone thinks he is catching a hold of the core of humanhood, he is missing it *per definitionem*.

A status for the embryo has to be built on the complexity and the uncertainty of what it is exactly, and seriously take into account our moral intuitions. Once this is accepted, we have to look for some acceptable premises concerning embryos in order to gather the largest consensus possible, but with no hope of reaching unanimity.

2. Is the Human Embryo a Person?

Many discussions around the status of the embryo ask whether the human embryo is a person or not or try to argue that the human embryo is or is not a person. They do this as if the answer to this question would give a solution to every or most of the ethical issues involving embryos and foetuses and close the debate. Consequently, in the landscape of bioethics, we find many kinds of theories, each of them attempting to produce more convincing arguments about the personhood of embryos.

On one side of the spectrum, scholars and many church representatives assert that the embryo is a person 'from the beginning', that is either from the moment of conception, or not much later, after implantation.[1] Some of them do not claim directly that it *is* a person, but ask rhetorically "how could a human individual not be a human person?".[2] The basis of the argument is usually continuity of development, potentiality and the

47

D. Evans (ed.), Conceiving the Embryo, 47–54.
© *1996 Jean-Marie Thévoz. Printed in the Netherlands.*

presence of a human genome.[3] I will refer to this standpoint as the conservative standpoint.

On the other side of the spectrum one finds other scholars claiming that embryos cannot be persons, either because they lack sensitivity to pain[4], or because they are not yet self-conscious and autonomous.[5] "Foetuses, infants, the profoundly mentally retarded, and the hopelessly comatose provide examples of human nonpersons" Engelhardt says.[6] They cannot be persons, though they are human, because they lack the "capacity to be self-conscious, rational, and concerned with worthiness of blame and praise".[7] Let us call this point of view the radical standpoint.

3. Difficulties of These Two Polarised Positions

Both the conservative and radical standpoints raise many difficulties. They do not provide a satisfactory account of the differences and the similarities of the human embryo with respect to fullgrown adults.

On one hand, the conservative position cannot see how the actual differences between a two day old embryo and a child or an adult have any moral relevance, even if the differences do not mean that human embryos deserve no respect or protection at all. The moral decision-making process is able to consider special interests of non-personal beings without depriving them of all rights or interests.

On the other hand, the radical point of view does not take into account seriously enough the moral common-sense of valuing entities on other grounds than their intrinsic capabilities or values.[8] Moral common-sense cannot be disparaged simply on grounds of irrationality or inability to present rational arguments. Actually, if morality is one of the most prominent abilities of persons, as neo-kantians like to assert, the common and spontaneous expressions of this morality cannot so easily be downgraded and scorned.

I have briefly described here some of the specific weaknesses of these two standpoints. Nevertheless, I think that an approach to the status of the embryo through the person argument has far more worrysome built-in flaws.

4. Intrinsic Difficulties With the Issue of Embryos As Persons (Or Non-Persons)

To define the issue of the status of the embryo as the problem of whether it is a person or not reduces this issue to a problem of classification. That is, on one hand we have the class of persons, on the other the class of embryos, both clearly defined and circumscribed. The practical problem becomes to know whether the class of embryos belongs to the class of persons or not. Actually, it is possible to classify only entities that are defined at the same level. For instance, only from biological definitions of various species, and biological definition of (say) a beetle, is it possible to assign a beetle to its correct species; likewise, only from moral definitions is it possible to assign an entity to its correct moral status.

The problem with the question whether the embryo is a person or not, is that we are simultaneously trying to know if it belongs to the class of persons *and* looking for its own definition. This means either that we are building an *ad hoc* definition to ascribe to it a moral class, or that we would like to use its presumed belonging to the class of persons to construct the moral definition it needs to enter it. A circular process is created from which we are unable to exit.

No biological enquiry about the embryo can result in any moral evaluation. Any moral evaluation of a developmental step of the embryo comes from a prior investment of moral value into the biological process. For instance if someone argues that the embryo becomes a person from the time at which neocortical activity is discernible, his choice is arbitrary from the scientific view point, because no piece of scientific data can imply that neocortical activity is the special feature of personhood. But he can argue that from his moral point of view mental capacities are what gives sense to personal life and therefore ascribe value to the foetus as soon as it shows some mental capacities. This chosen value given to conscious life is invested at this particular biological time (namely when neocortical activity is discernible) and motivates this particular moral choice. The value predates its ascription to a particular biological timing, and does not emanate from scientific observation. Consequently, one can say that to give value to the embryo is always dependent on a prior value-laden choice. Therefore, one should always state 'because I value genomic uniqueness / continuity in the process of development / transcendental ensoulment / cortical activity / moral capacity / etc., I think that the embryos should be protected from the biological point of fertilisation / individuation / etc'. Unfortunately, the value-laden choice is *a priori* and is difficult to argue for rationally (it seems to belong to pro-attitudes).

Even if we put aside the problem of 'developing persons' (embryos, foetuses, infants), the definition of what constitutes a 'person' is not easy and meets the same obstacles. Among living adults, are there any who don't qualify as 'persons'? People holding the conservative view deny it, others holding the radical view assert it, mentioning people with serious mental deficiencies or complete lack of consciousness.

There are at least three types of definition: essential, descriptive and conventional. I think that we cannot give either an essential, or a descriptive, or a conventional definition of either embryos or persons to construct a status for the embryo. Essential definitions are metaphysical and therefore cannot claim a social consensus in a pluralist society. Descriptive definitions are useful only in order to compare identical objects or differentiate dissimilar ones. From a descriptive definition, embryos and adult humans will always be dissimilar, but that does not mean anything from a moral point of view. Conventional definitions would best suit the prospect of finding a status for the embryo. The problem is that conventional definition presumes agreement or consensus and this is exactly what is missing. Moreover I would fear a conventional definition made for discriminatory purposes, namely sorting out who is or is not a person. Who will draw the line and where?

Many scholars have tried to give a definition of the person, some of them very competently. The resulting problem is that too many definitions are proposed. Should the requested definition define a standard type? But what are the accepted deviations from the norm? Should the definition be comprehensive? But on which criteria is it possible to describe the frontiers of personhood?

There is radical disagreement on how to define the person. The result is a complete lack of consensus on whether the embryo or other marginal entities belong to the class of persons or not.

To try to break this deadlock, I would like to propose formulating the question in another way: Why do we give such a value to human beings? I think that there are some rational answers but also others that, without being frankly irrational, are more emotional or linked to another kind of knowledge than rational and scientific observation. One of the latter kind I would like to develop is the idea that human beings are valued because it is indeed impossible to define or delimit them.

Human beings can be said to be a lot of things ... and much more. It is impossible to say and to know what we are. Each time somebody claims that he has come up with a definition of man, something tells us that he has missed his point. What has been defined is not a person, but a particular image of man.

I think that it is an error to try to define personhood in order to draw a line between persons and non-persons. Even more, we cannot give a definition of what humanhood, or a person, is. Every time we think we have arrived at a good definition of humanhood, we can be sure that we have missed the point we aimed at. If humanhood is the sum of very special characteristics that make every human being so valuable for him/herself, every attempt to define it will reduce that person to an object subject to description. Surely one reason we value persons so much is because they cannot be reduced to any kind of list of characteristics and qualities. Human beings are far beyond any possible description and comprehensive depiction. Martin Buber expressed this idea in saying that every person is a 'Thou'.[9] Any definition can only bring about an 'It' which is surely not the person. Indeed, there is a kind of arrogance inherent in each contending assertion that it has succeeded in defining the person.

5. Finding Other Ways

If we think that man is irreducible to his manifestations and appearances, that he is invaluable in view of a dimension that is not tangible and perceptible by any other means than moral intuition, then we have to renounce attempts to define him. We must change our way of looking at him and the way we speak of him as a person.

It follows that it is necessary for speaking of humans to use the same kind of rhetorical precautions we take in theology to speak of God. We know that nothing we can say about Him can approach any of His characteristics. Thus the prohibition of drawing images of God. Every claim to define God includes its own disclaimer. In a sense we must act in the same way with humanhood. We cannot come close to it in any way. It is in this sense that humans are made in the image of God. To say that human beings are made in the image of God means that, like Him, we are unable and must not attempt to draw images or definitions of persons.

The only way to capture the real presence of a person is to enter into a loving relationship with him/her. Any other approach will objectivise the subject we are observing, reducing him/her to an object that can no longer be called a person.

6. Reasoning in a New Context

Renouncing the attempt to define humans or persons does not give us a content for or a practical status of the embryo. It indicates only that we are to move from the supposed firm ground of rational (but non practicable) demonstration to another ground of discussion, more akin to common moral reasoning. The new ground upon which we have to build a status for the embryo has to deal with uncertainty, complexity, relationships and moral intuitions.

Uncertainty. The impossibility of giving an objective definition of what is an embryo or what is a person implies that we have to deal with uncertainty in our moral decisions or whenever we ascribe some values to something. Uncertainty does not mean total relativism, but openness to other opinions and arguments. It also means that every ethical consideration and decision has to take into account a certain margin of error.

Complexity. We must take into account the very complexity of persons, minds, moral life, and decision-making processes. It would be simplistic to pretend to resolve moral issues through definitions and classifications. We know through psychology, sociology, and philosophy how complicated the human mind is. Motives of action are not crystal clear. We are influenced by a range of factors over which we have only a limited power (the subconscious, social control, etc.).

Relationships. Moral considerations and values are not always and only related to objective and intrinsic qualities. More often than not, values are ascribed subjectively to things or entities because of personal relationships.[10] The subjective link established with a particular entity is what gives it value. This may be the case with very early embryos, namely when prospective parents expect them to become their children. On the contrary, spare embryos from parents who have had all the children they wanted might be less valued.[11]

Moral intuitions. Rational knowledge and philosophical reasoning are not the only way of approaching reality. The world's perception of human beings is more wide-ranging. Human beings also have a moral perception and understanding of things and situations. These are what I call moral intuitions from common-sense. We cannot disregard this dimension of human beings without diminishing their moral character, although common-sense must also be challenged by philosophical reasoning to avoid prejudice.

Moreover, if we are to take seriously the claim that persons have moral abilities, even if most of them are unable to express them in a rigorous and theoretical manner, we cannot dismiss their moral intuitions too easily.

7. Where Do We Go From Here?

The grounds for moral consideration concerning embryos must be reversed. As it is impossible to define from a rational and impartial point of view the intrinsic value of embryos (cf. uncertainty), we must change the place in which we look for values. The status of the embryo must be based on our own moral sense as persons. I do not think of each of our various and individual moral points of view, but of the fact that people who have to do with embryos are adult autonomous beings and as such have a moral sense. At least, this is what theories valuing persons on a basis of autonomy contend. Those deciding the fates of embryos are persons, sensitive to values and moral considerations. They are persons, and as such value-laden entities. When such persons enter into a relationship with other entities, they cannot help behaving in a value-prone way. These behaviours and values have to be evaluated from an ethical point of view, much more than a hypothetical and inaccessible intrinsic moral value of the embryo.

To sum up, modern moral philosophy cannot give a real content to the status of the embryo based only on rational and universal arguments. (A status, and its corresponding protection, that begins only when the child is self-conscious and autonomous is impractical and useless for policymaking concerning research on embryos and foetuses. And if the principle of beneficence can be filled with a concrete content only by 'communities' as Engelhardt contends, it is necessary to look for a content arising from something that falls short of being a rational and universal reasoning.) It is therefore certain that there will be no general consensus over the status of the embryo.

Therefore our task must be humbler and twofold. We need first for research and healthcare policymaking purposes, to sketch some kind of a status of the embryo, with some content to insure its protection, what I will call a 'minimal consensus' and, second, reflection on the meaning and consequences of a recurrent and irreducible conflict between opposing views of the status of the embryo, mainly the conservative and radical views.

Taking these in turn: to further a minimal consensus, we must engage in a step by step process to determine what tend to be the more consensual moral assumptions over our attitudes toward the embryo. One way to build a consensus on any point is to begin with common premisses receiving common approval. That is, to define a minimal consensus on premisses taken from both scientific and common-sense observations. I would like to present some premisses that might be approved by a majority of people, although they will never get approval from everyone.

A first set of these premisses is as follows:

(A) everybody now existing has developed from an embryo - continuity;

(B) not every embryo develops into a full human being - high failure rate;

(C) human embryos stem from human beings - shared origin.

There is a dialectic in our similarities and dissimilarities with embryos. An embryo (or the embryo out of which we grew) is not the same as ourselves now. Nevertheless, there is some kind of similarity between the embryo at an early stage and me now. We must take into account the dialectics between the two kinds of identity proposed by Ricoeur: identity-*idem* (sameness) and identity-*ipse* (selfness).[12] One aspect of the difficulties arising in building a status of the embryo is keeping clear the dialectics between these two identities (*idem vs ipse*) and not to confuse them. Indeed, I am not the same, either in terms of identity-*idem* or of identity-*ipse* as the embryo I was, and therefore there are good reasons for asserting that the two do not have the same value, but nevertheless I share something with it (the embryo) through time. Consequently we have something in common that deserves some respect as I myself deserve respect.

One can add additional premisses to the debate, which may still receive a rather large consensus as they stem from common moral intuitions. This second set of premisses is as follows.

(D) Embryos grow and gain new faculties and potentialities through time. The age of the embryo has moral implications.

(E) The human embryo deserves some protection. The burden of proof belongs to those who want to diminish or withdraw protection.

(F) Every embryo is the result of human intervention. But not all these interventions are equal and not all produce the same moral responsibility toward the embryo. The more voluntary and self-conscious an act, the more responsibility there is to be accountable for its consequences.

As soon as the first premisses have received a sufficient consensus we can proceed to build a set of criteria in order to help decision-making in issues concerning the embryo, short of a fully fledged ontological status of the embryo.

If this step by step process is conducted with sufficiently wide public debate, one can hope to escape extremely polarised standpoints and win some practical answers for pressing problems with a rather high rate of acceptance.

Moving now to the second part of our twofold task: we must acknowledge that this minimal consensus based on common sense and compromises, altough useful for policymaking, will satisfy proponents of neither the conservative nor the radical view. These two standpoints are implacably unreconcilable. Even a position of indifference saying 'let me alone and let me decide for myself' would certainly not be found acceptable from the conservative point of view, killing embryos being seen as homicide. On the other hand, not only the radical view but also more moderate views would not accept the prohibition of reproductive techniques they see as harmless, on the ground that some embryos might die in the process.

The question that arises and must be answered soon is: how can society cope with such lasting conflict in the long term?

Notes

1. Ford, Norman M, *When Did I Begin? Conception of the Human Individual in History, Philosophy and Science* Cambridge, New York, Cambridge University Press, 1988.

2. *Donum Vitae, Instruction on Respect for Human Life in its Origin and on the Dignity of Procreation* issued by the Sacred Congregation for the Doctrine of the Faith, March 1987. Quoted from Pellegrino, Edmund *et al* (eds), *Gift of Life Catholic Scholars Respond to the Vatican Instruction* Washington D.C., Georgetown University Press, 1990, p.12.

3. Cf. Thévoz, Jean-Marie, *Entre nos mains l'embryon* Recherche bioéthique, Genève, Labor et Fides, (Le Champ éthique 17) 1990.

4. Singer, Peter, *Practical Ethics* New York, Cambridge University Press, 1990.

5. Engelhardt, H. Tristram, *The Foundations of Bioethics* New York, Oxford, Oxford University Press, 1986.

6. *Ibid.*, p.107.

7. *Ibid.*

8. Cf. Millican, Peter J.R., 'The complex problem of abortion' in Bromham, David R., Dalton, Maureen E., Jackson, Jennifer C. and Millican, Peter J.R. (eds), *Ethics in Reproductive Medicine* Berlin, Springer-Verlag, 1992, pp.161-188.

9. Buber, Martin, *I and Thou* New York, C. Schribner, 1958.

10. Millican, *op.cit.*, p.178.

11. Thévoz, *op.cit.*, pp.252-254.

12. Ricoeur, Paul, *Soi-même comme un autre* Paris, Seuil, (L'ordre philosophique) 1990, pp.176ff.

5. THE HUMAN EMBRYO AND THE RELATIVITY OF BIOLOGICAL INDIVIDUALITY

Alex Mauron
Fondation Louis Jeantet de Médecine
C.P. 277, CH-1211 Genève 17
Switzerland

1. Conceptual Geography of Embryo Debates

Recently, in a talk-show on various ethical issues broadcast by the Italian-speaking channel of Swiss television, a professor of Catholic moral theology was debating with a secular humanist opponent on the issue of abortion. At one point, he advanced the following argument:

(A)   It is a rational question, which biologists should answer, whether the human zygote[1] is an individual of the human species.

There was no biologist on hand to provide the answer but there was a feeling among the participants that it would have to be "yes", and that this would somehow prove the whole point advanced by the moral theologian, namely that the human embryo has an unconditional right to life since conception. The other discussant was taken aback by this line of attack and it was clear that the theologian had scored a rhetorical point against his secular opponent.

Of course, being right and having the upper hand in public debate are two different matters, as we should know at least since Plato's *Gorgias*. The representative of the *laico*[2] camp was inexperienced and did not point out, for instance, that his disputant was constantly confusing "human individual" with "person". Yet the conflation of these two concepts is a standard move in the argumentation of those who defend the conservative viewpoint on the abortion issue and the personhood of the embryo. Nevertheless, I shall take this statement A as a starting point in examining the kinds of arguments presented in the status-of-the-embryo discussion. My general point is that much of the confusion of these discussions comes from the fact that the arguments that are often pitted against one another really belong to separate domains of discourse. This is especially true when biological statements are adduced to make a conceptual, metaphysical and/or normative point. Biologists and philosophers/theologians have interesting ways of talking past each other and I wish to explore some of them in this paper.

Firstly, one should notice that when one of the discussants in the talk-show brought

D. Evans (ed.), Conceiving the Embryo, 55–74.
© 1996 *Alex Mauron. Printed in the Netherlands.*

biology into the debate, he was drawing on a major source of intellectual authority in our society, namely science.   If you can somehow harness scientific discourse to 'energise' the philosophical or moral thesis you are trying to defend, the case is already half-won.[3] But of course we should query this particular appeal to biological categories and one way to start is to reexamine statement A after the confusion between 'individual' and 'person' is disentangled.   We have now two statements:

(A)   It is a rational question, which biologists should answer, whether the human zygote is an individual of the human species.

(B)   It is a rational question, which biologists should answer, whether the human zygote is a (human) person.

What are the problems with these statements? Starting with B, we can now see that it is plainly false.   It is none of the biologist's business to tell whether an embryo is a person.   'Person' is not a biological concept but belongs to metaphysical/descriptive terminology. It describes an element of reality that is metaphysical in the limited sense that it does not lie within the purview of a 'special' science like biology.   Various definitions of the person have been proposed by philosophers over the centuries, such as the well known one by Boëtius, taken over by Aquinas: *Persona est rationalis naturae individua substantia*. What sorts of beings exactly fit the definition of "an individual substance of a rational nature" has been a matter of philosophical debate to this day.
   On the other hand, statement A is more plausible.   Whether or not some piece of living matter can be characterised as an individual of a certain species is the kind of question biologists should in principle be able to answer.   Furthermore, the biologists answer may well be:

(C)   The human zygote is an individual of the human species.

as the participants in the television debate surmised.   But the exact standing of this statement is not as unproblematic as it seems.   One might ask whether this statement is simply a straightforward report stemming from some empirical research.   As we shall see later, there is more to it than just empirical fact. On the one hand, statement C is certainly *connected* to some empirical data, such as the fact that a new diploid genome is established at fertilisation and doesn't change (well, not much) afterwards. But as my analysis will show, it turns out that statement C is a *definition* of what constitutes a human individual rather than an empirical statement about zygotes and individuals.   Therefore, although C is a valid statement belonging to biological discourse, it is not an empirical finding but a statement making a conceptual or semantic point *about* some empirical data. For the time being, I will simply note that even within a given area of scientific discourse such as biology, one must be careful to avoid a confusion between empirical facts and conceptual/semantic statements.   The concepts of 'individual' and 'species' are especially liable to such confusions and yet they are the kind of basic biological concepts figuring most prominently in bioethics.

But let us go back to the distinction between 'individual of the human species' and 'person'. This distinction allowed us to sort out statements A and B as belonging to two different domains, namely the biological and the metaphysical-descriptive. But obviously debates on the status of the embryo really aim at establishing the truth of specific moral pronouncements, not just at quenching the proverbial academic thirst for clearing up conceptual minutiae. Arguments about whether embryos and zygotes are biological individuals, or persons (in one of many possible senses) are marshalled in order to make an essentially moral point: how one should treat zygotes and embryos and whether or not they have a right to life of some sort. So we are faced with three distinctive areas of discourse: the biological, the metaphysical-descriptive and the normative.

Certainly some may want to query the separateness of these three categories. For instance one could claim that the concept of person is really both descriptive and normative and that once we ascribe personhood to some entity, a whole string of moral presuppositions (right to life, for instance) are automatically attached to it. Still, at this point I assume that there is no compelling reason why this identification of the descriptive and the normative should be made *a priori*, without further inquiry. Even if it turns out that an entity has, say, a 'fairly serious' right to life if and only if that entity is a person, one could conceive of the relationship between the two classes (persons, entities having a right to life) as extensional identity. Some philosophers have upheld the concept of person as central and needed for establishing the ethical standing of the human embryo while others have disagreed.[4] I do not wish to enter into this particular controversy. My point here is only that, as a starting position, there are three distinct kinds of discourse being propounded in these debates. To sum up:

The biological level. My main interest in this paper centres on this one. I aim at showing that the concept of an individual is part of the theoretical armamentarium that we use to understand biological reality and that it is merely operational rather than substantive. This can be seen from the fact that its actual uses differ according to what sort of organism is being considered and, as a result, statements of the form 'entity X is an individual' are not open to refutation or confirmation in the same way as the truly empirical findings of biological science.

The metaphysical/descriptive level. This would include the various philosophical understandings of personhood, especially the idea of the person as an entity having experiences that are part of an individual biography. This is the concept that speaks most closely to the subject-matter of the philosophy of mind and beyond that, of psychology and neuroscience.

The normative level. Here 'person' is the traditional focus of ethical and legal concerns such as the ascription of value, of rights, of responsibility, of blame and praise. This tripartite classification is largely similar to the one proposed by D. Wiggins.[5]

2. A Few Confidence Tricks

Before we go on to explore the meaning of biological concepts relevant to the status-of-the-embryo debates, we should examine a few arguments that purport to solve the question in a single stroke of logic. The following argument is often found in popular writings of the 'pro-life' movement (this syllogism is analysed critically by L. Becker[6]).

Syllogism no. 1

This conceptus is a (living) being.
This conceptus is certainly human (it does not belong to another species).

Therefore, this conceptus is a human being.

Becker shows the fallacy by constructing the following syllogism:

Syllogism no. 2

This sperm is a (living) being.
This sperm is certainly human (it does not belong to another species).

Therefore, this sperm is a human being.

The fallacy is based on the semantic and syntactical ambiguity of the word 'human', which is a true predicate in the second premiss but then functions as a noun in the conclusion.

In a related context, Millican[7] mentions what he calls "hole-in-one" arguments in the abortion debate, i.e. arguments that purport to solve the whole problem in one single step, and gives the following example:

Syllogism no. 3

The embryo is a human being.
Killing human beings is wrong.

Killing the embryo is wrong.

This syllogism is valid but question-begging. In the words of Millican, "no opponents (of the right-to-life thesis) who have their wits about them are the least bit likely to accept the premises". A liberal confronted with this argument might presumably accept the first premiss but needs only to deny the second. He cannot be faulted for being manifestly unreasonable in denying that killing human beings is always wrong, since the matter in dispute is precisely the question whether embryos really are the sort of human beings that are unconditionally protected against killing. Like the confusion of 'individual' and 'person' by the moral theologian mentioned earlier, it is an example of the erroneous conflation of the three conceptual levels that I have listed before.

In order to clarify further the idea of three conceptual levels, we can ask whether it is possible to construct a 'pro-life' argument whose logically valid steps move in an orderly fashion through the three levels. This is the following 'hole-in-three' argument:

Syllogism no. 4A

A human organism is a human individual if and only if it is a diploid entity of the human species resulting from fertilisation.
The human zygote is a diploid entity of the human species resulting from fertilisation.

The human zygote is a human individual.

This is statement C, which I will also call the *zygote-as-individual* thesis.

Syllogism no. 4B

A human organism is a person if and only if it is a human individual.
The human zygote is a human individual.

The human zygote is a person.

This is a metaphysical-descriptive statement.

Syllogism no. 4C

A human organism has an unconditional right to life if and only if it is a person.
The human zygote is a person.

The human zygote has an unconditional right to life.

This is a normative conclusion, which I will also call the *zygote-as-person* thesis. At first sight, that designation might be more appropriate for the metaphysical-descriptive conclusion (4B) but usually the latter is simply a bridge towards a normative thesis. Therefore the 'person' in the *zygote-as-person* statement as I define it comes completely equipped with basic rights. The point of this paper is that the sequence of syllogisms 4A to C carries no intellectual authority, because there are problems with each of the three steps. Each one contains at least one premiss that can easily be denied without factual or logical contradiction.

3. The Biological View of Individuality

...the point of this story, I'll tell you right now.
Did you ever sit down and think about how
It is that each time a baby's born
It's a baby - not a rabbit or an ear of corn?

J. Herskowitz[8]

This ditty expresses a profound fact of life, obvious to normal adults, but which has always been a source of wonder for children, biologists and philosophers: living stuff is parcelled out as discrete blobs we call individual organisms, which can be classified as separate species and which reproduce according to their kind. Furthermore, these separate species are stable through generations (or so it seems at first sight if we discount for a moment Darwinian complications).

Life on this planet comes in discrete entities rather than as a continuous web of life-stuff. This is the material substrate of individual identity. This essential 'chunkiness' of living matter points to the centrality of the concept of individual. It underscores the idea of biological individuality as separateness: the problem of biological individuality does not address directly the issue of an organism's 'being', its ontological status, but rather the question of what makes an organism distinctive and separate from others, especially from such 'significant others' as parents, offspring and siblings. Furthermore, because of the basic facts of generation (namely that new individual organisms are generated by existing ones within species borders), the issue of individuality is also connected to the question of when a new individual can be said to come into existence. The blob of living matter writing this paper is quite certain that he has an identity of his own, separate from that of his parents, but has doubts about the earliest time at which that new identity existed. It is important to realise that these are difficult questions that should not be underestimated in the name of obviousness or common sense.

For a start, it must be emphasised that no particular concept of individuality can be applied uniformly and consistently throughout the living world. Some of the reasons for this appear if we try to unpack the many features that biological individuality must account for. Firstly, it is clear that there is more to being a biological individual than mere spatial unity and spatial separation from other individuals. Parasites and their hosts, as well as organisms living in close symbiotic association, are intimately connected. Plants which have the option of reproducing asexually can remain attached to their clonal offspring so that it becomes a matter of definition at what stage they are said to be two rather than one. Some organisms at the border between single-celled life and multicellular organisation[9] can be viewed either as closely-knit republics of single-cell organisms or as one multicellular individual. However, once we take on board our concept of stable species identities through reproduction as mentioned in Herskowitz' little poem, the concept of individual stands on somewhat firmer ground. For instance, a parasite and its host are separate individuals because they reproduce separately and therefore belong to separate genetic lineages. Furthermore, our concepts of genealogy and parenthood provide us with a genetic basis for constructing a conceptual barrier between parents and offspring. Consider the haploid-diploid cycle of a sexual species such as *homo sapiens* shown in Figure 5.1. There is an alternation between a diploid (two sets of chromosomes) stage that constitutes 'the individual' and a haploid (single set of chromosomes) stage consisting of the gametes. When gametes of opposite sex meet in fertilisation to form a zygote, they reconstitute a diploid set of chromosomes which is stably copied through the successive divisions of the zygote to form a clone of diploid cells which we call the grown individual. In a particular area of the adult individual's body (ovaries and testes), some diploid cells undergo meiosis which returns them to the haploid stage as sperm or oocyte, ready to meet and start another cycle.

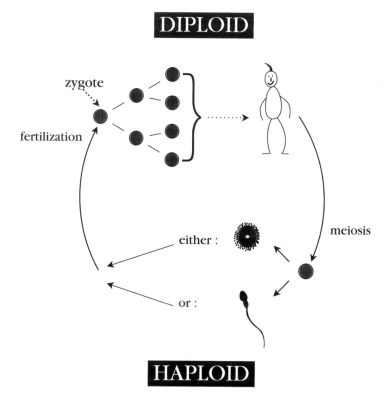

Fig. 5.1. Alternation between the haploid and diploid phase in *homo sapiens*.

It is tempting to see the interposition of random genetic change (involving the genome as a whole) as marking the border between successive individuals. But one must note that random genetic change occurs at two points in the cycle. Firstly, at fertilisation a new diploid genome arises from the combination of the parental haploid sets of chromosomes; secondly, meiosis involves a process of random reshuffling of genes between homologous chromosomes called genetic recombination, as well as a random assortment of chromosomes to separate gametes. Therefore, within one turn of the cycle, i.e. between parents and their offspring, Father Mendel's roulette spins twice. If genetic distinctiveness were the only thing at issue in the concept of an individual, sperm and oocyte would have to be regarded as individuals as well and each of us could be said to be, in a sense, his or her parents' grandchild. In fact, this is how plant biologists tend to see it in the case of certain algae (Figure 5.2), where the gametes

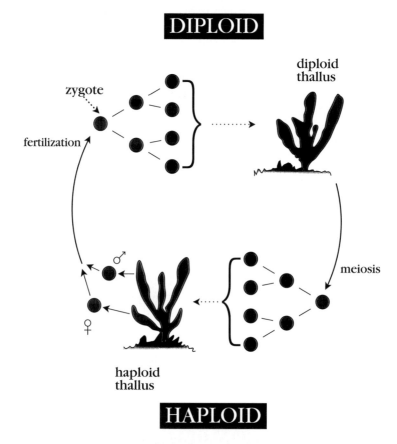

Fig. 5.2. Haploid-diploid cycle of algal species displaying an alternation of fully developed haploid and diploid stages.

divide many times and produce a 'plant' made of haploid cells, in a way that parallels the development of the zygote into a grown diploid 'plant'. Furthermore, in certain species the haploid and diploid plants look alike, so there is no reason to call one an individual and not the other. In this case, there is a symmetry between the haploid and the diploid phase of the cycle since both comprise a multicellular clone derived from a single cell, namely a gamete on the haploid side, a zygote on the other. Generally speaking, in the plant kingdom all the thinkable variations on this theme exist, including one where it is the haploid phase of the cycle which is clonally expanded and not the diploid (fungi). This is the very opposite as compared to the prevailing cycle in vertebrates.

In complex multicellular animals such as we, the cycle is asymmetric. Even though meiosis gives rise to gametes that are genetically distinctive as compared to their parent organism, there is no clonal expansion of haploid cells. In fact, a human gamete does not do much on its own except to await the happy reunion with its counterpart at fertilisation. So it makes good sense not to call human gametes individuals and yet to call a zygote an individual whereas it makes just as good sense to use the term individual for both the haploid and the diploid stage of algae. But what is this 'making good sense' all about? In fact, it points to the purely operational character of the biological concept of an individual. Biologists have (usually implicitly) decided to grant individuality to certain entities and to refuse it to others on various operational grounds within the context of a particular group of organisms. Furthermore, they did it in a way that is not really consistent across the living world[10], which further shows their lack of ontological commitment in using this definition. For it is a mere definition, as mentioned already when discussing statement C. To get a feel for the difference between it and a genuine empirical finding, compare the following two statements:

(C) The human zygote is an individual of the human species.
(C') Biology has recently discovered that the human zygote is an individual of the human species.

Whereas C can be accepted as reasonable, C' is faulty because it erroneously presents the individuality of the human zygote as a contingent empirical fact subject to being discovered by experiment in the same way as, for instance, the fact that:

(D) The p53 gene is involved in some forms of human cancer.

D is what I call a 'pure' empirical fact in the sense that it simply reports a finding and does not at the same time redefine the concepts of 'gene' and 'cancer'. Compare it with the following:

(D') It was recently discovered that the p53 gene is involved in some forms of human cancer.

D' is unproblematic, unlike C'. Another way to illustrate the difference is to imagine the following thought-experiment. Suppose that we live under a dictatorship which, for ideological reasons, would want to suppress either statement C or D. If C became taboo ('Anyone saying that the human zygote is an individual of the human species will be shot'), biologists would simply rearrange their terminology around this obstacle and reserve the term individual for later stages of development, without actually compromising their commitment to scientific truth. If however it was D that was suppressed ('Anyone saying that the p53 gene is involved in some forms of human cancer will be drawn and quartered') this would be a genuine suppression of scientific fact and cancer research would be drawn into something like a new Galileo affair. In short, denying C is epistemologically benign, whereas denying D would be tantamount to asserting a falsehood.

Operational definitions such as C are not discovered by experimental research, nor are they refuted by it. They are unfalsifiable and, in some sense, optional. Nothing of substance would be changed in the body of current biological knowledge if we did not accept statement C. In fact, we have (at least) three options:

1. We could stick to statement C.

2. We could reserve the term 'individual' for more advanced stages of embryonic development, as mentioned already, and use any of the various steps often referred to in the bioethics literature that tries to find a criterion for personhood in the descriptive and normative sense (primitive streak, formation of the neocortex etc.). This would be a narrow construal of the term 'individual'.

3. Conversely, we could adopt the 'botanical' usage described earlier. In that case, zygotes would be called individuals; sperm cells and oocytes would be called individuals too. But this shift in terminology would in no way commit us to any non-biological conclusions. We would not be compelled to call gametes persons (a descriptive conclusion), nor would we have to conclude that Onan's sin is mass murder (a normative conclusion).

In exactly the same way, the concept of individual adopted here, which entails the acceptance of statement C, does not commit us to any particular belief about the personhood of zygotes, nor does it have any bearing on whatever normative beliefs we happen to entertain about how zygotes are to be treated.

In conclusion, appeals to the biological individuality of the zygote carry none of the weight that genuine experimental findings would have. In fact, we can now see more clearly how some of the statements in embryo debates that purport to draw on scientific authority are flawed and purely rhetorical. Conservatives often claim that science has proved that the zygote is a person. When faced with the objection that science cannot possibly prove this (since personhood is not a scientific matter), they retreat to the supposedly consensual statement that, at the very least, science has proved the zygote to be a biological individual and they conclude that this fact must have some moral import.[11] But we have seen that science doesn't prove even that and, as a result, nothing compelling follows from it on the moral level.

4. The Hunter and the Jain

Another popular 'pro-life' argument that is connected to the same fallacy is the tutiorist argument advanced, among others, by the magisterium of the Catholic Church. This is an interesting argument because it takes into account the controversies about the standing of the human embryo and their lack of closure. Also this argument is rhetorically quite powerful. By advancing this argument, the believer (in the zygote-as-person thesis) in effect tells the non-believer: 'If you have the slightest doubt about the issue that divides us, then you must see things my way'. If the tutiorist move is successful, it compels non-believers to switch over to the other side and regulate their (and society's) behaviour on a view-point that they do not really share.

One must note that what I called the zygote-as-person thesis advanced by the most conservative wing within the Church does not represent official teaching. Taking seriously the uncertainty surrounding the precise nature of the early embryo, the Church proposes to play it safe, as it were, and to treat the embryo *as if* it really were a person. In other words, it regards the zygote-as-person as sufficiently reasonable that we would be grossly negligent in not acting as if it were true. The analogy often proposed is as follows. A hunter sees something moving in the bush; is it a rabbit or a human being? If the hunter shoots and kills a person, he would be found guilty of manslaughter because he should have abstained from pulling the trigger in view of the empirical uncertainty about what exactly he saw moving in the bush.

'Empirical uncertainty' is the key idea here. Whether the shape moving in the bush is a rabbit or a man is a matter of fact. It could be settled by empirical investigation and until the result is in, one is justified in speaking of probability (in the modern sense)[12] and of risk. But what about the zygote-as-person thesis? Is it a statement to which we can assign a probability (again, in the ordinary modern sense that relates to factual uncertainty)? No, because its truth or falsity is not a factual matter, something that 'is the case' and could be settled by empirical inquiry. There are two reasons for this. As we have seen, even the much weaker *zygote-as-individual* thesis is not something that can be confirmed or disproved. Talk of zygotes and embryos as individuals is reasonable, but nothing more. But in addition, the more radical *zygote-as-person* thesis involves the metaphysical-descriptive and normative levels as well. So the uncertainty about the zygote's standing is not an ignorance about whether something is the case in the world out there but about what conceptual framework is appropriate to speak about it, and about how we should value it.

The tutiorist argument conflates empirical ignorance with conceptual uncertainty. The former can be dealt with in terms of probability, risk assessment and prudential considerations. We can decide to forgo some action that may have a bad outcome, because we have figured out - or made conjectures about - the risk, i.e. the magnitude of the bad effect and the probability of its occurrence.[13] Conceptual uncertainty is quite another matter. We cannot apply the ideas of probability, risk and prudential calculus to such non-factual issues. *To do so confuses plausibility of opinion with probability of fact.* Of course, when faced with conflicting interpretations of the zygote's standing, it is tempting to ask which opinion is most likely to be right. But this is basically a meaningless question if it implies some sort of underlying fact that could be discovered, at least in principle. There is no right-making element in the world out there that could make one opinion win out against the others. And again, if this is the case at the biological level already, it is even more obvious at the metaphysical-descriptive and normative levels.

At this juncture, the tutiorist might perhaps concede the point that empirical and conceptual uncertainty are distinct but question the relevance of this distinction. Uncertainty might have two different origins. Yet uncertainty it remains; whatever causes it, it imposes a duty of prudence upon us. In other words, there might be something like conceptual and moral prudence, that compels us in ways similar to empirical prudence.

I believe that such a generalised duty of prudence cannot have much force in a society that takes moral pluralism seriously. Certainly, some forms of prudence are praiseworthy, even obligatory, in any society. But these forms of prudence - or of obligatory non-maleficence as it were - will be limited to the avoidance of harms that are generally acknowledged as such. Now consider the predicament of a pluralist society. In such a society, the world of empirical fact is the only one all of us share to the fullest extent. Since as existing physical individuals we are connected by cause and effect, it makes sense to ask for empirical prudence and condemn negligence about factual risks and harms, irrespective of creed or philosophical or political opinion. It makes sense to indict and pass sentence on careless hunters, reckless drivers, absent-minded pharmacists and drowsy air-traffic controllers. But the status of the embryo belongs to another world, the world of philosophical and religious opinion where the closure of debate cannot be effected by recourse to empirical finding. Of course, this is not to say that in this second world, rational discussion is impossible, only that whatever progress the debate makes is based on an area of consensus that is partial, provisional and constructed, rather than discovered out there in the world of fact. Outside this area, pluralism reigns, no matter whether it is acknowledged or suppressed.

Empirical ignorance is the stuff of probability and risk-avoidance, in short of prudential conduct and moral responsibility in case of negligence. Philosophical and moral uncertainty is the stuff of pluralism and a free society acknowledges this. To illustrate this point, let us construct an analogy for conceptual and moral uncertainty, just as the hunter's story exemplifies empirical uncertainty.

The Jain religion of India involves an extreme reverence for life. The Jain are strict vegetarians and some devout Jain are even said to avoid eating at night lest they swallow an insect, or to sweep the ground before them while walking to avoid killing bugs or other small animals. Theirs is a world-view that sees an important moral transgression in killing organisms that are not human and who are quite unlike persons in the usual sense of the word. In this, it differs importantly from the moral views of the average Indian or the average Westerner. If we were tutiorists, the very existence of the Jain outlook would create a serious philosophical and moral dilemma. Either the small bugs who are at risk of being stepped on have a right to life and then we should be earnestly concerned about it, or the bugs are a miniscule moral issue (if any at all) and so we are let off the hook. Who is right? Clearly, no amount of factual investigation will ever tip the balance one way or the other. Should we not try to save the bugs too, on the outside chance that the Jain might be right after all? No, because prudence about probable facts is one thing, pluralist debate about moral opinions quite another.

Could it be then that the Jain's concern for 'lower' animals is too bizarre to be taken seriously? Apart from the fact that this would be derogatory to the sincerely-held beliefs of millions, this world-view may well appear less unreasonable than the zygote-as-person view to many contemporary philosophers of a Benthamite persuasion. They might argue that insects at least have the basic neuronal equipment underlying sensation (even if talk of 'pain' is probably an anthropocentric illusion), which is more than could be said for the human zygote or early embryo. Furthermore, how reasonable is the zygote-as-person thesis? If taken literally, it has some counter-intuitive consequences to say the least. Any contraception that prevents implantation rather than fertilisation is tantamount to murder. This is the case for the IUD, postcoital and injectable contraceptives. In addition, since one in two conceptions fails to result in a pregnancy, there is - at the very least - one pre-implantation death of a person for every baby born. Pre-implantation death becomes the first cause of death in this world and would seem to claim our most pressing medical concerns. We would perhaps have to rearrange our research priorities towards fighting this tragedy and away from cancer, AIDS, cardiovascular disease, malaria and other such trifles. The legal scholar G. Annas has imagined a situation where a two-month-old child and seven embryos stored in liquid nitrogen are present in a laboratory. There is a fire and you can save either the baby or the seven "pre-born persons" as some would call them. Would you hesitate?[14] To quote Annas: "those who equate embryos and children show little respect for children".

Going back to the Jain, we see that the minority point of view they represent cannot be summarily dismissed. In this predicament, what should a society that values pluralism, such as India or ours, do? The Jain should be (and in fact are) free to practice their beliefs. They should be free to try and persuade the rest of us to see things their way. However, they cannot impose their views on non-believers if they want to be peaceful participants in a secular social order. One could imagine that this is psychologically hard on some of them. After all, the bug that gets squashed under a miscreant's foot had the same right to life as its congener that was saved by the Jain's broom. But that is the name of the game. Any member of a liberal, non-theological society that entertains idiosyncratic moral beliefs must come to terms with the fact that many people unthinkingly trespass on his cherished moral rules and that he is not

68   Alex Mauron

permitted to impose them on infidels except through honest persuasion. He must allow
that some harm will be done (from his point of view) to avoid the greater harm of
imposing illegitimate moral and/or legal authority on 'moral strangers', to use H.T.
Engelhardt's well-known phrase.[15]

5. The Problem of Twinning

The purely operational nature of the zygote-as-individual statement is not the only
reason why it cannot do the work that defenders of a personal standing of the human
embryo want it to do. The problem of twinning further underscores how the biological
concept of individual as used so far (and again insisting on its operational and optional
character) differs from the person concept or more generally with any ordinary sense
of the word 'individual' which would map one-to-one onto the person concept. The
problem of monozygotic twins is often misunderstood and goes like this: For several
days after fertilisation, the embryo can split in two and give rise to twins.[16]
Furthermore, there is nothing preordained in this splitting process; it is not hardwired
genetically, for instance. So if we use the zygote-as-individual thesis, the genealogy
of monozygotic twins looks like this (Figure 5.3):

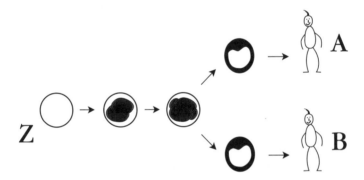

Fig. 5.3. The problem of twinning. The zygote Z splits into two embryos A and
B that eventually become persons A and B.

an individual zygote Z gives two individual embryos A and B, which then go on to
become 'the same' persons A and B. If we believe, as we should, that grown
monozygotic twins are separate persons, then A is not identical to B. Therefore the
following identity cannot be true:

Z *is identical to* A *is identical to* B.

The zygote cannot simultaneously be the same individual as A and as B since the latter two are separate. In other words, individuality as defined by statement C (the zygote-as-individual thesis) does not map one-to-one onto the concept of person as it applies to born humans. Yet another way of saying the same thing is that individuality as defined by statement C is not stably conserved along embryonic development.

This much is trivial and accepted by everyone. It is the significance of this fact which is controversial. Some moral theologians who think in Aristotelian-Thomist terms logically conclude that an embryo can be a person only at the primitive streak stage of embryonic development, after the last chance for twinning is gone.[17] Other theologians, subscribing to the selfsame Aristotelian-Thomist views disagree. To them, the majority of us who have no twin sibling are persons from fertilisation and the others can be accommodated by construing twinning as a process of clonal reproduction.[18] On this interpretation, Z reproduces asexually to give the twins A and B, but they are persons all of them. Maybe Z survives as A, while B is a 'new' person, or maybe it is the other way round. So the couple who generated zygote Z could consider one of its children to be a grandchild. There is no end to the semantic games one can play, but then, under the latter view, one must accept that the genealogy of individuals and of persons in the ordinary sense are different.

To anyone not committed to a belief in a soul or in substantial forms (for those are the beliefs underlying these speculations) all of this must be rather meaningless. In a way, one is basically free to use the terms 'individual' and 'person' as one likes. But one is not at liberty to change the laws of first-order predicate logic. Either one subscribes to the zygote-as-individual concept (statement C) and agrees that it is not congruent with the ordinary concept of person as applied to born humans; or one uses the narrower construal of individual as arising after the possibility of twinning is gone (primitive streak), in which case the numerical identity between individuals and persons is restored, but one must then accept that the zygote is not an individual. Whatever option one takes, it turns out to be impossible to take the moral intuitions that attach to personhood and 'pump' them back, as it were, onto the zygote. Merely redefining 'person' as the sort of human being that arises at fertilisation will achieve nothing. It simply creates a word - let's call it 'DNA-person' - making the statement 'the zygote is a DNA-person' tautologically true. But the connection with the ordinary sense of person is thereby lost and from the statement 'the zygote is a DNA-person', one cannot infer the statement 'the zygote is a person (in the ordinary sense)'. You cannot have your cake and eat it too.

6. Conclusion

We can now recapitulate our analysis in terms of the 'hole-in-three' argument presented in part 2. Syllogism 4A is reasonable but not compelling, because it is based on a premiss that is a reasonable, but optional, definition of biological individuality. We have seen that there are at least two other options: the 'botanical' definition of individuality that considers gametes to be individuals; and the narrow construal of individual that 'starts' later in development so as to map one-to-one onto the born organism. The definition used here, i.e. the zygote-as-individual definition, is probably the most convenient one for purposes internal to parts of zoology and to human biology (but not to plant biology or the study of lower invertebrates, nor - I would claim - to bioethics). This is because it takes into account two major biological considerations. First, it is a genetics-based definition that takes genetic distinctiveness as a necessary (but not sufficient) constituent of individuality. Second, the zygote-as-individual takes into account the asymmetry in the life cycle of animals, where only the diploid phases constitute 'the body' in the usual meaning of the word. It is also congruent with the ordinary view of the succession of generations and does not compel us to redefine parents as grand-parents, for instance. However, this individuality concept does not go all the way towards a one-to-one correspondence with the common-sense view of the body because it cannot account for monozygotic twins. That is the price to pay for holding on to a genetics-based concept of the individual. For if we choose the last option, which basically means to define the individual by moving *backwards* from the born organism as far as we can go without encountering the twinning problem (about 14 days post-fertilisation), then we lose the grounding of individuality in genetics. Again there is no way to win on all counts. No amount of conceptual gerrymandering will change the fact that identical twins are genetically identical while being separate persons.

Steps 4B and 4C will be dealt with very briefly, as they correspond to the issues most extensively discussed in the bioethical literature. Ascribing personhood to human individuals and to these only (4B, 1st premiss) is a massively metaphysical statement that can be, and has been, disputed by philosophers and theologians alike. For instance both contemporary utilitarianism (P.Singer) and neo-kantian moral philosophy (H.T.Engelhardt) disagree with it, for largely opposite reasons. Definitions of the person are a dime a dozen and one cannot hope to assert or refute convincingly this assumption without entering into explicit debate with them. Finally, the connection between personhood and ascription of rights (4C, 1st premiss) is not one that can be smuggled in under the false pretences of obviousness. Perhaps we have here an illustration of a non-controversial interpretation of Hume's is-ought barrier: we must make apparent all our moral presuppositions as such, rather than pretend that we are reading them off from some factual datum. In the end, we cannot avoid a thorough investigation of the rich nexus of anthropological, ethical and symbolic associations that come with concept of person. Nothing short of that can provide a "moral baseline"[19] on which to articulate a moderately consensual view of the embryo's ethical standing.

The use of scientific authority to buttress a strong ethical standing of the embryo is bound to fail. More specifically, there is nothing compelling about the postulated link between a genetics-based individuality concept on one side, and a personhood concept that speaks to the anthropological and moral concerns underpinned by the ordinary sense of 'person' on the other. One might wonder why many theologians and lay intellectuals continue to stick to this hopeless conceptual framework. There could be at least two reasons.

The first is the pressure existing in a secular ethical forum to find a baseline for one's position that is acceptable to all and, for better or for worse, scientific discourse is often thrust into that position. This is even more tempting for those who accept the tutiorist logic, for then rigorous scientific proof is not required, but only scientifically-inspired plausibility. This is typical of the official Catholic teaching that (correctly) denies that genetic arguments can be final on metaphysical and theological matters such as the existence of a soul, but still holds that scientific data provide a "valuable indication".[20] The purpose is not actually to convince non-believers that the embryo is really a person but simply to suggest that 'there might be something in it' and that we should therefore compromise with this view to a large extent. In fact, it is unlikely that more than a small minority actually understand and believe the straight zygote-as-person thesis.[21] To many conservatives, this position may rather be something like a bargaining chip, used to push the societal consensus on such issues as abortion and access to genetic and reproductive services towards a more restrictive position.

The second reason is more philosophical and I offer it as a mere conjecture. Thomist theologians are used to thinking in hylomorphic terms. Even though hylomorphism has been discredited as an approach to natural phenomena since the 17th century, it has still an important function in theological thinking. The idea of substantial forms is thought to mediate between a belief in a spiritual soul and the 'personalist', (allegedly) monist account of man's nature that is so important to the Catholic world-view. In other words, hylomorphism is thought to allow a belief in the soul while still holding Platonic dualism at arm's length. Within this mind-set, the reception of modern genetics and molecular biology is bound to raise false hopes and misunderstandings. This is because there is an unmistakably Aristotelian ring to the language of molecular biology, especially in its popularised versions.[22] Talk of the genome as an organism's 'blueprint' or 'master-plan', of DNA as a genetic 'program', an unmoved mover who gives birth and form to the body's structure and functions, all this is bound to be associated with Aristotelian and Scholastic ideas of matter and form and perhaps to suggest in hopeful minds the excessively optimistic notion that a wholesale revival of hylomorphism is possible. The desire to hook on to the bandwagon of a science, genetics, that is both highly fashionable and presumed to be philosophically congenial must then be irresistible.

Believers in the zygote-as-person thesis are the Jain of the Western world. Theirs is an implausible, but respectable, minority view. It ought to be respected to the extent that it does not infringe on the rights of others. Believers in the personhood of the embryo are free to practise their beliefs and to forswear abortion and IVF for themselves. They may even have a right to see their beliefs accommodated in public policy if no other liberty-rights are affected. But they cannot stand in the way of other person's rights to non-interference in private procreative decisions such as abortion and the use of reproductive services for legitimate medical reasons.

The zygote-as-person thesis has no serious claim on scientific validity. Defenders of women's rights, of basic liberties in procreative matters and of the freedom of scientific research should not let themselves be intimidated by it. They should advance their case in explicitly moral terms rather than let themselves be drawn into discussing alleged facts which only hide specific moral presuppositions.

Acknowledgements

Valuable comments by Dr. Bernard Baertschi, Prof. Bernardino Fantini, Dr. Knut Ruyter and Dr. Jean-Marie Thévoz are gratefully acknowledged. This paper is part of the 'Bioethics Project' of the Louis Jeantet Foundation for Medicine.

Notes

1. Embryological terminology is notoriously vague. There is no clear-cut border between 'zygote', 'embryo' and 'pre-embryo'. I will use the term zygote to refer to the result of completed fertilisation, aware that there is a conceptual uncertainty about what counts as completion and what exact stage should be seen as crucial, see my paper 'What developments of embryo research would be philosophically challenging?' in this volume.

2. 'Secular humanist' might be the closest translation; but the sociology and implications of the antagonism between Roman Catholicism and secular thinking in Latin countries is very different from the relationship between religion and secularity in the Anglo-saxon world.

3. By the way, it is common to fault scientists for trespassing on the limits of their expertise by making broad pronouncements on extraneous (often ethical) topics. But more often than not, scientists and non-scientists alike, whenever they have a religious or philosophical agenda, will be tempted to use bits and pieces of scientific information in a purely instrumental way. So if you hear someone say '... and anyway science has proven that X', don't believe X without really looking into it!

4. Baertschi, B., 'La place et le rôle de la personne en bioéthique' *International Journal of Bioethics* 4 (3), 1993, pp.187-198 and references therein.

5. Wiggins, D., 'The person as object of science, as subject of experience, and as a locus of value' in Peacocke, A. and Gillett, G. (eds), *Persons and Personality* Ian Ramsey Centre Publication No. 1, Oxford, Basil Blackwell, 1987, pp.56-74.

6. Becker, L., 'Les limites du concept d'être humain' in *Cahiers Science-Technologie-Société; Ethique et Biologie* Paris, Editions du CNRS, 1986, pp.135-156.

7. Millican, P., 'The complex problem of abortion' in Bromham, D.R., Dalton, H.E., Jackson, J.C. and Millican, P. (eds), *Ethics in Reproductive Medicine* Berlin, Springer, 1992, pp.161-188.

8. Herskowitz, J. and Herskowitz, I., *Double Talking Helix Blues* Cold Spring Harbor, N.Y., Cold Spring Harbor Laboratory Press, 1993.

9. A well-known example is the slime mould *dictyostelium*.

10. There are more profound reasons why the biological notion of individuality is in philosophical trouble nowadays. They are related to its role in evolutionary theory. As long as the individual is seen as the sole unit of natural selection (as posited by classical neo-Darwinism), individuality seems to be a fairly substantive, non-arbitrary concept. Recent developments challenge this thesis, however, and tend to view individuality as derivative and itself a result of contingent evolutionary events (see for instance Buss, Leo, *The Evolution of Individuality* Princeton, N.J., Princeton University Press, 1987). This may force us to be somewhat more nominalistic about individuals and also makes an interesting parallel to the fate of the species concept under Darwinism, particularly the population thinking of the 'New Synthesis' of the thirties and forties. Species were dethroned from being set types or essences to become something more like 'individuals' in the logical sense (i.e., individuals as opposed to classes), because a species in the modern sense is basically a historically situated object (a single branch on a cladogram, to speak the house jargon). For a discussion of why biological species should be regarded as individuals, not classes, see Ridley, Mark, *Evolution* Cambridge, Mass., Blackwell, 1993, chap. 15.

11. Here is a telling example taken from a comment on the extremely restrictive German law on the protection of the embryo by Cardinal Lustiger, Archbishop of Paris: "[The German law] while refraining from legislating *a priori* on all legal and moral matters, nevertheless admits an irrefutable biological fact which constitutes the minimal definition one can give of the human embryo, namely that *'specific human life exists from the time sperm and egg meet (...). The embryo refers to a fertilised human cell capable of development from the moment the nuclei fuse'*. For that simple reason the embryo has a right to protection and nothing less than establishing such protection can contribute to coherent legislation" (interview in *Le Monde* 12 January 1994, my translation).

12. The concept of probability has an interesting history that involves science as well as moral theology. In the 16th and 17th centuries, major schools of moral theologians confronted with rising divergences on moral issues devised the idea of 'probable opinion' to break the deadlock in the face of conceptual and moral uncertainty. Their important and sophisticated theories of casuistry (probabilism, probabiliorism) were sharply and rather unfairly criticised by Blaise Pascal, who also happens to be an early pioneer of probability calculus, see Jonsen, A.R. and Toulmin, S., *The Abuse of Casuistry: A History of Moral Reasoning* Berkeley, University of California Press, 1988). However, it seems that this casuistic tradition has little bearing on current Magisterium pronouncements on moral matters. According to a present French supporter of this tradition, a truly probabilistic attitude would emphasise personal moral deliberation as opposed to the tutiorist's short-circuiting of the individual conscience in the name of 'playing it safe' (Valadier, P., *Eloge de la conscience* Paris, Seuil, 1994).

13. Strictly speaking, the strong version of tutiorism would seem to disallow prudential calculus, if it mandates *infinite prudence*. Under this view, as soon as the risk attached to some action is non-zero, one should refrain from acting.

14. Annas, G., 'A French homonculus in a Tennessee court' *Hastings Center Report* 19 (6), 1989, pp.20-22.

15. Engelhardt, H. Tristram, *The Foundations of Bioethics* New York, Oxford University Press, 1986.

16. This is partly a reflection of the totipotent character of early blastomeres, the separation of which provides one of several known mechanisms involved in monozygotic twinning in humans; see for instance Gilbert, S.F., *Developmental Biology* third edition, Sunderland, Mass., Sinauer, 1991, p.97. The converse event of twin embryos fusing into a single one and giving rise to a single person, albeit very rare in humans, also exists, and can be experimentally studied in what are called *allophenic* mice (cf. *ibid.* pp.94-96).

17. Ford, N., *When Did I Begin?* Cambridge, Cambridge University Press, 1988.

18. Crosby, J.F., 'The personhood of the human embryo' *Journal of Medicine and Philosophy* 18, 1993, pp.399-417.

19. Millican, *op.cit.*, p.166.

20. The Catholic Church, Congregation for the Doctrine of the Faith, *Donum Vitae Instruction on Respect for Human Life in its Origin and on the Dignity of Procreation* Vatican City, Libreria Editrice Vaticana, 1987.

21. This includes the late French physician J. Lejeune, whose testimony in court on behalf of frozen embryos is reported by Annas, *op.cit.*.

22. Some pioneers of molecular biology who had an interest in philosophy saw this clearly. This is the case of Max Delbrück, who even added the tongue-in-cheek proposal to give a posthumous Nobel Prize to Aristotle for inventing molecular biology (Delbrück, M., 'Aristotle-totle-totle' in Monod, J. and Borek, E. (eds), *Of Microbes and Life* New York, Columbia University Press, 1971, pp.50-55, p.55.

6. HUMAN INDIVIDUATION AND MORAL JUSTIFICATION

Martyn Evans
Centre for Philosophy and Health Care
University of Wales, Swansea
Singleton Park
Swansea
Wales

1. The Claim

Those who want to object to embryo experimentation *because it destroys a particular or identifiable human life* would be on much safer ground were they to argue that a particular human life begins not at fertilisation but at around day 14 after fertilisation. By that time, *totipotency has been lost*, and the development of the primitive streak precludes the embryo from *becoming two or more different individuals through twinning.*[1]

[In such arguments i]t is not the individual formed at fertilisation that is an entity deserving of moral status: such an individual is present only beyond the time at which twinning or recombination can occur. The concept of individuality is more stringent than in the arguments for fertilisation [as marking moral status] and is applicable only 'when it is irreversibly settled whether there will be one, two or more individuals'.[2]

2. Overview

The claim expressed or referred to in these two extracts is that the life that is ended in the destruction of the very early embryo is not an individual life.

Roughly re-cast as a formal deduction (a useful way of handling the various arguments which we shall encounter) the argument which embodies this claim is as follows:

Argument A

(i) Destructive experimentation is morally justifiable if the lives that it ends are not those of individual human beings *(All Des.[not-I] is J)*;

(ii) early human embryos are not individual human beings *(E.s are not-I)*;

D. Evans (ed.), Conceiving the Embryo, 75–85.
© 1996 *Martyn Evans. Printed in the Netherlands.*

(iii) from (ii), ending the lives of early human embryos does not involve ending the lives of individual human beings *(Des.[E] is Des.[not-I])*;

therefore,

(iv) from (i) and (iii), destructive experimentation on early human embryos is morally justifiable *(Des.[E] is J)*.

Justifying destructive embryo research on the basis of this claim would rely on establishing both the *truth* of this Claim and also its *force*.

Clearly one can deny the truth of premiss (i), even whilst accepting the truth of premisses (ii) and hence (iii). I ought to say immediately that such a denial is incorporated in the final position taken in this paper, although I also believe that the arguments for premiss (ii) are neither decisive nor a matter for empirical science, which it seems that some of their proponents take them to be. Is 'an individual life' picked out in a value-neutral way by science, or is it a social concept whose denotation is liable to moral dispute? At least *prima facie*, it is the second of these alternatives that better explains the persistent public debate about the status of the early human embryo.

However, the claim about the life of the early embryo must involve an account of what such a life *is*, if it is not an individual life. For instance the life must be importantly like the 'life' that might be constituted by other organised living human tissue (such as a bodily organ), or other living cells (such as sperm cells). At any rate the life must be 'non-individual' human life.[3] Accordingly, our acceptance of the claim might be compelled empirically, if there is an empirical or *factual* difference between non-individual life in this sense and an individual life. In this case we need to know exactly what the difference is, and we need to be told how to look for the difference and how to identify and describe it when we see it.[4] Alternatively if there is no such factual difference, our acceptance of the claim would have to form a part of our sharing a certain *conception* of the nature of the early human embryo, and this would mean that the claim about there being no individual life in the early human embryo was finally not an empirical claim at all but a kind of value judgement.

It is not *prima facie* likely that embryologists are presenting the claim as a value judgement (as distinct from an empirical description), and my impression of embryologists' writings on this subject is that they present it instead as a factual matter.[5] Initially, at least, it is as an empirical claim that it should be judged. However, in the remainder of this paper, I will set out what I think is the logical case for seeing the claim as a conceptual one; in the light of this I will end by considering what response, if any, is forced upon us by either the conceptual claim itself, or by the logical arguments which could be marshalled in its support.

3. How Might the Claim be True?

For the claim to be true as the result of embryological studies, it looks as though its truth or falsity must be an empirical matter: as though the claim would have to be an empirical one for it to have any force. The larger justification whose core is in fact premiss (ii) of argument A, above, looks like an appeal to science.

Well, suppose it *is* an empirical claim; then in this case it must be either true or false. The evidence for its truth may be positive (i.e. something *other than* an individual life is observable in the conceptus such that it excludes the presence of an individual life: for instance, all the biological material in the conceptus is accounted for, and is seen to constitute something which is empirically not an individual life and, ideally, is incompatible with its being an individual life); or the evidence may be negative (i.e. no material which could biologically constitute an individual life is observed, and there is no reason to think we ever could observe such material in the conceptus).

But we must also consider that the claim might finally be a conceptual one, that cannot ultimately be maintained as an empirical matter. One aspect of the matter illustrates this, namely the allegedly indeterminate or *stochastic* nature of early embryonic development. This stochastic development is sometimes cited as a ground, though not the only ground, for denying the individuality of the early embryo. I say 'allegedly' because the indeterminacy may be a function either of the phenomena themselves or of the limits of our present knowledge. The implications of stochastic development are that given stages in embryogenesis are underdetermined by their own prior stages but, since science tends to abhor the suggestion that there can be effects without causes, these implications deserve scrutiny. For instance we must ask whether it can be demonstrated whether or not there is some as-yet undisclosed feature in either the conceptus or the maternal environment or some interrelation between the two which governed the fate of cells, where those cells both (a) occupied some spatial position and (b) were undisturbed by the experimenter. If this cannot be demonstrated either way, then the claim about stochastic embryogenesis is not falsifiable, and is not an empirical claim but is rather a way of *conceptualising* the early embryo.

3.1. THE RELATION BETWEEN EMPIRICAL CLAIMS ABOUT STOCHASTIC DEVELOPMENT AND LOGICAL CLAIMS ABOUT THE IDENTITY OF INDIVIDUALS

Prima facie, the empirical claim about indeterminate or stochastic development can be lodged independently of the logical claim about the identity of individuals. I *think* that the reverse is true as well: a logical point about the identity of individuals need not presuppose any actual developmental processes, and hence we can consider the two kinds of claim quite separately on their merits. We shall do so, shortly, below. First let us notice that the logical point about identity could be silent on the question of whether there is any pre-disposing (even pre-determining) feature of a given early embryo to become twin foetuses. The logical point would rely on the supposition that a pre-determining feature in an early embryo did not *constitute* there being two lives at that point. And if there are not, for that or for some other compelling reason, *two* lives then neither can there be *one* life either, because of the logical requirements of identity.

Of course if one challenges this then one is in effect denying one of the *premisses*, in this case the minor premiss, of the logical claim. Here is the general form of the logical claim in syllogistic guise:

Argument B

(i) Individual lives occur only within the continuous living existence of single entities *(All I.s are W)*;

(ii) the living existence of the early human embryo is outside (prior to) the continuous living existence of a single entity *(E is not W)*;

therefore

(iii) the living existence of the early human embryo does not count as, nor fall within, an individual life *(E is not an I)*.

Obviously if one denies any of the premisses of the claim then one does not meet the claim on its own terms. (I tackle the minor premiss here largely because I feel intimidated by the major premiss. Holland, I think, does indeed take on the major premiss[6], even having accepted that the early life of monozygotic twins is not plural in the way that the later life is. His contention is that the early life is nonetheless identical with the later, and is at the earlier stage *one individual* where it is later two. But the attempt is tortuous and I don't think satisfactory, even for Holland.)

3.2. THE EMPIRICAL CLAIM CONCERNING STOCHASTIC DEVELOPMENT

There are two senses in which 'stochastic processes' are asserted: (i) is a weak sense in which the relation between present and previous states of a system is simply *too complex* to be described in anything other than probabilistic terms; whereas (ii) is a strong sense in which present states of a system are *not determined by* previous states. The trouble with (i) is that it seems not to provide the sort of ontological (and hence, supposedly, moral) discontinuity between earlier and later stages of embryonic development which is claimed; the trouble with (ii) is that it seems at odds with what science can tolerate in that it involves events which are without causes. I suppose that if (ii) were true then it would involve a pretty striking ontological discontinuity, although whether that entails a moral discontinuity requires further argument.

In particular, if stochastic embryogenesis is true in this strong sense (ii), the question is whether the claimed moral conclusions about the permissibility of destructive embryo research really do follow. Of course there is a sense in which they cannot strictly follow, since they begin with premises which are at least supposed to be independent of value and discoverable by scientific embryology. However proponents of those conclusions will argue that stochastic embryology constrains the ontological descriptions that we can apply at various stages (in particular, 'individual', 'human being', 'human embryo' are disbarred at different stages) and that it is *these ontological descriptions* which carry the contested moral weight. The moral conclusions therefore *do* follow, according to this view, from the stochastic development, via the mediation of the ontological descriptions which are allowable at different stages of embryogenesis.

Resisting *this* line of argument would therefore amount either to contesting the provenance of the alleged constraints on description, or to contesting that those descriptions exhaust the range of moral objects. (This last manoeuvre, certainly legitimate, suggests something which we are steadily establishing: that finally the success or otherwise of the Claim must be judged against moral convictions and not against deductive rigour. But we shall reflect on this in conclusion.)

*

The denial of individuality does not rest on these grounds alone, as I have conceded. Other grounds concern the idea of 'a spatially defined entity that can develop directly into a foetus'[7] and the idea of a discontinuity in development between the so-called pre-embryo and the foetus itself.[8] Again these grounds deserve sceptical scrutiny, since it is one thing to deny that something is an individual at all, and quite another to deny simply that something is not the same individual as a later individual. The claim of discontinuity in identity needs to be open to falsification if it is to be a genuinely empirical claim. I shall explore the suggestion that it is, by contrast, a further way of *conceptualising* the early embryo.

3.3. A REFINEMENT OF THE CLAIM ABOUT STOCHASTIC DEVELOPMENT: THE ARGUMENT FROM TOTIPOTENTIALITY[9]

Argument C

(i) Living tissue of a given species, whose component cells are presently totipotential with respect to their future development and function, does not constitute an individual of that (or any other) species *(All T is not-I)*;

(ii) the cells of the early human embryo are totipotential *(E.s are T)*;

therefore

(iii) the early human embryo is not an individual of the human species *(E.s are not-I)*.

This won't do, in the sense that it obviously is an individual *something*, and the 'something' is obviously of the human species. So *what sort* of something is it? The notion of the individual in one sense could be removed entirely, since every descriptively isolable phenomenon could be an individual something. For instance the twelve-to-sixteen-cell embryo, or morula, is also an individual; so what is at stake is perhaps the difference between what a morula *is* or *counts for* as distinct from an embryo of greater development.[10]   Maclaren's reference to the post-differentiation embryo as a 'spatially defined entity' illustrates a comparable point; on whose definition is this such an entity where a morula is not? (It is one thing to say that the morula is a clump of cells and quite another to say that it is a clump of cells *and nothing more*.) Moreover, what difference is made by the fact that things *are* of different sorts? Specifically, what happens when something changes from an F to a G, where F is asserted to lack a moral status enjoyed by G? We see this kind of question posed elsewhere (as in disputes concerning the moral status of the foetus, the newborn generally, the mentally impaired, the comatose, the PVS patient, and the 'brainstem dead' patient) but it might be objected that at least these are all indisputably individual human lives, and that there is a qualitative difference about the *difference* here claimed, where *this* difference can somehow be contrasted with those other differences.

Since the early human embryo is then after all obviously an individual something-or-other, the point that defenders of the claim wish to establish is that the early human embryo is not an individual *human being*. Therefore what is needed is a modified argument C_1:

Argument C_1

(i) Living tissue of a given species, whose component cells are presently totipotential with respect to their future development and function, does not constitute an individual being (in the sense of an individual member of a species) *(All T is not-I[B])*;

(ii) the cells of the early human embryo are totipotential *(E.s are T)*;

therefore

(iii) the early human embryo is not an individual being of the human species, that is, it is not an individual human being (in the sense of an individual human being) *(E.s are not-I[B])*.

Here the conclusion is apparently closer to what supporters of the claim want to have. Whilst the truth of premiss (i) is not obvious to the scientific layman, perhaps it could be something that is empirically established by science. As we can see from Mauron's discussion[11], biologists use different senses of the notion 'individual', and not all of them conform to the sense of 'individual' in ordinary use, as when we talk about individual human beings (or, more familiarly, individual *people*). However there is a further assumption in the parentheses in premiss (i), concerning who are the 'we' who would fail to acknowledge a totipotential cell mass as an individual human being. The 'we' in question are primarily the scientists themselves, since few laymen would encounter either the cell masses in question or descriptions of them or judgements concerning them. It seems to be a matter for the social sciences to determine whether the convictions of embryologists can readily be generalised to cover the parentheses in the conclusion (iii) such that there is some definite 'sense in which we acknowledge an individual human being', where 'we' refers more generally, that is, *outside* the discourses of embryology, law or philosophy - and such that the rest of us would, like the embryologists in question, refuse to acknowledge the early human embryo as an individual human being. (Holland has addressed the question of whether there is any obligation to regard the adult form of a species as the archetype of an individual of that species, and observes that at any rate biologists are *not* under any such obligation.[12])

There is one feature of individual human beings, however, that virtually no-one would deny; namely that individual human beings have separate, unique identities. They may often share characteristics; they never share identities, whatever may be claimed in science fiction or espionage thrillers. In this respect, there can be no doubting that the constituency of opinion grandly referred to in the previous syllogism as 'we' must, certainly, include us all. Let us, then, now consider the strongest of the Claim's supporting arguments.

3.4. THE POSSIBILITY OF BECOMING TWINS - THE 'NUMERICAL IDENTITY' OBJECTION

The 'numerical identity' objection is a way of reaching the conclusion of Argument C_1 above but without using, because without *needing*, the precautionary reference in parentheses to who acknowledges what. As we'll see, it is a clearly logical argument, and does not even appear to rely on extending the empirical conclusions of developmental biology into ordinary public usage:

Argument D

(i) All individual human beings have a continued numerically single identity *(All I.s are S)*;

(ii) early human embryos have the potential to become twins or higher-multiple siblings *(E.s can be M)*;

(iii) multiple identity and single identity are mutually exclusive *(All M.s are not-S)*;

(iv) from (ii) and (iii), early human embryos have no continued numerically single identity with their resulting foetus(es) *(E.s are not-S)*;

therefore

(v) from (i) and (iii), early human embryos are not individual human beings *(E.s are not-I)*.

On the face of it, the argument is compelling. If it has a weakness, one might be found in the jump from premisses (ii) and (iii) to premiss (iv), specifically, with the move from what *can* be true *of some embryos* to what *must* be true of them all. As the lawyers say, 'Hard cases make bad law', particularly when harnessed to the problems of imperfect knowledge, or to the fallacy of generalisation as it bears on the question of the *epistemic* force of these relatively few cases of monozygotic twinning (as distinct from the vast majority of embryos which either fail to develop at all, or survive and develop into a single foetus). Note, however, the risk of making a trivial response to Argument D by concentrating one's fire on this possible weakness: it is as much an act of faith to suppose that some distinguishing feature *will* emerge via future research, earmarking those relatively few embryos destined for twinning, as it is an act of faith to suppose the process to be genuinely stochastic in the strong sense.

We must recognise that these cavillings, in the face of a generalisation which may after all turn out to be empirically justified, look uncomfortably like cowardice. *What if* premiss (ii) can after all sustain the leap to premiss (iv), in the light of new knowledge?[13] Acts of faith are no response at this stage. It seems that the proponents of the general Claim (concerning the justification of destructive embryo research) have established a crucial part of their case, namely premiss (ii) in Argument A, above - from which that argument's premiss (iii) straightforwardly followed. Given this, then, what *is* the force of the Claim that we have been examining?

4. The Force of the Claim

Can we now accept the premisses of the original Argument A, yet still resist its conclusion? In retrospect, we have accepted them all except the crucial, first, major premiss - that *if no individual lives are ended*, destructive research is justified. Now it seems that our resistance to the conclusion of Argument A *must* stem from resistance to the major premiss - in effect, from simply not holding the moral view embodied therein. We may accept that no individual lives are, in fact, ended, and *still not* believe - as the Claim requires us to believe - that destructive research on human embryos is justified in virtue of that fact. That is, we may concede that an *ontologically significant* stage in human development is reached at individuation, as presently described.[14] Yet unless the descriptive constraints, imposed by this stage upon its predecessor(s), rule out significant moral objects among the predecessor stage(s), then we are back to the familiar problem that non-normative premisses cannot entail normative conclusions. (Roughly, if the premisses are normative then they are not wholly discoverable by science. If they are not, then there is no contradiction in accepting the ontological conclusions but rejecting the moral conclusions.)

The last question to be faced, then, is this: *Do* the constraints on possible descriptions rule out significant moral objects in the predecessor stage(s)? It will be seen immediately that this is not an empirical nor even a conceptual but a *moral* question, and answers to it constitute a moral view. The trouble with moral views is that people can disagree over them, and since the hopes of those putting forward the logical objection concerned the overcoming of moral disagreement, those hopes are bound to be disappointed. Disagreements over the right way to conceptualise the embryo will collapse back into the very disagreements over moral status that are supposed to be *settled by* claims such as the one we are considering. *The evidence that goes into establishing the individuation claim is typically not innocent of the views which the claim embodies, and which the claim is supposed to uphold.* This is of course not a necessary truth: it is a somewhat empirical assertion I lay against those versions of the claim (with their supporting evidence) which I consider. It invites a requirement, though: evidence for the various versions of the individuation Claim ought to be inspected in the way that I attempt, and the evidence ought to survive that inspection if it is to be taken seriously as independent support for any version of the Claim. Perhaps to some extent this is a task for social scientists rather than (or at any rate as much as) for philosophers, although I hope to have shown already that philosophical inspection is very much to the point.

Supposing that it turns out that the rest of us would, like the embryologists in question, refuse to acknowledge the early human embryo as an individual human being. Faced with accepting this conclusion, best established by Argument D, our next question is to consider what happens when we are forced to give up that description (the ordinary sense of 'individual human being') with reference to the early human embryo - what happens, that is, if we accept the truth of the claim that 'no individual lives are ended'. Have we now a compelling reason to think that destructive research on human embryos is morally justified?

The answer to this hinges on whether we think 'individual human being' to be an *inclusive* or an *exclusive* moral category. This should not surprise us. Why have the proponents of the Claim been anxious to deny that the early embryo is an individual human being? Not, finally, because continuous numerical *identity* is in itself an important problem, but because it is meant to guide us to the morally-relevant *properties* of the early embryo, properties which we are then meant to find insufficient to impeding destructive embryo research. But people, notoriously, disagree over what moral relevance different properties have; and in the case of embryo research no less than in the case of debates about brain death, the proper treatment of the comatose and so forth, science cannot tell us what we must find morally compelling. Logic can, of course, challenge us to consider whether our *unreflective* use of certain descriptions is sustainable.

If we are logically forced to accept an argument compelling us to give up the unreflective use of certain descriptions, we are also forced by logic to choose between (a) changing our moral view, since the morally significant descriptions cannot any longer apply;   and (b) seeing 'new' descriptive categories (for instance, the pre-individuated human embryo) under presently-existing, and moreover significant, moral descriptions or categories.   Logic might force us to make a choice between these alternatives, and indeed I think that our analysis has shown that it does;   but, like science, logic cannot direct us as to which way we should choose.

Acknowledgements

I am grateful to Rolf Ahlzén, Donald Evans, Keith W. James, Göran Lantz, Alex Mauron, Neil Pickering, Frances Price and Hugh Upton for remarks and suggestions made to me during the course of preparing this paper.

Notes

1. Kuhse, H. and Singer, P., 'Individuals, humans and persons: the issue of moral status' in Singer, P., Kuhse, H., Buckle, S., Dawson, K. and Kasimba, P. (eds), *Embryo Experimentation* Cambridge, Cambridge University Press, 1990, pp.65-75, p.68 (my emphasis).

2. Dawson, K., 'Segmentation and moral status: a scientific perspective' in Singer *et al* (eds) *op.cit.* pp.53-64, p.54.   Dawson's final sentence quotes Ramsey, P., 'Reference points in deciding about abortion' in Noonan, J.T. (ed.), *The Morality of Abortion* Cambridge, Mass., Harvard University Press, 1970, pp.60-100, p.75.

3. Maclaren seems to suggest an entity which is simply not the *same* individual as the later individual; the reference to co-extension is puzzling (Maclaren, A., 'Prelude to embryogenesis' in Bock, G. and O'Connor, M. (eds), *Human Embryo Research: Yes or No?* London, Tavistock Publications, 1986, pp.5-17, p.14 and p.15). Kuhse and Singer make the same allusion when they say that "the zygote that gave rise to me and I, the adult, are not the *same* individual - the *former* is a unicellular being totally devoid of consciousness..." (Kuhse and Singer, *op.cit.*, p.66, emphasis added).

4. It is here apparent how science is dependent on philosophically contestible concepts.   The notion of an 'individual' is much more obviously a philosophical than a scientific notion; to rescue it from philosophy, the embryologists need to give us a defensible scientific definition of 'individual', *and* show why we should accept it as proper to human beings.   In this, as Holland argues (Holland, 1991, cf. note 6) they cannot *as biologists* assume that it is the human adult which offers the paradigm.

5. See for instance Edwards, R., 'The Human Embryo' in Edwards, R., *Life Before Birth* London, Hutchinson, 1989, p.49; Marshall, J., 'The case against experimentation' in Dyson, A., and Harris, J. (eds), *Experiments on Embryos* London, Routledge, 1990, pp.55-64, p.58; Maclaren, *op.cit.* pp.11-12 and pp.14-15; and Austin, C.R., *Human Embryos* Oxford, Oxford University Press, 1989, p.17 and p.18.   These authors, incidentally, are by no means entirely in agreement with each other as to how the early embryo should be viewed; their common characteristic is that they take the question as either actually *being* or, in Austin's case as *hingeing upon* essentially factual matters.

6. Holland, A., 'A fortnight of my life is missing: a discussion of the status of the pre-embryo' in Almond, B., and Hill, D. (eds), *Applied Philosophy* London, Routledge, 1991, pp.299-311.

7. Maclaren, *op. cit.*, pp.11-12.

8. *Ibid.*, pp.14-15.

9. This is the essential ground of what Kuhse and Singer take to be the decisive argument, concerning numerical identity, against ascribing the moral status of individual human beings to early embryos; Kuhse and Singer, *op. cit.*, p.68).

10. Even embryologists disagree over the proper denotation of 'embryo' - consider the version put forward by Austin (Austin (1989), p.17).

11. See Alex Mauron 'The human embryo and the relativity and biological individuality' in this volume.

12. Holland, *op. cit.*, p.301.

13. I mean, for instance, the compelling establishment of a paradigmatically random process at work - something comparable to the radioactive decay of atoms where, I am assured, we can find present states effectively unrelated to previous states, and the disappearance of causation in any recogniseable sense. (I am grateful to Dr Keith W. James for this suggestion.)

14. As if the previous controversies were not enough, not all embryologists think that individuation is satisfactorily established even by fourteen days: see Dawson, *op. cit.*, pp.55-61.

PART TWO

Moral Values in Social and Cultural Contexts

7. CONTRACEPTION AND THE MORAL STATUS OF THE EARLY HUMAN EMBRYO

Stephen Beasley
Community Pharmacist
R.A. Hopkins Ltd.
152 Sundon Park Road
Luton
Beds LU3 3AH
England

1. Introduction

1.1. THE BACKGROUND: THE POST-COITAL ('MORNING AFTER') PILL (PC4)

How may we treat the early human embryo? Should human society be willing to afford to it some degree of protection? Do we need to know precisely what it is, in order to answer these questions? If so, is it already a human being, a human individual, or is it rather some sort of 'pre-person' with the inherent potential to later become a person in a fuller sense?

   The question as to when the life of a human being can properly be said to have begun has perplexed the minds of scientists, philosophers and theologians for many years. More recently, pharmacists have become embroiled in the conceptual confusion surrounding the issue as a result of the Department of Health's announced intention of investigating the possibility of allowing the post-coital contraceptive pill to become available to the public without prescription (via pharmacists, at least in the first instance.)[1]   A steering group set up by the Royal College of Obstetricians and Gynaecologists, chaired by Sir Stanley Simmons was later said to be broadly in favour of such a move.[2]   This news generated much correspondence in the *Pharmaceutical Journal* as to the appropriateness of these plans, and the underlying causes of disagreement are not hard to discern. When does the life of a human being begin? Mr. P. McCrystal writes, "The real issue for the pharmacist is whether he should co-operate in a transaction which has a high probability of causing the expiration of a new human life ... That human life begins at conception is well proven. In health promotion for women who have conceived there are two patients for the pharmacist to consider, not one".[3] In a similar vein, Mr. J.A. Lane writes, "A new human being, genetically complete, exists from the moment of fusion of male and female gametes, irrespective of implantation".[4] On the other hand, Ms.K.E. Godfrey writes, "Ms. Shaw refers to PC4 as an abortifacient which, quite clearly, it is not, since the drug prevents

89

D. Evans (ed.), Conceiving the Embryo, 89–118.
© 1996 *Kluwer Law International. Printed in the Netherlands.*

implantation of an ovum if it were to have been fertilised, which may not necessarily be the case. A foetus will never exist, therefore talk of an abortifacient is nonsense. It is time these pharmacists who object on the grounds of their perceived morality got a grip on reality and put their sanctimonious and judgmental attitudes out of their professional lives".[5] This final comment which seeks to bring a divide between a person's moral convictions and their professional action caused others to react. Mrs. M.E.M. Martin wrote, "there are many community pharmacists who embrace the pro-life ethos but recognise that the standards and beliefs by which they themselves live cannot be imposed on others ... ".[6] Miss. C. Breewood agrees, "It must be said that the duty of every pharmacist is to their customers, not just to their own conscience. Pharmacists should not use their professional position to ram their personal beliefs down everyone else's throat".[7] Others disagree, arguing that pharmacists are of course not obliged to supply just anything the public thinks is right or good. Mr. A.G.M. Madge writes, "We are enjoined that medicines are not mere articles of commerce. The pharmacist's conscience is a precious gift that delineates pharmacy as a profession. How many times in the past has the role of the pharmacist with his conscience and judgement been in advance of codes and laws?"[8] Miss. A. Terry is forthright in rejecting the view of Ms K.E. Godfrey, who, she writes "seems to take the view that pharmacists should leave their consciences at home when they go to work. This is entirely unreasonable".[9]

Of course, there are other areas of moral concern for those advocating the greater availability of the post-coital pill (PC4), such as how does the pharmacist know the patient is telling the truth: is she in fact many weeks pregnant? And will the public come to view PC4 as a form of family planning alternative to other forms of contraception? However, in tackling the basic confusion in the above correspondence, I shall need to address two questions: firstly, 'is the taking of PC4 a form of *contraception* at all?' If it is true that the life of a human being begins once fertilisation of the ovum is complete, then to deliberately prevent its implantation in the uterus is to end a life that has begun, not to prevent one from starting. On this view, the taking of PC4 is an early form of abortion, as is the use of the intra-uterine device (IUD) which works by a similar method. If one concludes that this is morally reprehensible, then it follows that the implications for embryo research and *in vitro* fertilisation are also drastic. The second question I shall need to address is 'do we really need to know when a human life begins anyway?' I shall suggest that our answer to this question may well depend on our own 'worldview' - the element of subjectivism which is inherent in us all.

It is my intention to espouse two differing views: the first is theistic i.e. based on the premiss that God does indeed exist and that human life is valuable to him from its beginning (and by implication ought to be to mankind); the second arguing from the opposite non-theistic stance. I shall argue, in the first case, that significant, though not absolute, rights of protection should be assigned to the embryo after implantation at Day 14, the time when cell differentiation and gastrulation occurs i.e. when the primitive streak of the early embryoblast is formed; and that before this time no human person exists. In the second case, I shall propose a different set of criteria for valuing the existence of a human being and will conclude that a weaker and more graduated form of moral significance be assigned to the embryo, from a stage in the development of the nervous system (the beginnings of sentience) and increasing steadily during foetal development.

It will thus be my aim to indicate that in neither case does the use of PC4 or the IUD jettison the life of a newly formed human being and therefore these are indeed contraceptive methods rather than means of abortion. However, it will become clear that if one believes that the newly implanted human life is indeed a person in the eyes of God, having an eternal destiny, then one's attitude towards that life from implantation onwards is likely to be vastly different from a non-theistic view and this will have major ramifications for the later-abortion issue.

1.2. EMBRYOLOGICAL FACTS AND HUMANISTIC AND RELIGIOUS VALUES

Is the embryologist in a position to inform the rest of society of just when a human life begins? What is not in dispute are the facts of embryology: male and female gametes fuse and give rise to an unpredictable and unique chromosomal genotype, which, if free of major intrinsic defect and given favourable environmental circumstances, will develop into one (or more than one) human being. What is more controversial is the interpretation of these scientific truths. What science is unable to tell us is whether the newly fertilised ovum is, by virtue of its unique human genotype and self-generating capacity, already a human being and will go on becoming what ontologically it already is, or whether the zygote is rather the substrate from which a new individual will arise over the ensuing days or months. The entity we call variously the zygote, early embryo or blastocyst (after the first cell divisions) is certainly human, in the sense that it possesses a human genotype, and it is unquestionably living - it exhibits all the biological signs of being a live human cell(s). However, simply being human by type and alive is not sufficient to establish that the early embryo is a living human being. It may instead be the case that it is simply a multiplying collection of human cells which may later become a human being. If this is the case, our use of language may need to be amended, conception occurring at a later date than fertilisation of the ovum, whereas we currently speak of the two as the same event.

C.E.Curran is one of many writers who agree that "Biological, genetic or scientific data alone will not be able to solve the problem of when truly human life begins ... ", it is rather "a philosophical or human judgement ... ".[10] In a similar vein, Daniel Callahan says, "Biological data ... do not carry with them self-evident interpretations. There are no labels posted by God or nature on zygotes, primitive streaks or fetuses that say 'human' or 'non-human'".[11] Implicit, then, is the need to bring human deliberation and judgement to bear upon the raw data of embryology. This can lead to quite divergent views, as is well illustrated by theologian Paul Ramsey (who is well acquainted with the facts of embryology) and consultant geneticist Caroline Berry: Ramsey says, "in all essential respects the individual is whoever he is going to become from the moment of impregnation [of sperm into ovum] ... his subsequent development cannot be described as becoming someone he now is not ... ".[12] Berry disagrees however, saying, "A person must be more than the sum of his or her genes"[13], and referring to the genotype urges the Christian to ask "does this printout bear the image of God?"[14]

Daniel Callahan continues, "it will be evident that people not only have the right, but are forced to bring extra-scientific values and conceptual systems to bear on the facts ... the way we interpret reality will depend upon our prior choice of some particular set of terms with which to do the interpreting".[15] Each person seeking to "interpret reality" comes with his own set of beliefs, his own "worldview". It is improbable that any of us can approach a subject like this totally objectively, divorced from the influences of culture or personal belief: we each need some frame through which to view and categorise the world around us. The very term "embryo" is likely to be value-laden and to provoke from us some subconscious moral response according to our particular frame of reference. Our use of the term is likely to reflect the culture or sub-culture of which we are a part, whether ethnic, Christian or feminist etc. Zbigniew Szawarski observes, "In the moral usage the term "human embryo" always conveys a moral message. It expresses a moral tradition specific for a community the speaker belongs to".[16]

As indicated earlier, it is my intention to look as dispassionately as possible at two quite different ways of seeing our world. The question of religious belief is not one that can be decided by rational argument. Theism which is not irrational and yet places faith in God's existence in a way that goes beyond rationality, as in the case of Christianity, is an example of a worldview providing one particular frame of reference through which to observe and categorise the world. It is likely to divide a man from his neighbour on many moral issues including the one presently under consideration, and in this paper I hope to take equally seriously the theistic and non-theistic worldview, though I recognise I may not be able to entirely disrobe myself of my own subjectivism. It would be simplistic, however, to think that in the case of the moral and ontological status of the early human embryo that Christian belief, or lack of it, neatly divides opinion into two uniform camps. On the contrary, Christians are divided as to when exactly a human being comes into existence, and of course secular philosophers hold almost every conceivable position as to when the developing embryo/foetus acquires moral significance. But though there are exceptions, a theistic worldview is likely to place value upon the developing embryo at an earlier date than the secular, because the former is more often concerned with beginnings, whereas the latter may look rather for points of significance in a human being's development.

2. The Theistic Search for the Moment of Conception

Religious systems are of course many and various, but it is through the monotheistic and specifically Christian, Conservative Protestant way of seeing the world that I now wish particularly to enquire. Uniting both Roman Catholicism and biblical

Protestantism is the fundamental belief in a Supreme Being, a Creator, the Originator of our universe and the Designer of every human life. The universe thus turns out to be a moral universe, derivative of a moral God. Central also to all Christian doctrine is that Mankind, alone amongst animal species, is somehow made in God's image, the *imago Dei*.[17] This image is variously understood as being constituted in man's capacity to enter into a relationship with God, or in man's created character as a rational, creative and moral being, or both. A physical image is certainly not part of orthodox Christian doctrine, as God is portrayed in scripture as a spiritual being.[18] It is incumbent upon Christian believers to give the highest respect to the life of a fellow human being, from the very moment that life begins. Whilst the injunction 'Do not kill' may not be absolute for the Christian (there are biblical principles which sanction the taking of life in certain circumstances) the injunction to 'love your neighbour as yourself' would seem to apply from the earliest moments of a human life.[19] The question a Christian needs most fundamentally to ask in this case, is just when does a human life come into existence? Precisely when does a human person with an eternal destiny begin to exist, created by an Almighty God? For once this being is in existence, given this designed and moral world, then human agents ought not, perhaps excepting the most extreme of circumstances, intervene to snuff out this life.

Now it is my contention that current Roman Catholic (and most of current Protestant) thinking is in error in concluding that fertilisation is evidently or most reasonably, the moment of conception of a human life. I wish to defend the view that a human being does not come into existence before implantation and the beginnings of cell differentiation. My argument is founded on the following considerations: the dependency of the embryo on the mother for its continuing development; the high natural wastage of fertilised ova; the instability of the blastocyst in terms of the phenomena of twinning and recombination; and the totipotentiality and undifferentiated nature of the pre-implantation embryo. My argument will not entail a search for the moment of 'ensoulment', though it will assume a certain view of the soul that differs from the Aristotelian 'rational soul' or a model of the soul which assumes that the soul can be introduced into a pre-existing human person (as in the concept of delayed animation). At one time the Roman Catholic Church looked to the moment of quickening (the first maternal perception of foetal movement) as the time when God gave the foetus its soul and hence when its truly human life began.[20] However, to conceptualise the soul as something that God adds in to the human being at some subsequent moment in his/her life is to misunderstand the Hebraic way of speaking about the soul. David Atkinson, Chaplain at Corpus Christi College, Oxford argues, "You do not 'have' a soul, in a sense you are a soul; likewise, you do not 'have' a body, in a sense you are a body. The various aspects to our make up (heart, soul, body, flesh, spirit) are ways of speaking about the whole of us".[21] In other words, for the purpose of this present work, I shall adopt the view that from conception onwards, (the true moment of conception, that the human being is both an ensouled body and an embodied soul, and thus to search for a moment of ensoulment is misguided.

2.1. FERTILISATION AND THE MOMENT OF CONCEPTION OF A HUMAN LIFE

It is time for me to begin to be more specific in explaining my argument, and to consider likely objections. The zygote is often assumed to have the capacity for self generation because of the inherent character of its genotype, and this had lead many such as Ramsey, quoted earlier, to assume that the formation of this genotype is doubtless the moment a new human individual is formed. In 1989, Bedate and Cefalo argued that the embryo, prior to implantation, is, in fact, incapable of self-generation independent of genetic messages transmitted from the mother. They assert,

> The information used for the development of a human embryo involves more than the zygote's chromosomal genetic information, namely, the genetic material from maternal mitochondria, and the maternal or paternal genetic messages in the form of messenger RNA or proteins. In terms of molecular biology, it is incorrect to say that the zygote possesses all the informing molecules for embryo development; rather, at most, the zygote possesses the molecules that have the potential to acquire informing capacity ... In the process of differentiation the embryo interacts with the mother: there is no doubt that both biological systems receive information from each other ... Where does the information necessary for [differentiation] come from? Some type of interaction between molecules of the zygote and extra-zygotic molecules must occur ... In summary, the zygote makes possible the existence of a human being but does not in and of itself possess sufficient information to form it. The formation of the embryo depends on a series of events that will have to occur during the course of the ontogenesis, some of which are outside the control of the genetic programme.[22]

Now, it is true that certain aspects of Bedate and Cefalo's paper, from which the above has been abstracted, have been shown to be inaccurate, namely their belief that hydatidiform moles and teratomas were the result of a lack of, or deficient, interaction between the zygote and maternal genetic information. Later work has shown that such malignancies are more likely, though perhaps still not always, the result of abnormal genes within the zygote itself, in which case it could be said that these abnormal cells do not possess a truly human genotype.[23] However it remains that, to date, no-one has disproved their basic premiss which is that the cells of the newly implanted embryo cannot properly begin to differentiate without interaction with the mother's genetic information. If this is so, then it seems that a good case can be made that prior to implantation, the multiplying cells of the human blastocyst are no more than the building blocks of the future human individual, rather than the individual being already present by virtue of the genotype. The implication is that without such interaction between the zygote and the mother, some of the zygote's genes will remain switched off and thus be incapable of proper, further development.

It might be countered: 'Isn't this simply akin to asserting that an embryo can't develop fully without its mother, that's nothing new!?' This can miss the point that we are seeking to distinguish between an embryonic human being that is floating around the fallopian tubes and uterus looking for a home to grow up in, and a collection of cells that may become a human being if they can interact with the mother once implanted in the uterine wall. The distinguishing feature may lie in the difference between seeing the uterine wall as simply a channel of nutrients for a being that already exists or seeing it as the passage way of a genetic key which is able to bring about a transformation of the embryo into a human being. *In this case Day 14 would turn out to be Day 1 and the moment of conception.*

Before proceeding further, it is worth pausing to note, that for many, it is significant that the passing of a signal from the newly-implanted embryo is nature's way of indicating to the mother that a pregnancy has begun. David Atkinson has suggested that instead of enquiring when personhood begins, we should instead consider when parenthood begins.[24] Caroline Berry seems to concur when she says, "implantation is a crucial stage, and some would say that conception should be considered to occur at the time of implantation rather than at fertilization, as it is only now that the new organism becomes related to its nurturing mother".[25]

A second type of argument in favour of implantation and gastrulation as the correct time of conception is the high rate of wastage of fertilised ova. Berry believes this to be in the region of 50% of all fertilised ova[26], the mother being totally unaware that during menstruation she is parting company with what is or might have been a human being. Now it may be immediately be objected that many of these lost ova contain lethal abnormalities that are the cause of their failure to implant, and further that their lack of viability indicates the absence of a truly human genotype. In other words, many of these lost fertilised ova, if fertilisation equates to conception, might fail to qualify as human beings in any case. But the fact remains that a significant number of apparently otherwise healthy embryos fail to implant. What are we to say in this case? If one believes that the creation of a genotype is to create a human being with an eternal destiny, then one seems bound to conclude that large numbers of human beings pass into a spiritual realm beyond this physical world, without ever having lived a life in this world, (excepting their brief, detached life *in utero*). The rate of loss drops dramatically once implantation is complete and cell differentiation initiated; from this point, if I am correct in suggesting that conception occurs during the time of cell differentiation, then Christian belief would seem to demand that human life which fails *in utero*, will survive in terms of an after-life. What seems counter-intuitive and can only be speculative as related to scripture, is that God is populating heaven with a vast army of ex-preimplantation human individuals who have never seen the light of day, who have never properly lived a life. As I have read the arguments of those favouring fertilisation as the correct moment of conception, I have encountered a strange silence on this issue, not an alternative perspective or the overt embracing of what I consider an implausible position.

A third line of argument against considering fertilisation the moment at which a human being begins his/her life is based on the fact that prior to the laying down of the primitive streak (i.e. the time of cell differentiation or 'restriction' as it sometimes known) the embryo has the ability, perhaps genetically encoded, to divide, and thus lead to the existence of more than one human individual, both sharing the same genotype. There is also laboratory evidence that some animal embryos can be recombined to form just one single embryo. If one were to maintain that a human being begins at fertilisation, one is bound to say that, in twinning, somehow, one human individual (ensouled, on my understanding) divides and becomes two. Can one human individual divide into two and retain its own identity, whilst 'budding' another human individual? There is the immediate problem of knowing which half of the resultant pair of twins is the original. Norman Ford has proposed that one solution is to declare that the original embryo in a real sense dies in giving rise to two daughter embryos, with the implication that these twins are in fact the grand-daughters of the mother giving birth![27] Others see no need for such convoluted thinking, Augustine Regan being one who sees no problem in maintaining that one human individual can remain intact whilst giving rise to its genetic double.[28]

Teresa Iglesias responds to these kinds of objection forthrightly: "the organic mechanisms of natural monozygotic twinnings are not yet fully understood and known; there are good indications for believing that they are genetically determined and hence that the two beings emerge as *two* from conception ... ".[29] Iglesias is saying that both individuals are present in the fertilised ovum, and she does not accept that one divides and gives rise to the other: they merely separate. Yet it is hard to conceptualise one human embryo that is really two, if only we had the right spectacles through which to see its particular gene winking at us, unless we revert to a dualistic approach where, upon division, the soul(s) is added in. However, Iglesias has a strong case when she asserts, "recombination of full embryos to form a single chimeric one has not been proved to occur naturally, either in humans or in any other mammalian species ... ".[30] Were this otherwise, it would be hard indeed to argue that two human individuals are combining, one dying, or perhaps both giving rise to a new individual. Since it is so that recombination may not occur naturally, I will not attempt to place any weight on this form of the argument. What, however, we are left with is a general impression of the fluidity and seeming lack of stability of the early embryo. It seems hard not to agree with Ford that the final establishing of human individuation is the moment when a human being properly comes into existence. He says, "There cannot be a human person present if the conditions required for the presence of any ontological individual cannot be satisfied".[31] Thomas Shannon and Allan Wolter agree: "An individual is not an individual, and therefore not a person, until the process of restriction is complete, and determination of particular cells has occurred. Then, and only then, is it clear that another individual cannot come from the cells of this embryo".[32]

This undetermined nature of the cells of the pre-implantation embryo is a matter which persuades many that no human being is yet in existence. During the first three days of cell division following fertilisation, the cells retain their pluripotentiality. This means that any one of them, if extracted from the rest, is capable of forming a new human individual itself, i.e. it becomes a zygotic equivalent in and of itself. The pluripotential cells of the morulla have no apparent relation with one another, their association maintained only by a membrane called the *zona pellucida*, thus leading to an impression that this early stage in embryonic development is more comparable to a loosely connected, multiplying collection of cells, than to a self-generating human individual. Norman Ford sees great significance in this:

> There is very little evidence of intrinsic unity, or the presence of a single organism, in the first cleavages of the cells in the human embryo. Their membranes merely touch within the *zona pellucida* ... It is the *zona pellucida* that gives the appearance of a single organism or unity by holding the eight distinct individual cells together. It prevents them from coming apart and sticking to the walls of the fallopian tube and protects them during their journey to the womb. Prior to implantation, and more obviously when there are no more than eight blastomeres, each cell takes in its own nutrients, thereby showing autonomy in a vitally significant way. This would indicate that each blastomere, at least up till the eight-cell stage was a distinct ontological individual, even if the life span of each blastomere consisted of less than twenty four hours.[33]

Ford is searching, once more, for a point where individuation can properly be said to have taken place, and finds in these considerations yet more evidence to substantiate his conclusions with regard to twinning and the lack of final individuality. Moreover, the fact that the majority of the cells of the blastocyst eventually become part of the extra-embryonic tissues, upon differentiation, is a further consideration that many find difficult to assimilate into the fertilisation equates to conception view. There seems no way of predicting just which of the earlier cells of the blastocyst will eventually become the cells of the embryoblast, this being dependent upon spatial positioning within the implanted embryo and complex information transfer and cell migration during the process of gastrulation, once the embryo is in the maternal environment. In simple terms, most of what we look at down a microscope when we observe the pre-implantation embryo, will never become the embryo proper, but will end up as extra-embryonic and placental material that will be discarded once their function is completed. Can, then, the pre-implantation embryo be a living human individual when the majority of its cell mass is yet to be jettisoned? Teresa Iglesias sees no problem here, asking, "Are not the 'afterbirth', i.e. placenta and membranes, much needed organic parts of the whole being which are developed for its sustenance as other parts are?"[34] The difference that might easily be glossed over here, is that other parts of the human body which are produced and then lost, like layers of skin, whilst a part of us form a vital part of the ontological individual, and not a mere appendage to the outside world, more like an oxygen mask. The undifferentiated embryo forms a mass of tissues which are not part of itself and from which it will finally disassociate itself.

Iglesias consistently maintains her stance over the early embryo, seeing a human individual present from the zygote stage. She makes the following four propositions

a. Living beings are organic wholes; as such they can shed parts (cells) which may become parts of other organisms.
b. Living beings can shed parts (cells) which may become new organic wholes themselves, either on their own, or in combination with others.
c. Living beings can be deprived of or damaged in substantial organic parts and yet regulate or regenerate themselves to continue to develop as well-functioning wholes.
d. Living beings (of mammalian species) as *whole beings* neither divide from nor fuse with other whole beings, but their parts which they can shed. ... there is no 'fusion' or 'splitting' of living beings as total wholes ... Every living being is individual, i.e. organically individuated in all its dimensions from its generation to its death. The early embryo as a living whole is an individual stable organism.[35]

What are we to say, though, of the pluripotential cell, taken from a 4-cell human embryo and left for half an hour before being introduced to another different 4-cell embryo? If left a single cell it would multiply and become an individual in its own right. In Iglesias's terms, it would be, for this half hour a human being. But then it is introduced into another 4-cell embryo, it thus loses its individuality, and again, if Iglesias is right, are we not bound to say that a human being has just died, even though the cell that it is, lives on? I suspect Iglesias is likely to reply that such a thing is most probably not a natural occurrence, and thus of little value in discussing. Still, once again we are left with the impression that pluripotentiality within the *zona pellucida* lends itself more toward a lack of individuation rather than the existence of a stable organism.

To summarise, thus far, I have reasoned that each of these four types of argumentation are capable of casting doubt on the view that conception occurs at the time of fertilisation, and when seen conjointly are good grounds for asserting that there is only a minute possibility that a human person comes into existence prior to implantation and restriction. I say 'only a minute possibility' rather than 'no possibility' because we are dealing with the interpretation of scientific data rather than in matters of empirical observation alone. There remains just that slim chance that in a mysterious world created by a God who has not made all things known to his creation, that He might just be populating heaven with persons who have never lived a life (as we know it); the human genotype just might bear the image of God; twins just might share one set of chromosomal material at the outset of *both* their lives; science just might yet be proved wrong in the matter of maternal genetic dependence, or its importance marginalised; a human individual just might begin its life as a composite of embryonic and extra-embryonic material; and the *zona pellucida* just might be God's way of ontologically individuating a new human life. This is not to undermine my arguments, but to indicate that we are not dealing in matters of proof.

Before continuing to consider more closely some rival views of the early embryo, I pause to note a certain implication that follows from viewing the human person as both an embodied soul and an ensouled body. The implication is just that it makes no sense to speak of an entity as a 'potential' human being/person. Within my stated theological frame of viewing a human being, there is either a person there in the eyes of God or there is not: a person's life has either begun or else the person does not yet exist, there is merely an opportunity for such a life to exist - an opportunity that perhaps contains within it a God-given role of human responsibility alongside his own creative role. If one acts to prevent conception by using conventional contraceptive techniques, then one is not committing murder nor do we consider the sperm and ovum just prior to fertilisation a 'potential' person; instead one is acting to prevent a life from beginning. Similarly, if conception occurs during the time of cell differentiation, then to act to prevent implantation is not to murder, nor is it to snuff out the life of a potential person, it is to act to prevent the life of a person from beginning in a way which is no more reprehensible than preventing the sperm and ovum meeting in the first place. Unless one holds to the Roman Catholic view that all contraception is wrong and that sexual intercourse must never be divorced from the real opportunity for procreation, then it is hard to see how one is acting in a way contrary to God's revealed will. To prevent implantation of a blastocyst is not in this view to end a life for which God had an eternal purpose, but to prevent a life from beginning in a way which accords with the measure of creative responsibility that God has assigned to Man. Man chooses with the free-will which is his created inheritance to refrain from acting to produce a new human life: this does not upset God's sovereign purpose or prevent a life from being that God has eternally willed that there should be; rather a life that God never planned that there should be is prevented from being by an act of Man who has been created with the free-will to choose, who is choosing not to end a life (which would doubtless be a sinful act), but who is choosing not to be a partner in beginning a life. I shall look again at the question of potentiality later.

2.2. RIVAL THEOLOGICAL POSITIONS

Most Christian theists have chosen fertilisation of the ovum as the most likely time for conception.   Those who argue this way normally base their arguments on the significance of the formation of the human genotype, as discussed earlier, or on the alleged absence of a later moment of developmental significance in foetal life. Nigel M de S. Cameron raises the further issue of the doctrine of the Incarnation as supportive evidence for the embryonic beginning of the life of a human person. He asserts

> ... the doctrine of the incarnation of Jesus Christ accords with the common sense reading of the biological evidence that the act of incarnation took place not in Bethlehem where the baby was born, but before ever the journey to Bethlehem began. God became incarnate in an embryo, in the supernatural fertilisation of an ovum ...   For God to become man in embryo therefore requires that man in embryo already bears the image [of God] and absolutely forbids the possibility that

in the early stages of his biological life the divine image can be absent.[36]

My question is, 'just how do we know what happened within Mary's womb?' Did one of her ova become fertilised by a divine act? If so, does that demonstrate that the life of Jesus Christ incarnate had begun or did that (ensouled) life begin after implantation? Another alternative is that an implanted embryo appeared within Mary by a divine act, even if this was one of her own fertilised ova. We are seemingly on the shaky ground of speculation. Cameron also seems to assume that the divine image does reside in the human genotype - that a human being is the sum of his genes. I do not dispute that the composite man/God implicit to the Incarnation requires Man to be made in God's image, but God did not 'take over' a normal human embryo, he was supernaturally involved with it from the beginning - the genotype of Jesus Christ being an amalgam of the human and the divine. Yet the Person of Jesus Christ need not yet reside within this genotype; rather the life of the incarnate Christ may have begun at the point of cell differentiation and restriction. In other words, whilst agreeing that from conception proper, the ensouled human being bears the image of God, I do not see that necessitates the assertion that image was present from fertilisation, or that any human cell bears that image, in and of itself.

Is it true, then, that there is no moment between fertilisation and birth that will bear the moral burden of declaring the existence of life prior to that moment as the "life" of a non-person? This view is expressed well by Roger Wertheimer, "going back stage by stage from the infant to the zygote, one will not find any differences between successive stages significant enough to bear the enormous moral burden of allowing wholesale slaughter of the earlier stage while categorically denying that permission of the next stage".[37] Does this argument necessitate an equal moral status for both the zygote and the infant? One reposte to this conclusion comes in the form of Donald VanDeVeer's argument: "The fact, if it is a fact, that the requisite differences do not exist between successive stages does not show that they do not exist between non-successive stages".[38] VanDeVeer illustrates his view with the person who slips gradually into insanity: at no particular moment can we suddenly say that the person has crossed the threshold - the sanity/insanity boundary, but we can look at non-successive stages in this slide from sanity and declare there has been a definite change. Now, VanDeVeer wants to use this argument to draw attention to the vast difference between the undifferentiated blastocyst and the late foetus, concluding that this difference does support the moral burden of declaring the former as some sort of pre-person. My purpose in raising this argument is to argue that even if it is not possible to pin-point the moment within the process of gastrulation and restriction when the life of a person begins, it is possible to argue that there is a point of distinction between the non-successive stages of the free-floating blastocyst (prior to implantation) and the early embryo undergoing the cell differentiation where the primitive streak is laid down. Conveniently sandwiched between these stages is the stage of implantation itself.

I am not arguing that implantation is *the moment* of significance, but I am pointing out that it divides non-successive stages in the development of the embryo in such a way that may divide the life of a human person from the existence of cells which are the substrate of that life. Thus, I do not wish to take issue directly with the views of those like John Stott who says "implantation changes only the environment of the foetus, not its constitution"[39]; the moment of implantation does not effect in and of itself the necessary changes within the embryo that may begin the life of a person, but rather, on the view I have outlined, the phenomenon of implantation may trigger a series of informational processes which over the next few days result in the beginning of a human life. VanDeVeer's non-successive stage argument can then be used to argue that there is a difference in ontology between the implanted embryo undergoing gastrulation and the pre-implantation blastocyst.

Within the Christian theological worldview I am considering, there are not many proponents of a later dating for conception. Some have argued for the moment of birth, the time when the baby inhales its first breath, based on the Genesis record that God breathed the breath of life into Adam.[40] But this view is rejected because of the weight of scripture passages referring to the life *in utero*, particularly those relating to the Incarnation itself. Others, such as Thomas Bole, think that biological integration and the settling of individuality at the time of restriction is insufficient to establish the beginnings of human personhood. Bole is looking rather for sufficient psychological integration, saying, "the rational soul cannot be present in material insufficiently organised to manifest rational operations".[41] However, all attempts to identify such sufficient psychological integration in the pre-rational foetus are bound to be limited to identifying levels which are but precursors of rational activity. Similarly, if one asserts that the foetus is sufficiently psychologically integrated at eight weeks old to receive the soul, why not be prepared to go back further to the beginnings of the laying down of the primitive streak, which will similarly give rise to rational functions after further development. More fundamentally, Bole's concerns arise out of that view of the soul which is more akin to the rational mind, in terms not unlike Aristotle's hylomorphism. If man is from his earliest beginnings both an ensouled body and embodied soul, there is no necessary reason to insist on an intact and perhaps functional nervous system, rather the spiritual aspect of man can develop alongside his physical nature.

In summary, I have described a view of the beginnings of human life which seeks to identify the moment when that life begins in the eyes of the God of Christianity. Such a moment does not belong to the data of biblical revelation, but there are good reasons to doubt that this life can exist before the process of cell differentiation and restriction begins. The process of implantation serves as a boundary between the non-successive stages of the undifferentiated blastocyst and the embryoblast undergoing gastrulation, and thus it may be argued that no human person exists prior to implantation, even though one cannot identify a single moment during or at the completion of gastrulation when a human embryo becomes an ensouled human person. This view of personhood is of course to be contrasted with the traditionally Lockean view which emphasises functional rationality; rather, personhood is viewed teleologically, a person having a definite beginning and an infinite future. The implication of this view for the debate over PC4 is that the pharmacist who wishes to take the Christian worldview seriously can have a high degree of confidence that PC4 is a contraceptive method, not a means of abortion.

3. The Non-theistic Search for When Human Life Begins to Matter Morally

Let us now begin to explore a totally different worldview: God does not exist, the human individual together with the world he inhabits are the chance products of impersonally caused physical events. Human life is not sacred in any religious sense, and there is no need to speak of man possessing a soul, though we may choose to speak in an abstract way of his mind. Given this frame through which to view the world, I intend to argue that we need not assign moral significance to the human foetus before its capacity for sentience. I am not saying that we need to argue that the life of a human being *begins* at the threshold of sentience, only that the life of a human being need not be considered of moral significance in and of itself, before its capacity for sentience.

L.W. Sumner adopts a similar approach to Donald VanDeVeer in stressing the important contrast between non-successive stages in prenatal life, saying, "Views which deny the relevance of this factor deserve to command no more than minority support … A moderate and differential view of abortion is capable of drawing the commonsense distinction between early and late abortions, and of showing that such a distinction is neither shallow nor arbitrary".[42] Sumner, however, seems to be in the minority in going on to assert, "The threshold of moral standing is that area of the continuum through which sentience fades into non-sentience … ".[43] The exact timing of such a threshold is uncertain, Sumner referring to the necessary physiological structures needing to be in place, some time in the second trimester; however, it is within the nature of my argument to insist that this be the *earliest* time that modern science conceives sentience to be a possibility. Although electrical activity can be detected in the brain stem at 7 weeks gestation, connections would appear to be necessary between the thalamic fibres and the neocortex for pain sensation, these appearing at 22-23 weeks. Many scientists, however, are of the opinion that sentience is not present before 26 weeks because it is only around the 25th week that thalamic fibres form synapses with cortical neurones. According to this understanding, in order to be quite sure that sentience is absent, one would have to opt for a time of approximately 24 weeks gestation. However, a more conservative scientific opinion would still opt for a time of about 6 weeks, as the foetus is able to react to certain stimuli during the 7th and 8th weeks.

But why sentience as a threshold? My argument will depend upon identifying features of the foetus that call for a protective response from the moral community, in other words, I shall ask, at what point of development does the human foetus begin to exhibit properties that cause us to empathise with it, value it, and relate to it as one of ourselves. This line of argument will need to rebut the view that the embryo, prior to sentience, is valuable because of any inherent potentiality to acquire such properties, along with views that point to other significant characteristics in prenatal life. I also need to defend this view from those proposing the limits of morally relevant human life be based on the concept of personhood as construed in terms of functional rationality.

What property or properties, then, ought to evoke a moral concern that seeks to protect the embryo/foetus and grant it certain rights to life? It is my contention that it is not enough that the early foetus looks a bit like us. This does matter to some who begin to sense a moral repugnance at the thought of abortion once the foetus develops past its 'large tadpole' shape. But just what has changed within the constitution of the foetus to justify such a change in our attitude towards it? We are seeking to identify a stage in the development in the foetus whereby moral respect is warranted by virtue of the actual acquisition of a morally relevant property. I propose that such a property is the ability to feel pain. Such ability evokes a response of compassion and empathy from us because it is an experience that we know and relate to well. Before the foetus acquires this ability we are able to relate to it only in terms of what it will one day experience and become, not because of what it presently is. Now I must concede that were the foetus to be carried externally on the mother's body for all to see, that we may feel quite differently about abortion carried out at 3 weeks and 6 weeks gestation. This is not because we feel that the foetus has become a human being during this time, since we may argue that it is a member of our species in its own right once gastrulation is completed. Our emotions over the abortion of a 6 week foetus are more likely based on the sense of waste when more is assembled of what we one day will count as of value. Before an artist begins to paint his masterpiece, he must first assemble his canvas, paints and brushes. As we follow this time of preparation, so the greater our sense of loss would become if the project were to be interrupted. If much of the background colour were added on to the canvas before any of the valuable detail were in place, it would still be in no way a valuable piece of artwork, but our sense of loss would be the greater if the project were terminated at this point. It would be naive to suggest that were the foetus to be carried externally, that our emotional involvement with it would not increase steadily throughout the period leading up to the sixth week, but the question remains, 'what property has the foetus acquired through this time that demands a moral response from us, in such a way that we assign some degree of protection to it, even against the mother's desires?'

Cora Diamond argues for the importance of the notion of 'humanness' in ethical thinking. Her argument is not based on being fellow members of the human species alone, but on the imaginative links between human beings who empathise in being sharers of the experience of having a human life to lead. She refers to such practices as the offering of hospitality to strangers (in other cultures) as a right expression to our "commonality of need and joinedness of fate".[44] Now I would argue that such empathy is most realised in our shared experience of pain, and that when a human foetus acquires such ability, then our emotions are rightly elicited, rather than on a superficial level of physical appearance. Hence a case may now be made that the human foetus should be assigned some moral status once sentience is achieved. Up until this point, even at week 6, the foetus merely has the potential to acquire such ability. My argument can also be illustrated in the following way: we may rightly value a piece of artwork, and even though we may not like it personally we may still value its features and the skilled work that has gone into its production, and we would therefore, rightly, have a sense of outrage were that piece of art to be vandalised or destroyed. This can be so, even though we may not think that such pieces of art ought to be maximally produced. In other words we can value what already is in existence whilst not thinking it would necessarily be a good idea that such entities be multiplied maximally. Similarly, it does not seem inconsistent to argue for the value of a human foetus once sentience is achieved, whilst not necessarily thinking that the number of sentient foetuses ought to be maximised or that it would be a good idea for all pre-sentient foetuses to reach sentience.

Diamond sets forth her ideas in such a way as to defend them from the charge of 'speciesism' from the ranks of such philosophers as Peter Singer. Diamond does see a definite place for a right moral concern for non-human animals, though she warns that to disregard our humanity as of any moral relevance is likely to alienate us from what we truly are and from the naturally human focus through which we see the world and ourselves. This echoes the sentiments of Baroness Warnock who says, "I would argue ... that the concept of 'speciesism' as a form of prejudice is absurd. Far from being arbitrary, it is a supremely important moral principle".[45] Thus, if we allow that there is a right place for a moral solidarity within our own species, we may assign a moral status to the sentient human foetus whilst denying a similar status to the sentient chimpanzee foetus, though it remains a matter warranting further deliberation as to just when we begin to assign a moral status to the chimpanzee and at what point of development, if at all, we would allow this status to 'trump' that of the sentient human foetus.

Let us return now to the question of potentiality. Should we value the human foetus and grant it some moral status prior to its possession of sentience on account of its inherent potentiality to acquire such ability together along with all other relevant characteristics of adulthood? Many have argued for the importance of potentiality in moral considerations of the early human embryo/foetus. Robert Joyce insists that the zygote itself is as fully a human person as you or I. He says, "every living, individual being with the natural potential, as a whole, for knowing, willing, desiring and relating to others in a self-reflective way is a person ... Therefore the human zygote is an actual person with great potential".[46] In terms reminiscent of Tertullian theology, he further argues, "No individual living body can become a person unless it already is a person. No living being can become anything other than what it already essentially is".[47] This seems to bring together arguments for ontological individuality with potentiality equalling actuality. I do not need to take issue with the former notion that the living individual remains what it essentially is throughout its lifetime. But does potentiality equate to actuality? Joyce makes this point explicitly, "A person's potential to walk across the street is an actuality that the tree beside him does not have".[48] In other words, Joyce is arguing that the zygote has an intrinsic potential by virtue of its particular genotype, to do what only a human being can do. The actuality consists in its unique nature. This argument seems weak because it is necessary, but insufficient, to say that the actuality lies in the individual's nature alone. This potentiality may be sufficient to differentiate the human zygote from any other entity, but somehow fails to convince me that I should grant actual moral status to an individual on account of what it may become. The early foetus, assuming it is free of serious defect, has the potential to reach the time of sentience and beyond, but it may not do because of reasons external to itself. Logic seems to dictate that potentiality is not the same as actuality. It is not clear that I must value a thing because it may become something valuable one day. Similarly, it does not seem inconsistent to maintain that the human race need not be enlarged maximally, as discussed earlier. The early foetus, then, is arguably a human being with the potential to develop fully into what it already is by nature, but this potential need not be seen in terms of present actuality or valued in the same way as actuality. Similarly, it is often argued that a person who will grow up to be Prime Minister, need not be valued or be granted rights equivalent to Prime Ministerial rights by virtue of what he may become.

Edward Langerak wants the potential person to be assigned at least some minimal claim to life, even though this will be inferior to the claim of an actual person. He argues that this respect is due in proportion to the respect elicited by the actual persons they will become, after all, we do give respect to dead human bodies on account of the persons they were.[49] The problem with this argument is that there is an asymmetry here in that what we value about the life of an ex-person (e.g. his thoughts, experiences and actions) has not been experienced at all by the early human embryo/foetus; in other words, the experiential content of prenatal life prior to sentience is not something that evokes a similar sense of moral respect, and why ought I to think that experiences after sentience should necessarily come to be realised. Once they exist I may value them, but before they exist, I may rather wish that they did not exist at all, and certainly not feel constrained to value what is merely tentative and hypothetical.

This is perhaps another way of saying that a human being, prior to sentience, though a member of the human species, cannot be said to have an interest in its own survival. If it has a right to life, it can only be a conferred right - conferred by the moral community. My argument leads to the conclusion that the moral community need not see the pre-sentient human foetus as one of its number, nor need grant it a right to life or other rights which follow from it having its own interests. Up until the point at which it can experience pain, the human foetus cannot be said to have an interest in having or avoiding any experience at all. It may have the potential to have such experiences, but there seems no real reason why the moral community should want its numbers increased, or the number of its valued experiences increased, even though it counts rational experience a valuable thing.

Is it possible, then, to harm a human being prior to sentience? This is a very good question. The pre-sentient human foetus may have no interests of its own, but if it undergoes structural damage, for example, as the result of drugs taken by the mother which are toxic to the foetus, then the future person may meaningfully declare, 'I was harmed during my pre-sentient existence'. The implication is that we may need to assign the early foetus a degree of moral respect, not on account of what it presently is, but because of what it may become. For whilst it has no interest in its continuing survival, the future person will have an interest in not having been harmed whilst in a pre-sentient phase. This seems to me to be one form of potentiality argument that does carry some weight, but it should be noted that it is not an argument that precludes abortion prior to 6 weeks, but that society should be responsible in caring for the foetus during this period, assuming that it is to be allowed to come to term. Roslyn Weiss argues along similar lines when she says, "We have duties with respect to beings, even if they have no rights against us".[50] Weiss argues that a potential person can be harmed, it can be a victim. I would reply that such harm is only experienced by the future person, and if it turns out that that person never survives prenatal life, then there has been no harm, there has been no victim. In summary, the pre-sentient foetus has no interests in its own survival, and any degree of respect we give to it is because of consequentialist considerations for the future person.

Many philosophers make the distinction between a human being and a human person, based on the Lockean view of personhood which emphasises functional rationality. The limits of personhood may thus not extend to the boundaries of human life, rather, a human being may enter into the phase of being a person, and possibly depart from it before his life's end. A.O Rorty says, "The idea of a person is the idea of a unified centre of choice and action, the unit of legal and theological responsibility".[51] A person, in these terms, is characterised by the ability to make self-aware, rational decisions for which he may be held responsible and accountable. The person is self-reflective and able to consider himself as himself through time. In support of this concept of personhood, Peter Singer says, "The belief that mere membership of our species, irrespective of other characteristics, makes a great difference to the wrongness of killing a being is a legacy of religious doctrines".[52] In Singer's view, it is not what type of being you are by nature that counts, it is whether you possess, at any given moment in time, the requisite features of rationality. Within this concept of rationality, for many, it is the capacity to have conscious experiences that is of paramount importance. Roland Pucetti says, "It was Lucretius' contention ... that good or harm can accrue only to a subject of conscious experiences ... I am inclined to think Lucretius was right about this, that personal life is ineluctably shorter at both ends than the life of the organism which is the biological substrate of the person".[53]

It soon becomes apparent that a view of the person is being constructed which excludes all prenatal life as well as the life of the adult human being who slides into dementia or is in a persistent vegetative state. Harry Frankfurt makes it clear that it is a person's capacity for second-order volitions, to wish to have a different set of preferences and objectives to those he currently possesses, that marks him out.[54] Charles Taylor agrees, saying that only a person can raise the question, "Do I really want to be what I now am?"[55] Michael Tooley is clear that a right to life should only be granted to a being that has the capacity to desire its own continuing existence: he says in conclusion, "not all members of the species *Homo sapiens* have a right to life".[56]

If this concept of personhood is used to draw boundaries as to who is a proper object of moral concern, then, of course, my proposal for the time of sentience appears far too early, unless one allows that we widen the criteria to include the laying down of the nervous system which is the substrate of rationality and conscious experience, but this is not the intention of those who advocate personhood as a moral category. Indeed, Tooley goes as far as to argue for the justification of infanticide as well as abortion, because the human newborn is clearly not self-aware and rational in the terms outlined above. So, need we go along with Tooley, Singer and others who would declare the sentient human foetus and even the late-term foetus or newborn to be a human being outside of a moral category of humanity which possesses a right to life? I think not. Not simply because of my proposal of another set of criteria for when we should start to value and protect a human life, but because of inherent flaws in the concept of personhood under discussion, and because the boundaries of the concept are ill-defined and liable to abuse.

Daniel Dennett outlines a first difficulty for this construal of personhood when he points out the difficulty of being able to confidently say just what are the necessary and sufficient conditions a being needs to satisfy to qualify for personhood. He says that the concept of personhood is inescapably normative, and "Human beings or other entities can only aspire to being approximations of the ideal, and there can be no way to set a passing grade that is not arbitrary".[57] For others too, it is the line-drawing exercise at the boundaries of personhood that gives rise to concern: once a line is drawn, the moral dilemma is not solved, we are still left wondering about the moral status of the being that lies just beyond the boundary. Dennett also sees a circularity when personhood is used as the basis of assigning moral responsibility i.e. when we declare a person culpable because he was acting of his own free will and knowing what he was doing. What Dennett is pointing to is that the very grounds of declaring moral culpability are reasons to doubt whether the conditions of personhood are actually fulfilled in any given instance: is the person guilty, or is he a person at all?

Loren Lomasky rejects the personhood criterion, saying, "no debate over normative issues is likely to be advanced by determining whether some affected party is or is not a person".[58] The reason is that in our society a newborn baby simply does have the right to life, and therefore any concept of personhood which insists on the ability to perform a certain feat which is based on a higher degree of rationality is simply in error. Tooley would doubtless retort that this societal attitude needs to be revised and re-educated, but this would be no easy task as Lomasky makes clear, because birth represents a 'quantum leap forward' in terms of social bonds and relationships, the baby now being identifiable and re-identifiable as an individual.

As has been argued previously, a duty of obligation can be owed to those who are unable to claim any rights, i.e. a wrong can be effected, not just when a right is violated, but when an act adversely affects a victim. In this way, we may have a duty of obligation to those outside the category of personhood, or society may choose to confer rights on those who are less than full persons, as Norman Gillespie argues, "being a person is a sufficient but not necessary condition for having rights ... less than full persons can have rights, and these rights can be unjustly violated".[59]

Our history books should warn us against the danger of any group within a society declaring another minority group sub-human, or less than full persons. The opportunities for prejudice and oppression are blatant. To declare the late foetus, the infant and the Alzheimer victim as outside of personhood, when using that very category to decide who may have the right to life is to create a dogma which could be mercilessly exploited. It is not that we should reject the features of functional rationality as attributes of great value, but rather, that they are not in a position to demand our exclusive attention. Instead, a valid moral concern can be elicited from us in knowing that a young member of our own species is in pain. This concern may be at a more primitive level than that envisaged by, for example, Loren Lomasky when he speaks of the importance of our relationship with the infant, but as Roger Wertheimer has argued, "I am suggesting that what our natural response to a thing is, how we naturally react to it cognitively, affectively and behaviourally, is partly definitive of that thing, and is therefore partly definitive of how we ought to respond to that thing".[60] The natural response to a sentient foetus in pain is a moral response, to what I have proposed to be a morally relevant property. This seems, in turn, to define a limit to the moral concern for the human foetus, unless we allow as morally relevant properties membership of the human species, or potentiality to acquire morally relevant properties.

4. Pluralism and Respect for Conscience

I began by arguing that, given a Christian theological worldview, it was important to locate with reasonable certainty the time at which a human life begins. I argued that this life could not reasonably be said to exist prior to gastrulation, and that implantation served as a convenient developmental phenomenon which gives the divide between the non-successive stages of the differentiating embryoblast and pre-implantation blastocyst. I then argued that, given a non-theistic worldview, it is not necessary to identify the moment at which the life of a human being begins, but rather, the moment at which the foetus acquires some significant and morally relevant property. I have proposed and defended the idea that sentience is such a property.

I will now explore how each of the views I have espoused might respond to a feminist critique, and then proceed to enquire what dialogue, if any, is possible between such widely differing views, and how such discussion is influenced by our own lack of objectivity. I will also consider the objection of Germain Grisez that we should not kill any human embryo unless we are totally sure there is no human person present, the implication being that we cannot be sure.

Let us begin with a brief survey of the feminist position. The basic claim of feminist thinking is that pregnancy needs to be approached in a woman-centred way, not a foetus-centred way. In other words, it is allegedly a mistake to think of the foetus as an individual in its own right whilst it remains part of its mother's body. Feminists are divided in their attitude to IVF and other new reproductive technologies, some seeing them as furthering the autonomy and independence of women, others viewing them as the product of a medical profession that is misogynist and 'foetalist'. Patricia Spallone thus labels both anti-abortionists and IVF practitioners as foetalists, saying, " ... both sorts of fetalists subordinate women to their fetalist values".[61] Spallone is clear that in the calculus of pregnancy, there is really only one person to be considered, and that is the mother. She says,

> An embryo or fetus is not a disembodied individual, as fetalists represent it ...
> We reject defining the embryo as unconnected with the woman who carries it.
> We reject the identification of embryos as separate entities with separate interests,
> whether by anti-abortionists, doctors, scientists, lawyers, politicians, ethicists or
> theologians ... The term 'status of the embryo' is about the power of men, of the
> state, and of medicine and science over women ... The right to abortion is not
> dependent on certain circumstances [i.e. medically defined abnormalities etc.]:
> it is our absolute and essential right to have control over our bodies.[62]

Laura Purdy agrees in rejecting the medical view of seeing the foetus as the 'second patient', saying, "Fetuses, after all, are not yet persons ... ".[63] One obvious result of this way of thinking is to render as meaningless the search for life's beginnings or the moment of conception. Spallone makes this explicit: "The question of the beginning of human life has been, and continues to be, a reflection of sexist thinking and practice. It has been and continues to be a criterion to judge and control women's reproductive behaviour".[64]

How, then, might we defend the foregoing arguments against such a critique? The Christian theistic defence will rely heavily on the notion that human life does indeed begin *in utero*, and that much is plain from the doctrine of the Incarnation and the many passages of scripture where individuals refer back to life in the womb as part of their present life. That argument makes clear that human life, once conceived, is of value to God, and therefore we are morally responsible as stewards and custodians of that life. The Christian desire to grant rights of protection to the unborn child, it might therefore be protested, is not the result of sexist and misogynist thinking (unless we go as far as to claim that the whole idea and design of women as the bearers of pregnancy is the product of a misogynist Creator), but is the simple desire to protect a human life which is of value to God (whether that life turns out to be male or female). If it were the case that the human male bore the child, then the Christian position ought to be no different at all. Any view of human personhood that denies such personhood to the life of the foetus is foreign to the Christian worldview. So, to the Christian theist, it remains of central importance to try to identify the beginnings of human life, and from that point to support the view that, medically, there are now two patients to consider, not just one. Whilst Patricia Spallone may be unimpressed that theologians are ready to define the embryo as a separate entity, with separate interests to the mother, the Christian is likely to reply, 'but what if God defines it that way?'

The non-theistic argument does not rely on arguments which try to identify the beginnings of human life, though it does reject the notion of rational and functional personhood as already mentioned. The main defence of this argument is to appeal to the moral relevance of sentience in a being which is obviously human, and who is able to feel pain in a way which is independent of its mother's feelings. In other words, our non-theist may ask the feminist, just what is it that exists within the mother and is experiencing pain in its own right? The foetus may not be a person as construed in terms of functional rationality, but once it possesses sentience, then how can we continue to maintain that it has absolutely no interest in its own pain-free life, or how can we resist defining it in an way independent of its mother? The feminist may reply, as Spallone does, that any pain suffered by the foetus is minimal in comparison to the pain experienced by the woman who undergoes painful medical interventions or wants a termination.[65] However, this is not the same as saying that the pain of the foetus is of no consequence at all: if there is pain being experienced by one of our species, then do we not have some sort of obligation to relieve it, or to try to prevent it? Surely, from sentience onwards, we cannot do just anything we like with the foetus, as the whim may take us. Even if one rejects any definite moral obligations toward the sentient foetus, then at the very least, ought we not to see acting in its interests as an act of beneficence? It is hard to understand the hardened logic of those who so emphasise the woman's wellbeing over the interests of the foetus, that pain being experienced by the foetus is considered of no account at all.

Laura Purdy raises a good point when she argues that is absurd to insist that a woman make huge sacrifices for her foetus, when she would not be required to do the same for her two year old child.[66] It does seem incongruous that women have been forced to undergo major invasive surgery to save the life of their foetus, when the law would never force parents to undergo bone-marrow transplantation or organ donation in order to save their already-born children. This seems a good guide to legislation: a woman may choose freely to make great sacrifices to save or benefit her foetus, but care should be taken to balance the interests of both parties. However, in the same way in which the state seeks to protect the child from its negligent or hostile parents, then it does seem not disanalagous to seek to protect the sentient foetus also. It may be argued that the parents do have some moral obligations towards their foetus, and that within certain defined limits that society might expect them to fulfil these.

What the above discussion serves to illustrate is that each person comes to the abortion debate, as to a debate on any moral issue, with his own history, his own cultural background and his own frame of reference through which he sees the world. It is in the nature of pluralistic societies that moral dilemmas are subject to debate by parties who hold widely divergent views of how to interpret the world around them. As indicated earlier, each individual is forced to interpret even raw scientific data by a process involving a set of non-scientific, philosophical presuppositions, and even the term human embryo itself is likely to be value-laden and thus colour any subsequent discussion of its ethical status. This point is well made by Anthony Fisher,

Modern philosophers of science have exposed some of the assumptions behind naive inductivism and shown how illusory are the classical distinctions between fact and interpretation, neutral objective science and committed, subjective metaphysics. They have identified the 'theory dependence of observation' and shown that the presumed objectivity of the scientific observer actually reflects considerable personal involvement, commitment and, accordingly, interpretation.[67]

With this kind of entrenched subjectivism as part of each person debating the moral status of the early human embryo, it would seem that even the modest goal of understanding the thinking and arguments of other parties is no mean accomplishment, let alone coming to appreciate that another person's way of seeing things may be equally valid to one's own. But let us suppose that the non-theist perfectly understands the theist's position, and the theist likewise understands that of the non-theist. Let us further suppose that, having understood each other's arguments, that they each agree that were they to lose/gain faith in God, that they would then take up each other's stance on the moral status of the early human embryo. What then would these two individuals have to say to one another in a dialogue on this issue, and how might they legislate together for a pluralistic society?

Firstly, in truly understanding one another's position, they may both have to acknowledge their own subjectivism. For the Christian, there is a necessary subjective aspect to faith in God, even though he may feel that objectivity is also derived from biblical revelation. The non-theist may also acknowledge his own history and past experience of painful situations that colour his views as to what may count as morally relevant properties, even though he may hold fast the notion of pain as a reasonably "objective" and universally disvalued experience. Of course, both parties may take issue with what the other holds as valuable (there may be instances where pain is the pathway to a greater good, as in the apparently painful and necessary struggle of the butterfly emerging from its cocoon, or it might be asserted that human life may not be valuable when lived with major handicap), but let us suppose again that both parties are sympathetic to each other's subjectivism, and that they appreciate the internal consistency of each other's worldview.

Now, both parties are agreed that prior to implantation, that the embryo cannot be said to possess a right to life or have an interest in its own continuing survival. The theist is reasonably confident that no human person exists prior to implantation, and the non-theist is sure that the embryo during this stage has no property requiring the moral community to confer a right to life upon it. However, both are likely to agree that harm may accrue to a future person if this early embryo is exposed to noxious circumstances, and therefore, they may wish to grant certain rights of protection, both to implanted embryos and their mothers. Both parties may wish to legislate against certain harmful laboratory procedures being performed on embryos which are to be implanted and similarly seek to protect the potential mother from exposure to toxic substances and/or radiation, where there is the possibility of conception. Again, both parties are agreed that contraceptive techniques which seek to prevent implantation are morally acceptable, because, on the one hand it is believed that no human person yet exists, and on the other, that no harm can be said to be done to a being in its pre-rational and pre-sentient phase, if its life ends whilst still in this phase.

After implantation, the theist is faced with the very real possibility that a human individual now exists, and that its life is sacred. The Christian is now likely to want to assign significant rights of protection to this life. Different Christian traditions have expressed different views as to the degree of this protection. Roman Catholic pronouncements have gone so far as to deny the mother life-saving treatment in order to save the life of the embryo/foetus. More often, it is only when the life of the mother is threatened or in the situation where rape has been committed, that abortion is thought permissible. In liberal traditions, then other adverse situations affecting the mother and family might be considered as well. The seriousness of the circumstances permitting the termination of a new human life are understandable when one sees this life as the result of the creative act of God, and precious to him. For abortion to be the preferable course of action, one needs to be sure just how much worse the other course of action actually is. Many Christians would thus feel great sympathy and admiration for the victim of rape who chooses to bring the baby to term (and likewise if she also intends to care for it afterwards). Similarly, many Christians, when faced with the choice of whether to abort in order to save their own lives (as in certain types of uterine cancer) may choose to sacrifice their own life.

The Christian would thus want to legislate to protect the post-implantation embryo from abortion on perceived flippant grounds. The degree of protection will vary according to the Christian tradition being observed, but it is likely that this early human life will be afforded a degree of protection not dissimilar to that afforded to a late-term foetus. There may be some protocol in place for just what might count as grounds for permissible abortion, but there would be no requirement to opt for abortion on those grounds. How might the non-theist respond to such proposals? The non-theist is not interested in when a human life begins, he may well concede that it has begun just as the theist claims. Yet until the sixth week of pregnancy, the foetus remains insentient. He wants abortion to be freely available on request up to the sixth week, because he is sure that no harm will be done, there will be no victim. The Christian may reply to the contrary, and may challenge the non-theist to at least legislate as if there were the possibility that a human person is present or that God will one day judge him for his presumptuous act. Now, it is unlikely that the non-theist will heed the latter advice, for why should he change his course of actions on this one issue, just because God's existence is possible, if he is not going to be consistent and change his behaviour on many other issues as well? Neither may he heed the former plea, because he is convinced that it is not simply being alive as a human being that is to count morally. He may well reply that the Church may wish to legislate for its own community, but should not impose its views more widely. The Christian, however, will probably see the withholding of such social intervention as morally irresponsible. The views of our two parties seem irreconcilable, and would probably mean that were the theist and non-theist *forced* to legislate for the wider community, then a compromise date of about four weeks in order to begin introduction of certain rights of protection for the foetus, would be the preferred option (though viewed as unsatisfactory by both parties). For the

Christian this would be a damage limitation exercise, and for the non-theist, it would mean that a significant number of women would be denied access to abortion services in an apparently needless way.

At week six, the non-theist begins to view the foetus as an object rightly evoking the concern and protection of the moral community. What degree of protection might this be? Once again, any answer to this question will probably be arrived at by balancing the relative harms of pain experienced by the foetus being aborted, with the pain experienced to the mother or other family members as the result of the pregnancy continuing. The details of how one might legislate on such an issue would doubtless be the subject of much heated debate. The point is, that the degree of protection afforded to the foetus is likely to increase as pregnancy develops, not simply because the degree of sentience increases, but because there is growth in all other attributes and further bonding between the foetus and its parents. Contrary to the Christian position, it seems a commonly held moral intuition that a late-term abortion is a greater loss than an earlier one. It may also be the case that some supporters of the sentience-point of view may not wish to afford the late-term foetus the same degree of protection given by most Christians to the newly implanted embryo, but this follows from the logic of the underlying positions.

What then of the case made by Germain Grisez, that if one is prepared to kill an entity, not knowing for sure that this entity is not a human person, then this is precisely the same as being willing to kill a human person? Grisez puts it this way:

> In being willing to kill the embryo, we accept the responsibility for killing what we must admit *may* be a person. There is some reason to believe it is - namely the *fact* that it is a living human individual ... *To be willing to kill what for all we know could be a person is to be willing to kill it if it is a person ... If one is willing to get a desired result by killing, and does not know whether he is killing or not, he might as well know that he is killing.*[68]

Now this argument is no doubt more troublesome to the theist than the non-theist. The theist has examined all the relevant scientific data, and is reasonably, but not completely, sure that no human person exists before implantation. There remains just a tiny doubt that a human person might be present from fertilisation. The question in need of an answer, then, is just to what extent will the theist allow such a tiny doubt sway his judgement and actions. But firstly, he may rightly take issue with Grisez' assertion that to kill what may be a person is no different to killing with a definite knowledge. The theist is entitled to reply that when the likelihood of there being a person present is incredibly small, then this makes a huge moral difference to an act where the odds are, say, equal in either direction.

Some have likened the situation to that of the hunter who, on seeing some movement in the bushes, is unsure whether it is some wild game, or his friend. It is said that he is under an obligation not to shoot, until he is perfectly sure that it is not his friend. What makes this kind of argument less straight forward, is when further details are

added[69]: the hunter's friend was behind him only a few minutes beforehand, it is
therefore highly unlikely that he has been able to cover the ground unobserved by the
hunter to where the movement in the bushes now is; furthermore, the hunter and his
family are both starving, they need to eat today, and game is rare in the area to which
they are confined, and so on. These kind of details do make the illustration more
analogous to the question of whether a human person is present prior to implantation.
A broad sweep of all the relevant data has convinced the theist that it is highly unlikely,
and there is a great deal at stake if he chooses to act as if there might be a person
present. He would need to take a moral stand against the IUD, PC4 as well as embryo
research and many of the new reproductive technologies.

In summary, the theist may reply that he remains reasonably confident that no human
person is present prior to implantation and that there is indeed a great moral difference
between ending the existence of an entity that is most unlikely to be a human person and
what he knows to be a human person. It needs to be born in mind that any such killing
is not being done for sport, but to further the happiness and wellbeing of actual persons.
He may also reject Grisez' notion that a living human individual is present, because he
is able put forward the case against individuation being established prior to cell
differentiation. As said earlier, the non-theist is unlikely to be moved by Grisez'
arguments. He is sure that being alive as a human individual is not a matter of intrinsic
value, and thus there is no inconsistency in maintaining that it is legitimate to end the
life of a human being in its pre-sentient phase.

The conclusions of this discussion for the pharmacist wishing to know if it is morally
acceptable to sell PC4 to the general public, are therefore as follows: a good case can
be argued that the pre-implantation embryo is not yet a human individual. This is likely
to be a conclusion of most interest to the pharmacist of theistic persuasion, though not
exclusively.   I have argued that the non-theist should most reasonably hold the
possession of sentience to be the earliest morally relevant property that requires the
moral community to assign rights of protection to the foetus (in and of itself), and
therefore the non-theist can be confident that the sale of PC4 cannot be said to harm any
individual, because, even if a human individual is present, harm can only accrue to the
future person, who in this instance will never exist. The theist, also, can be reasonably
confident that PC4 is a means of contraception, not of abortion, because it is acting to
prevent a life from beginning, not by ending a life that has already started. Yet there
remains for the theist the tiny nagging doubt sown by Grisez: there may just possibly
be a human person present from fertilisation, and that may be enough to sway some
from selling PC4, even though a pregnancy may cause considerable distress to the
family concerned. Of course, in most geographical situations, the patient will simply
go to the next nearest pharmacy to buy PC4, or get it prescribed by the doctor, but this
may not always be possible.

Notes

1. Cf. *Pharmaceutical Journal* 251, November 1993, p.693.

2. Cf. *Pharmaceutical Journal* 252, February 1994, p.281.

3. McCrystal, P. [correspondence] *Pharmaceutical Journal* 253, September 1994, p.299.

4. Lane, J.A., [correspondence] *Pharmaceutical Journal* 253, September 1994, p.299.

5. Godfrey, K.E., [correspondence] *Pharmaceutical Journal* 253, August 1994, p.272.

6. Martin, M.E.M., [correspondence] *Pharmaceutical Journal* 253, September 1994, p.394.

7. Breewood, C., [correspondence] *Pharmaceutical Journal* 253, September 1994, p.394.

8. Madge, A.G.M., [correspondence] *Pharmaceutical Journal* 253, October 1994, p.478.

9. Terry, A., [correspondence] *Pharmaceutical Journal* 253, September 1994, p.332.

10. Curran, C.E., 'Abortion: contemporary debate in philosophical and religious ethics' in Reich, W.T. (ed.), *Encyclopaedia of Bioethics* New York, Macmillan Free Press, 1978, pp.17-24, p.17.

11. Callahan, D., 'The "beginning" of human life' in Goodman, M.F. (ed.), *What Is A Person?* Clifton, N.J, Humana Press, 1988, pp.29-55, p.32.

12. Ramsey, P., 'Reference points in deciding about abortion' in Noonan, J.T. (ed.), *The Morality of Abortion: Legal and Historical Perspectives* Cambridge, Mass., Harvard University Press, 1970, pp.64-100, p.66.

13. Berry, C., *Beginnings: Christian Views of the Early Embryo* London, Christian Medical Fellowship, 1993, p.15.

14. *Ibid.*, p.10.

15. Callahan, *op.cit.*, pp.33-34.

16. Szawarski, Z., 'The "Embryo" Usage' Working Paper for European Commission research project Fertility, Infertility and the Human Embryo plenary conference, Barcelona, October 1994, p.4 (published as 'Talking about embryos' in this volume).

17. See Genesis 9.6.

18. See Atkinson, D., 'Some theological perspectives on the human embryo' in Cameron, N.M. de S., *Embryos and Ethics* Edinburgh, Rutherford House Books, 1987, pp.43-57, pp.46ff.

19. See Exodus 20.13 and Matthew 19.19.

20. See for example Spallone, P., *Beyond Conception: The New Politics of Reproduction* Basingstoke, Macmillan Education, 1989, p.36.

21. Atkinson, *op. cit.*, p.56.

22. Bedate, C.A. and Cefalo, R.C., 'The zygote: to be or not be a person' *Journal of Medicine and Philosophy* 14, 1989, pp.616-645, pp.642-644.

23. See Cahill, L., 'The embryo and the foetus: new moral contexts' *Theological Studies* 54 (1), pp.129-142, p.136.

24. Atkinson, *op.cit.*, p.55.

25. Berry, *op.cit.*, p.14.

26. *Ibid.*, p.13.

27. Ford, N., *When Did I Begin?* Cambridge, Cambridge University Press, 1988, pp.120-121.

28. Regan, A., 'The human conceptus and personhood' *Studia Moralia* 30, 1992, pp.97-127, p.122.

29. Iglesias, T., 'What kind of being is the human embryo?' in Cameron, *op.cit.*, pp.58-73, p.70.

30. *Ibid.*, p.70.

31. Ford, *op.cit.*, p.85.

32. Shannon, T. and Wolter, A. 'Reflections on the moral status of the pre-embryo' *Theological Studies* 51, 1990, pp.603-626, p.614.

33. Ford, *op.cit.*, p.137.

34. Iglesias, *op.cit.*, p.67.

35. *Ibid.*, p.71.

36. Cameron, N.M. de S., 'The christian stake in the Warnock debate' in Cameron, *op.cit.*, pp.1-13, pp.12-13.

37. Wertheimer, R., 'Understanding the abortion argument' *Philosophy and Public Affairs* 1, 1971, pp.67-95, p.83.

38. VanDeVeer, D., 'Justifying "wholesale slaughter"' in Feinberg, J. (ed.), *The Problem of Abortion* second edition, Belmont, Ca., Wadsworth, 1984, pp.65-70, p.67.

39. Stott, J., *Issues Facing Christians Today* Basingstoke, Marshall, Morgan and Scott, 1984, p.285.

40. See for example Gardner, R., cited in Stott, *op.cit.*, p.286.

41. Bole, T.J., 'Zygotes, souls, substances and persons' *Journal of Medicine and Philosophy* 15 (6), 1990, pp.637-652, p.648.

42. Sumner, L.W., 'A third way' in Feinberg (ed.), *op.cit.*, pp.71-93, p.93.

43. *Ibid.*, p.85.

44. Diamond, C., 'The importance of being human' in Cockburn, D. (ed.), *Human Beings* Cambridge, Cambridge University Press, 1991, pp.35-62, p.53.

45. Warnock, M., '*In vitro* fertilisation: the ethical issues' *Philosophical Quarterly* 33 (132), 1983, pp.238-249, p.241.

46. Joyce, R., 'Personhood and the conception event' in Goodman, *op.cit.*, pp.199-211, p.199.

47. *Ibid.*, p.204.

48. *Ibid.*, p.202.

49. Langerak, E., 'Abortion: listening to the middle' in Goodman, *op.cit.*, pp.251-263, p.256.

50. Weiss, R., 'The perils of personhood' in Goodman, *op.cit.*, pp.115-126, p.121.

51. Rorty, A.O., 'A literary postscript' in Rorty, A.O. (ed.), *The Identity of Persons* Berkeley, University of California Press, 1976, pp.309-312, p.309.

52. Singer, P., *Practical Ethics* second edition, Cambridge, Cambridge University Press, 1993, p.150.

53. Pucetti, R., 'The life of a person' in Goodman, *op.cit.*, pp.265-280, p.265.

54. Frankfurt, H., 'Freedom of the will and the concept of a person' in Goodman, *op.cit.*, pp.127-144, p.129.

55. Taylor, C., 'Responsibility for self' in Rorty, *op.cit.*, pp.281-299, p.281.

56. Tooley, M., 'In defence of abortion and infanticide' in Feinberg (ed.), *op.cit.*, pp.120-134, p.124.

57. Dennett, D., 'Conditions of personhood' in Rorty (ed.), *op.cit.*, pp.175-196, p.193.

58. Lomasky, L., 'Being a person - does it matter?' in Feinberg (ed.), *op.cit.*, pp.161-172, p.161.

59. Gillespie, N., 'Abortion and human rights' in Feinberg (ed.), *op.cit.*, pp.94-101, p.98.

60. Wertheimer, *op.cit.*, p.56.

61. Spallone, *op.cit.*, p.34.

62. *Ibid.*, p.35, p.39, p.55 and p.35.

63. Purdy, L., 'Are pregnant women fetal containers?' *Bioethics* 14 (4), 1990, pp.273-291, p.278.

64. Spallone, *op.cit.*, p.36.

65. *Ibid.*, p.52.

66. Purdy, *op.cit.*, p.278.

67. Fisher, A., '*When Did I Begin?* revisited' *Linacre Quarterly* 58, 1991, pp.59-68, p.60.

68. Grisez, G., *Abortion: The Myths, the Realities and the Arguments* New York, Corpus Books, 1970, p.306 and p.344.

69. See also McCormick, R., 'Who or what is the pre-embryo?' *Journal of the Kennedy Institute of Ethics* March 1991, pp.1-15, p.11.

8. TALKING ABOUT EMBRYOS

Zbigniew Szawarski
Centre for Philosophy and Health Care
University of Wales, Swansea
Singleton Park
Swansea
Wales

The question 'What is the human embryo?' can be answered in several ways. When we ask what is the essence of the designate denoted by the term 'human embryo' we look for a definition of the human embryo; we try to find a certain definite set of relevant characteristics which is constitutive of the human embryo distinguishing it amongst other things from the class of all embryos. However, there is another possible approach. Here we do not ask for the relevant characteristics of the human embryo as an entity but we try to grasp the meaning of the concept of 'human embryo' by noting the role of the term in discourse. Whatever strategy we choose, whether we look for a definition of the human embryo, or whether we try reflect upon all possible usages of the term, in both cases we face the same essential problem: how the dispositions of the observer determine what he considers relevant or irrelevant characteristics of the human embryo. The main thesis of my paper is the belief that the dispositions and the social context of the observer determine the usage of the word. Therefore, there is no universal usage of the expression 'human embryo'. Whenever that concept is used it is related to a particular community which is using it in the way specific for that community.

1. The Moral Usage: the Human Embryo as a Member of the Moral Community

When we endeavour to identify the concept of the human embryo in its moral usage we are trying to decide what makes the embryo a member of the moral community. We assume that we have moral obligations only towards those beings which share with us some morally relevant characteristics. If, for example, sentience is a morally relevant characteristic then it means that sentient beings deserve some respect or are the subject of moral obligations. Thus, the extent to which the human embryo (or an animal) resembles a normal human being is both the explanation and the main reason why we should treat it in a certain way. However, different people offer different reasons for attributing or denying moral status to the embryo. These are the most typical approaches.

119

D. Evans (ed.), Conceiving the Embryo, 119–133.
© 1996 *Kluwer Law International. Printed in the Netherlands.*

The embryo is a human person and belongs to the moral community. This is the most radical approach, central to the moral doctrine of the Catholic Church and reiterated in all the recent fundamental documents of the Church.[1] What makes us human is that we are conceived and born by human parents. At the moment of conception a new human being comes into the world and from that specific moment it is a member of the human community.

> My conviction is that the human embryo is a human person, a being of human nature with an eternal destiny. I take this conviction to be true, and grounded on biological knowledge, philosophical reflection and the Christian faith and way of life which I share with other Christians in the community we form as a Church.[2]

It is not my aim to examine all the metaphysical and scientific presuppositions of this approach. What is really important in this context is that it does not acknowledge any moral difference between successive stages of human development. 'Human person', 'human being', 'human individual', 'unborn child', 'human embryo', or 'human zygote' denote the same entity which preserves exactly the same moral status throughout its life span beginning from the very moment of conception.

> The terms 'zygote', 'pre-embryo', 'embryo', and 'fetus' can indicate in the vocabulary of biology successive states of the development of a human being. The present Instruction makes free use of these terms, attributing to them identical ethical relevance, in order to designate the result (whether visible or not) of human generation, from the first moment of its existence until birth.[3]

The most striking consequence of this approach is a moral claim of complete solidarity with our unborn progeny. Whatever the biological status of the human embryo is it is something more than a cluster of cells. And though contemporary theologians and moralists disagree about the exact moment of our coming into being[4] it does not have any substantial impact on the moral attitude towards the human embryo - it has intrinsic moral value, it is one of us and it should be protected by law and morals.

The embryo is a thing. This is a relatively new usage. As a matter of fact it was generated by modern reproductive technology in which the embryo has left its natural surroundings and become an object of manipulation. Created as the extracorporeal embryo it can be transferred, frozen, stored, banked, used; it is the object of selection, quality control, and disposal. Though it is an evident case of human life it does not have the full moral status of a human being. A good example of this usage is provided by Peter Singer and Deane Wells.

> We therefore make the following proposal. The internationally recognized criterion for the permissibility of using the vital parts of another human body is brain death. Total brain death, the complete absence of all brain functions,

indicates that the heart, kidneys, the pancreas, and other organs may be removed for transplant purposes. If the medical profession (and indeed the Churches) recognize a body's lack of a functional brain as sufficient grounds for declaring that there is no living person existing in that body, and the body may therefore be used as a means to worthwhile ends, then why not use the same criterion at the other end of existence? We suggest that the embryo be regarded as a thing, rather than a person, until the point at which there is some brain function.[5]

The rationale of Singer and Well's position is simple. If the moral community encompasses only those beings which are able to experience pain or pleasure, and it is obvious that a being cannot be sentient unless it has a developed brain, then the functioning brain is the morally relevant characteristic of the embryo. The zygote or the frozen embryo cannot feel any sensations so in this sense they remind us more an amoeba or a thing than a developed human organism.

The human embryo is not a thing but it is a potential member of the human community. Human potential is something which gives the embryo a moral value making it at least a potential member of the human community. 'Human potential', 'potential person', 'potential humanity' - these are the categories which are usually used to describe the status of the embryo. An excellent example of this approach to the human embryo is the following quotation from Leon Kass:

> The human blastocyst, even the blastocyst *in vitro*, is not humanly nothing; it possesses a power to become what everyone will agree is a human being....The blastocyst is not nothing, it is *at least* potential humanity, and as such it elicits, or ought to elicit, our feelings of awe and respect. In the blastocyst, even in the zygote, we face a mysterious and awesome power... *The human embryo is not mere meat; it is not just stuff; it is not a thing.* Because of its origin and because of its capacity, it commands a higher respect.[6]

This is a very attractive approach and indeed very few people would challenge the moral claim that it is wrong to destroy human potentiality. The problem is however that it is not clear what human potentiality is and when precisely the embryo acquires human potential or becomes a potential person. These two concepts are by no means identical and one may claim that though embryos acquire human potential at the moment of fertilisation nevertheless they become potential persons at the moment of implantation or even later when the primitive streak is formed.

The human embryo is neither a human person, nor a thing, nevertheless it has a certain value and should be treated with respect. This is a sort of compromise position between Singer and Wells and Kass. The embryo is more than a thing but less then a fully fledged human person and there are good reasons to treat it with greater respect than any other human organ or tissue. This approach has gained quite wide acceptance recently, particularly in the U.S.A., and is aptly represented by the following quotation:

> The embryo may, however, be accorded respect on grounds other than what it is
> owed by virtue of its present biological status. Although neither a person nor an
> entity possessing interests, it may be the subject of duties created to demonstrate
> a commitment to human life and persons generally. Justice may not require that
> we grant the embryo rights, but we may choose to treat the embryo differently
> than other human tissue as a sign of respect for human life generally. Since the
> embryo is living, human, and has the potential to become a person if transfer
> occurs, it activates sentiments in much the same way that dead persons and
> cadavers do. Thus, as long as the basis for evaluation is clear and embryos are
> not given the full respect accorded persons, it may be desirable to assign embryos
> a higher value than accorded to other extracorporeal human tissue in order to
> symbolize respect for human life. Such symbolizing is an essential part of any
> human community, and helps constitute and identify the community's values.[7]

The fact that we are inclined to grant a higher value to the embryo does not mean that
it has to be an instrinsic moral value. We respect a national flag or other national
symbols not for their moral but mainly for their symbolic value. It is then quite natural
that we should precisely regulate what may be done with human embryos. It may or
may not exclude some forms of experimentation or genetic engineering.[8]

The embryo is not a human person though it is a member of the human community.
This is a bizarre and somewhat self-contradictory usage but it deserves to be recorded
as it comes from on of the most distinguished authorities in modern embryology -
Clifford Grobstein:

> The preembryo clearly merits the same respect accorded to all other human cells,
> tissues, and organs. This means that its significant human character - its kinship
> relationships as well as its genetic individuality - should be neither neglected nor
> denigrated. Beyond this general status, however, the preembryo requires
> additional special concern for its potential to become an infant and eventually a
> full person. However, if that potential no longer exists, for whatever reason, the
> value of the preembryo as a member of the human community should still be
> recognized and conserved. This means, among other things, that the preembryo
> should be accessible to carefully considered research, providing that the research
> supports substantial medical objectives and the proposed plan for the research has
> been approved by a suitable review body. Failing achieving its highest potential -
> to become a full person - the preemebryo can thus realize part of its human
> heritage and potential by fulfilling a significant and unique role in the human
> family.[9]

Speaking about embryos which have lost their potential Grobstein means those embryos generated *in vitro* that would not be transferred back into the woman's womb. They are of course biological material too valuable to be discarded. As an object of ethically reviewed research they can nevertheless contribute to the development of humanity and apparently it is their *role to do so*. Paradoxically the human community, as seen by Grobstein, seems to consist mainly of humans who are first of all research subjects. The only possible sense in which the embryo, although not a person, can belong to the human community is simply by being a valuable human research subject.

I have presented just a few quotations from the recent literature. They are enough, however, to make some general observations possible.

(a) In its moral usage the term 'human embryo' always conveys a moral message. It expresses a moral tradition specific to the community the speaker belongs to. So the meaning of the expression 'human embryo' when it is used by a Catholic nun from 'the Christian community formed as a Church' may be radically different from the meaning of the same words when they are spoken out in the scientific community of embryo researchers. The same words express different moral attitudes and different ideas of what constitutes a human or moral community. It may happen of course that an embryologist is simultaneously a true believer and belongs in fact to two communities; obviously his usage of the term will then be decided by his moral and religious beliefs and so will the scope and methods of his research.

(b) Although probably most of us will grant a moral status to the human embryo, the meaning of that status and the reasons justifying it may be in principle very different. But whatever the choice of the morally relevant property (or properties) of the embryo, it is always a moral choice.

(c) If we accept that no moral conclusion can be deduced from empirical or metaphysical statements alone, then whatever the empirical (or metaphysical) argument brought into debate to endorse a moral position, it can never be the conclusive reason. It is always what C.L.Stevenson would call a 'supporting reason' only.[10]

2. The Scientific Usage: The Human Embryo as an Object of Research

The aim of science is true description and explanation of facts. If we ask an embryologist what is the proper object of his research he will probably characterise a process of generation and development of the embryo. It is not an accident that Robert Edwards needed five pages to define the human embryo.[11] It is impossible to explain adequately when the individual human life begins unless one describes precisely consecutive stages of that life from the moment of fertilisation to the moment of birth. What is interesting, however, is that the object of embryological research is always a physical object which can be described in the pure language of science. To what extent the scientific description of the human embryo is value neutral, is the question I would like to discuss later. However, scientists hardly ever have any doubts about what they *see* in their labs. If the object of research is a very early embryo, it is normally seen simply as a 'collection of living cells'[12], 'a simple cluster of human cells'[13], 'the mass of dividing cells'[14], 'hollow ball of cells'[15], 'little clump of cells'[16], 'a human cellural aggregate'[17], 'a multicellural assembly'[18] etc. but the researcher does not see any human person there.[19]

This does not mean of course that all researchers see exactly the same or assign the same significance to particular stages of embryonic development or, what is more relevant, that they will use the same terms to describe successive stages in human development. One might think that more than 20 years of growth of reproductive technology was quite sufficient to produce a clear, precise and consistent terminology. It is commonly accepted that there are three main stages in the process of embryogenesis:

- pre-embryonic: from the moment of fertilisation to implantation;
- embryonic: from the moment of implantation to the end of the 8th week;
- foetal: from the 8th week to birth.[20]

However, different terms and definitions are offered to describe particular stages. Here is a modest selection of the most important definitions proposed by different scientists and professional and legislative bodies. I have arranged them in the chronological order to show precisely how difficult it is, even in science, to get a consensus with respect to the most essential terms. The more we know about the earliest period of embryogenesis the more difficult it is to make a decision about what is the most suitable term to denote a particular stage of growth. It was quite recently that scientists realised that the term 'human embryo' is an ambiguous one.

The ambiguity arises because the word 'embryo' is also used to denote the *whole of the collection of cells* formed by repeated division of the fertilized egg during the first two weeks or so, although only a few per cent of these cells are destined to become the embryo proper; by far the greater number of them will turn into extra-embryonic tissue and ultimately into the structures that are discarded as the afterbirth. Furthermore it is indeterminate which particular cells will form the embryo proper. The embryo proper is first recognizable at about the 15th day after fertilisation when a specialised region of cells called the 'primitive streak' first appears. Before that stage, it cannot be said that a definitive embryo exists; *the product of conception is a structure* of which a small and undetermined part will - if development proceeds normally - form a 'primitive streak' and later an 'embryo' in the sense in which the word is generally understood, and later again a 'foetus'.[21]

For upwards of 2000 years embryo has been used to denote the growth of the organism in the womb from the time of the first formation of the body parts until their completion followed by the fetal stage in which the completed baby grows to viability. Now that science has revealed a vital pre-embryonic stage of cellural activity before organogenesis can begin an appropriate name should be given to it. Pre-embryo seems a proper name to describe this stage of development.[22]

I shall use the term pre-embryo to refer to the first three major stages of development: the earliest stages of cell division (the so called cleavage stages), the blastocyst (when the pre-embryo is a hollow ball of cells) and the stages of implantation up to the formation of the primitive streak.[23]

Fertilisation does not produce an embryo. The introduction of a sperm into an egg stimulates cell-division. Those dividing cells might produce an embryo but may well not. The term pre-embryo allows for the possibility. The term embryo is, at this stage, incorrect.[24]

With some caution, we intend to use three key terms as follows:
Pre-embryo: the product of conception, from fertilization to nidation, i.e., up to implantation in the uterine cavity. This stage lasts about 10 days.
Embryo: the product of conception during the stage from implantation in the uterine cavity up to six weeks after fertilization.
Foetus: the product of conception from the end of the embryonic stage to birth.[25]

A preembryo is a product of gametic union from fertilization to the appearance of the embryonic axis. The preembryonic stage is considered to last until 14 days after fertilization. This definition is not intended to imply a moral evaluation of preembryo.[26]

In this Act, except where otherwise stated -
(a) embryo means a live human embryo where fertilisation is complete, and
(b) reference to an embryo include an egg in the process of fertilisation, and for this purpose, fertilisation is not complete until the appearance of a two cell zygote.[27]

Zygote: the fertilized egg until approximately 14 days of development; from two weeks to eight weeks of development the developing entity is termed an embryo; from eight weeks to birth is termed fetus.[28]

The language of science is never rigid and ossified but gradually evolves following the growth of knowledge. It is quite natural then that traditional basic terms, like 'zygote', 'embryo', 'foetus' will have to be redefined or new terms introduced. Robert Edwards used the term 'embryo' or 'pre-implantation embryo', A.Huxley suggested the term 'embryo proper' to distinguish the embryo proper from the extra-embryonic tissue. G.Dunstan coined the term 'pre-embryo' which was later promulgated by Ann McLaren and the British Voluntary Licensing Authority but for political and moral reasons rejected by British Parliament and British feminist movement.[29] For the time being, the situation is peculiar. The Canadian 'zygote', the American 'pre-embryo' and the British 'embryo' denote exactly the same cluster of cells, the same entity, the same organism, or exactly the same object of research. It is not a normal thing for the scientific community to use three different terms, depending upon the country in which the research is being carried out.

If the term 'pre-embryo' had concerned a particular stage in the development of mammals other than humans it would be very unlikely that anybody would have paid any attention to it. However, when the term 'human pre-embryo' was introduced it brought at once serious accusations of moral and political manipulation. The term has been challenged both by Catholics[30] and feminists.[31] Even some biologists were sceptical about the biological significance of it.[32]

Two fundamental issues were at the base of the whole controversy. First, the question of the meaning of the word 'human'; is the biological concept of humanity identical with the moral one? If the embryo is a human being, is it automatically implied that it has full moral status? The second question was more complicated and concerned the continuity or discontinuity of our individual being. If we ask this question and count our continuity from the moment of implantation, then our decision to talk in this way is something more than a simple description or explanation; it is a decision about the metaphysical significance of that particular event. One can of course refer to various moral, or religious reasons to justify that decision. But the biologist who does so is changing his social role - he speaks then mainly as a moralist, as a member of particular moral or religious community. The debate about the moral status of the embryo clearly demonstrates how difficult it is to draw any sharp line between our roles. It is not only impossible but also morally undesirable.

3. The Medical Usage: The Embryo as an Object of Medical Intervention

In the medical context the embryo is treated mainly as a means of bypassing parental infertility or simply as a patient. When it is a patient the medical intervention may be expected at different stages of embryonic development before implantation, e.g. to control culture conditions during pre-embryo growth, or to control the process and results of cryopreservation and assist in reproductive hatching of the pre-embryo.[33] However, the most relevant medical interventions are biopsy, genetic diagnosis, and microsurgical manipulation of the genetic composition of the embryo. In this sense the embryo may be treated for some congenital diseases.[34] It is interesting to note that another possibility of correcting defective genes in the pre-embryo, germ line gene therapy, is still in the experimental stage and is not possible with human embryos. However, as in science, there is no universal medical usage of the term 'human embryo'. The decision to proceed with or to end research on the extracorporeal human embryo is a moral decision and even those who tend to consider the human pre-embryo as a patient usually deny it full moral status.[35]

4. The Legal Usage: The Embryo as an Object of Conflict

A recent story from America illustrates well this particular usage. A Mr and Mrs Davies had tried for several years to have a baby with help of *in vitro* fertilisation. After several unsuccessful attempts they decided to adopt, but for various reasons failed with this too. However, the new technology of cryopreservation encouraged them to make another attempt to beget a child of their own. In 1988 nine eggs were aspirated from Mrs Davis and fertilised with Mr Davies' sperm. Two of the resulting embryos were implanted in Mrs Davies. The other seven were frozen. Unfortunately, neither of the implanted embryos resulted in pregnancy. The problem arose when the couple decided to divorce and both parties were trying to secure their rights over the frozen embryos. A more complete account of the story can be found in Steinbock.[36] Enough has been told to see that what is at issue is the legal status of the frozen embryos and the possibility of solving the conflict.

  The law can refer in this situation to different legal paradigms and suggest thoroughly different solutions. If one accepts that extracorporeal human embryos should be treated in the same way as unborn children, then perhaps the rights of the mother should prevail. If the extracorporeal, frozen embryo is treated as a property of both parents[37], then absolutely different options are possible. One may also argue that though it is neither a person, nor a property it has nevertheless some symbolic value and is owed our respect and protection by the law.[38] Whatever the legal decision is, it is always based on some moral assumptions and reflects to some extent the original moral uncertainty. Lawyers generally agree that the human embryo should have a special status. But the nature of that status depends on the legal and moral perspective of the community from which the lawyers come. In some countries deliberate destruction of pre-embryos may not constitute a criminal abortion, in some others the law may drastically restrict access both to abortion and assisted procreation. The growing number of legal cases in reproductive medicine (at least in the U.S.A.) proves how difficult it is to resolve conflicts over human embryos.

5. The Commercial Usage: The Embryo as a Sweet Object of Desire

For many couples and individuals who cannot or do not want to conceive a baby in the natural way assisted procreation offers the only chance to have a child and they are ready to bear substantial costs to have their wish fulfilled. The reproductive technology and services thus become the objects of a market economy. This is not the proper place to discuss all the arguments for and against commercial surrogacy. Suffice it to say that the human embryo is now the object of legal contracts and commercial transactions.

  Here we are, actively pricing motherhood - it costs about $1,000 to purchase a spare embryo, another $10,000 to "rent a womb," and then we have it. What is the meaning, what the value of motherhood? $11,000 on the open market. And once the priceless is priced, market considerations take over. How long before the brokers in this business, the men who have books of women's pictures to show prospective purchasers, follow the cattle industry in seeking higher profits? With cattle, profits have been increased by planting more valuable embryos in less valuable breeders. Can we look forward to baby farms, with white embryos grown in young and poor Third-World mothers? Price goes down, labor costs are saved, and profit goes up. But who profits here? In whose interests are we developing our technology? Where is the profit in commodifying life?[39]

There is, indeed, a growing demand for artificially conceived babies. According to Andrew Kimbrell:

> U.S. baby brokers have arranged the birth of over four thousand babies through commercial contract, charging customers between $30,000 and $45,000 per child. While the sale of these children has barely made a dent in the reported 2.3 million cases of infertile couples in this society, it has been profitable for many of the brokers, bringing in close to $40 million to the baby sellers. ... In the hands of these new entrepreneurs, childbearing, once of the most important and revered of all human activities, is fast becoming a profitable and highly visible commercial business.[40]

But if the human embryo becomes the object of commercial transactions then the language of trade applies. Both parties bound by the contract have some rights and obligations and the contract usually specifies the qualities of the expected product. A surrogate mother may for instance be legally obligated to terminate her pregnancy if the baby is of a different sex than that specified in the pregnancy contract.

6. The Ideological Usage: The Embryo as a Friend or Foe

Paradoxically, the feminist approach is reminscent of the Catholic position. For the Catholic church all the terms denoting particular stages of embryonic development have exactly the same moral relevance. For feminists it does not really matter what definition of the human embryo is proposed and how the successive stages of its development are named. Christine Overall, for example, consistently uses the term 'embryo/fetus'.[41] The most important issue is whether modern reproductive technology enhances or diminishes the reproductive freedom of woman. From that point of view the feminist movement displays a wide spectrum of approaches: from a liberal position generally approving artificial reproduction and pregnancy contracts to emphatic denial and condemnation of so-called male-generated and male-controlled technology. Those who, like Laura Purdy, approve using reproductive technologies, emphasise mostly their pragmatic value: whether fertile or infertile, a woman may have a baby whenever she wants, women may exchange their reproductive services, and even lesbian couples may have babies without engaging in sexual relations with males.[42] On the other hand, the radical feminism, centred around the movement called FINNRAGE, highlights the ideological function of reproductive technology. It is an instrument of oppression and exploitation of womankind. A typical account is the position of the British feminist Patricia Spallone.

> A pregnant women is herself whole. Being woman-centred rather than embryo-centred, feminists reject the identification of disembodied embryo. We reject defining the embryo as unconnected with the woman who carries it. We reject the identification of embryos as separate entities with separate interests whether by anti-abortionists, doctors, scientists, lawyers, politicians, ethicists or theologians.[43]

> The term 'status of the embryo' is about the power of men, of the state, and of medicine and science over women. The state and medical scientists - the keepers of ideology and the makers of technology - collude to construct a meaning of the embryo as 'natural', hiding its misogynist history. They construct the image of the embryo as essential, central to the ethics and the technology. The myth of the unencumbered, free-floating embryo, and the identification of IVF embryos as the subject of reproduction are tricks against women. The use of the 'biological facts' to define the embryo protects medical scientists and their interests. This should be obvious since medicine and science has defined the terrain - embryos, pre-embryos, isolated fetuses - from their own point of view in the first place. Their fetal-centred point of view, their fetal-centred technology, and their authority as 'experts' on reproduction place women's physical bodies at the service of fetus-oriented medical scientists. The women's health movement wants to see the orientation of medical science changed to consider women as the central subject of pregnancy.[44]

The language of feminism is generally the language of alienation, exploitation, oppression, and war. If women, having lost control over their bodies, have indeed become the object of manipulation by "child production engineers" (as Gena Corea has it[45]) then of course it is quite natural to fight against all the oppressing "technodocs", "Rambo doctors" and "pharmacrats".[46] Thus whatever the proposed definition of the human embryo is, it is absolutely irrelevant as the embryo however defined will be always a tool of oppression in male dominated and man controlled reproductive medicine.

7. Is There Any Proper Usage of the Concept of the 'Human Embryo'?

It is evident that what has so far been presented is simply a collection of different usages of the term and it seems to be very difficult (if possible at all) to offer any inductive and substantial generalisation of those usages. This is quite understandable as the list is far from being complete and the more experienced student of the language could suggest a plethora of other usages. It might, for example, be interesting to analyse how potential parents and practitioners see the result of *in vitro* fertilisation or to record some other, more exotic usages. Happily that sort of full evidence is not necessary to prove my thesis. And the thesis is simple: there is no single proper usage of the concept 'embryo'. 'Embryo' is an open concept (in the words of Weitz[47]) and it may be used according to different criteria in different linguistic and social contexts to deliver radically different meanings. Though all the interested parties may talk about the same entity - the product of human conception at its earliest stage - they may see, select, and describe absolutely different aspects of it.

The concept of aspect is crucial here. We talk about an aspect of an object if we want to stress its similarities or relations to some other objects. Talking about an aspect of a thing is then identical with talking about the thing as it is seen from a certain perspective, from a certain point of view or in a certain particular context. Sometimes we apply the concept of status to emphasise that we are talking about a thing from a certain particular point of view. When we talk about the *ontological, moral*, and *legal* status of the human embryo, in each case we refer to different conceptual categories or different conceptual contexts. And as the language of ontology is thoroughly different from the language of law and morals there is no unified and single proper usage of the term. What is, for instance, the status of the extracorporeal human frozen embryo? Is it a frozen thing or a frozen person? As it is frozen it is certainly more like a thing than a human person. We do not normally use the language of killing in talk about things. But if it is really similar to a thing does this mean that it may without moral qualms be flushed away or discarded? If it can be discarded, what is wrong with selling it? Is it an object of custody (as an unborn child) or simply the property of its parents? The problem is that we try to compare persons with objects and their features without having a common measure. Is a frozen embryo more a thing or more a human person? How is it possible to find a rational answer to this question?

It is not clear to what extent the choice of aspects is the result of rational decision. It is then quite natural that biologists perceive the objects of their research absolutely differently from theologians or feminist activists. The biologist wants to know what happens when, for example, human sperm meets human egg. The theologian wants to explain the metaphysical or moral significance of that fact. And the feminist may want to protect women against technological intrusion into their privacy. All the parties have vested interests in the description and interpretation of the same fact and again their interests are incommensurable. But even if we try to explain or interpret the meaning of the fact within the same perspective we cannot avoid some bias. Is having the human DNA in its cells a morally relevant characteristic of the frozen embryo? Are there any morally relevant characteristics of the pre-embryo? It is enough to contrast the Catholic and feminist positions to see how deep and how radical is the moral disagreement about the moral status of the embryo. The different interests, the different hierarchies of values, the different social and political contexts and, most important, the different perceptions of the same facts, make these two approaches absolutely irreconcilable.

We cannot escape some subjectivity in our perception, description, and interpretation of the human reality. This is best seen in the language we use to describe the relation we have to our world. We can make language more precise, we can offer new, more exact and sophisticated definitions, but we cannot escape our humanity. And it is this precisely which colours all debates about the meaning and significance of the language used to describe the earliest stages of human life.

Notes

1. Congregation for the Doctrine of the Faith, *Instruction on Respect for Human Life in its Origin and on the Dignity of Procreation* Donum Vitae (22 February 1987) London, Catholic Truth Society, 1987.

2. Iglesias, T., *IVF and Justice: Moral, Social and Legal Issues Related to Human Fertilization* London, The Linacre Centre for Health Care Ethics, 1990, p.86.

3. Congregation for the Doctrine of the Faith, *op.cit.*, p.3.

4. Contrast, for instance, the views of Cahill, Ford, and McCormick. Ford, N., *When Did I Begin?* Cambridge, Cambridge University Press, 1988; McCormick, R.A., 'Who or what is the preembryo?' *Kennedy Institute of Ethics Journal* Vol. 1, No. 1, March 1991, pp.1-15; Cahill, L.S., 'The embryo and the fetus: new moral contexts' *Theological Studies* Vol. 54, No. 1, pp.124-142.

5. Singer, P. and Wells, D., *The Reproduction Revolution* Oxford, Oxford University Press, 1984, p.98.

6. Kass, L., 'Ethical issues in human *in vitro* fertilization, embryo culture and research, and embryo transfer' in Ethics Advisory Board, Department of Health, Education and Welfare, *Appendix: HEW Support of Research Involving Human In Vitro Fertilization and Embryo Transfer* Washington, D.C., US Government Printing Office, 1979, pp.6-8 (quoted in Gorovitz, S., *Doctor's Dilemmas* New York, Oxford University Press, 1982, p.175) emphases in original.

7. Robertson, J.A., 'Embryos, families and procreative liberty: the legal structure of the new reproduction' *Southern California Law Review* 59 (5), July 1986, pp.933-1041, pp.974-975.

8. Cf. Robertson, J.A., 'The question of human cloning' *Hastings Center Report* 24 (2), 1994, pp.6-14.

9. Grobstein, C., *Science and the Unborn. Choosing Human Futures* New York, Basic Books, Inc. Publishers, 1988, p.82.

10. Stevenson, C.L., *Ethics and Language* New Haven, Connecticut, Yale University Press, 1944, pp.30-31.

11. Edwards, R., *Life Before Birth* London, Hutchinson, 1989, pp.49-54.

12. Grobstein, *op.cit.*, p.67.

13. *Ibid.*, p.77.

14. Congress of the United States Office of Technology, *Infertility. Medical and Social Choices* Washington, D.C., US Government Printing Office, May 1988, p.387 (Appendix. J. Glossary).

15. MacLaren, A., 'Why study early human development?' *New Scientist* Vol. 110, No. 1505, 24 April 1986, pp.49-52, p.49.

16. Seller, M.J., 'The human embryo: a scientist's point of view' *Bioethics* Vol. 7, No. 2/3, 1993, pp.135-140, p.138.

17. Grobstein, *op.cit.*, p.67.

18. *Ibid.*, p.82.

19. Cf. Seller, *op.cit.*, for a generally excellent paper on these matters.

20. E.g. Braude, R.P. and Johnson, M.H., 'The embryo in contemporary medical science' in Dunstan, G.R. (ed.), *The Human Embryo. Aristotle and the Arabic Traditions* Exeter, University of Exeter Press, 1990, p.209.

21. Huxley, A., 'Research and the embryo' *New Scientist* Vol. 106, No. 1451, 11 April 1985, p.2.

22. Dunstan, G.R., quoted in Gunning, J. and English, V. (eds), *Human In Vitro Fertilization. A Case Study in the Regulation of Medical Innovation* Dartmouth, Aldershot, 1993, p.58.

23. MacLaren, *op.cit.*, p.49.

24. Voluntary Licensing Authority, *The Third Report* London, 1988, p.22.

25. Glover, J., *Fertility and the Family* London, Fourth Estate, 1989, p.94.

26. The Ethics Committee of The American Fertility Society, 'Ethical considerations of the new reproductive technologies' *Fertility and Sterility* Vol. 46, No. 3, September 1986, Supplement 1, p.vii.

27. U.K. Human Fertilisation and Embryology Act, 1990, Part 1, sec. 1, in Jones, M.A. and Morris, A.E. (eds), *Blackstone's Statutes on Medical Law* London, Blackstone Press Limited, 1992, p.188.

28. Canada. Royal Commission on New Reproductive Technologies, *Proceed With Care* Vol. 2, 1993, p.1174.

29. Spallone, P., *Beyond Conception* London, Macmillan Education, 1984.

30. Iglesias, *op.cit.*, refers to the term as a "cosmetic semantic".

31. Cf. Spallone, *op.cit.*

32. Kimber, S., 'IVF and manipulating the human embryo' in Dyson, A. and Harris, J. (eds), *Ethics and Biotechnology* London, Routledge, 1994, pp.93-120.

33. Shenker, J.G., 'Pre-embryo: therapeutic approaches' *Annals of Medicine* 25, 1993, pp.265-270.

34. Bonnicksen, A.L., 'The embryo as patient' in Humber, J.M. and Almeder, R.F. (eds), *Bioethics and the Foetus. Medical, Moral and Legal Issues* Biomedical Ethics Reviews, Totowa, N.J., Humana Press, 1991, pp.145-170.

35. For example, Schenker, *op.cit.*, p.269.

36. Steinbock, B., 'The moral status of extracorporeal embryos' in Dynson and Harris (eds), *op.cit.*, pp.79-92. Cf. also Clayton, E.W., 'A ray of light about frozen embryos' *Kennedy Institute of Ethics Journal* Vol. 2, No. 4, 1992, pp.347-359.

37. Andrews, Lori B., 'Control and compensation: laws governing extracorporeal generative materials' *Journal of Medicine and Philosophy* Vol. 14, 1989, pp.541-560.

38. Cf. for example: Steinbock, *op.cit.*, Robertson, *op.cit.*, Andrews, *op.cit.* and Annas, G.J., 'Redefined parenthood and protecting embryos. Why we need new laws' in Campbell, C.S. (ed.), *What Price Parenthood? Ethics and Assisted Reproduction* Dartmouth, Aldershot, 1992, pp.33-35.

39. Rothman, Barbara Katz, 'Reproductive technology and the commodification of life' in Baruch, E. Hoffman, D'Adamo, A.F. and Seager, J. (eds), *Embryos, Ethics, and Women's Rights* New York, The Haworth Press, 1988, pp.99-100.

40. Kimbrell, A., *The Human Body Shop* San Francisco, Harper, 1993, p.100.

41. Overall, C., *Ethics and Human Reproduction. A Feminist Analysis* Boston, Allen and Unwin, 1987, e.g., Chapter 3 'The embryo/fetus', pp.40-67.

42. Purdy, L.M., 'Are pregnant women fetal containers?' *Bioethics* Vol. 4, No. 5, October 1990, pp.273-291.

43. Spallone, *op.cit.*, p.39.

44. *Ibid.*, p.55.

45. Corea, Gena, *The Mother Machine* London, The Women's Press, *passim.*

46. This is probably the best description of what is called 'Rambo' medicine in feminist medical ethics: "Rambo medicine is based on male heroic technical prowess that requires more high tech, more high drama, more high publicity, more high funding and more high risk for women, with little immediate success - but, of course, the *promise* of it. Rambo medicine, like a messianic religion, is always promising a future that is yet unrealized. Rambo medicine is the medical eschatology of things to come" (Raymond, J.G., 'Of eggs, embryos and altruism' in Hynes, P.A. (ed.) *Reconstructing Babylon. Essays on Women and Technology* Bloomington and Indianapolis, Indiana University Press, 1991, pp.82-91, p.88.

47. Weitz, M., 'Open concepts' *Revue Internationale de Philosophie* 1972, pp.86-110.

9. CULTURAL PRO-ATTITUDES, REPRODUCTIVE ETHICS AND EMBRYO PROTECTION

Vassil Prodanov
Institute of Philosophical Research
Sofia 1000, Patriarch Evtimii 6
Bulgaria

The development of common European regulation of assisted procreation and embryo protection depends on the existence of common European cultural space, on the availability of shared European values underlying positions concerning biomedical ethics. It is well known that the availability of shared American values of the American nation does not prevent 'culture wars'[1] over the family, art, law and politics and even terrorist acts when it concerns the pro-choice movement and the 'right to life'. The question is which kind of regulation would prevent European 'culture wars'.

Any period in the development of human society is connected with differences in the demographic behaviour of people regulated by certain values and norms. These values and norms prescribe, demand, and control phenomena such as parenthood, infanticide, celibacy, childlessness, and abortion. Accordingly, the novelty resulting from the new technologies in the reproductive behaviour of people cannot be comprehended and evaluated in the framework of an abstract and absolute moral system. The moral meanings and intuitions concerning the application of new medical technologies for treatment of infertility cannot be based just on one or two axiomatic principles but are rooted in the whole body of the culture. This body of culture facilitates the respective content and perceptions of the general categories constituting the social construction of reality - 'normal' and 'abnormal', 'natural' and 'unnatural', 'artificial' and 'pervasive'.

1. Value Presumptions of Any Logical Solution

There are various logical solutions of the problem concerning the moral status of the embryo. Which of them will be chosen depends on the special social context of the family and child in any country and the resultant perception of the 'need' for regulation of assisted procreation and embryo protection.

From a logical point of view all debates concerning the moral status of embryos can be subsumed under several groups of solutions:

1. The embryo is a person. This means that embryos and persons have one and the same moral position and moral rights. To adapt Kant's words: 'The embryo is a goal in itself'. The embryo has a right to life.

D. Evans (ed.), Conceiving the Embryo, 135–148.
© 1996 Kluwer Law International. Printed in the Netherlands.

2. The embryo has nothing in common with any person. It has the ontological position of a thing and does not possess any moral standing. The embryo is not a goal in itself, and it has no right to life.

3. The embryo is something intermediate between person and thing. The gradualist position, for instance, takes this line, claiming that because the embryo is a potential person, it has some moral status, although not the same as a mature person. This status grows with development of the embryo. Naturally, the questions what are the rights of the embryo at its various stages of development, in what sense does the protection of the embryo in the course of its growth in the living process become morally more important, and when does it attain the right to life, can be raised.

4. For some period (for instance its first 14 days) the embryo is not a person and has no moral rights but later it becomes a person with the relevant rights.

These four types of solution could be achieved by four possible approaches.

Approach 1. Search for some specific biological features of the zygote, embryo, and foetus from which to infer their moral standing. But it is impossible to find something moral in biological characteristics in themselves. This would be to make a jump from facts, descriptions, and indicative statements to values, prescriptions, and normative statements. As a result this approach becomes an example of the "naturalistic fallacy".[2]

Approach 2. Take for granted that there is some general ontological category or substance whose moral standing is self-evident or proved in some way. One may then try to find in the embryo the same ontological or descriptive features as in this general category. If they are found, it can be inferred that these ontological characteristics are necessarily connected with the same moral status. This general category in all debates is that of person. If the embryo is a person, it has moral rights and moral value. In this approach one comes up against the questions what is a person and what is the proof that there is a necessary connection between ontological and moral characteristics of the person - problems of philosophical anthropology and general normative theory. Lack of analysis of this problem might suggest that the underlying idea is that there is some neutral definition of person which could be applied to the embryo. For instance, person is defined as a rational being, or as a being in the image of God, or as an individual able to act autonomously, or as a subject having moral standing, etc.[3] In all these cases the implicit proposition is that the descriptive characteristics such as 'rational', 'in the image of God', 'autonomous', etc. are intrinsicly connected with a high moral value. Some comprehension of an available link between the description and moral standing of a person is regarded as self-evident.

Here the problem is whether a unified or sufficiently complex notion of person is possible given that there are different notions of person in the various accounts and that they look incommensurable. The sociologist would say that person is a sum of social roles or an assemblage of social relationships; the psychologist that a person is a subject of consciousness, self-consciousness, desires, interests, etc; legal theory will hold the idea of person as a legal subject; the moral philosopher may define person as a bearer of rights and obligations; philosophical anthropology will identify a person as something with such characteristics as the capacity to speak human languages and to make choices about its future, to organise communal actions in accordance with some freshly negotiated plan, and to recognise itself as one creature among many having a history, a character, a hope of change, etc.   These are different discourses and it looks impossible to take any one of them as an independent ontological ground on which to assert some other aspect of the person, especially if it is normative.   The same holds for the embryo which is variously used as a moral, scientific, medical, legal, commercial, ideological, etc., concept.   These different notions of embryo and person look incommensurable.   It seems logically impossible to infer one aspect of the person or embryo from any other one.   Any attempt to make such inferences leads to some form of reductionism or the 'naturalistic fallacy'.   In fact, certain values (attitudes, pro-attitudes) are the grounds of any approach to the person or to the embryo and they must become the possible starting point of any unified study.   The sociologist, psychologist, philosopher, ethicist, economist, and jurist start from value presumptions that are specific interdisciplinary matrices of everyday perceptions.

Approach 3.   Propose some general normative theory.   Such an approach has three different but necessary steps.   The first one is the search for a factual or ontological correspondence.   The second one is taking for granted some concept of person with correspondence between respective ontological and moral characteristics.   The third step is the application of some general normative theory.   For instance, one may explain that a person is a subject of desires or interests and that the general normative theory grounds morality on desires or interests.   Anyway, if the general normative theory overcomes the gap between 'is' and 'ought', it would be possible for a moral philosopher to take some neutral ground and act as expert in the moral area for the general public and try to change some public perceptions of moral matters.

Approach 4.   Accept that all our discussions on the moral standing of the embryo are value-laden and have some hidden presuppositions.   This will involve the recognition that it is not a rational understanding of the biological facts so much as our moral intuitions which nourish the debate.   The different positions concerning the moral standing of the embryo will be seen as expressions of various pro-attitudes.[4]

All our efforts to find how at some stage of development of the fertilised egg some moral standing grows look unconvincing.   It does not matter whether fourteen days, three months or some other time after the fertilisation process is taken to be the point for this jump from biological to moral status.   It is difficult to capture any such process of transition.   The same difficulty exists in any attempt to link the biological age of the developing human being with its legal or political status and the respective legal and political rights.   There are, for instance, no convincing arguments why a young person gets legal and political status at 18, 19, 20, 21, etc.   In some sense we find here the same situation as in the well-known paradoxes of Zeno of Elea: *viz.* how to describe the process of change, movement, and development. Just as we are not able to understand when Achilles will outrun the tortoise or how the arrow goes from one place to another, the movement from a biological entity to moral standing looks inexplicable. What, then, is the character of the relationship between the biological and non-biological aspects of an embryo? Are our pro-attitudes connected with the biological aspect of the embryo by some necessity or regularity, or are they accidental? I should mention that the famous "is-ought" gap does not denote a lack of necessary connection at all but only a lack of logical connection of formal inference of moral status from biological status. There are indeed three other types of necessary connections between them:

1. The inference of "is" from "ought" or the logical dependence of biological status on moral status. I hold that this kind of dependence is possible. If one presupposes that the embryo has a moral position and right to life, these will demand as logical consequences actions protecting the biological existence and development of the embryo. If the moral rights or obligations are reasons for some actions, these actions have to bring forth some facts.

2. Causal or factual dependence of moral status on biological status. This type of connection is also possible and does exist. For instance the foetus engenders sympathy or moral feelings if it is perceived as a potential child.

3. Causal or factual dependence of biological status on moral status. If moral status implies some actions, they inevitably bring forth some causal events and implications for biological status.

One purpose of our discussion is to find a rational basis for moral and legal regulation of actions concerning the embryo. If however our pro-attitudes prevent the achievement of such a rational basis, raising again the old 'is-ought' question, the only reasonable direction in which to look for answers is the analysis of the character, functioning and origin of ideological or value pro-attitudes.

Our vision of the embryo and its moral standing is a social construction rationalising our pro-attitudes. But the question is what is the origin of the pro-attitudes. Undoubtedly they have different causes but some of these are important, others insignificant. One could say that the meanings we assign to the word embryo depend on the linguistic context in which case the major task would be linguistic clarification. But the possible and existing moral visions of the embryo are not indefinitely many and we can identify only three of them: (1) the embryo has the same moral standing and rights as a person; (2) the embryo has a moral standing but it is different (lower) than the moral standing of a person (logically, it is possible that someone could hold that the embryo has a higher moral standing, but I have not come across anyone who does hold this yet); (3) the embryo does not possess any moral standing and one cannot attribute to it any moral rights.

One can say that these are the possible moral paradigms which are found as rationalised positions arising from pro-attitudes or moral intuitions in everyday or mass consciousness. The predicament of contemporary western cultures is that all possible paradigms can be found in the same society and that these differences present great problems if one wants to reduce them to a common denominator and work out some acceptable regulations. People in modern society are often uprooted from their original cultures and it is difficult to find a link between their visions of the embryo and some identifiable culture. Their pro-attitudes look like their personal visions, like subjective emotions, rather than expressions of a moral position of some culture or social group engendered by some social conditions and having important functions for the social group. Given this, we need to go deeper to find the social conditions and social functions assigning the meanings of the different moral paradigms to the embryo. What I would like to highlight is the fact that it is neither the individuals nor philosophical reflections which determine any moral vision of the embryo but rather the general activities and ways of life of social groups. These general activities and ways of life might be analysed in various frames of reference. The most appropriate is that based on the difference between 'civilisation' and 'culture'.

2. Civilisation as a Basis of Reproductive Ethics

Under civilisation differences I have in mind cross-cultural peculiarities brought about by identical technological and economic structures. To put the point figuratively, civilisation differences are 'vertical', they are connected with successive stages of historical development - agrarian, industrial and postindustrial civilisations, to use terms adopted by Toffler: 'first wave', 'second wave' and 'third wave'.[5] On the other hand, cultural differences are immutable, ahistorical and in some sense 'horizontal', they pass through successive stages of the civilisations.

Our time is a period of shift of civilisation preconditions of morality and in particular of reproductive ethics, assisted procreation and protection of the embryo. This shift is intertwined with changes of family relations, gender roles, division of labour, parenthood, kinship links, etc.

Reproductive ethics of *agrarian civilisations* corresponds to a lack of medical technologies, high birthrate and high mortality. The values of this 'wave' stimulate the birth of more children and attempts to control and confine conception are in principle condemned. Characteristic of reproductive ethics in this context are traits like: (i) moral values and norms which praise and appreciate giving birth to more children; (ii) childhood is not seen as a peculiar stage of individual development and children are considered to be small adults, which is why, for instance, infanticide is not regarded as a different offence from homicide; (iii) society is not child-oriented, placing special value on children, but may be described as a 'civilisation of adults'[6]; (iv) the process of reproduction is inseparable from family relations and sexual relations, sexual relations independent from reproductive relations being more or less reproached and children born outside family relations are regarded as 'bastards'.

The reproductive ethics of the *industrial societies* has different dimensions: (i) it is intertwined with processes of decreasing birth rate and mortality, and corresponds to them; (ii) a separation of sexual and reproductive relations is developed and moral rules justify family planning and contraception; (iii) children are not considered as completed adults and childhood as a special stage of human development emerges; (iv) there are child-oriented societies where the value of children grows enormously; (v) giving birth to an unlimited number of children alone is not a good, but their upbringing becomes more important; (vi) parental love towards children as valuable in themselves is given a higher status than the previously prevailing functional evaluation.

Bulgarian society reached this second stage between '40s and '80s. Only a few minority groups like gypsies and Turks living in the countryside kept their pre-industrial reproductive ethics of high birthrate, and abstention from abortion, though in conditions of decreasing mortality.

Today the world is in a transition stage between a reproductive ethics of the second 'wave' and *postindustrial (information, third wave) societies*. Peculiar to such societies are characteristics such as the following[7]: (i) crisis of the typical nuclear family and a shift to various new forms of family relations; (ii) growth in the number of the people choosing what comes to be known as a 'child-free' life-style. We then find in the developed world a massive shift from 'child-centered' to 'adult-centered' homes. The child looses its dominant position and takes a less privileged place. (iii) Processes of return of labour from offices and plants to home is taking place and it changes family relations. This leads to a situation in which young people and children are brought into socially and economically productive roles, making child labour again morally acceptable and creating again conditions for blurring of childhood as something separate from the stage of adulthood. (iv) The new procreative technologies like IVF, gamete and zygote intra fallopian transfer, prenatal diagnosis, genetic therapy, all forms of assisted procreation, make possible not just a separation of sexual activity and conception - and, respectively, sexual and reproductive ethics - but the distribution among many subjects of the process of reproduction - genetic, carrying and nursing mothers and fathers. Thus numerous stages of human reproduction may be separated and regulated by different moral codes.

There are different cultural reactions to these trends. For example, Toffler points out that:

> In the field of values we need to begin removing the unwarranted guilt that accompanies the break up and restructuring of families. Instead of exacerbating unjustified guilt, the media, the church, the courts, and the political system should be working to lower the guilt level. ... Values change more slowly, as a rule, than social reality. Thus we have not developed the ethic of tolerance for diversity that a de-massified society will both require and engender. Raised under Second Wave conditions, firmly taught that one kind of family is 'normal' and others somehow suspect, if not 'deviant', vast numbers remain intolerant of the new variety in family styles. Until that changes, the pain of transition will remain unnecessarily high.[8]

3. The Cultural Basis of Reproductive Ethics

The real situation concerning the regulation of procreative activity and the protection of the embryo in Europe today is much more closely connected with cultural than civilisation differences.

A widespread understanding is that in principle in the past a homogeneous and unitary moral tradition has existed, especially with regard to the relationships between doctors and patients, while the modern person is left without a solid moral basis and a settled moral system. This predicament needs further specification. First, there is not only one moral tradition at any stage of the development of mankind. Numerous cultures and moral systems once coexisted separately, and rarely came into contact with one another. The moral absolutes are inside concrete traditions. The modern world just makes the likelihood and intensity of contacts much stronger. Second, in our time the individual is much more free to choose his own worldview or philosophy as a frame of reference, but inside this worldview and philosophy he may have moral absolutes and instruments for decision making. For instance, in the context of a communitarian or social-democratic political and moral philosophy, based on the idea of justice, a much more active social policy towards the availability of assisted conception services is possible. In contrast, a liberal individualistic philosophy does not justify governmental intervention in regulation of procreative activity and assisted conception. But any philosophy is a kind of rationalisation of the much more complex totality of meanings of the various cultures.

If during the industrial age a process of growing unity of human culture and an erasing of cultural differences took place, an opposite trend is currently occurring. Europe is increasingly becoming economically and politically a united space, but concurrently there is a growth of cultural diversity. The breaking up of the old regimes in Eastern Europe and the end of the 'cold war' between two great ideological forces have brought to the fore the deeper cultural differences between people. Samuel Huntington has even suggested that the coming new big clashes are likely to be between the Western, Confucian, Japanese, Islamic, Hindu, Slavic-Orthodox, and Latin-American cultures or civilisations.[9] Their differences are fundamental and the growing interactions between them enhance the feelings of common identity inside each of them. The 'velvet curtain' between cultures has replaced the iron ideological curtain. Their structures are so stable and longstanding that even the deepest changes of modernisation leave room for their influence. The old ethnic divisions again grow in importance. The world is becoming increasingly multicultural. The pro-attitudes of each of these cultures with their moral systems towards fertility and infertility, assisted conception and embryo research are varied. The intensive interactions between contemporary cultures do not make their distinctions less important but even strengthen them. Accordingly, the opportunities for common regulations of assisted procreation and protection of the embryo diminish because it is impossible to find morally or culturally independent descriptions of the human person and embryo.

The most general cultural distinctions in Europe among the regulations of assisted procreation are along the following lines.

(i) Moving from the Western to the Eastern part of the continent we go from more individualistic to more collectivistic value systems, with societies increasingly relying on governments and governmental regulations.

(ii) There are intensive distinctions of cultural divisions based on religious traditions. In the area of biomedical ethics these are greater than in other areas. Europe is strongly divided between its Catholic, Protestant and Orthodox parts.

The *Catholic tradition* is especially strong in the areas of nursing, charitable hospitals and wards, and it has the most developed normative systems of medical ethics. That is why it has an extremely active moral position towards reproductive issues and tends to impose strong prohibitions on the application of the new medical technologies in the area of human reproduction.

The *Protestant* moral tradition is more individualistic emphasising human freedom, and leaves much more room for personal decision and personal morality in respect to the appropriate use of the means and techniques of family planning and medical assistance in procreation.

The *Orthodox tradition* is characteristic of Bulgaria, Serbia, Macedonia, Greece, Romania, Russia, The Ukraine, and Byelorus. In regard to its role in morality several points are important. (i) It has no legal tradition, unlike the Catholic Church, and leaves the matter of law and regulations to the state. The Orthodox Church does not impose its rules on the state but is used to supporting the rules of the state because in principle it is subordinate to the rules of the state. (ii) Its authority as moral legislator is weak in comparison with the authority of the Catholic Church. It pays much less attention to preaching than to altar service because what is important for it is not so much moral influence and education but a mystic unity with God. (iii) It does not have strict prohibitions like the Catholic Church concerning family relations and sexual morality. For instance, in contrast to the Catholic Church it allows divorce. (iv) It has charitable activity but its traditions concerning nursing activity are much weaker.

As a result in the Orthodox countries the Church does not pay attention to abortion as a moral phenomenon and its attitude to contraceptive methods and assisted procreation is more or less morally neutral. Having in mind that for the last fifty years the health care systems in almost all Orthodox countries were state funded, we can understand why the regulations in the medical area, including assisted procreation, are seen through a nonreligious and paternalistic prism. Health and children are seen neither as personal and private phenomena nor as transcendental religious values but as important social values.

There are several types of opposition underlying the values that prevail in different countries that can explain the different cultural reactions to assisted procreation and protection of the embryo: rights versus the common good, individualism versus communitarianism, freedom versus equality, autonomy versus paternalism.

Rights versus the common good. If the Western tradition is strongly connected with the individual rights of people who arrange their relations through appropriate contracts, in the Eastern European Orthodox countries the traditional pro-attitudes emphasise the common good (common interest) which is accepted as something given, not a result of a contract, but of established tradition, historical development, and writings of the 'classics of Marxism', etc. In fact contractarian and naturalist views of morality are in opposition. In some cases in the foreground is the common good of the family and kinship; in other cases, large social and political entities such as nation, class, party, and state. If we take just the deepest pro-attitudes, we might draw a very simplified picture and say that in the Western liberal world people need their individual rights and to be protected from abuses by the state or other large entities. In Orthodox Eastern Europe people need virtues in order to pursue the common good ('common interests', 'state interests') and to serve their social and political institutions. Here, reproductive ethics should be subordinated to the common good and abortion is permitted if it complies with the general interest of the community.

Individualist versus collectivist pro-attitudes. These are connected with different conceptions of person and personhood. The former see the person as a bundle of rights and the question of when this person begins becomes a question of when those entitlements accrue to him or her. The latter understand the person as a bundle of his social identities, affiliations and roles. Marx's dictum that "the human essence is no abstraction inherent in each single individual. In its reality it is the ensemble of the social relations"[10] here seemed self evident. The opposition between bearer of rights and bearer of social relationships is so strong that until the late '80s the political thinking and the mass consciousness of the Orthodox countries developed without a notion of individual rights. At the same time, the notion of qualities (virtues) of the socialist type of person was ubiquitous. Any person takes his essence and his views from the existing society, class, group and community.

There is a well known distinction between the Western (political, inclusive) and the Eastern (cultural, exclusive) notion of nation. We can draw a similar distinction between inclusive, liberal and exclusive, nonliberal notions of morality as well. It is possible to include everyone in the liberal moral community because this community is fundamentally a result of individual choice and agreement as to the appropriate social contract. The Eastern moral community is exclusive, however, because participation is not considered to be a result of personal choices but a product of past development, of 'objective regularities'. Being members of society, people carry with them the most important characteristics of this common morality. They share these characteristics not as a result of personal choices, but because they are born into some particular national group, ethnic community and cultural tradition, and are affiliated with it.

Freedom versus equality. Freedom is a central notion of Western liberal culture. Equality is much more prominent in the Eastern type of thinking. If one starts in the United Kingdom and goes to the East, he will find increasing readiness to sacrifice freedom for equality and to accept some kind of welfarist or corporativist ideology. These are deeply rooted attitudes. This egalitarian thinking was the ground of totalitarianism in Europe before the Second world war. It was the ground also of the totalitarianism of the left.

It is true that the notion of freedom was widespread and often invoked in the former communist states. But its meaning differed totally from that of the liberal conception of freedom. In the language of the Eastern Orthodox people the ideas of social freedom - liberty of the nation, of community - were much more entrenched, while in the Western part the accent is on individual freedoms. In liberal Western thinking freedom is first of all lack of coercion, of compulsion, or necessity, while in Eastern European thinking it is knowledge, a voluntary acceptance of necessity and actions taken in the light of that necessity.

Autonomy versus paternalism. Autonomy is one of the most important notions of Western political and ethical thinking. Until recently, it didn't even exist in the language of socialist thinkers, politicians, or common people in Bulgaria and most of the other Eastern Orthodox countries. It was used sometimes in the sense of national or territorial autonomy but never as a notion of autonomy of the individual, autonomy of the person.

It is true that the notion of paternalism is also missing from the language of the East, but its content is ubiquitous in the form of people's expectation that different collective bodies will take care of them, that is, in individuals' dependance on collective bodies - governments, parties, officials, physicians, etc. In the Orthodox world or the Byzantine cultural area the State always has been a mighty force and one of the strongest paternalistic institutions in human history. That is why neither the term nor the content of the concept of autonomy, the foundation of Western bioethics, could be found in Eastern Orthodox Europe. But that means these cultures lack the deep soil in which bioethics must be planted and raised.

In his work concerning Greek and Roman reflection on sexuality, Michel Foucault sketched out four dimensions of ethical analysis: ethical substance (what persons work on to transform themselves, e.g., desires, pleasures, images); the mode of subjection (the way one relates to rules and their form of legitimacy, e.g. custom, divine law, moral exemplar); the forms of elaboration (the practices by which one works on oneself, e.g. renunciation, self-decipherment, confession); and the telos (the ultimate aim of self-mastery, e.g. purification, tranquility, detachment).[11]

Let us use these four aspects of ethical analysis in order to clarify the Orthodox cultural attitude to reproductive ethics:

a) Determination of the ethical substance: the focus of moral attention is moral action. The person becomes a moral subject by being brought up by some community; one is a moral subject only as a conscious individual who is perceived not as a holder of rights and freedoms but of obligations. That is why neither the gamete and zygote nor the embryo and foetus are subjects of moral relations.

b) Mode of subjection: one subjects himself to a moral code first of all because he is a member of a group and the collapse of this group brings about moral crisis and excessive forms of utilitarian behaviour as has been evident during recent years.

Nowadays this is strengthened by the fashion of a pervasive market ideology.

c) Form of ethical work: industrious labour is considered a major way to transform oneself into an ethical subject.

d) Telos: being a reputable man, living a life without shame, having social success. In this context morality is mainly an external and social phenomenon. Accordingly, individual moral self-reflection and search for some 'soul' of the person before birth are not so important. The current moral debate in Western bioethics concerning the moral dilemmas of assisted procreation looks like a curious exercise of the mind, a luxury of the wealthy Western world.

During recent years all these questions of reproductive ethics are seen against the background of an enormous economic and moral crisis. In this situation we might expect to find an abortion debate in Catholic Poland and Hungary, but not in Orthodox Bulgaria, Romania, or Russia. A decrease of the standard of living has led to a vast increase in the number of abortions on demand. Their number in Bulgaria is twice that of the number of births; in Romania the ratio is four to one and the killing of the foetus is considered not a moral but a practical question. People do not want to have children and the birth rate in Bulgaria is very much down - 9.9 per 1000. A quarter of children are born out of wedlock. Because of malnutrition new born babies are between 200 and 400 grams below the normal weight. In 1993 in Bulgaria about 89,000 children were born, and almost 5000 had serious and incurable inherited diseases. There is a trend for many children from charity houses to be adopted by foreigners - principally Americans. The collapse of values and the poverty of some social groups are restoring the ancient practice of infanticide, and from 20 to 30 new born children have been murdered annually in recent years. Between 2000 and 3000 are mutilated because of their parents' negligence each year.

Almost 12% or between 200,000 and 300,000 families in Bulgaria are sterile. IVF has been practiced since 1988 by two medical teams. One alone of them contributed to the birth of 45 children. Since 1989 the government has been unable to finance this activity. Currently it is paid for privately, and because the cost is about 800 dollars it is affordable only for very wealthy people. In the context of the current moral system, it is much more a market than a moral phenomenon.

4. The Moral Norm 'Thou Shalt Not Kill' and the Moral Standing of the Embryo

The cultural pro-attitudes in the Catholic part of Europe require strong regulations concerning assisted procreation and protection of the embryo. The pro-attitudes in the Protestant part prescribe less regulation. In the Orthodox area of Europe we have noted that these are not moral but predominantly practical questions subordinated to individual and social needs and interests. Bearing in mind the tradition in this part of Europe, I will suggest a communitarian normative position.

The question that seems to underlie the debate on the moral status of the embryo is whether the embryo has the same right to life as the person or (to put it another way) whether the moral norm 'thou shalt not kill' is applicable to the embryo in the same sense as to the person. But the problem is that the right to life or the moral norm 'thou shalt not kill' cannot be an absolute frame of reference. The moral codes and legal systems of all societies admit of different types of violation of the right to life, and exceptions from the norm 'thou shalt not kill', for instance in situations of self-defence, duelling, sacrifice and self-sacrifice, the death penalty, and during wars. The real question is what are the social conditions, what is the social frame of reference, of these exceptions. The right to life is not a conclusion of the logical analysis of moral philosophers. Accordingly, it cannot be justified by logical means. It is brought into existence not through certain logical premises, but through corresponding social causes. The filling of the gap between "is" and "ought" cannot be done by logical necessity, but only by causal necessity.

What is the nature of this causal necessity when it concerns the right to life and the norm 'thou shalt not kill'? There are some common interests of human communities and boundaries of existence of these communities, some general conditions securing the survival of these communities. My main point is that the major purpose of the norm is not the survival of the person but the survival of the community. From this point of view in real societies rather than in philosophical reflections, ethical theories and political slogans, it is the higher value of the life of the community, and not of the separate individual, that counts. That is why in all moral systems various communities demand sacrifices by members, for example, that they die in wars in defence of these communities. But the opposite situation of a person demanding the sacrifice of the community in order to be protected looks impossible and morally absurd.

The actual content of the individual right to life depends on two major social necessities. First, the protection of the existence of some communities (family, tribe, nation, state, etc). Their protection can require the right to life in some situations and its absence in other situations. Infanticide or killing of older people may be applied in this context.

Second, the content of the right to life depends also on the borders of the community in which the relevant moral code is applied. In the ancient world these borders were some tribal or local groups, some estates, etc. These are the social relations facilitating the emergence of the individual person with a respective right to life. For a long time, until the turn of this century, women were not persons in the same sense as men and were deprived of the right to vote. However, one could say that from the time of Kant the moral imperative to treat any individual human being as a goal in itself, as if every person embodies the whole of mankind, has spread as a universal norm. Nevertheless, even Kant did not see the right to life and the moral norm 'thou shalt not kill' as absolute, and he was a supporter of the death penalty.[12]

So we reach the conclusion that the right to life is a relative right and the value of life is a relative value and in situations of value conflict between the value of a personal life and the protection or well-being of the society, community, group, nation, state the value of the personal life is lower and morality can require deprivation of the right to life. Even the most rigid individualist, who rejects any holistic vision of social life, would agree that in order to protect his own life he needs a state and community protecting this his right, in some cases even at the price of the life of other persons.

We could say that the embryo has some value as a potential conscious human being. But the problem is what this value is. If there are some cases when real persons can be deprived of the right to life, in which cases should this deprivation be applied to the embryo? What should be our vision of the right to life of the embryo from the point of view of the social necessity which determines the content of this life. Again, it should be the protection and well-being of the community. Some global trends are also important in this context.

I will draw attention to several value conflicts which put limitations of the right to life of the embryo, making this right relative. The first is the conflict between the right to life of the embryo and the right to life of another person - for instance the pregnant mother. The actual self-conscious and indisputable moral subject, a result of much more social effort, embodied in her abilities, capacities, attitudes, values, social relationships and investments, possesses higher social and moral value then a future person.

The second is the conflict between the right to life of the embryo and the opportunities for survival or a tolerable life of the future conscious person where, for instance, it is well known that soon after his birth the infant will die from cancer or hunger in a country like Rwanda. Population control may be a more humane and moral perspective than the alternative of suffering from starvation and terminal disease.

Third and finally, is the conflict between the right to life of the embryo and the survival and well-being of the community of now living persons. If demographic explosion threatens to violate the rights to life and well-being of actual persons and endanger their existence, and the survival of the whole community or even the whole of mankind, then population control and deprivation of the embryo's right to life is morally justified. The survival and continuation of the existence of the community is a higher value.

Notes

1. Hunter, James Davison, *Culture Wars: The Struggle to Define America* New York, Basic Books, 1991.

2. Cf. Moore, G.E., *Principia Ethica* Cambridge, Cambridge University Press, 1959, pp.10-16.

3. See Lomasky, L.E., 'Concept of person' in Becker, L.C. (ed.), *Encyclopedia of Ethics* Vol. II, New York, Garland Publishing Co., 1992, pp.950-955.

4. In this context I agree with Donald Evans who in his paper 'Pro-attitudes to pre-embryos' (in this volume) holds that philosophical reflection might not enable us to resolve disagreement of this kind because it is in itself characterised by similar disagreements. For this reason only a minimalist programme of regulation in a unified Europe is possible.

5. Toffler, A., *The Third Wave* Toronto, Bantam Books, 1980.

6. Aries, P., *Centuries of Childhood: A Social History of Family Life* New York, Vintage, 1962.

7. Toffler, *op.cit.*, pp.208-225.

8. *Ibid.*, p.224.

9. Huntington, S., 'The clash of civilizations' *Foreign Affairs* 72 (3), 1993, pp.22-49.

10. Marx, K. and Engels, F., *Selected Works in Two Volumes* Vol. II, Moscow, Foreign Languages Publishing House, 1955, p.433.

11. Foucault, M., *The History of Sexuality* Vol. 1, London, Penguin Books, 1978-86.

12. Kant, I., (trans. Ladd, John) *The Metaphysical Elements of Justice* Indianapolis, Bobbs-Merrill, 1965 (1797), pp.99-107.

PART THREE

Personhood and the Human Embryo

10. IS THE HUMAN EMBRYO A PERSON? NO

Maurizio Mori
Politeia. Centro per la formazione in politica ed etica
Milano
Italy
Editor *Bioetica. Rivista Interdisciplinare*

1.

The issue of whether the human embryo is or is not a person seems to be the most crucial one in current debates on the morality of interventions in reproduction such as abortion and of *in vitro* fertilisation (IVF). Even IVF involves the death of some embryos, and for this reason it can be associated with abortion so that those who oppose abortion can mount a criticism of IVF on the same grounds: they hold that both practices are immoral because from conception the embryo is a person and therefore any embryo's destruction is a form of homicide. Since in western societies there is a widespread agreement about condemning homicide, it is clear why what I call the 'embryo-question', i.e., the question whether or not the embryo is a person, has a central position in the debate concerning assisted reproduction.

In this paper I want to show that the correct answer to such a question must be negative: human embryos certainly are *not* persons. It would follow, if the framework of current discussions were the only possible one, that no strong criticism could be raised against IVF or against abortion, and that the whole issue would be immediately solved. However, I want to show that the current framework of discussion is not the only one possible, and that the source of disagreement in debates about assisted reproduction need not be the embryo-question at all (which can be solved, as I try to do). Disagreement is more fundamentally over a quite different issue, to be precise, over the duties we may have concerning the reproductive process. In order to accomplish my task it will be best to start by presenting a wider analysis of the assumptions underlying the current framework of discussion.

2.

The general framework of current debate on reproductive issues is strongly dependent on the following three claims made by critics of IVF:

A. that the embryo is a person from conception, and therefore any embryo's destruction

151

D. Evans (ed.), Conceiving the Embryo, 151–163.
© 1996 *Kluwer Law International. Printed in the Netherlands.*

is immoral being a form of homicide;

B. that if the embryo were not a person, it wouldn't deserve any protection at all and therefore all destruction of embryos would be permissible;

C. that scholars deny that the embryo is a person because they are misled by their passions.

The first two claims lead to an either-or choice, so that the framework of current debate can be represented by the following scheme:

Is the embryo a person?

yes	no
It ought to be protected as much as any other person	It deserves no protection at all
Any destruction of an embryo is a form of homicide	Any destruction of an embryo is a licit act

This diagram shows very clearly the polarisation of current discussion on this issue. As we can see, the major question is whether or not the embryo is a person, and such a question creates an either-or situation: any attempt to avoid answering 'yes' or 'no' constitutes a kind of escapism. Moreover, the diagram makes it clear also that the embryo-question revolves around a *descriptive* issue, since values and duties are immediately dependent on a descriptive answer and subsequent to it. In this sense a wide consensus over the norm prescribing a strong protection of persons is assumed. I think that this last assumption is plausible, and therefore it is plausible to say that according to this perspective the controversy is a descriptive one.

The last claim listed above is of a different sort, since it points out that the passions involved in the debate are so intense as to lead people to give a wrong answer to the descriptive question. Such an answer should be very easy to give and should be as immediate as any empirical answer. The failure to give such an answer is

a good example of the impact that an ideology can have on scholars. If abortion were not a practical issue, none would doubt that for genetics and embryology it is a sure datum that from the moment of conception, with the appearance of the zygote, there is an *individual* endowed with its own structure and distinct from the mother's organism on which it is dependent. Biologically speaking this individual has within itself the 'programme' which will be developed in the course of its existence.[1]

I'll return at the beginning of next section to the significance of this claim, but for now I want to observe that the whole framework of the current debate is misleading because it disregards the possibility that the embryo may deserve strong protection *even if* it is not a person. This respect could be as strong as that owed to a person, or even stronger. If this observation makes sense, then the real issue is not whether or not the embryo is a person, but whether or not there is a special duty concerning respect due to the natural reproductive process. On this account, the controversy is not over the *descriptive* part but over the *normative* one: passions are so intense as to create confusion over the whole issue, and they prevent a clear understanding of the proper role of the various aspects of the issue. In order to make this confusion visible, I will start by showing why the position according to which the embryo is a person from conception is untenable. Later I will suggest a different (and more adequate) framework of discussion.

3.

Those authors who claim that the embryo-question calls for an immediate answer hold that contemporary scientific knowledge is *per se* sufficient to give such an answer. This is exemplified in the above quotation of a Catholic theologian, very influential in Vatican circles. His belief is that biology provides sufficient evidence to justify saying that from conception it is certain that "a human nature is *really* (*virtually* or *actually*) given".[2]

It is important to remark that according to this argument - which from now on I shall call 'the scientific argument' - scientific knowledge *directly* solves the embryo-question and that such knowledge is by itself sufficient to give a positive answer to the question. I wish to underline this point because it is here that the argument goes astray: the argument is faulty because it is impossible that science alone can solve the embryo-question, and this is simply because it is not a *scientific* question.

The fundamental basis of my statement is that in order to give an answer to the embryo-question (i.e., the question whether the embryo is or is not a person) one must have a definition of 'person', and any problem concerning the notion of person will not be merely a scientific problem. It follows that, since science cannot (logically) provide an answer to a question which is not merely scientific, it cannot (logically) provide an answer to the embryo-question.

There are (at least) two justifications for my claim that the concept of person is not a scientific one. The first reason is a 'formal' one - 'formal' because it concerns the nature of definitional problems as such *in general*. From the 'formal' point of view we can observe that a definition sets limits to a certain field of inquiry. From this alone it follows that problems concerning definitions do not belong to the field defined, but to study at a higher level. Problems concerning basic definitions of any specific science do not belong within such a science, but to a more general study that we used to call 'philosophy'. On this account, underlying any specific science there is a 'philosophy', and definitional problems represent some of the most important philosophical questions underlying any particular science.

'Philosophy' is here conceived as a general study concerned with a whole world-view: when a specific science establishes itself, it needs a precise and well-defined field of inquiry where a critical methodology is applied. On the other hand philosophy has no similar limitation to its sphere of inquiry and its task is to interpret various pieces of empirical knowledge so as to fit them all together in a grand harmonic perspective. In this sense, a definition is like a single piece of a grand mosaic of which we have to discover the overall shape.

An analogy with a jig-saw puzzle can be useful: in such puzzles we have to order different pieces so as to form a certain shape, and some pieces can be placed quite easily while others require a great deal of attention. Sometimes it happens that in order to place a piece we have to change everything and start the puzzle over again from the beginning. Something analogous happens with definitions: some definitions can be established easily, while others raise the most difficult problems because a slightly different formulation may require a complete change of the whole world-view (i.e. the whole shape of the puzzle). From this 'formal' point of view, we can at least say that problems concerning the definition of 'person', along with all other basic definitions in general, difficult to establish or not, are in any case *philosophical* (and not at all scientific) ones.

The second reason supporting my claim is 'material', because it is about the *specific* problem concerning an adequate definition of the notion indicated by the term 'person'. As I shall argue more extensively later, the concept 'person' as commonly used in western societies refers to something which 'transcends' the natural world (and therefore the field of mere science). On this account science cannot provide any immediate answer to the embryo-question, but rather scientific data must be interpreted in the light of an adequate definition of the embryo. Using an old (but still very useful) way of speaking, one can say that a person is a unity of a *body* and a *soul*. From this material point of view, we can say that science can inform us about the body but cannot say anything about the soul, which does not pertain to its field: as is stated by the Sacred Congregation for the Doctrine of the Faith "it is not up to biological sciences to make a definitive judgement on questions which are properly philosophical and moral, such as the moment when a person is constituted or the legitimacy of abortion".[3]   Any attempt to proceed as if science could make such judgements entails a category mistake, since two different levels of discourse are therein confused.

Therefore, from both points of view, no scientific knowledge *per se* can provide an argument for the thesis that from conception the embryo is a person. This conclusion is convergent with a long and honoured tradition accepted for centuries in western culture according to which for several weeks after fertilisation the conceptus is not a person. According to this Aristotelian-Thomistic perspective, the rational soul can be infused only when the matter (body) is adequately formed, and therefore only after some time after conception. As a matter of fact it is interesting to remark that, historically, even if abortion was severely punished by law, it was not usually considered homicide but was classified as a different form of crime.[4]

4.

Holders of the thesis that from conception the embryo is a person object to this historical observation by saying that "it was the paucity of the biological information available"[5] which in the past led many authors (such as Aristotle, Aquinas, etc.) to hold that the embryo was not a person. They claim that such authors could change their position and that "in the light of our present biological information, we cannot avoid concluding that Aquinas *today* would have considered the human embryo from conception a *homo*, ... a human person".[6] The basis of this position is that at fertilisation new DNA is formed which encodes the genetic programme of the person and therefore we have to accept that the embryo is a person.

Leaving aside the problem of whether or not formation of a new piece of DNA is by itself sufficient to determine that there is an 'individual' organism[7], there is a more general argument showing that this basis is inadequate to justifying its alleged conclusion. We know that DNA, as such, is organic matter. It will follow that, if its occurrence were sufficient for the existence of a person, we would have to conclude that persons are mere 'natural entities', which is contrary to what we assumed in the definition of 'person'. In other words, if biology alone could solve the embryo-question, then, since biology like any science deals with natural events, we would be unable to escape the conclusion that persons are nothing more than a "conglomeration of transformed groceries", as is indeed claimed by biologists holding some version of so-called 'strong materialism'.[8] It may be that strong materialism will turn out to be a sound view, but this would compel us to reframe our whole current world-view, a move that holders of the thesis that the embryo is a person are unwilling to do.[9]

There are also more specific mistakes in the arguments supporting the claim that the embryo is a person. One of these mistakes is clearly to be found in Teresa Iglesias (from whom we have already heard) in the following passage:

> [T]he development of personal abilities (self-awareness, ...) does not come about independently of our organic development. There is no reason for affirming that those powers are something 'added on' at any particular stage. ... we must admit that whatever powers we have now ... [they] are a *manifestation* or a development of the powers we had from the beginning.[10]

I have emphasised the word 'manifestation' because - as Max Black remarks[11] - many words ending in '-tion' (though not only these) have a special (and misleading) characteristic of shifting meaning: so, for instance, 'destruction' may mean both (a) the *process* of destroying something, and (b) the *product* of the result of such activity.

Analogously, 'manifestation' may mean both the *process* of manifesting something, for example the act of showing my gratefulness to someone, and the *product* resulting from such an act, in this example the specific words that I pronounced or gesture that I made. Now the two are clearly different, and it is unfortunate that the same word is used in both cases, because this ambiguity produces a common fallacy called the 'process/product fallacy'. When Iglesias writes that "whatever powers we have now ... [they] are a manifestation ... of the powers we had from the beginning" her argument is a clear instance of such a fallacy because 'manifestation' is used to mean both the process and the product.

A second mistake implicit in arguments like that of Iglesias can be easily identified if we consider the words of another author who holds a similar position to her. Angelo Serra S.J. asserts that

> already from the first moment ... are contemporarily present, and developing, the central structures which at a certain stage will appear as the primitive streak. At any point of development there already exists the unity which will later be defined as the foetal-placental unity. ... Single events are seen by our eyes as discontinuous ... but each of these events is nothing but the instantaneous *expression* of what was already formed from the first moment.[12]

Probably, even in this case, the word 'expression' leads Serra into the trap of the process/product fallacy, but here it is more interesting to examine another aspect of his argument. Serra says that even if our eyes do not see it clearly, from the first moment the whole organism already exists, which - mainly for didactic reasons - will later be called by different names.

Serra seems, then, to believe a modern version of preformism, that is, of the idea that biological development is nothing more than growth in size of a *homunculus* which is existent in miniature and complete from the beginning. In the eighteenth century preformists held that the *homunculus* was hidden in one gamete, and some claimed to have seen *homunculi* by means of a microscope. Contemporary preformists hold that it is hidden in the DNA formed at fertilisation. Serra confirms this interpretation of his position when he notes that our imperfect eyes see single events of embryological development as discontinuous, but that this fact should not prevent us holding that a complete *homunculus* is already there from fertilisation, waiting only to grow in size, and that if we had more perfect eyes we would see it as such.

However, we know that preformism is an indaquate view, because biological development is not mere growth in size of what is already existent, but involves the formation of new traits and the emergence of new characteristics, i.e., it is 'epigenetic'. Preformism seems appealing because of its simplicity, but - as Theodosius Dobzhansky noted

> on closer examination the simplicity [of preformism] proves deceptive. Although the instructions of the developmental processes are 'preformed' in the genes, in the same sense as the instruction for a computer are in the perforations of the computer tape, the development of the embryo is epigenesis, formation of a new

body which was not present earlier as an individual.[13]

On this account, we can conclude by observing that it was not "the paucity of biological information" (as Iglesias and others claim) that led Aristotle, Aquinas and many others to hold that the embryo at first has a vegetative life, then a sensitive one, and finally - when the brain is formed - a rational one, but that they took an epigenetic (and correct) view of biological development.

5.

Up to now I have shown that the 'scientific argument' as a method for answering the embryo-question is invalid: it relies on mere scientific knowledge and confuses two different issues by trying to give a scientific answer to a question which is not scientific. Moreover, I have pointed out other mistakes involved in the stronger (counterfactual) claim concerning one possible answer to the embryo-question. However at this stage of our inquiry it is important to try to understand why such misleading 'scientific arguments' have appeared (and to many still appear) to be so attractive as to establish a position on the issue.

Undoubtedly, many reasons might be given in explanation of this attractiveness, but here I want to examine a specific reason connected to scientific debate. As a matter of fact, up to the end of the 1950s, the traditional (Aristotelian-Thomistic) view was very common and as late as the mid-sixties a well-known Jesuit said that "modern science has resuscitated the old theory of successive animation of the human embryo".[14] However, scientific evidence for the 'successive animation' view seems to have depended on a literal interpretation of Ernst Haeckel's famous 'recapitulation theory'.

According to this theory "ontogenesis recapitulates philogenesis" so that each individual in its embryological development passes through the stages of the evolutionary process. So, a human person first is a vegetable, then an animal of various species, and finally a member of humankind. Since Haeckel's theory was accepted as a 'scientific truth', the whole question seemed to belong to science. Moreover, it should be pointed out that Haeckel's theory received a 'literal' interpretation because the passage concerning different stages was intended as a *biological* change in the sense that the embryo was at first a plant of some sort, then a fish, a bird, a mammal of successively different kinds, right up to the human species.[15]

Even though this theory had been vigorously criticised since the '30s, it was so popular and its influence was so profound that even in 1952, in the great *Enciclopedia Medica Italiana*, it was stated that in the second period of its development (after the third week) "the embryo ... does not present the characteristics which are proper to the *human species*", and only later can it be considered "as belonging to the *human species*".[16]

If we consider this 'scientific' background ('scientific' is in inverted commas for obvious reasons) and the fact that in the '60s and early '70s the crucial question about the embryo was formulated as 'When does human life begin?', then we can understand why scientific knowledge seemed to be immediately and directly relevant. Information about DNA proved that from the beginning the embryo was *human*, i.e., that it belonged to the human species, and this seemed enough to conclude that the embryo was a person from conception. So in the early 1970s it was rather common to emphasise the fact that "from the time of fecundation there is no genetic change. *But without genetic change there can be no change of species*"[17], and still now for many authors this is the most relevant information.

However, what biological knowledge actually shows more clearly than before is that the literal interpretation of Haeckel's theory is untenable and false, but it shows nothing more than that. So, we can accept that in the embryological process there is no change analogous to a change of species, but hold also that this is no evidence at all for the conclusion that the embryo is a person from conception. At any rate we have explained why scientific knowledge seemed to be so relevant, and this may in turn help to understand the general framework of the current discussion in the field.

6.

So far I have criticised the position which holds that the embryo is a person and I have tried to make clear where it goes astray. Now I want to take more positive steps. To do this it is not enough to show that the arguments supporting the thesis that the embryo is a person from conception are invalid, and I want to give positive arguments showing that the embryo is not a person. My plan is to agree that the embryo-question is a *descriptive* one, but think of the process in a more complex way.

If we examine the problem carefully, we see that there is no possibility that the embryo is a person. This can be shown once a Thomistic definition of 'person' is accepted, according to which a person is an *individua substantia rationalis naturae* (an individual substance of rational nature). I think that this definition is valid not only because it has had a long and honoured existence, but also because it states the two minimal requirements involved in the notion of 'person'. In fact this definition gives the two necessary conditions which are jointly sufficient. These are (i) *individuality*, and (ii) *rationality*.

Let us examine them briefly.

Individuality. This is the property which is proper to an indivisible organism. Organisms are generally composed of many parts, some of which can be removed without any crucial change, while other parts have a different role because if they are removed (or damaged) the individual organism dies. On the other hand there are also other kinds of organism, such as colonies for instance, which lack individuality, so that their parts can be removed or split without causing the organism's death.[18]

Rationality is a property indicating that persons are entities which are *qualitatively* different from other living organisms. Other authors prefer to call this property by a different name ('symbolic capacity' or 'self-consciousness', for instance) but these are details irrelevant to our main problem. What is important is the fact that 'rational entities' are not mere 'natural entities', but they are *non-natural* or, probably better, *trans-natural* entities'. On this view human persons are rooted in organic nature, but they are *qualitatively* different from the rest of organic nature and are *irreducible* to it.

There are two different general ways of explaining this difference. Some think that rationality is an attribute of a special *substance*, the soul, which is spiritual and *transcends* organic nature. Others think that rationality is a peculiar property *emerging* from the high degree of complexity reached by some organisms, so that, even if the new level of existence is *irreducible* to lower levels belonging to mere organic nature, there is no need to presuppose a special *substance* to explain the existence of such a property. Since both perspectives concur in emphasising that persons are qualitatively different from the rest of biological nature and irreducible to it, and this idea is a basic tenet of western culture, we need not decide in this paper which of the two is 'better', and we can simply distinguish them by saying that persons *transcend* organic nature or are *emergent* from it.

If we accept such a definition of 'person' (as I think we must, unless we are to revise our whole world-view) then it is even clearer than before why from a 'material' point of view the embryo-question is a *philosophical* question, and not a scientific one. 'Philosophy' is here conceived either as an inquiry about metaphysics (in the traditional meaning of the term, i.e., the study of being, including of a spiritual substance different from matter), or as an inquiry which examines a field beyond the natural, a field which is about the categories of our thinking. In this sense philosophy belongs to the 'social sciences', or 'humanities', or *Geisteswissenschaften* as they are sometimes called.

Now that we have an adequate and precise definition we can establish whether or not the embryo is a person by seeing whether or not it meets the requirements stated by the definition.

Does the embryo meet condition (a) concerning 'individuality'? Empirically we know that up to the fourteenth day after fertilisation, if we split an embryo in two parts, far from dying it gives origin to two different organisms. Therefore, it is an empirical fact that, during its first days, the embryo fails to meet the individuality-condition required by the definition of 'person'. Someone may say that, in that case, killing the embryo is the killing of many individuals, i.e., something similar to mass-murder. However, this would be a mistake, originating in a wrong application of the category of individuality to an entity which does not yet present such a property. It would be better to speak of 'a sub-individual', i.e., something like a worm, which has a spatial boundary but is not an individual.

Does the embryo meet condition (b) concerning 'rationality', at least after having reached individuality? Some authors think that it is almost impossible to answer this question because, being a 'non-natural' or 'trans-natural' property, rationality seems to be an impalpable and subjective requirement. There is some truth in such a contention, in that it is difficult to state occurrences of the actual exercise of rationality. However, we need not to go so far in our analysis of the issue, and I think that the 'rationality-condition' can be satisfied more objectively.

We know that *empirically* a necessary condition for the occurrence of rationality is the presence of a human brain: if there is no brain adequately formed and functioning, we are sure that there can be no rationality. On the other hand, if there is a brain adequately formed and functioning, there might be rational processes, and we grant it the benefit of the doubt. In this way, our answer to a question concerning the 'rationality-condition' depends on physiological criteria, which are definite and objective. It is not our task, in this paper, to establish exactly *when* the rationality-condition is met, but we can confidently hold that it is not met during the first weeks after fertilisation. And given that the second condition for personhood is not met, we can conclude with certainty that the embryo is not a person.

It is important to remark that in my argument scientific knowledge does not prove that the embryo is *not* a person, but a proper interpretation of scientific data in the light of an adequate definition of 'person' leads to the conclusion that without doubt the embryo in its first weeks is *not* a person. In other words this conclusion is not drawn *directly* from scientific knowledge (as in the invalid argument I earlier criticised), but it is *indirectly* drawn through a definition.

7.

If the current framework of discussion (represented in the diagram) were correct, then - if our analysis is sound - we would have to conclude that embryos deserve no moral protection at all. But here the third possibility mentioned above becomes relevant: it is possible that embryos deserve protection, even if they are not persons. On this account the reason justifying our having a duty toward the embryo depends on our having a general duty regarding the naturalness of the reproductive process. As a matter of fact, in the western moral tradition the idea of an absolute duty of respect toward the natural reproductive process has been part of the general 'sanctity of life' tradition. So not only abortion was forbidden, but also various other kinds of sexual 'offences', such as homosexuality and contraception.

It is important to observe that, according to this view, the duty concerning the reproductive process is an absolute one, i.e., a duty which admits of no exception at all. If it were not absolute, then in all likelihood such a duty would be overridden by other stronger duties relevant to the situation, such as the duty to increase one's well-being, or to look after the welfare of one's children. It was this notion of an absolute duty which surrounded the whole field of reproduction with an aura of sacredness which prevented any sort of human intervention until very recent times. So, for instance, contraception was strongly opposed for nearly a century, and it was only in the 1960s that it became accepted by most people (even if not all, as Roman Catholics are still against it).

I mention the case of contraception because the question of its prohibition is particularly important for our discussion, and for two reasons. First because in recent years in western society there has been a profound change of attitude toward contraception. At the beginning of this century it was still prohibited (sometimes even by law), while now it is reckoned to be permissible. It is observed that by means of contraception we can control the number of children and space them more conveniently, with a net advantage for the children themselves, their parents and the whole of society. So what seemed to be an absolute prohibition became a *prima facie* prohibition which is almost always overridden by stronger considerations.

Second, the case of contraception is important because contraception is a direct interference with the natural course of the reproductive process, in that it is an act causing the death of human life at an earlier stage than the embryonic one. Given this, the same moral principle which regulates respect due to the early embryo should regulate contraception's moral permissibility. Indeed, there is a quantitative difference between the two interventions dependent on their different degrees of complexity, and this may influence our view of the gravity of the acts. However, both interventions are qualitatively of the same kind and therefore subject to the same judgement.

We are at the end of our inquiry: the crucial issue is not whether the embryo is or is not a person, because such a question has a precise and definite answer: no. The crucial issue is, then, about the kind of duty we have toward the reproductive process. If we think that there is an absolute duty to respect the naturalness of such a process, then the embryo deserves very strong protection, possibly stronger than the one deserved by a person. But in this case we have to hold that even contraception is absolutely forbidden, a conclusion that to many seems unacceptable. However, it is still possible that the majority of people are wrong on this point, and that the Roman Catholic position is the correct one. I do not discuss this issue here, and it requires a separate inquiry: I want only to make clear the logical framework of the controversy. On the other hand, if we think that there are only *prima facie* duties toward the naturalness of reproduction, then we can justify contraception as well as destruction of the human embryo in certain circumstances. There can still be some constraints on what we may do, but they must be justified by means of a principle different from the one forbidding 'homicide'.

Notes

1. Cottier, G., *Scritti di etica* Piemme, Casale Monferrato, 1994, pp.213-14.

2. *Ibid.*, p.220.

3. Sacred Congregation for the Doctrine of the Faith, *Declaration on Procured Abortion* No. 13, 1974, (I quote from Flannery O.P., A., (ed.) *Abortion and Law* Dublin, Dominican Publications, 1983, p.7).

4. So, for example, under the 1930 Italian criminal law, abortion was classified as a crime against the "sanity and integrity of the race", and not as a homicide (cf. Titolo X).

5. Iglesias, T., 'What kind of being is the human embryo?' in Iglesias, T., *IVF and Justice. Moral, Social and Legal Issues Related to Human In Vitro Fertilisation* London, The Linacre Centre, 1990, p.108.

6. *Ibid.*, p.109.

7. The idea that at fertilisation there is an 'individual' is keenly criticised by many, for example by the theologian N. Ford, in his *When Did I Begin?* Cambridge, Cambridge University Press, 1988.

8. For a good defence of a modern version of 'strong materialism' one can refer to Australian philosophers such as D. Armstrong, *A Materialist Theory of the Mind* revised edition, London, Routledge, 1993.

9. For a more detailed analysis of this point, see my paper 'Il diritto alla vita e il paradosso della posizione antinti-abortiista: un'analisi filosofica' *Rivista internazionale di filosofia del diritto* 1979, pp.172-221. In any case I do not reject strong materialism as such, but claim only that it is not consistent which a widely accepted view, and that it must be abandoned by those who accept such a perspective.

10. Iglesias, T., 'The human being and the right not to be killed' in Iglesias, T., *IVF and Justice, op.cit.*, p.79.

11. This remark may be found in Black, M., *Critical Thinking. An Introduction to Logic and Scientific Method* New York, Prentice-Hall, 1946, p.178. Similar observations are in Hospers, J., *An Introduction to Philosophical Analysis* second edition, Routledge and Kegan Paul, London, 1967, p.15.

12. Serra, A., 'Dalle nuove frontiere della biologia e della medicina nuovi interrogativi alla filosofia, al diritto e alla teologia' in Serra, A., Sgreccia, E. and Di Pietro, M.L. (eds), *Nuova genetica ed embriopoiesi umana* Milano, Vita e Pensiero, 1990, pp.13-95, p.78 (my translation; emphasis added).

13. Dobzhansky, T., 'On gods of the gaps' in Dobzhansky, T., *The Biology of Ultimate Concern* London, Rapp and Whiting, 1969, p.29.

14. Zalba S.J., M., 'The Catholic Church's viewpoint on abortion' *World Medical Journal* 1966, p.92. Zalba was Professor of Moral Theology at the Gregorian University in Rome. Other authors held at the time a similar position, and among them I can mention here only the following: Lanza, A., *La questione del momento in cui l'anima razionale è infusa nel corpo* Roma, Edizioni Universitarie, 1940, p.303, which is certainly the most thorough analysis of the problem that I know of; in English the most relevant book is Messenger, E.C., *Theology and Evolution* London, Burns and Oats, 1949 (and 1952). Other authors in this line are the following: Hugon, E., *Philosophia naturalis* Paris, Desclee, 1934, Vol. II, pp.508-516; Sertillanges, A.D., 'La creazione dell'anima umana' *Quaderni di Roma* I, 1947, pp.301-308; Gedda, L., 'La questione dell'infusione dell'anima nei gemelli' (1949), now reprinted in Gedda, L., *Problemi di frontiera della medicina* Torino, Borla, 1963, pp.93-99; Josia, C.G., 'Infusione dell'anima umana nel feto' *Perfice Munus!* 1951, pp.15-30; Hering, H.M., 'De Tempore animationis foetus humani' *Angelicum* 28, 1951, pp.18-29; Hudeczek, M.M., 'De tempore animationis foetus humani secundum Embryologiam hodiernam' *Angelicum* 29, 1952, pp.161-181. Even J. Maritain defended this position, see 'Vers une idèe Thomiste de l'èvolution' *Approches sans entraves* Paris, Fayard, 1973. I could list many other authors, but for further information a good and impartial survey of the discussion can be found in Gentili, E., 'Il momento dell'animazione razionale. Studio sistematico' *La scuola cattolica* 1964, pp.221-240.

15. On this issue, see the interesting remarks by Giuseppina Pastori, a pupil of Agostino Gemelli ofm., the founder of the Catholic University in Italy, who claimed that for decades many scholars accepted Haeckel's theory as evidence for mediate animation theory. Cf. Pastori, G., 'Intervento' in Polli, E. and Bettinelli, C., (eds) *Aborto: diritto o crimine?* (Abortion: A Right or a Crime?) Milano, Ferro, 1972, pp.149-152, p.150.

16. Andreassi, G., entry 'Embriologia umana' in *Enciclopedia Medica Italiana* Firenze, Sansoni, 1952, col. 1659. For criticism of Haeckel's theory, cf. De Beer, G., *Embryos and Ancestors* second edition (the first edition was published in 1939), Oxford, Oxford University Press, 1951.

17. Miller, C.E., 'Abortion: good science = good morals' *The Holiletic and Pastoral Review* 1970, p.760. For a similar quotation, see the very influential paper (at least in the Italian debate) written by Bompiani, A., 'Individualità biologica e dignità umana del concepito' *Rivista del clero italiano* 1972, p.197.

18. For an excellent analysis of some problems concerning this issue it is still useful to read the book written by Raffaele, F., *L'individuo e la specie* Firenze, Sansoni edizioni scientifiche, 1941 (first edition 1905).

11. HUMAN EMBRYOLOGY AND THE CRITERION OF MORAL STANDING: SOME PHILOSOPHICAL AND ETHICAL PROBLEMS

Alicja Przyłuska-Fiszer
Zakład Historii Medycyny i Filozofii
Akademia Medyczna
ul. Złota 7
00-019 Warszawa
Poland

1. Introduction

Embryo research, transplants and new reproductive technologies are, like abortion, difficult topics for the moral philosopher. The difficulty is not just that strong views are held on both sides of the ethical debate. The problem is that the issue of embryo experimentation is interlocked with some of the most difficult general problems of moral philosophy and metaphysics. One of the main issues in discussion of the philosophical and ethical aspects of embryo research, transplants and new reproductive technologies is the problem of the status of the embryo. That is very much the same problem as the one we are familiar with in the abortion debate. Some philosophers propose the use of three key terms pre-embryo, embryo, and foetus, to distinguish between the different stages of development of the entity to which the term 'embryo' applies, but none of these definitions is intended to prejudge any moral issues.[1]

This question of status is often reduced to the question of whether the early developmental stages of human beings, i.e., the human fertilised egg, embryo, foetus and infant, are persons or not. Many scholars take it for granted that only persons have moral rights, including the right to life, and that all human beings are persons, or at least potential persons. This belief allows them to think that the answer to the question about the rightness or wrongness of embryo research is strictly related to the issue of the humanity of the entity in question, i.e. to the criteria for being a human being. It is for this reason that the ethical debate on abortion, embryo research and new reproductive technologies is often concentrated upon the question of when human life begins.

The aim of this paper is to show that the concept of human as well as the concept of person is essentially a philosophical one, and that it cannot help us with resolving any of the moral problems of modern medicine without additional, ethical assumptions. Most of these assumptions are presupposed by the radical conception of moral standing. Thus what we really need is an analysis of what moral standing is. Only in that way we can find reasonable and convincing answers to the following questions: what is

D. Evans (ed.), Conceiving the Embryo, 165–172.
© 1996 Kluwer Law International. Printed in the Netherlands.

wrong with killing human beings or persons? do or do not pre-personal human beings belong to our moral community? and what are our moral obligations towards unborn human beings?

2. On the Definition of 'Human'

As Mary Anne Warren[2] has pointed out, the term 'human' has two different senses: the genetic sense of 'human' and the moral sense of 'human'. In the descriptive sense of 'human', which she calls the genetic one, there are no doubts that we are human beings from conception, because 'human' means simply a 'member of Homo Sapiens'. But it does not follow that we are human beings from conception in the moral sense, i.e. a full member of the moral community. The concept of human is essentially philosophical. Let us distinguish two questions: the first is of when human life begins, and the second of when it requires full respect. It is possible to hold that all human beings in the moral sense are human beings in the genetic sense and *vice versa*. It is also possible to hold that some genetically human beings (embryos, irreversibly comatose 'human vegetables') are not human beings in the moral sense. We should answer the question, as Feinberg says[3], of whether the two classes of 'human' correspond exactly.

In the moral debates on the standing of the human embryo let us distinguish three basic criteria or sets of basic criteria for human beings. These are, first, the genetic criterion; second, the birth criterion; and third, development criteria. Each of these may have several meanings. According to the conservative view we become human beings at the moment of conception. Some Catholic theologians say that scientific evidence has shown that human life begins at the time of conception and obviously a foetus has full moral standing from the very beginning. However, attempts to justify our moral beliefs on scientific grounds have to fail, because - as is well known - one is not allowed to derive normative propositions from descriptive ones. Furthermore, in debates on the standing of the human embryo one is tempted to forget that the biological concept of individuality is operational and context-dependent. That is why it should not be treated as an appropriate grounding for the philosophical idea of personhood or as a basis for ethical considerations.[4] Nevertheless the conservative criterion I mentioned above can be understood in a different way if we assume, as Norman Ford does, that fertilisation is not the beginning of the development of the human individual but rather, represents the beginning of the process of the zygote's cell progeny becoming one or more human individuals. Ford concludes that a human individual cannot begin before the appearance of the primitive streak about 14 days after fertilisation.[5]

On the other hand Ford thinks, that

> even if it were certain that the early human embryo was not a person, I would morally disapprove of interrupting the generative process by aborting preimplanted

human embryos and destructive experiments on human embryos.[6]

This condemnation of early abortion as well as destructive experiments on embryos confirms the supposition that we should seek an argument for the conservative ethical position outside biology.

Most pro-choice liberals think that the foetus's legitimacy as a holder of rights is in doubt and assume that a human product of conception is not immediately a human in a moral sense.[7] This opinion allows them to deny the moral consequences of destructive experiments or the abortion of a foetus. The strong version of this view is represented by a feminist medical ethics, which claims that the value of foetal life is contingent upon the woman's free consent and subjective acceptance. The foetus must be invested with maternal valuing in order to become human. The feminist pro-choice position accepts a process of 'humanisation' through personal consciousness and 'sociality'.[8] According to this view, the foetus has no moral standing at all, so - as a consequence - abortion and destructive research on human embryos becomes morally acceptable. The acceptance of the birth criterion for being a human being relies upon a very controversial thesis, according to which it is external factors which give value to an unborn human. If we think, as I do, that the future child acquires an intrinsic value before birth, in its prenatal life and if we furthermore take for granted that this value does not depend on anybody's will or desire, then it would be wrong to ignore the interests of the foetus.

Similar conclusions can be drawn from the next position which I call development criteria. According to it there is a morally significant dividing line somewhere between a zygote and a viable foetus. Several philosophers hold that we should take a moderate position, which distinguishes between the earlier and later foetus's moral status. The most important development criterion is brain activity. The reason for that is that it recognises the analogy between the beginning and the end of life. The moment of beginning corresponds to the moment of death according to whether there is any brain activity or not. The main problem with developmental criteria is that we do not have any reason to choose one rather than another, as between, for example, implantation, gastrulation, the presence of all organs, completion of the brain structure, quickening, viability and birth. At each point - as Callahan says - the being in question is still far more potentiality than actuality.[9] Another problem is how a biological basis could be grounds for our moral policy.

On the liberal view a foetus has no moral standing; on the conservative view it has full moral standing. Pro-choice liberals say that 'the right to life' is dogma and cannot be subjected to rational analysis or argument. I think the same can be said about the liberal view that a foetus is a part of the woman's body and does not have any rights. As Marquis has argued:

A sketch of standard anti-abortion and pro-choice arguments exhibits how these arguments possess certain symmetries that explain why partisans of those positions are so convinced of the correctness of their position, why they are not successful in convincing their opponents, and why, to others, this issue seems to be unresolvable.[10]

None of these positions can answer in a proper way the question of when potential human beings become members of our moral community unless we have a much wider and deeper conception of the idea of moral standing.

3. On the Concept of A Person

Some philosophers think that we can bridge the gap between the normative and the descriptive sense of 'human' if we simply distinguish between two things: the concept of a person, and the concept of a human being.[11] There is no general agreement between philosophers as to understanding the concept of a person, but most of them at least agree that 'person' means an entity which has moral rights, including the right to life, and which therefore should be treated as a full member of the moral community. The problem of the status of the embryo is understood in terms of when the foetus becomes a person. The attempt to draw a boundary line between persons and non-persons is hopeless until we have a criterion of personhood. That is why an ethical debate on the standing of the human embryo can usually be expected to concern the question of necessary characteristics of a person.

   It seems to me that this approach is unhelpful in the same way as the foregoing one, because the concept of a person is not only ambiguous but also has been subject to change in the course of the history of philosophy and has different historical meanings. Three issues are crucial here. In the first place, the concept of a person does not have to be restricted only to human beings, it is possible to hold that some persons are not members of Homo Sapiens (God, angels, devils, higher animals such as chimpanzees[12]). As Feinberg has pointed out to be a 'person' is "to be the sort of being who could have rights and duties without conceptual absurdity".[13] Second the concept of 'person', as with the term 'human', has both a normative (moral or legal) and a descriptive (commonsense) sense. It is not enough to establish a set of characteristics that are rooted in the commonsense concept of personhood, such as for example consciousness, a concept of self, self-awareness and rationality, and try to say what the relation is between having these properties and being a person in the moral sense. Our decision to choose such traits must be defended in the manner appropriate to moral claims. Third, since the concept of a person is a normative one, there is no empirical procedure for discovering which side is correct. The definition of a person is a result of philosophical and ethical decisions concerning the value of life, of humankind and of human persons. That is why it is a philosophical illusion that normative moral principles and specific rights and obligations can be derived from what is essential to the concept of a person.[14]

   The decision to say when the foetus becomes a person is a moral decision, for which we should have moral reasons. Indeed, we do not need to know if the foetus is a person or is not. What we really want is an answer to the question of how we should treat the early developmental stages of human beings. The proper moral question concerns what it is that makes killing wrong and what we ought or ought not to do. I think, and it is not only my opinion[15], that facing up to this question is a simpler and better way of resolving the moral problem at issue.

4. A Criterion of Moral Standing

One of the approaches to resolving the problem of what makes killing wrong is an analysis of what moral standing is. The status of the foetus is related to a wider normative criterion of moral standing. It is Sumner who believes that the main point in discussions of abortion and embryo research is to establish a criterion of moral standing, which should have meaning not only for foetuses but for all other creatures too.[16] It seems to me that the answer to the question of what a criterion of moral standing is could help us to say what is wrong with killing and therefore what kinds of beings can have moral status. A criterion of moral standing should not be mistaken for the concept of person. Its role turns out to be more important since it purports to provide us with a theoretical and moral basis for all our moral valuation.

In the history of moral philosophy we can find four possible candidates. We can attribute full moral standing to the paradigm person on the grounds that she/he is, first, intrinsically valuable; second, alive; third, sentient; or, fourth, rational.[17] The first criterion cannot be accepted without an appropriate theory of intrinsic values. The second one seems to be too wide to be a predominant idea in our practical moral life, though it plays a principal role in Albert Schweitzer's ethics of reverence for life. Sumner supports the third option when he writes

> ... if morality has to do with the promotion and protection of interests or welfare, morality can concern itself only with beings who are conscious or sentient. No other beings can be beneficiaries or victims in the morally relevant way.[18]

The criterion of rationality has a long philosophical tradition and has usually been understood as the widely acclaimed component of the humanistic ethical program.[19] According to this tradition human dignity is presumed to be founded on such merits as reason and conscience. Several philosophers who belong to the consequentialist and utilitarian tradition have pointed out that this approach turns out to be an unacceptable particularism and deserves the label of 'human speciesism'.[20] From the practical point of view the criterion of rationality seems also to be too narrow since it denies moral standing to so many human beings, for example newborns, and the severely abnormal etc. That is the reason why rationality is usually treated as a sufficient but not necessary condition of moral standing.

A most promising middle path between a criterion of life and a criterion of rationality is a criterion of sentience. This position is defended for example by Feinberg, Regan,

Singer, Sumner, Warren, Steinbock and others, who assume that the possesion of interests (and thus sentience) is the criterion of moral standing.[21] We can call it *the interest view*, based on the "interests principle" which Feinberg proposes as an answer to the question "what kinds of being can have moral rights".[22] Feinberg's central insight - that interests are essential to rights - can be applied to moral status as well.[23] The possession of interests is both necessary and sufficient for 'moral status'. It means that we should attribute moral standing only to those creatures who could have interests, i.e., we owe moral duties to only and all those beings capable of having interests; no other beings can be harmed in the morally relevant way. Interests are compounded out of beliefs, aims, goals, and concerns. The interest view allows us in addition to give an answer to the question of what makes killing wrong. Killing someone is *prima facie* seriously wrong because the killing inflicts the greatest possible loss one can suffer - the loss of one's future.

5. Research on Embryos

If we have a criterion for moral standing, we can answer the question whether a foetus is the sort of entity that qualifies as a subject of morality. Particular views should be defined by selecting the natural characteristics whose gradual acquisition during normal foetal development carries with it the acquisition of moral standing. What are the thresholds? How is moral status acquired? Is it acquired gradually or all at once? One possible answer is to be found in Steinbock's book *Life Before Birth*.[24] She argues that the capacity for conscious awareness is a necessary condition for the possession of interests and then uses the interests view to defend a pro-choice position on abortion. Embryos (the unborn during the first weeks of gestation) and early foetuses do not have interests, they will acquire interests once they are born or even late in pregnancy, once they become sentient. Thus, we are not morally required to consider their interests because foetuses do not have them. And so, although Steinbock accepts a woman's right to choose abortion, her point of view is closer to the moderate than to the liberal position. The interest view entails the belief that our moral opinion of embryo research and abortion should at least partly depend upon the level of a foetus's development.

What is the role of this argument in justifying destructive research on embryos? Is destructive research on embryos justified in virtue of the claim that no life with moral standing is ended? The concept of moral standing is very important in defining our moral obligations towards other creatures, nevertheless we should not forget that our obligations do not have to be symmetrical with moral rights. It is possible to hold that destructive embryo research ought not to be tolerated, even if we believe that the foetus lacks full moral standing. It might be objected that only those beings who possess the special property (the capacity for awareness) can have moral importance. In debates on the standing of the human embryo, the attempt to use the differentiation between full and less than full moral standing as a decisive argument against embryo research are quite common. A typical argument admits that even if it were true that the embryo could not be a moral agent it should be treated as a moral subject. That would mean that we can have moral obligations towards the early developmental precursors of human beings, including the obligation not to kill them and not to perform destructive research on them, even if it is nonsense to speak of their rights. Two arguments are crucial for this opinion. First, the symbolic value of human life and the slippery slope argument, according to which the use of embryos for experimental research is a step in the direction of harmful research on persons and a loss of respect for human life. Second, the argument from potential, that even if the foetus lacks an actual right to life, its potential personhood may constitute a reason against killing it.[25]

It seems to me that the differentiation between entities having full and less than full moral standing, for example moral agents and moral subjects, is problematic. On the other hand it seems possible to have moral duties which are not grounded on the rights someone has 'against' us. Ultimately the delineation of the range of the creatures whose good we will take into account in our activities is a question of moral decision. For that reason, even if we assume the interests view, we should be very careful in deciding which form of embryo research and transplants we would like to accept.

Notes

1. For example, Glover, J., *Fertility and the Family* London, Fourth Estate, 1989, p.94.

2. Warren, M.A., 'On the moral and legal status of abortion' in Hunt, R. and Arras, J. (eds), *Ethical Issues in Modern Medicine* Palo Alto, California, Mayfield Publishing Company, 1977, pp.159-178, p.168.

3. Feinberg, J., 'Abortion' in Regan, T. (ed.), *Matters of Life and Death* New York, Random House, 1980, pp.183-216, p.186.

4. Mauron, A., 'The human embryo and the relativity of biological individuality' in this volume.

5. Cf. Ford, N., *When Did I Begin?* Cambridge, Cambridge University Press, 1988, pp.164-177.

6. Ford, N., 'When Did I Begin? - A Reply to Nicholas Tonti-Filippini' *Linacre Quarterly* Vol. 57, No. 4, 1990, pp.59-66, p.65.

7. Macklin, R., 'Liberty, utility, and justice: an ethical approach to unwanted pregnancy', *International Journal of Gynecology and Obstetrics* Suppl. 3, 1989, pp.37-49.

8. Cf., for instance, Callahan, S., 'Abortion and the sexual agenda' *Commonweal* 25 April 1986, pp.232-238, p.233, and Sherwin, S., *No Longer Patient. Feminist Ethics and Health Care* Philadelphia, Temple University Press, 1992, pp.108-111.

9. Callahan, D., *Abortion: Law, Choice and Morality* London, Collier-Macmillan Ltd, 1970, pp.364ff.

10. Marquis, D., 'Why abortion is immoral' *The Journal of Philosophy* Vol. 86, No. 4, 1989, pp.183-202, pp.183-184.

11. For example, Feinberg, *op. cit.*

12. Cf. Singer, P., *Practical Ethics* Cambridge, Cambridge University Press, 1979, p.98.

13. Feinberg, *op. cit.*, p.186.

14. Cf. Rorty, A.O., 'Persons and *Personae*' in Gill, C. (ed.), *The Person and the Human Mind. Issues in Ancient and Modern Philosophy* Oxford, Clarendon Press, 1990, pp.21-38.

15. See also Marquis, *op. cit.*, and Hare, R., 'Abortion and the Golden Rule' *Philosophy and Public Affairs* Vol. 4, No. 3, 1975, pp.201-222.

16. Sumner, L.W., *Abortion and Moral Theory* Princeton, New Jersey, Princeton University Press, 1981, pp.26-39.

17. *Ibid.*, p.129.

18. *Ibid.*, pp.136-137.

19. Lazari-Pawłowska, J., 'Kręgi Ludzkiej wspólnoty' (The Reach of Human Solidarity) *Etyka* 18, 1980, pp.200-218.

20. Cf. Singer, *op. cit.*, pp.48-71, and Ryder, R., *Speciesism: The Ethics of Vivisection* Edinburgh, Scottish Society for the Prevention of Vivisection, 1974.

21. Feinberg, J., 'Human Duties and Animal Rights' in Morris, R.K., and Fox, M.W. (eds.), *On the Fifth Day: Animal Rights and Human Ethics* Washington, Acropolis Books Ltd., 1978; Regan, T., 'Introduction' in Regan, T. (ed.), *Matters of Life and Death* second edition, New York, Random House, 1980, pp.3-27, p.23; Singer, *op. cit.*, p.12; Sumner, *op. cit.*, chapters 4 and 5; Warren, H.A., 'Do Potential People Have Moral Rights?' *Canadian Journal of Philosophy* 7, 1977, pp.275-289, p.289; Steinbock, B., *Life Before Birth. The Moral and Legal Status of Embryos and Foetuses* Oxford, Oxford University Press, 1992, pp.9-13.

22. Feinberg, J., 'The Rights of Animals and Unborn Generations' in Blackstone, W. (ed.), *Philosophy and Environmental Crisis* Athens, Georgia, University of Georgia Press, pp.43-68.

23. Cf. Steinbock, *op. cit.*, p.10.

24. *Ibid.*

25. Cf. Feinberg (1980), *op. cit.*, pp.193-196.

12. EMBRYOS AS MORAL SUBJECTS AND LIMITS OF RESPONSIBILITY

Knut W. Ruyter
Center for Medical Ethics
University of Oslo
Norway

1. Introduction

I take it that ethics must be anchored in a common morality and that most of us tend to argue in terms of typical cases. This approach tends to be conservative, but it is not exempt from rebuttals or changes. I submit that this way of reasoning is helpful in discussing matters of practical importance and leaves room for dialogue in an attempt to decide what status embryos should be accorded and which responsibilities we have towards them.

Today there is substantial disagreement and considerable doubt about the moral status of the embryo. The last twenty years show evidence of challenges to traditional norms and of radical changes, which have led to adaptations of some forms of ethical gradualism. The most obvious example is the legalisation of abortion on demand before 12 weeks in most European countries, due mainly to an emphasis on the self determination of women. The indirect consequence of this is that the foetus is not accorded independent legal status during the first trimester. In moral terms it means that the autonomy of women overrides the interests of the foetus, and that the foetus, by definition, must be accorded less moral status than the woman.

The foetus is, however, accorded gradually increasing status and protection from the second trimester. Abortion is no longer available on demand in Norway, but is selective and dependent for example on the approval of a hospital committee. The acceptable reasons for requesting an abortion increase in gravity with the length of the pregnancy. At the point of viability the foetus has traditionally been accorded full legal status.[1]

There are two new developments in medical technology that challenge the relative acceptance of abortion in most countries. At the end of the pregnancy, neonatology has forced the point of viability down from 28 weeks to about 22 weeks. What is actually meant by viability is uncertain, but it is clear that foetuses from about 22 weeks and onwards may survive with the intensive assistance of medical therapy, though with a substantial risk of serious defects. With this development it is obvious that the traditional line between late abortions and infanticide has been crossed. To resolve this problem some legal scholars suggest lowering the threshold for late abortions to about 22 weeks.[2] At the beginning of life, conception may take place outside the body, as a

D. Evans (ed.), Conceiving the Embryo, 173–192.
© 1996 *Kluwer Law International. Printed in the Netherlands.*

result of *in vitro* fertilisation. This new intervention makes it necessary to decide what moral status is to be accorded to a fertilised egg. Most have decided in favour of some 'special respect', though laws and guidelines are under constant revision.

Both these developments show that the moral weight of self determination has important limits. Besides, the assignment of limited moral status to the foetus in the context of abortion is not transferable to the area of fertilised eggs *outside* the body. In this context their status cannot be limited on account of self determination.

In this paper I will address only the question of the moral status of the embryo outside the body, with the intent of arguing for a position which accepts some understanding of continuity as a fact of human life from beginning to end.

In any case, there is substantial disagreement about the moral status of the early embryo. Most of these discussions hinge on the problem of whether or not the embryo is a person. Some hold that it is a person or, if this cannot be sustained, that it should be treated *as if* it were a person.[3] Others hold that it is not a person, for a variety of reasons (e.g. the enormous natural prenatal loss, the lack of particular individuality and the possibility of twinning, the absence of a recognisable body, the absence of mental capability or of the capacity to feel pleasure or pain) so we may sacrifice it for a variety of purposes (such as abortion and experiments).[4]

On the basis of these different opinions and decisions various terminologies are formed, which are not neutral. It is important to pay attention to this, since terms are value laden and often reflect the position one wants to defend and thereby presuppose a judgement. Those who use terms like 'child' or 'foetus' tend to hold restrictive positions, while those who use terms like 'pre-embryo', 'fertilised egg', 'thing' or 'little clump of cells' are inclined to defend more liberal practices. The same will be true in the case of research on embryos. The more restrictive positions will often refer to this type of research as 'destructive' or 'consuming', while more liberal positions will refer to e.g. 'invasive' research. The choice of terms does not only reflect scientific knowledge, but also underlying values. Scientific knowledge may of course contribute facts that may be morally relevant, but they are not neutral in themselves.[5]

The various terms and their underlying presuppositions are far from trivial. It is probably fair to say that the opinion one has about the moral status of the embryo will have decisive significance for how one judges medically assisted conception, since the handling of embryos outside the body for various purposes will entail that a large number of embryos are destroyed.

In regard to *therapy*, it seems necessary to accept that a large number of fertilised eggs are left to die, owing to the fact that it is common to fertilise more eggs than are needed for an embryo transfer and that fertilised eggs are selected according to criteria that one hopes to be somewhat predictive of success. An attempt was made to resolve some of the problem of waste through the process of *cryo preservation*. However, half of the frozen fertilised eggs are destroyed in the process of either freezing or thawing. In regard to *research*, it seems necessary to accept that embryos are destroyed in the process of investigation or as a result of not being found fit to be transferred to a woman. Many argue for a definite need to do research, both for the improvement of therapy and for general knowledge of embryology. If a fertilised egg is a person none of these activities may be deemed morally acceptable. If a fertilised egg is not a person, all of these activities may be considered morally acceptable. The early embryo is either treated as a person, or as a thing.

I think that the either-or position is false. The first attempts to claim too much, while the second claims nothing. It seems both are counter-intuitive and neither represents a common acceptable standard. Contrary to the views of many who hold that the embryo is not a person, it does not follow that we do not have any moral responsibility toward it.[6] On the contrary, it is possible to be of the opinion that an embryo is not a person and still claim that we have substantial moral obligations towards it.

This insight is to varying degrees expressed in the way various nations have chosen to regulate medically assisted conception. In regard to research it is e.g. expressed by recommending caution and introducing several specific cautionary rules. These regulations may be seen as attempts at striking a balance between the either-or positions.

It is unlikely that an attempt to reach a moderate balance will satisfy any of the either-or positions, but it seems to be a feasible alternative for the construction of an answer which may meet with common acceptance.

I will suggest an answer by considering the analogical extension of moral standing from typically accepted cases to disputed cases, in the context of commonly accepted guidelines for research. I propose to pursue discussion under four heads: analogical extension of moral status; embryos as moral subjects; caution by limited moral responsibility; and research on embryos. My tentative conclusion is that embryos may be considered to be moral subjects towards which we have significant, but limited responsibility.

2. Analogical Extension of Moral Status

As in any casuistic method - or dialectical argument - the first step is to see and define a clear case of which there is a fairly high degree of certainty and agreement.[7] The next steps proceed by analogical extension to areas of greater uncertainty and disagreement. I think this approach might be helpful in practical reasoning, both to see if there is ground for common understanding and how that might be extended to disputed areas, and, if disagreement cannot be overcome, as an analytical instrument to understand how and why people differ.

As a common moral ground in a secular context it seems reasonable to consider the universal declaration of human rights to be acceptable to all or most people. The declaration states that "all members of the human family" are recognised as having equal dignity and equal basic rights. The members are also described as *persons*. They have *inherent dignity* and are recognised by three criteria: persons are (1) born free and are endowed with (2) reason and (3) conscience (Article 1).[8] These criteria may be interpreted as actual skills, but I will suggest in the following that it is more reasonable to interpret the criteria as including persons who have abilities for free action, reason and conscience or have lost them. Abilities exist irrespective of whether they are or have been actual skills. The declaration purports to attribute equal dignity to all human beings, or very nearly all.

In an instructive way the Norwegian philosopher Jon Wetlesen distinguishes between moral *agents*, moral *persons* and moral *subjects*.[9] These distinctions make it possible to differentiate between the notion of a moral agent, who has actual skills, and a moral person, who has the ability to be a moral agent, regardless of whether this is an actual or only a potential or lost skill.

In a casuistic method this may be interpreted as follows. The moral agent represents a paradigmatic example for all agents on the basis of the recognised opinion of the universal declaration of human rights. In step two the opinion is extended to encompass moral persons, who are not agents, but who have abilities or have lost them. In other words, all agents are also persons, but not all persons are agents. In step three the question of moral status is extended to moral subjects, who are not persons, but who are not exempt from the moral responsibility of agents.

As Wetlesen rightly notes, if one must be a moral *agent* to have equal inherent dignity, then many human beings will be excluded from the class of moral persons, such as neonates and small children, foetuses and embryos, as well as the severely mentally retarded and the severely senile.[10] Some defend this position, especially if dignity is interpreted as actual autonomous skills, but I suppose, as does Wetlesen, that this would not reflect a commonly accepted opinion. A reasonable interpretation of the declaration assigns equal human dignity to all moral persons, irrespective of whether they are agents or not.[11] It means that moral persons will include human beings who have abilities or have lost them. This will e.g. include premature neonates, the severely mentally retarded and comatose patients.

On this rendering it seems clear that all human beings, or nearly all, ought to be included in the class of moral persons and be assigned inherent dignity and equal rights.

At the same time it seems that the recognised opinion about human dignity is relevant only to those who are born, including those foetuses that are viable. The universal declaration does not seem to have had any intention to say anything about human dignity before viability. There is as a result great doubt and disagreement about the status of human life before viability, that is about such entities as fertilised eggs, embryos, foetuses, and possibly also anencephalic newborns, and whether they fall inside or outside the class of moral persons.

Some assume that human life before viability falls inside the class of persons, and therefore has the same claim to protection as persons. Others find this improbable, and presume that moral status as persons can be ascribed only later in pregnancy, e.g. at the second trimester or at birth. This opinion has longstanding roots in our culture and may be ontologically justified in the Aristotelian-Thomistic tradition, on the basis of theories of delayed animation or of formation.

It is in this discussion that there may be another advantage to the distinctions presented by Wetlesen. Forms of human life not included in the category of moral persons, may be considered *moral subjects*. Wetlesen's argument, based on the analogical extension of moral status, is especially developed in relation to animals and all living organisms as subjects, but I assume that the same kind of reasoning may be applied to human life which is not defined as person.[12] In a possible analogical extension the responsibility of the agent may depend on abilities which are similar, and which may vary in degrees compared to the paradigmatic measure for human dignity. As in all analogical reasoning, the strength of the arguments will depend on morally relevant similarities and differences.

There are presumably two ways of arguing for this analogical extension. It may be argued on the basis of abilities that are somehow manifest and observable, but not yet actual skills. This type of reasoning may lend itself to assessing gradual moral status. It may also be argued on the basis of abilities that are not manifest, but only present as potential abilities. In the next section I will examine various analogies and disanalogies between moral subjects and moral persons on the basis of abilities that are manifest.

To sum up, moral subjects do not share equal inherent dignity with persons, but this does not mean that they are without dignity. Along a spectrum in an analogical extension subjects may be accorded gradually less dignity and have gradually less claims to protection, on the basis of morally relevant differences.

3. Embryos as Moral Subjects

For the sake of the argument, I assume that we agree that all moral persons have equal inherent dignity. I take it that we may rely on the example of the Declaration provisionally, until we have sufficiently strong reasons to rebut it in terms of revisions or changes. If embryos are deemed to fall outside the class of persons, this must be justified by morally relevant differences that have a substantial degree of probability.[13]

If we reason within this framework each relevant similarity between a paradigmatic example and a contested case will provide a ground for a pro argument for a similar treatment, and each relevant difference will provide a ground for contra-argument; that is, a pro-argument for a different treatment.

I suggest that morally relevant differences must be sought in relation to the criteria suggested by the universal declaration of human rights, as I interpreted them as abilities of identity, consciousness and conscience. I will right away emphasise that such a determination is bound to be somewhat arbitrary. It will depend on thresholds of the criteria (what is the minimal manifest characteristic of an ability) and degrees of relevance (more or less different). These determinations may also lead to various resolutions, dependent upon whether criteria are related to biological substance or to an understanding of human life as a continuous developmental process.

3.1. BORN FREE

The declaration uses the term "born free" as a criterion which characterises a person. An embryo or a foetus is neither born nor free, in the sense that it can live independently outside the body of the mother. This criterion may be interpreted as another way of phrasing the longstanding legal understanding of independent existence at viability as a marker of full legal status.

On this basis it might be argued that there is a morally relevant difference between born and unborn human life, between the visible and the invisible, even though, as we have seen it has become increasingly difficult to draw the line between born and unborn. If the criterion "born free" is accepted as a dividing line for a morally relevant difference, it will mean that human life before birth or viability does not acquire independent status as a moral person, but should be considered as a moral subject.

3.2. BIOLOGICAL SUBSTANCE

In relation to the other criteria for being a person, there are at least four aspects that are biologically significant, and, I think, morally relevant. These are the enormous loss of fertilised eggs prior to implantation; the possibility of twinning; the lack of differentiated individuality; and the need for genetic information from the mother to guide development, even after the genotype is established. All these aspects must be considered. If they can be accepted as morally relevant differences, it also follows that embryos may be treated differently from persons.

First, there seems to be agreement among scientists that at least seventy percent of all eggs fertilised in natural cycles do not develop toward a viable child. Most of them die prior to implantation.[14] With such an enormous natural wastage it doesn't seem reasonable to assume that fertilised eggs are persons with inherent dignity.[15] When there is a certain waste of embryos in research or IVF treatment this may then also be deemed morally acceptable. Against this one may of course object that it may not be relevant to compare a high natural risk of loss to a risk of waste produced as a result of human intervention. Where human intervention is accepted, there is usually some attempt to prevent or minimise natural risks, not imitate them. The argument from waste does not in itself create the ground for claiming that embryos should be treated differently from persons.

The second, and I suppose a more substantial, morally relevant difference, seems to require that abilities of persons must presuppose that the embryo has developed into a differentiated and indivisible individual. According to the current interpretation of embryology this is not the case during the first fourteen days. It is emphasised that at this stage all cells are pluripotent, i.e. if they are separated, each one of them may develop toward a viable person. Cells at this stage may also divide spontaneously into two or more embryos with identical genetic constitutions, or cells from two or more genotypes may fuse into one embryo, which can develop into an individual person who represents a mosaic of more than one genotype.[16] If a differentiated and indivisible human life is accepted as a prerequisite for the capability of persons, there cannot exist a particular individual human life before this time.[17]

A third possible morally relevant difference seems to be that the abilities for rationality and conscience are not present at such an early stage. Capacities for rationality will be present in the development of the brain and of the nerve system. These will develop on the basis of the formation of the primitive streak which takes place after the fourteenth day.

A fourth morally relevant difference may be found in the fact that the early embryo is not genetically distinctive. It is dependent upon the mother's messenger RNA directing the initial steps of embryonic development. It is not until the 4-8 cell stage (after six days) that the early embryo is genetically distinctive. As of this time the embryonic genome is activated and assumes full control of further development[18], while the embryo remains of course totally dependent upon nutrition from the mother.

One interpretation of these biological facts may indicate that an embryo cannot have the manifest abilities of a person prior to implantation (6-8 days) or prior to the formation of the primitive streak (about 14 days), due to lack of developmental individuality and rational ability. Both these timelimits relate to the notion of individuality, albeit in different ways. It may not be philosophically significant to discuss the extent to which maternal signals are important for early development (as Suarez and opponents seem to imply). It seems however significant that the boundary between mother and embryo is unclear. In the words of Alex Mauron the directing of maternal mRNA represents a kind of "overlap between generations".[19] This overlapping seems to undermine any manifest capability for individuality in the embryo. As Alex Mauron shows in his paper in this volume a similar conclusion can be reached in relation to the primitive streak stage.[20] The issue here is the connection between individuality and sameness. Since the primitive streak roughly corresponds to the disappearance of the last opportunity for twinning, this also seems to undermine any manifest capability before this stage.

On the basis of criteria related to biological substance it seems feasible to argue that an embryo at this early stage neither has manifest abilities of individuality or reason, though there is potential for both. It is, however, difficult to see that potential abilities should be accorded full moral weight.[21] Thus it seems reasonable to conclude provisionally that it is hardly probable that an embryo is a person. In the analogical extension attempted here, it seems that the morally relevant differences are dominant.

This provisional conclusion does not give any answer to the question of what value an embryo should be accorded on the grounds of its being a moral subject. In a number of statements from national committees it has been emphasised that embryos ought to have a special status.[22] From this the idea is also derived that embryos should be treated with (profound) respect, though not with the same respect as that accorded to persons.

It is, however, not clear what 'special status' entails and how profound respect is translated into action. It seems reasonable to accord the embryo and the foetus increasing moral status up to viability, in line with increasing morally relevant similarities pursuant to manifest abilities such as individuality, bodily form, brain activity or a sufficiently developed nervous system.

We could, as Wetlesen suggests, assume that all moral subjects have some degree of inherent dignity equal to or less than 1, but greater than 0.[23] Value 1 is ascribed to all moral persons. It follows that all other moral subjects have some degree of moral value which is proportional to their degree of similarity with moral persons. The determination of value along a continuum from one to zero will be disputed. Some will assume that the embryo as a moral subject should be ascribed a value close to 1, while others will assume that it will be close to zero.

3.3. DEVELOPMENTAL PROCESS

Against this way of determining morally relevant differences, it may be argued that there is no stage in the development of nascent life which is so significant that it, in itself, can determine what may be considered a morally relevant difference. Neither fertilisation, individualisation, implantation, an ability to feel pain, having bodily form, showing brain activity, spontaneously moving nor any particular degree of development of the nervous system may be said to be a sufficient marker event of either skills or abilities which separately or in combination can constitute significant features or, as it is often said, qualitative changes or stages, in the developmental process. The features represent only passing stages in a continuous development of the capacities deposited in the cells from the time of fertilisation.

As far as I can ascertain the connection to a paradigmatic understanding of human life as a process has two possible outcomes. Either the analogy is extended back to the first stages of a human life that is species specific and genetically unique, or it is not extended at all beyond the limit of viability, with reference to the criterion of being born free.

The first possibility entails that embryos and foetuses must be accorded the same moral status as persons, since there are no (acceptable) morally relevant differences, which separately or in combination, are sufficient to the conclusion that an embryo or a foetus has a different status from a born, moral person. Some have drawn such a conclusion. The German philosopher Robert Spaemann has for instance emphasised that the foundation of human dignity must be independent of criteria of abilities or qualities. The respect for human life as person must be expressed in the encounter with all life which is bred by human beings.[24] This conclusion has far reaching implications. Presumably, it will mean that all destruction of embryos ought to be avoided.

Within the paradigmatic understanding of human life as a developmental process, it may also be possible not to extend the analogy of moral status beyond the limit of viability/birth. Also in this case it is possible to avoid a qualitative evaluation as to when and how abilities are present. I think none of these approaches are satisfactory. Even if we admit to a continuous process of development, the section above does illustrate that many discontinuous changes occur after fertilisation. Whether any of these changes amount to morally relevant differences depends on whether the achievement of a certain level of development can be discerned from the characteristics of abilities mentioned. Above I argued that they do. Precise markers according with the presence of these abilities are however not easily discernible. Establishing a marker will be somewhat arbitrary, but not totally arbitrary. The marking will be determined by reasonable assessments of what constitutes the minimum abilities necessary for personhood.[25]

As is obvious from the way of probabilistic (and practical) reasoning proposed here, it is not possible to reach a clear and unambiguous answer. There are a number of reputable opinions, with different degrees of probability and acceptability. Nevertheless, it seems reasonable to draw the provisional conclusion that it is not very probable that embryos outside the body have - or should be accorded - the same status as moral persons. It is thus far more probable that embryos are not moral persons, but moral subjects, in the terminology of Jon Wetlesen.

This is a relatively modest conclusion, which continues to be encumbered with substantial doubt and disagreement. Reasonable doubt about degrees of probability should indicate that it is feasible to say only that some actions are 'more right' than others, and that there will be a certain freedom to choose between various alternatives.

Even if it should be possible to establish a very probable opinion which is accepted by most, it will not give any precise or unambiguous answer to the question what we may do with embryos, which are created to fulfill various desires and interests of moral agents.

The asymmetric relation between agents and subjects, which arises from the fact that human life may be created outside the body, ought to urge caution. This is anchored in the probable opinion that the embryo is a moral subject, which is more than a thing or a tissue that may be discarded at one's own discretion. In an embryo there are the beginnings of human life which, under favourable conditions, will lead to a moral person. A gradually increasing status ought to give occasion for a certain respect. As an expression of this type of respect it seems reasonable to restrict strong personal and professional interests on the part of moral agents. In the latter domain there are obviously justified worries and uncertainties about whether it is possible to control research and therapeutic possibilities. This is due to the fact that it has proved extremely difficult to stop any medical development, which has given some valuable data and some therapeutic benefit, even when expected negative consequences or abuses are detected.

4. Caution by Limited Moral Responsibility

In a classical tutioristic (cautious) way of thinking it is of decisive importance to be clear about what a reasonable doubt is related to. This point of view admonishes caution in cases of insecurity and doubt. The chief concern of tutiorism is that one should not resolve doubts probabilistically if the life of a (possible) person is at risk. As long as there is doubt, one may not risk taking a human life.

In line with this several authors have concluded that any reasonable doubt must count for the benefit of the embryo, i.e. we should treat the embryo as if it were a person. This is also the conclusion in Ford's book:

Wherever there are reasonable doubts about the personal status of the early
embryo, moral principles, ... require that the human embryo from conception be
treated as a person.[26]

This interpretation of a cautious (tutioristic) approach corresponds to the one found in
Donum vitae.[27] Of greater interest in a secular context is that it also corresponds to
statements made by some national committees and legislators. One of these is The
National Committee for Medical Research Ethics in Norway, which in 1990 published
Research on Fetuses.[28] According to the cautious rule of descending order, which is
worked out in this statement, the Committee concludes that the ethical guidelines for
research on human beings, which apply to research on *born* persons should be adopted
for research on foetuses.[29] Being on the lowest step in the descending order foetuses
must be considered "an extremely weak group in the research context".[30] Foetuses shall
not only be treated as if they are born persons. The research community has indeed
"even greater obligations - to foetuses as subjects of research than to other groups of
born potential experimental subjects".[31]

It seems possible to substantiate such conclusions by reference to some of the well
known examples of reticence and caution, drawn from the tradition of casuistry. When
a hunter is uncertain as to whether there is an animal or a human being moving at the
edges of the wood, there is an obligation not to shoot. When a pharmacist is in doubt
as to whether a bottle contains the medicine stated on the label, there is an obligation
to refrain from giving it to customers. It's a question of following the more secure path
morally (*via tutior*). These examples seem to resemble the situation which we confront
in the case of the status of the embryo. Ergo, caution mandates that the embryo should
be treated as a person.

This may be seen as a reliable and trustworthy conclusion, but I think it is erroneous.
This is mainly due to the fact that Ford and others ignore both that the doubt does not
concern facts, but reveals an ontological uncertainty as to the status of the embryo as
person, and the lack of discussion of degrees of doubt. Above I have attempted to
argue that there are strong reasons to be of the opinion that it is hardly probable that
an embryo is a moral person, even if it is possible. It seems then that the doubt must
be correspondingly small. The more probable opinion is therefore sufficient to
according embryos a different status than persons and to justifying different treatment
of embryos.

In the case of embryos there is ontological insecurity and doubt, which cannot be
resolved, either factually or theoretically. In the apparently comparable cases of the
hunter and the pharmacist, there will always be occasion to verify the factual
circumstances. This will never be possible in the case of embryos outside the body.
It seems unreasonable that factual and theoretical doubts should be converted into
morally certain opinions, which give rise to even greater obligations than we usually
have to born persons.

The factual and theoretical doubt which exists about whether embryos may be included
in the interpretation of the Declaration of Human Rights of the inherent dignity of the

born human being, cannot bring forth a (perfect) duty always to choose the most secure course of action - by e.g. prohibiting all invasive research or all abortions or all IVF therapies which may involve the destruction of embryos.[32]

In addition to this Ford and others have not considered whether the degree of doubt may be morally significant. Ford refers to "reasonable doubts", while the Norwegian Committee cited earlier has not even expressed any doubts about the rightfulness of the extension of its descending order. Ford does not give any further explanation as to what is meant by "reasonable", but he has elsewhere claimed that if his thesis, concluding that an embryo is not a person, cannot be shown to be "certainly true", even the slightest doubt will bring forth an obligation to treat the embryo as a person from the moment of conception.[33]

In light of casuistic traditions Ford's conclusion is surprising. There was usually never any requirement for true or absolute certainty. Rather there were requirements for sufficient internal and external certainty to justify a course of action. As we have seen a sufficient degree of certainty is determined by reputable opinions that a great majority can follow and accept. When there are solid and convincing arguments in favour of concluding that it is highly dubious that an embryo can be a moral person, this cannot bring forth an obligation to choose the most secure path of action.

It seems therefore that Ford and others must base their conclusion on some form of a negative doubt. In a religious context this may be expressed as follows: immediate animation is probable, because one can never prove the opposite. In a secular context it may be claimed that there are not any substantial morally relevant differences between those who are born and those who are unborn, which can also be difficult to repudiate.

Nevertheless, there is cause to emphasise that precautions (e.g. in the form of tutiorism) are always related to positive doubt.[34] In this case it should indicate that it is highly improbable that an embryo can be considered a moral person. Even within such a rigorous approach as tutiorism, it cannot be claimed that a negative doubt can be considered a sufficient ground for extending the understanding of moral person, or ethical guidelines for protecting human research subjects, to include embryos. If so, it would mean that if there is even the slightest possibility for the slightest doubt, the case must be resolved by choosing the most secure course of action. This is a highly unreasonable interpretation of even the most cautious approach to moral matters, or indeed most other matters.

In this case, with sufficient positive doubt, it seems justifiable to suggest that the safer course must not be followed. Rather, probabilistic reasoning shows that there is substantial positive doubt about the status of the embryo and that it is highly improbable that embryos can be persons.

The understanding of the ontological status of embryos, which is argued here, limiting the analogical extension of moral persons, cannot exclude in principle the claim that some forms of embryo research, or wastage of embryos in therapy and abortions, may be ethically acceptable.

Above I have emphasised that it doesn't follow from this provisional conclusion that embryos have no value at all. I suggested that they ought to be considered to be moral subjects, which deserve respect from moral agents. It is with respect to their status as moral subjects that the basic regard for caution may be converted into a limited *prima facie* obligation, as well as a willingness to build in some level of safety margin. Both are suggested to ensure that we err on the side of caution. I think many will find this acceptable, in order to search for consensus about specific areas of utilisation and measures for protection[35], though there will of course remain problems about settling on definite markers. The 14-day limit represents a cautious approach, which gives sufficient protection from research on a particular, individualised and identifiable embryo. Proponents of different moral beliefs, e.g. that sentience constitutes a minimum claim to consideration, will find this approach far too cautious. If embryos are sentient at 18-20 weeks, their caution in erring on the safe side may be arbitrarily set at a 28-day limit, which provides sufficient protection against the possibility of an embryo suffering during experimentation.[36]

5. Research on Embryos

The proposed precautions make it possible to utilise the ethical guidelines developed for the context of research on human persons, though they may need some adjustment, as to the principle of estimated risk.

To begin with, it is morally important to determine what type of research is important and whether it is necessary. In the context of research on embryos it is relevant to distinguish between invasive research and research of systematic observation. By invasive research I understand the type of research which entails intervention in an embryo, with the result that these embryos are discarded. By observational research I mean the type of research which includes systematic observation, but does not result in the destruction of embryos.

Both types of research may serve various legitimate purposes. The first area will concern general basic research. This may be aimed at increasing general knowledge about embryology, immunology and genetics, in relation to e.g. increased understanding of the mechanisms of fertilisation and of the detection of genetic abnormalities. The Norwegian White paper mentions this area of research explicitly[37], but, like many other countries, Norwegian authorities place important restrictions against any use of embryos in basic research aimed at changing embryonic genes and creating identical individuals (cloning) or animal-human hybrids.

It is worth noting that scientists express the opinion that basic research "will probably pay a modest role"[38], i.e. it may not be very important, since most of what is interesting in early human development can be discovered by studying development in other vertebrates and mammals. One cannot, of course, preclude the possibility that there are specific features of human embryogenesis that are unique to human beings[39], but these may represent small (and insignificant) details that can hardly claim to represent necessary knowledge.

The other purpose of research is related specifically to the improvement of existing methods of IVF aimed at offering a more successful therapy and the introduction of new procedures aimed at treating conditions that are at present untreatable. In the light of relatively poor success rates research of this type, aimed at the improvement of technology and methods, seems far more important. For responsible clinical practice basic knowledge is not directly tranferable to the development of human embryos in vitro, or to questions about which embryo cultures, temperatures, choice of embryos, time of transfer, time of freezing, etc. are most conducive to success.

It seems clear that a good deal of this research does not entail invasive procedures. It may be claimed that observational research in the form of systematic observation and monitoring of embryos, the analysis of culture medias, and the induction of superovulation, represent necessary research which has given important results. As Mauron points out, this type of non-invasive research has e.g. made it "possible to define predictive criteria for choosing which embryos are most likely to develop normally and should therefore be transferred" back to the woman.[40]

On the basis of this discussion it may be useful to develop a taxonomy[41], which suggests that there should be increasing requirements for the significance of a research project in order for it to be accepted ethically, for each descending step in the diagram.

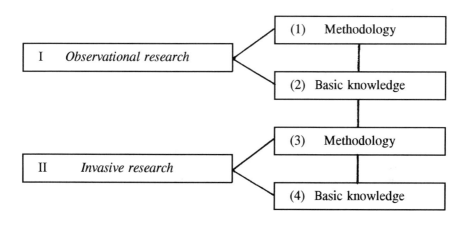

It seems reasonable that all types of research shall follow generally accepted scientific principles and ethical guidelines, with regard to the proposed protocol, review of previous trials, expected results and, if applicable, the consent of the woman/couple.[42] Both types of observational research (1, 2) seem clearly acceptable, if they fulfill standard requirements for research.[43] This may not be sufficient in the case of invasive research (II), because it overexerts the framework for commonly accepted risk assessments in research ethics. As a result of invasive research embryos will be significantly damaged and will be discarded. At the same time we cannot apply the same risk assessments to moral subjects, as we do to moral persons. The injuring and discarding of embryos remain a disvalue, which must be balanced against the significance of the research and the need for its results.

It may be inconsistent to prohibit all types of invasive research, as long as some clinical practice is based on this type of research, and as long as therapeutic methods are used which entail that a large number of embryos are discarded or destroyed. At the same time, and since invasive research is disputed, further precautions may be taken, leading to suitable caution and making it possible to evaluate the research. The aspired-to caution also gives embryos limited protection.

Invasive research limited to methodology. First, the area of invasive research may be limited to research specifically related to methodology (3). The limitation is however open to several interpretations. In a restricted sense methodological research is research which aims solely at improving existing methodology or developing new procedures in the use of IVF. The purpose of the research will in this case be directed only to medically assisted conception. In a broad sense methodological research includes all types of methods that may be related to the treatment proper, such as e.g. genetic screening of embryos in vitro (preimplantation diagnostics), development of germ line gene therapy or the development of new contraceptive methods to prevent implantation. My discussion in this context is limited to methodological research in a restricted sense.[44]

Non-invasive research. Second, there are very many areas of methodological research that do not entail invasive procedures. It is often sufficient to observe embryos by analysing different culture medias for adequate nutrition and embryo viability, trying various stimulation controls and freezing protocols.

There will, however, remain areas of methodological research which cannot be done without intervening in the embryo. This may for example apply to the development of new procedures, such as micro injection of sperm into eggs or freezing of unfertilised eggs. It is argued that these procedures must be evaluated for safety before embryos created using them are transferred back into women, and this may be done sufficiently only by invasive procedures, even after successful laboratory tests with animal models.[45] The first of these procedures raises the possibility of the clinical use of the method to assist couples where the man has severe problems of semen quality. (Up to now the only treatment available was donor insemination.) Successful freezing of eggs and fertilisation after thawing may eliminate the present practice of freezing embryos.

It is thus plausible that the concrete gain of research, which is obtainable through invasive research, may offset the destruction of embryos. This presupposes that the gain cannot be obtained in any other way.

Special requirements. When these points are taken account of, one may also consider further factors as elements in a cautious use of embryos in invasive research. As with many other countries, which endorse this type of research, the Norwegian White paper suggests "special requirements" as conditions for approval. Research should be carried out only on surplus embryos, which are not older than 14 days, and those embryos that are used in research must not be transferred back to the woman.[46] It is easy to concur with the two latter conditions, but the first one is far more troublesome.

In many countries there is an emphasis on the distinction between surplus embryos and embryos that are produced for the purpose of research. Surplus embryos may be understood as those fertilised eggs that are superfluous after the completion of a treatment cycle. The discrepancy arises from the fact that up to twenty eggs may be fertilised from one stimulation cycle, while only two to three fertilised eggs are transferred back to the woman. Since most of the surplus fertilised eggs are cryopreserved for the benefit of patients for later replacement, the surplus is often restricted to those that are unused after the expiration of the limited time for cryopreservation (and to those of such poor morphology that they are not selected for cryopreservation). These may then be thawed and used for invasive research.

The caution which is suggested in this proposal will contribute to the restriction of the material available for research to those embryos that are left over after the conclusion of treatment cycles or the expiration of the time for cryopreservation. This proposal will also delimit this type of research from all types of animal research. Animals, which are used in research, are produced solely for the sake of research. The limitation also prevents eggs being harvested from other women than those who seek treatment.[47] The disadvantage of the limitation is that it is difficult to prevent women seeking treatment being susceptible to undue pressure to give up so-called surplus embryos for research.

At the same time it is clear that so-called surplus embryos are also created (or produced), though not primarily for the sake of research. The existing surplus is not conditioned by natural processes, but deliberately produced. If this is so, namely that embryos shall, to the extent possible, be used only in the context of treatment, a surplus may be avoided. This can be done for example by fertilising only the number of eggs which can be safely transferred back to the woman. Surplus eggs may also disappear as a result of the development of improved treatment procedures. In both cases the result will be that there is no surplus available for research.

To restrict research to surplus embryos also implies that there is a good deal of research that cannot be done. The type of research that can be done may be of relatively limited value, because there will be only multipronucleate (4-8 cell) embryos available. Nevertheless, research on spare embryos may yield useful information about the blastocyst stages (4-6 days), culture medias and alternative techniques for cryopreservation. The type of research that cannot be done will for instance relate to new treatment procedures in the case of male factor infertility, which may for example be attempted by depositing semen inside the egg by various techniques of micromanipulation.[48] In this case there is no purpose to doing research on surplus embryos. If poor quality semen are to be used in treatment, it seems to presuppose and require that invasive research is done to assess efficacy and safety. This type of research may yield significant results. In the long run it may lead to a diminished need for donor-insemination, including avoidance of some of the additional ethical problems implied in using donors.

I doubt whether there is a morally relevant distinction between the use of surplus or produced embryos in vitro. In my judgement the morally relevant difference is between invasive and observational research. To the extent invasive research is deemed acceptable the question of whether the research is done on surplus or produced embryos seems subordinate. Making use of produced embryos in invasive research will require clarification as to which women may be asked to give consent to give eggs for the sake of research. In accordance with commonly accepted guidelines for research ethics, the regard for women as patients should suggest the greater suitability of asking healthy adult women volunteers to give eggs, e.g. in conjunction with sterilisation. Their eggs may be fertilised with random semen to produce embryos for the sake of research. Whether invasive research as such is acceptable must be determined by the significance and need of this type of research, within the restraints proposed here.

Approval by research ethics committee. To ensure that any type of embryo research is significant and necessary, proposed research protocols should be submitted to a research ethics committee. With the exception of changed risk evaluation in regard to moral subjects, it seems that the remaining guidelines for research projects may equally be the basis for this type of research.

To the extent that this type of research is commonly acceptable, it carries with it one important advantage, that is that research centres must develop research protocols which are conducted according to reliable and scientific standards. It seems beyond doubt that there has been much unsystematic, observational research of the trial-and-error sort in clinical attempts to improve the techniques, without making the results available for scrutiny. For a research-based and responsible IVF practice it seems far more preferable for research to be subjected to the same standards as are commonly accepted in research ethics.

Prior evaluation by a research ethics committee also has the advantage that the interests of patients may be attended to, in order, among other things, to avoid patients being unduly pressured. It is possible to require written information for patients, and proper consent, on the basis of a research protocol. It is especially in regard to the interests of patients that it may be worthwhile recruiting eggs from healthy volunteers for the purpose of invasive research.

Acknowledgements

The author wishes to thank Svein Aage Christoffersen, Alex Mauron and Jon Wetlesen for critical comments on earlier drafts of this paper, and the Norwegian Research Council for its financial support.

Notes

1. The condition of viability has been central especially to legal reasoning, where it is stated that a foetus has no independent status and cannot acquire independent rights unless it obtains an independent existence. Various terms are used, such as capability to be born alive or born alive. Regardless of terms they are not easy to define precisely and they are open to various interpretations.

2. See e.g., Syse, Aslak, *Abortloven. Juss og verdier* Oslo, Ad Notam Gyldendal, 1993, p.309.

3. This opinion is held by, for example, The Catholic Church, Congregation for the Doctrine of the Faith, *Instruction on Respect for Human Life in Its Origin and on the Dignity of Procreation* Vatican City, Libreria Editrice Vaticana, 1987, and by some national committees.

4. This may of course be substantiated on philosophical grounds, supported by scientific knowledge. The classical Thomistic definition of personhood, "individuus subtantia rationalis naturae" may be interpreted to exclude embryos from personhood, since they may not be said to be individuals and they have no cortex. What conclusions may be drawn from the lack of moral status varies however. Mary Seller says e.g. that "[research on embryos] is not a problem for me because I do not consider the very early human embryo a human being". See 'The human embryo: a scientist's point of view' *Bioethics* 7, 1993, pp.135-40, p.139. Helga Kuhse and Peter Singer emphasise the idea that until any prenate has "the capacity to feel pleasure or pain...[it] does not have any interests and, ... cannot be harmed - in a morally relevant sense - by anything we do". See 'Individuals, humans and persons: the issue of moral status' in Singer, P., Kuhse, H., Buckle, S., Dawson, K. and Kasimba, P. (eds), *Embryo Experimentation. Ethical, Legal and Social Issues* Victoria, Australia, Cambridge University Press, 1990, pp.65-75, p.73. In the Thomistic tradition such a conclusion would not be evident. It is likely that proponents would consider research on embryos to be a moral problem, though not as serious as the taking of the lives of persons. This may be conjectured from traditional views of abortion. An early abortion before 40 or 80 days was considered a moral problem, but it was also deemed to be a less serious offence than later abortions. (In a religious context the difference was distinguished by referring to venial or mortal sins.) The same may be said about legal traditions, with their ancient demarcation of 'the capability of being born alive' as the characteristic of a human being with the full status of person. Before the time of viability damage or destruction to a foetus would be considered a 'great misprision', while it would be considered murder after viability.

5. A very interesting illustration of this is the various court decisions in *Davis v. Davis* in the U.S.A. concerning the moral status of seven embryos and the question of custody. Cf. *Davis v. Davis* The Ciruit Court for Blount County, Tennessee, at Maryville, 21 September 1989; The Court of Appeals of Tennessee, Eastern Section, 13 September 1990; The Supreme Court of Tennessee at Knoxville, 1 June, 1992.

6. In this I agree with Maurizio Mori who says "[I]t is not true that *if* the embryo is not a person, *then* we have practically no obligations towards it". See his 'Genetic selection and the status of the embryo' *Bioethics* 7, 1993, pp.141-48, p.142; and Solbakk, Jan Helge and de Cuzzani, Paola, 'Anfang und Ende des Lebens: Ecksteine für eine Ethik medizinischer Forschung' *Medizinische Klinik* 88, 1993, pp.595-98, p.598.

7. Jonsen, Albert R. and Toulmin, Stephen, *The Abuse of Casuistry* Berkeley, CA, University of California Press, 1988. See also Ruyter, Knut W., *Kasuistikk som saksbasert problemløsning i medisinsk etikk* (Casuistry as case based problem solving in medical ethics) (dissertation) Oslo, Universitetet i Oslo, 1995.

8. At the same time various forms of 'status' are rejected as grounds for different treatment for being morally irrelevant, for instance sex, race, religion, political convictions, and ownership of property.

9. Wetlesen, Jon, 'Moral status in environmental ethics. Exploring alternatives to anthropocentrism in a discourse ethics' unpublished manuscript, 1993.

10. *Ibid.*

11. The reasonableness refers to the context of the Declaration, which was drafted in the aftermath of the Second World War, to wit the heinous crimes against weak and vulnerable prisoners and against mentally retarded persons.

12. Wetlesen gives himself an indication of the possibility of this in Wetlesen *op. cit.* p.29. See also Gunnar Skirbekk for a very similar approach, arguing on the basis of a paradigmatically unique ethical standing for humans, discussing arguments in favour of an ethical gradualism between humans and other mammals. He also thinks that medical interventions into borderline cases of human existence have forced us to adopt a certain gradualism within the human species. See his 'Ethical gradualism?' in Gilje, N. (ed.), *Modernitet: differensiering og rasjonalisering* Bergen, Ariadne forlag, 1990, pp.26-74, p.30.

13. Probability is here used as an evaluative term of opinion in moral discourse, referring both to arguments in favour of the opinion, and to acceptance of the opinion by many or by experts. This usage is to be distinguished from the understanding of numerical measurements of probability, which underlie decision theory, e.g. in terms of statistical inferences.

14. See Chard, T., 'Frequency of implantation and early pregnancy loss in natural cycles' *Baillière's Clinical Obstetrics and Gynaecology* 5, 1991, pp.179-80.

15. More than twenty years ago the German theologian Karl Rahner asked whether moral theologians had the courage to hold on to the moment of conception as the moment for the beginning of individual human life, in the light of scientific knowledge reporting that more than 50% of all fertilised eggs will never succeed in attaching themselves to the womb: "Will [the moral theologian] be able to accept that 50% of 'human beings' - real human beings with immortal souls and eternal destiny - will never get beyond this first stage of human existence?". See 'The problem of genetic manipulation' *Theological Investigations* Vol. IX, New York, Herder and Herder, 1972, pp.225-52, here p.226, n.2.

16. See Grobstein, Clifford, *Science and the Unborn* New York, Basic Books, 1988. Identical twinning is said to occur in about one of each 270 pregnancies, while only a dozen or so human chimeras have been documented. See e.g. Moore, K., *The Developing Human* third edition, Philadelphia, PA, Saunders, 1982.

17. For a similar argument couched in theological terms, in relation to delayed animation, based on the conviction that the soul may not be infused before human life is 'formed', see Donceel, Joseph, 'Immediate animation and delayed hominization' *Theological Studies* 31, 1970, pp.76-105; Mahoney, John, *Bioethics and Belief* London, Sheed and Ward, 1984; Dunstan, G.R., 'The human embryo in the western moral tradition' in Dunstan, G.R. and Seller, M.J. (eds), *The Status of the Human Embryo. Perspectives From Moral Tradition* London, King Edward's Hospital Fund for London, 1988, pp.39-57; Ford, Norman M., *When Did I Begin?* Cambridge, Cambridge University Press, 1988; McCormick, Richard, 'Who or what is the preembryo?' *Kennedy Institute of Ethics Journal* 1, 1991, pp.1-15.

18. This was one of the finds of one of the first research projects on embryo experimentation. See Braude, P., Bolton, V. and Moore, S., 'Human gene expression first occurs between four and eight cell stage of preimplantation development' *Nature* 322, 1988, pp.459-61. As a basis for arguing that the moral status of the zygote must be different from the moral status of person, see Bedate, Carlos and Cefalo, Robert, 'The zygote: to be or not be a person' *The Journal of Medicine and Philosophy* 14, 1989, pp.641-45. Others have

submitted evidence to show that the embryo does not receive any message or information from the mother. See Suarez, Antoine, 'Hydatidiform moles and teratomas confirm the human identity of the preimplantation embryo', *The Journal of Medicine and Philosophy* 15, 1990, pp.627-35. Most disagree with Suarez on this point, but there is substantial disagreement over to what extent the embryo is dependent upon information from the mother.

19. Personal communication from Alex Mauron, 23 August 1994.

20. Mauron, Alex, 'The human embryo and the relativity of biological individuality' in this volume.

21. This is disputed, but at least one possible conclusion among several. Cf. Holm, Søren, 'The moral status of the pre-personal human being: the argument from potential reconsidered' in this volume.

22. See Department of Health and Social Security, *Report of the Committee of Inquiry into Human Fertilisation and Embryology* (the Warnock Report), London, Her Majesty's Stationary Office, 1984, p.27 and p.63.

23. Wetlesen, *op. cit.*, p.137.

24. Cited by Jan-Olav Henriksen, 'Hvordan begrunner vi menneskeverdet?' *Aftenposten* 2 May 1990.

25. See also Buckle, Stephen, 'Biological processes and moral events' in Singer, P. *et al* (eds), *op.cit.* pp.195-201.

26. Ford, Norman, 'Ethics, science and embryos: weighing the evidence' [letter] *The Tablet* 13 January 1990, p.46; cf. also his 'The case against destructive embryo research' in Dawson, K. and Hudson, J. (eds), *Proceedings of the Conference: IVF: The Current Debate* Victoria, Australia, Monash Center for Human Bioethics, 1987, pp.90-95; and his *When Did I Begin?*, *op.cit.*, p.62. In the last the reference is rather to "prudential certitude".

27. Congregation for the Doctrine of the Faith, *op.cit.*.

28. The National Committee for Medical Research Ethics in Norway, *Research on Fetuses* Oslo, The Norwegian Research Council for Science and the Humanities, 1990.

29. *Ibid.*, p.24. By 'fetus' the Committee means all stages of foetal development, from the fusion of the egg and sperm to the completed birth.

30. *Ibid.*, p.21.

31. *Ibid.*, p.22.

32. The same argument can be made within a religious context, in which the time of animation decides full moral status. When there is serious doubt about ontological status, the doubt cannot translate into a certain moral opinion. See especially Tauer, Carol, 'The tradition of probabilism and the moral status of the early embryo' *Theological Studies* 45, 1984, pp.3-33; cf. McCormick, *op.cit.*, p.11; Mahoney, *op.cit.*, passim.

33. Ford, Norman, 'Ethics, science and the embryo' *The Tablet* 3 February 1990, pp.141-42; cf. also his 'The case against' *op.cit.*, p.94.

34. See e.g., Rahner, *op.cit.*, p.236.

35. In the following I treat only the use of embryos in research. Other areas are the use of embryos as part of treatment, including embryo selection and embryo cryopreservation.

36. Kuhse and Singer, *op.cit.*, p.74.

37. Ministry of Health and Social Affairs, *Biotechnology Related to Human Beings. Report No. 25 (1992-1993)* Oslo, Ministry of Health and Social Affairs, 1993, p.31. The English translation is an abbreviated version of the parliamentary report.

38. See e.g., Mauron, Alex, 'What developments of human embryo research would be philosophically challenging?' in this volume.

39. *Ibid.*, p.285, with reference to the work of Braude *et al* showing that embryonic genome activation occurs at the 4-8 cell stage, which is much later than in e.g. mouse development (Braude, P., Bolton, V. and Moore, S., 'Human gene expression first occurs between the four- and eight-cell stage of preimplantation development' *Nature* 332, 1988, pp.459-461).

40. Mauron, *ibid.*, p.287.

41. This is an attempt to classify various *types* of research, in line with common distinctions between non-therapeutic and therapeutic research. This may seem to be an obvious and simple point, but when for example the World Medical Association concluded that embryo research is acceptable in some circumstances, it does not say anything about the circumstances. See 'Helsinki statement on human *in vitro* fertilization' *Annals of the New York Academy of Sciences* 442, 1985, pp.571-2.

42. The latter requirement is tricky, since it is not always obvious who the subject is. In the following I presuppose that the embryo is the subject, but especially within category 2, in the area of clinical research, it is worth noting that the woman may also be considered the subject.

43. Broad spectrum basic research of this type may include endocrine studies and ovarian paracrinology.

44. The broad interpretation of methodological research raises a number of other ethical problems, which deserve a thorough and separate discussion in their own right.

45. See e.g., Trounson, Alan, 'Why do research on human pre-embryos?' in Singer *et al* (eds), *op.cit.*, pp.14-25, here pp.15-16. In clinical research the woman, to whom the embryo will be transferred, is also a research subject, with obvious interests of her own.

46. Ministry of Health and Social Affairs, *op.cit.*, p.33.

47. Other sources may be eggs from women donating eggs, or from women seeking sterilisation, or oogonia from aborted foetuses.

48. Such as microinjection, zona drilling, zona opening and zona cutting.

13. THE MORAL STATUS OF THE PRE-PERSONAL HUMAN BEING

The Argument From Potential Reconsidered

Søren Holm
Department of Medical Philosophy and Clinical Theory
University of Copenhagen
Blegdamsvej 3
DK-2200 N
Copenhagen
Denmark

1. Introduction

The moral status of the human fertilised egg, embryo, foetus and infant is at the centre of the bioethical debate on abortion, infanticide and the new reproductive techniques. This question of status is often considered under the heading of person or non-person, and this philosophical distinction has therefore acquired important performative aspects. To declare someone or something a person, is to include them in the moral community, and confer upon them all moral rights, including the right not to be killed. Whereas to declare someone or something a non-person is to say that they are to some degree outside the moral community and outside the realm of moral rights. Several philosophers have pursued this line of argument, and held that the property conferring personhood upon a being is some specific mental capacity (in this paper referred to as the radical view of personhood, or simply the radical view). This view is presented most fully in books by Engelhardt, Glover, Harris, Singer and Tooley[1], and has in recent years been defended in articles by numerous authors. Apart from Engelhardt these philosophers all belong to the consequentialist/utilitarian tradition and espouse some form of preference utilitarianism.

There is no absolute agreement between these philosophers as to the necessary and sufficient conditions for obtaining status as a person, but all the definitions put forward definitely exclude any human being before the age of about 6 months. As a consequence of this, abortion, foetal experimentation and even infanticide become morally innocuous if the procedure involved does not cause pain to the non-personal human being.

The radical view stands thereby in sharp contrast to the common-sense view which can perhaps best be described as gradualist, since it incorporates the notion that the moral status of a developing human being gradually grows, and that there is no specific point at which moral status is attained.

D. Evans (ed.), Conceiving the Embryo, 193–220.
© 1996 Kluwer Law International. Printed in the Netherlands.

It is tempting immediately to disregard the radical view and claim that it is a classic example of a *reductio ad absurdum*, that is the claim that any set of premises and philosophical ideas leading to the conclusion that infanticide is not only permissible in some highly specific circumstances but generally morally innocuous, *a priori* disqualifies itself from serious consideration.

This claim is, however, unlikely to persuade people holding the radical view of personhood referred to above, not necessarily because it is a bad argument, but because the proponents of the radical view hold that you must follow your ethical views to their logical conclusion, accepting all their consequences, however apparently counter-intuitive. If a counter argument is to be effective it will have to be intelligible to the people it is directed against, and must therefore in its constructive parts take its point of departure more or less within the ethical theories held by the proponents of the radical view.

Initially conceding that preference utilitarianism is the 'correct' conception of morality will lead to the demise of the project of discussing the moral status of the human embryo, because if preferences are the only thing that matters, then all beings without preferences (including many pre-personal human beings) are automatically excluded from moral consideration. But - as I will try to show - there is no obvious reason to make this concession. But to be convincing the argument has to proceed along mainly consequentialist lines. It is a debate where few conclusive and compelling arguments can be adduced on either side, so what we are engaged in is perhaps better described as rational persuasion.

1.1. THE RADICAL VIEW OF PERSONHOOD

The basic structure of the arguments employed in favour of the radical view on personhood is along the following lines:
1. There is a property X which makes a being morally important, or gives a being a right to life, or makes it wrong to kill a being.
2. For reasons A,B,C etc., X must be rationality, or a wish to live, or ability to conceive oneself as a being with temporal existence, or ability to understand simple moral arguments.
3. It can be shown that human beings below the age of Y lack X.
Therefore
4. Human beings below the age of Y are not morally important etc.

The argument from the potential of the pre-personal human being tries to dispute the first of these premises, by arguing for the claim that:
p1. A being which has the potential to become or obtain X has equivalent moral importance to a being which is or has X;
or
p1a. a being which has the potential to become or obtain X has sufficient moral importance to have a right not to be killed.
p2. Human fertilised eggs, embryos, foetuses and infants have the potential to become

or obtain X.

Therefore

p3. Human fertilised eggs, embryos, foetuses and infants are morally important etc.

To carry the field the proponents of the argument from potential have to show four things:

a. That it is not *only* beings which are or have X that can be morally important etc.

b. That being a potential X is morally important.

c. That adopting this view does not lead to logical inconsistencies.

d. That adopting this view does not entail even more counterintuitive actual consequences than the radical view.

Part 2 of this paper will concern itself with the problem of whether *only* having or being X is what gives moral importance. Part 3 will discuss what it means to say that some entity has potential to become something else. Part 4 will discuss if and why potential is morally important and part 5 will look at the consequences of adopting the argument from potential. Finally part 6 will sum up the arguments presented and try to state a coherent conclusion.

2. Desires and Moral Values

2.1. WHO HAS MORAL IMPORTANCE?

The initial obstacle that a proponent of the argument from potential has to overcome is to show, that it is not *only* those beings who possess the special property conferring personhood who can have moral importance. It is obvious that human beings in the early stages of their development are not persons in the requisite sense, and if it was true that *only* persons could have moral importance, then human beings in these early developmental stages could obviously have no moral importance.

Tooley puts forward a specific moral principle concerning the ascription of rights to show that a right to life can be ascribed only to persons. He states that:

> It is a conceptual truth that an entity cannot have a particular right R unless it is at least capable of having some interest I which is furthered by its having right R.[2]

From this he derives the idea that A has a right to X means the same as

> A is capable of wanting X, and if A does want X, others are under a prima-facie obligation to refrain from actions that would deprive him of it.[3]

It is clear that this principle restricts the holding of rights to those individuals which are at least capable of having desires, and as such it is a cornerstone of Tooley's constructive argument for his position. If the initial assertion of a 'conceptual truth' concerning the ascription of rights were correct, then the derivation of the want or desire description of rights might be correct.

That a desire for a state of affairs X is sufficient to bring about even a *prima facie* right to X can be true only if the concept of *prima facie* rights is stretched beyond its limits. It is absurd to claim that a murderer has even a *prima facie* right to kill, or a thief a right to steal, just because they want to perform these acts.[4] But this does of course not touch the assertion that a desire for a state of affairs X may be necessary to have a right to X.

It is important to realise that the derivation from the first principle relies on a specific narrow concept of interest, according to which a being can only be said to have an interest I, if it is capable of wanting I. But this seems to exclude a wide range of important interests and their corresponding rights. Although most six year olds are capable of wanting to go to school, many of them do not actually have this desire, and it seems strange that their right to schooling should depend on such a desire. And in general it is an invalid claim that a given right depends on a specific desire. If I have a right to the best health care available (for instance because I have bought the best available insurance policy), then I have the right to the best health care available, even though it may be a mode of treatment I cannot conceive of, and therefore cannot desire.[5]

It might therefore be suggested, that the following statement is more in agreement with the general conception of a right:

> It is a conceptual truth that an entity cannot have a particular right R unless it has some interest I (interest here used also in the non-psychological sense) which is furthered by its having right R.

Or to state it in terms of obligation:

> It is a conceptual truth that an entity cannot have a particular obligation O towards another entity unless this other entity has some interest I (interest here used also in the non-psychological sense) which is furthered by obligation O being discharged.

If it is possible to have an interest in a state of affairs without actually wanting it, then there is no logical reason to exclude the notion of obligations toward non-personal entities.

2.2. IS THERE MORE TO MORALITY THAN DESIRES?

Tooley and most other defenders of the radical view adhere to a uniform theory of value according to which all moral value can ultimately be reduced to one common currency (e.g. in Tooley's case desire satisfaction), but there are important reasons to doubt that this reduction is possible. There may be no common moral currency and in that case there may not be a single property which confers moral status within all moral spheres.

Thomas Nagel has consistently argued that the reduction of moral value to one common currency is only possible from the detached objective point of view, where all personal subjectivity is left behind.[6] This is the vantage point often sought by moral philosophers, but to claim that it is the only relevant vantage point may be a serious mistake. Every one of us is inextricably bound up in a subjective existence, and a morality which does not incorporate this subjective point of view is impoverished. This is most vividly illustrated when we consider the question of why life is valuable. Seen from the detached objective point of view, it is very difficult to establish any value in life, and the following four propositions become very plausible:

1. The real nature of things is that which is seen from a cosmic or ultimate perspective.
2. To view things rationally is to view them from the cosmic point of view.
3. When things are viewed rationally (i.e., from the cosmic point of view), they are seen to be lacking in value.
4. To attribute value to something is irrational.[7]

There are good reasons to try to attain some detachment from my present subjective existence, when I evaluate and weigh present desires against longterm interests and future desires, but proposition number 2. above is simply not true. The cosmic perspective is often irrelevant to the daily decisions we make, because it provides no guidance as to what acts to perform. If I have to choose between two flavours of icecream, it would be irrational to do it from the cosmic perspective, because it leaves out the very factors that are important to my choice (i.e. my preferences). My preferences are definitely subjective, but they are the very material upon which reason operates. There is therefore no possibility of excluding the subjective and claiming that rationality coincides with the objective point of view.

Nagel suggests that although agent-neutral consequentialism, derived from the objective point of view, is the correct description of a significant form of moral concern we owe to others, there may well be at least three types of agent-relative reasons, which enter the moral equation from the subjective point of view:

The first type of reason stems from the desires, projects, commitments and personal ties of the individual agent, all of which give him reasons to act in the pursuit of ends that are his own. These I shall collect under the general heading of reasons of autonomy (not to be confused with the autonomy of free will).

The second type of reason stems from the claims of other people not to be maltreated in certain ways. What I have in mind are not neutral reasons for anyone to bring it about that no one is maltreated, but relative reasons for each individual not to maltreat others himself, in his dealings with them (for example by violating their rights, breaking his promises to them, etc.). These I shall collect under the general, ugly, and familiar heading of deontology. Autonomous reasons would limit what we are obliged to do in the service of impersonal values.

Deontological reasons would limit what we are *permitted* to do in the service of either impersonal or autonomous ones.

The third type of reason stems from the special obligations we have towards those to whom we are closely related: parents, children, spouses, siblings, fellow members of a community or even a nation. Most people would acknowledge a noncontractual obligation to show special concern for some of these others - though there would be disagreement about the strength of the reasons and the width of the net. I'll refer to them as reasons of obligation, even though they don't include a great many obligations that are voluntarily undertaken.[8]

It is immediately obvious, that no single natural property gives moral importance within all of the three types of agent-relative moral reasons identified by Nagel. Being me is what gives moral importance in the realm of reasons of autonomy, being a member of the moral community gives moral importance in the realm of deontological reasons and standing in some partly natural, partly cultural relations to me gives moral importance in the realm of reasons of obligation. We may well follow Nagel in doubting that his typology of agent-relative moral reasons is correct in its present form, but if any agent-relative moral reasons are admitted as legitimate into our moral reasoning, then there is no *a priori* reason to believe that the properties giving moral importance will be coincident with the properties giving moral importance in the realm of agent-neutral moral reasons.

2.3. MORALITY AND NATURAL PROPERTIES

The properties advanced by the proponents of the radical view as the properties which divide between persons and non-persons are all, at least in theory, objectively discernable. We can devise tests to show whether a given being wishes to live or understands simple morality. It is often argued that natural stages and social rites occurring during the development of the pre-personal human being cannot form the basis for a moral difference, because only properties belonging to the being in question should matter "... since whether an entity is a potential person should depend only on its properties, not upon its relations to other things".[9]

But this may again be because of an unallowable reduction to the objective point of view. It is no good saying that the birth of the baby cannot conceivably give rise to a change in moral status, because it cannot matter whether the same being is inside or outside the woman's body (it not being a property of the being), if we actually know on the subjective level, that it does matter because it alters relationships and obligations. The ultimate objective description may not always be the one which gives the correct picture of reality or of the moral consequences of acts.[10] My evening meal may be described as a nice piece of gammon, or more objectively as a piece of dead pig's buttock, but it is not clear which of these two descriptions give the best picture of reality. And there is a huge difference between describing an act as 'stealing 4 grams of 14 carat gold' and 'stealing Mr. Jones's wedding ring' or between 'stealing 10 pennies worth of edible material' and 'stealing the last piece of bread in the life boat'. There is even a crucial moral difference between 'stealing one of goldsmith Jones's many wedding rings' and 'stealing carpenter Jones's only wedding ring'.

The morality of an act may crucially depend on the description from the subjective point of view. It is therefore not always a legitimate move to take a certain distinction and apply it in a thought example where specific features are changed. This is especially true if the example involves radical changes in the nature of the world or in well known natural processes. Our intuitive moral judgments are developed in and based on the world as it presently is, and if the world that we are asked to imagine is too different, no argumentative value can be placed on our judgment. The strangeness in the judgment may well reflect the strangeness of the imagined situation[11], as is probably the case when two such eminent philosophers as Michael Tooley and Richard Hare report diametrically opposed intuitions about Tooley's famous kitten example.[12]

Standing in a special relationship to somebody else or having a specific symbolic meaning is not a property of a given thing which can be detected by studying the thing in itself, but is a function of its existence in interaction with other things in the world. There is no way in which we can deduce directly from a specific arrangement of wood and gold that it is a religious symbol (e.g. a crucifix or a buddha statue), and thereby assess its true value, unless we allow its symbolic importance to enter our considerations. Likewise banknotes are just pieces of paper, and there is no way of discovering the difference in value between one issued by the Bank of England and one issued by the Confederate States of America just by paying attention to its purely intrinsic properties.

Some of the strongest, and therefore most important, relationships are formed within families, and yet we seem unable to give them any real moral value, as long as we proceed from the objective point of view. How can the simple fact that I am the son of these parents give us any special responsibilities towards each other. I don't owe my parents anything, and am only obliged to help them if we are still friends, and only to the extent that I would help other friends.[13] Henry Sidgwick was led towards the same conclusion but evaded it by stating "We not only find it hard to say exactly how much a son owes his parents, but we are even reluctant to investigate this".[14]

Seen from the first-personal subjective point of view, we know that these relationships matter, but from the objective point of view it is exceedingly difficult to show why.[15] From the subjective point of view, the most important consideration is probably the fact, that most pre-personal human beings originate because of decisions taken by persons, as a critic of Tooley has remarked:

> In the real moral world origins matter and so does the social context. In particular the fact that babies are produced by moral agents capable of voluntary obligations to them matters vitally. Tooley's procedure for determining a right to life is simplistic, and fatally so for the neonate. He seems to believe that all one needs to do is inspect a human infant or nonhuman adult for its right-making characteristics; but where babies come from is morally significant.[16]

It is undoubtedly true that some pre-personal human beings are created by accident, but most are either created deliberately or as a foreseeable by-product of certain pleasurable human activities, and all IVF embryos are of course created deliberately. Although being created deliberately is not an objective property of an entity, that can be detected by studying the entity in isolation, it is of no less moral importance.

What an entity is, and what determines its moral importance, is as the examples given above show, not only dependent on the properties of the entity, but also on its relationships to other entities. We cannot *a priori* discount any aspect of these relationships simply by claiming them to be 'not a property of the entity'. To do so will lead to the neglect of important aspects of the real world, and an impoverished ethics.

3. What is Potential?

The meaning of the sentence P: 'The entity X has a potential P to become Y', is essentially ambiguous until the precise meaning of the two concepts 'entity' and 'potential' and their interrelationship has been spelled out.

The concept of potential has strong interrelations with the concept of possibility, so we could try to explicate P as: 'It is logically possible for the entity X to become Y'. But since it is logically possible for most things to become most other things (e.g. for the moon to become a giant cone of strawberry icecream), this does not capture the meaning of the sentence.

A second try could then be to apply the concept of practical possibility and claim the meaning of P to be: 'It is practically possible for the entity X to become Y'. This seems to capture more of the meaning of P, but we then have to explain the exact concept of practical possibility used in this connection.

It will not do to exchange likelihood for practical possibility leading to 'There is a certain likelihood for the entity X to become Y', for though likelihood plays a role in the concept of potentiality it is only a minor role. It is perfectly possible to talk about the likelihood of actualising a potential, whereas it is plain nonsense to talk of the likelihood of actualising a likelihood.

When we talk about greater and lesser potentials we do not in common parlance mean greater or lesser likelihood of fulfilling the potential but the possibility of fulfilling greater or lesser potentials. A centre forward with great potential is a centre forward who may become extremely good at playing this position in a soccer team, while a centre forward with lesser potential will probably never be as good, although they may have the same likelihood of fulfilling their different potentials. In this sense potential is all or nothing, something either has or has not a certain potential.

We find, on the other hand, that likelihood has some role to play, since the ascription of potential seems to lose its sense if the actual likelihood of its actualisation is very low under any conceivable circumstances. It seems true that something cannot have the potential to become something else, if it does not have any possibility of becoming so (likelihood 0). It may however be impossible to state this criterion more precisely because every line drawn will be open to arguments of the *sorites* kind. But this of course does not indicate that no line can be drawn. The required likelihood for actualisation for a valid ascription of potential is probably very low, since we can make at least some sense of the suggestion, that an acorn which is presently part of someone's souvenir collection still has the potential for becoming an oak, even though its likelihood for being able to actualise this potential is very low.[17]

Another aspect of the notion of potential which is not captured by the substitution of possibility for potential is that for an entity X to have the potential to become Y, at least some steps in this transformation must be controlled or co-controlled by the entity itself; it must possess some intrinsic capacity for the development in question.[18] This excludes some practical possible transformations of an entity X from being constitutive of a potential of X. To take an example, the letters of the words of this paper could be rearranged so as to form a science fiction novel, but this possible transformation does not give this paper the potential of becoming a science fiction novel (or so I hope), because every step in the transformation would be externally controlled.

Kottow has argued, that potentiality in the case of living organisms should be understood as " ... the set of future developments that can be read out of the present state of an organism".[19] Using this definition Kottow describes two fallacies which in his view often affect the ascription of potential to a given entity, 'borrowing' and 'skipping'. Borrowing occurs when the potential of the entity in itself is conflated with the joint potential of the entity and its environment, and skipping when the potentialities of late and early stages in a given development are conflated, thereby ascribing greater potential to the earlier stages of development than is actually warranted by the properties of the entity at these early stages.

Kottow's description of the concept of potential is, however, problematic because it leads to the conclusion that potentiality can never be ascribed to any entity in a non-stable environment. It is probably correct that external influences cannot create potential, but they can certainly destroy it, and given the ubiquitous nature of external influences it seems doubtful whether any prospective states or actions can be directly derived *solely* from analysing a given being without the hidden premiss that the environment in which the being exists is stable and will not interfere with the development of the being. It is easy to think of examples of situations where such a stable environment exists, but difficult to find any which has any relevance to the development of biological organisms on earth. Even if such examples could be found, they would share in the alleged fallacy of borrowing, since they would borrow the property of environmental non-interference from the environment.

If any realistic content is to be left in the concept of potentiality, it is therefore necessary to allow requirements of certain states of the environment/nature to enter the ascription of potentiality. For biological organisms the first such requirement which springs to mind is the requirement of natural surroundings, leading to the statement: 'The entity X has a potential P for becoming Y, if given natural surroundings it is practically possible (or at least minimally likely) for X to become Y'. This move will inevitably be resisted by anybody who holds the view that ethical theory should encompass only the objective view. Such a person could, with some right, claim that the term 'natural surroundings' is inherently so vague and misleading that it would be impossible to agree on what constitutes natural surroundings; and that even if agreement could be reached, the natural surroundings, and thereby the potential and moral status, of a given kind of entity would be liable to change over time.[20] And seen solely from the objective point of view all this seems initially true. The whole raison d'etre of the human species appears to be the conquest and control of nature, and concepts like normality, natural kind, and natural development sound terribly outdated. It would be possible to incorporate this in ascriptions of potentiality as: 'The entity X has a potential P for becoming Y, if given optimal surroundings it is practically possible (or at least minimally likely) for X to become Y'. And 'optimal surroundings' could be given a clear meaning by defining them as the best surroundings which are currently available, given the present status of knowledge.[21] (On the importance of possible future developments, see below.)

But it is questionable whether it is necessary to give up all reliance on the concept of 'natural surroundings'. No ethical theory can escape making some assumptions about normality and the nature of the human species. A classical utilitarian relies on the 'natural' fact that all beings like pleasure and hate pain, and the preference utilitarian relies on the fact that all beings 'naturally' like getting what they want, and that they do not 'normally' change their minds or regret their enjoyment.[22]

It is also important to note that the claim that the sentence 'the entity X has a potential P to become Y' should be understood as 'given natural surroundings it is practically possible (or at least minimally likely) for X to become Y', does not rest on an identification of the natural as the morally best.

In the case of the developing pre-personal human being (especially if created *in vitro*) it is evident, that human decisions play a large role in determining whether or not the potential will be actualised. Humans decide whether an embryo should be implanted, discarded or experimented upon, or whether a foetus should be aborted or allowed to develop further. It has been pointed out, that the further development of embryos created *in vitro* requires active human intervention, and that any notion of 'natural development' is inapplicable to such embryos, whose potential is therefore fully determined by human decisions (thereby destroying any moral force of the notion of potential).[23] But if the interpretation of potential advanced above is accepted either in its 'natural surroundings' or 'optimal surroundings' form, then this objection loses its force, because, whereas it will then still be true that the actualisation of the potential of an embryo would depend on human interventions, it would not be true that the potential as such at any given point depended on human interventions.

The fallacy of skipping, as identified by Kottow, touches upon the epistemology of the ascription of potential, and can best be explained by referring to a point raised earlier about the relationship between potential and probability. If we say about a human foetus that it is potentially a great philosopher, we have committed the fallacy of skipping. It might be that it actually will develop into a great philosopher, but at this stage in its development we do not normally have sufficient evidence to put forward such a statement. It is no more likely to have the potential to become a great philosopher than to become a great athlete. If the parents of the foetus were both great philosophers or if we could detect 'philosophers' genes' in its DNA, then the ascription of potential would be more defensible. This example shows that we cannot in general ascribe potential if we cannot give reasons for the ascription. Every ascription of potential must rest on a rational explanation of why we believe this potential and not some other potential to be present.

A further problem is presented by the notion of 'distributed' or 'joint' potential. In what sense can we attribute potential to an entity consisting of two or more separate physical parts? And is there any sense in which sperm and egg taken separately (apart from the possibility of parthenogenesis) have the potential for personhood?

There seems to be no problem in ascribing potential to large conglomerates of people. It makes perfect sense to state that: 'Montgomery's army has the potential to defeat Rommel's army'.[24] But we cannot go from there to the statement that private Smith *qua* member of Montgomery's army has the potential to defeat Rommel's army. And even if we reduce the subdivisions of Montgomery's army into only two, armoured vehicles and infantry, it is still not true that either of these two subdivisions has the potential to defeat Rommel's army. This potential only exists because the subdivisions stand in a specific spatial and temporal relationship to each other. If Montgomery's armoured vehicles were in Cairo and not at El Alamein, his army would not have the potential to defeat Rommel. If the two parts of the army were not arranged in the proper spatial relationship, then it would not be possible to ascribe it the potential, since it would then involve the counterfactual 'if they were arranged so and so, then....'.

In the same way sperm and egg placed in the appropriate medium in a petri-dish can be said to possess the potential for personhood, because they stand in that relationship to each other which creates the potential. But if they are not spatially arranged so as to allow fertilisation there can be no ascription of potential, because an entity of the required kind has not been created. The claim made by Singer and Wells that "Everything that can be said about the potential of the embryo can also be said about the potential of the egg and sperm when separate but considered jointly"[25] is not true. A pair of sperm and egg, do not obtain potential for personhood just because we can *consider* them jointly. Our ability to consider things jointly is inexhaustible, but considering myself jointly with the gold in the Bank of England, does not in any way alter my actual possibility or my potential for paying my rent, and the fact that I can consider myself equipped with immense strength, the ability to fly and the ability to travel in time does not make me morally culpable for the demise of the Titanic. Likewise we can consider every single spermatozoon together with the one egg in the dish, but that does not make all 50,000 or so into potential persons. We know that only one fertilised egg will emerge from this dish, and that there is therefore (disregarding the possibility of later segmentation of the fertilised egg or embryo) maximally one potential person, although there may well be 50,000 possible persons. It is not sufficient to be able to consider a state of affairs - human beings can even consider states of affairs which are logically impossible - the state of affairs must also be practically possible for any potential to be created. The argument for the joint potential for personhood of sperm and egg could, however, also be put in the following way: sperm and egg have the joint potential to become a fertilised egg, a fertilised egg has the potential to become a person, therefore sperm and egg have the potential to become a person. The second premiss of this argument is assumed to be correct by most proponents of the argument from potential, and the only possibility of rejecting the argument is therefore to show that the first premiss is wrong. But how could that be? Every fertilised egg originates from a pair of sperm and egg, so if anything has the potential to become a fertilised egg it must be the pair of sperm and egg, because it is implausible to claim that nothing has this potential, since some eggs do actually become fertilised. This is further supported by the fact that it is not obviously incoherent to exclaim 'Oh, what a waste of potential!' after an intercourse where contraceptive measures have been used. At the same time it is obvious that not any given pair of sperm and egg has this potential, if there is no practical way in which they can be brought together (i.e. Cleopatra and Napoleon did not[26] have the joint potential to beget children, although they presumably had sufficient amounts of eggs and sperm between them). It is also the case, that although the sentence 'X and Y have the joint potential to become Z' is true now, this does not entail that the sentence 'X and Y will have the joint potential to become Z tomorrow' was necessarily true yesterday because, as Ockham realised in the 14th century, there are no necessary truth connections between the two sentences 'It is today true that X is the case' and 'It was yesterday true that X would be the case today'.[27] Ascription of potential is always prospective not retrospective, and from the fact that I am *now* able to see that something yesterday had the potential to become an entity which exists today, I cannot validly infer that I could or should have ascribed that potential yesterday. To take an example from the very similar language game of academic promise, from the fact that X is an eminent philosopher now, we cannot validly infer that she showed great academic promise as a student. Her tutors may very well, on the evidence they had at the time, have been justified in saying 'she is not really a very promising student'. It may well be the case, therefore, that at a certain moment in time there was nothing which had the potential to become a given fertilised egg, even though the spermatozoon and egg-cell, which would eventually meet, were both physically existant and mature. (For example, the sperm and egg from which I was conceived did not have the prospective potential to become a fertilised egg the day before I was conceived, if I was conceived as the result of an unplanned one night stand.) For any given pair of sperm and egg, we will have to produce reasons why an ascription of joint potential to them will be correct in the present situation. It does not, therefore, follow from the fact that some egg and sperm pair has the joint potential to become a fertilised egg, that egg and sperm as such have the joint potential to become a fertilised egg, and the first premiss above is therefore false. One could try to get over this problem by describing either sperm or egg as part of the natural surroundings for the other gamete, but it seems highly artificial to describe an entity carrying half of the genetic blueprint as a part of the environment, and one would have to oscillate between the 'joint potential' and the 'natural surroundings' description to explain the potential of sperm and egg.

The same sort of argument applies to the question of in what way the possibility of future technological progress influences the moral status of present entities. To take an example, does the possibility of the development of techniques to induce parthenogenesis in human egg-cells alter their present moral status? The first point to notice is that, even if parthenogenesis occurs in some animal species, there is no certainty that we will ever be able to produce it in human eggs. The possibility of parthenogenesis is therefore only a *logical* possibility and has as such no direct purchase on our moral judgments. If there is no way in which the future *logical* possibility changes our present *practical/real* possibilities then it is irrelevant to our moral responses.[28] The possibility that parthenogenesis will be available in the future does not, therefore, influence the present status of single human egg-cells. If, however, parthenogenesis should become possible, then every human egg-cell would become a potential person if the 'optimal surroundings' account of potential for biological entities is accepted, whereas it is unclear what its status would be under the 'natural surroundings' account.

Quinn has argued that parthenogenesis should not be conceived as a change in the egg, but as a transformation of the egg into a new organism with a different nature.[29] If this view is accepted then eggs would not be potential persons, even if parthenogenesis was possible. Singer and Dawson dismiss this argument, but seem to have misunderstood it slightly:

> … Warren Quinn suggests that in this situation the environmental agent producing parthenogenetic development can be treated as a prefertilization entity that is incorporated into the 'zygote' at the onset of development. In this way, he seeks to preserve the view that even if parthenogenesis occurs, the egg alone is not a potential person; it becomes a potential person only when parthenogenetic development has been triggered. But Quinn's suggestion does not succeed in marking a distinction between the egg and the embryo. For the embryo also needs a specific environment if it is to develop, and if the particular environment which leads to parthenogenesis is allowed to count as an entity for the purposes of denying potential to the egg on its own outside that environment, then the particular environment which leads to the development of the embryo must also be allowed to count as an entity, and we should deny potential to the embryo on its own outside that environment.[30]

What Quinn claims, if I understand him correctly, is that a given entity can rightly be said to *develop* into another entity only if the two entities share the same nature and plan, and that neither the egg nor the spermatozoon is of the same nature as the zygote and later developmental stages. His argument does not depend on describing the parthenogenic environment as an entity in contrast to the environment of the embryo, but on the claim that whereas the development of the embryo is development according to its nature and plan, the transition from egg to embryo is no part of the nature and plan of the egg but a radical transformation and the creation of a new form of life. Quinn's argument is therefore not defeated by Singer and Dawson's objections, but its plausibility rests on a set of specific assumptions concerning the nature of human gametes and embryos that are not widely accepted.

4. Why Value Potential?

It is a logical truth that the sentences 'X is A' and 'X is potentially A' are not equivalent. No syllogistic reasoning can therefore establish the link between 'X is potentially A', 'A has a right B' and 'X has a right B' without further premisses.

The first step is therefore to make it plausible that potential to become something may entail rights or give moral importance, thereby supplying the additional premiss 'X being potentially A confers on X the rights or moral importance of A'.

Several authors have tried to show that this step cannot be accomplished without introducing a logical error:

> What follows from potential qualification ... is potential, not actual, rights; what entails actual rights is actual, not potential, qualification. As the Australian philosopher Stanley Benn puts it, "A potential president of the United States is not on that account Commander-in-Chief".[31]

It is true that being a potential president of the United States it not sufficient to have an absolute claim upon the administrative prerogatives of the presidency, but this is not because intelligible claims cannot be made, but because the American legal system (not unwisely) is designed to ensure that only one claim to these wide ranging powers is *legally* recognised at any given time. Because of its very nature the presidency can be held by only one person at a time, whereas a great, although not unlimited, number of beings can hold (and exercise) a right to life simultaneously.

Benn's counterexample falsifies the premiss 'being a potential A always gives all the same rights as being an A', but this is not the only additional premiss which can be used in presenting a valid argument from the premiss 'X is potentially A' to the conclusion that X is as morally important as A, or that X has some subset of the rights of A.

In everyday life potential does play a role. Parents try to spot the potentials of their children and encourage the development of those potentials which they think will lead to greater fulfillment in the lives of their children. There even seems to be an obligation incumbent on parents to develop these potentials, sometimes even against the wishes or preferences of their children. Not encouraging the development of this kind of potential is incompatible with the role of parenting. It would be difficult to understand a parent who said 'I think my child has the potential to become a good musician, but we won't encourage her to develop this potential', if she did not carry on with saying 'because we think she will be better off if ...'. The child may at present have no preferences or desires for the development of a given potential, but we nevertheless often see encouraging this development as morally important.

But in our daily experience we also observe that whereas potential to become some things seems to give certain rights, other potentials seem to be considered insignificant. As John Harris has pointed out, one of my most certain potentials is the potential for being dead (it carries a 100% chance of being actualised), but nevertheless I am not, and would not like to be, treated as if I were already dead.[32]

Is there any dividing line between those potentials we take as valid reasons for action and those potentials we ignore? And if there is, are there then independent reasons why such a dividing line is defensible in itself?

A possible typology of morally important potentials could be in 3 x 2 categories (for a different typology see Seedhouse[33]) where one axis divides potentials into those which are potentials for morally good developments in the psychology of the entity, the morally neutral and those which are potentials for morally bad developments, and the other axis divides between potentials for developments causing harm to the entity and potentials for developments doing good.

	Harm	Good
Morally good		Development of morality
Morally neutral	Death?	Development of general potentials (artistic, scholarly, etc.)
Morally bad	Development of criminal potential?	Development of criminal potential?

Development of potentials causing moral goodness in the entity or good consequences for the entity is normally encouraged, whereas development of harmful potentials is resisted, and development of morally bad potentials actively discouraged.

Society does, then, see the potential for being dead as important, but it acts to prevent its actualisation through supporting and restoring health, since the actualisation of this potential is (normally) seen to be harmful for the entity. The promotion of morally good developments in the entity, the promotion of developments doing good to the entity, the prevention of morally bad developments and the prevention of harmful developments can all be seen to be beneficent actions. This typology of moral values can also explain why we do not act upon potentials for moral badness in the entity in the same way that we act towards actualised moral badness. For whereas it is arguably just to punish transgressors, it is unjust to punish beings who have not yet transgressed, and their transgressions should instead be prevented.

The fact that it is possible to explain our attitudes towards potential in this way still does not give an independent justification for why potential, and especially potential in non-personal entities, is important.

Richard Hare has suggested such a justification based on the 'Golden Rule'. He extends the rule from 'do to others as you would wish them to do to you' to 'do to others what you are glad was done to you', and then goes on to argue that as I am glad that my parents conceived me and did not abort me while I was only a potential person, I should take the same attitude towards other potential persons.[34] There is another possible extension of the Golden Rule, which perhaps is better suited to bring out exactly why potential persons are morally important. According to the Golden Rule we ought to do to others as we would wish them to do to us. There is obviously in many cases a time difference and a situational reference involved in the description of the act we ought to do and the act we would like done to us. It is not the case that we ought to do to others what we would wish them to do to us in our present situation. To give any worthwhile moral guidance the Golden Rule must therefore be extended to state that we ought to do to others what we would wish them to do to us if we were in the same situation as they are now.

Let us imagine that time travelling is made possible, and that I enter my parents living room just in the middle of a discussion about whether or not to abort this foetus, which I know will become me. Would I then wish to put in a word on behalf of the foetus? I think most of us would, and it follows that we ought to do the same for other potential human beings.

This example may be charged with trading on a confusion created by a conflation of the knowledge of my present personal existence and my previous pre-personal existence, and I would not like to put to much weight on it, but it is perfectly plausible to claim that if I was a foetus I would prefer to live on, and that the Golden Rule therefore enjoins me to let foetuses live on, if I have any say in the matter.

The argument has been attacked by Warren who claims that:

> As it stands, the principle that, other things being equal, we should treat others as we are glad we were treated appears to be irrelevant to the treatment of potential people. For personal pronouns like 'we' refer to people; we are essentially people if we are essentially anything at all. Therefore, if fetuses and gametes are not people, then we were never fetuses or gametes, though one might say that we emerged from them. The fetus which later *became* you was not *you* because you did not exist at that time. It was not you for the same reason that your dead body will not, or that your living body with the cognitive and perceptual centres of the brain permanently destroyed would not be you, namely, that you are a particular *person*, not just a particular human organism regardless of its stage of development or degeneration. So if it had been aborted nothing whatever would have been done to *you*, since you would never have existed. You cannot coherently be glad that you were not aborted, since in order for there to be a you at all, you cannot possibly have been. And therefore the Golden Rule as Hare

extends it does not proscribe abortion, much less contraception or celibacy.[35]

The claim, that I cannot coherently be glad that I was not aborted may be true, if the 'I' in the second part of the sentence is taken to be the person which I am now (but see below). But I can coherently be glad that the entity from which I emerged - which was the only entity from which I could ever emerge - was not aborted. The foetus which became me, stands in a quite different relation to me than my dead body ever will. I am not going to emerge from my dead body, and no part of my personality will depend on its properties or on the things that are done to it. It is true that I will never be in a position to grieve that I have been aborted, because I would then never have been. But this does not entail that I cannot be glad that I do exist, and be glad that the (positive and negative) acts necessary to bring this about were carried out.

Warren continues to explain why nobody is harmed if a potential person is aborted:

Merely potential people, or rather the people they might have become, are not, just as possible worlds are not, things that exist alongside the actual world in, as it were, a super-space that includes not only the actual but the possible. Or at any rate we have absolutely no reason to think they are. They are just things that might have existed, that is at some time were empirically possible, but which in fact do not, never did, and never will exist. And what does not exist and never will cannot be harmed or wronged or have its rights violated.

Why is this? Because harming someone, behaving wrongly towards someone, and violating someone's rights are all extensional rather than intentional concepts. I can think about Pegasus, but I cannot catch him, beat him, be unfair to him, or violate his rights. Mythical entities, which never did, do not now and never will exist, have no rights to be violated, and we have no duties or obligations toward such entities, simply because such entities cannot be acted upon in any way whatever, other than illusory, through the intentional medium of thought.[36]

We can all agree that our possible interactions with Pegasus are severely restricted by the fact that there is no possible way to bring him into actual existence. Pegasus is simply a mythical figure, and has no potential for actual being. But potential persons (at least of the biological kind we know of) are not mythical in the same sense as Pegasus. There is a great difference in ontological status between entities which are necessarily imaginary (like Pegasus), entities which are not presently existing but who could be brought into existence (like the embryo, when it is still not created from the separate bottles of egg and sperm), and presently existing entities, and this difference is not irrelevant to our moral assessment. We cannot interfere with the development of Pegasus (because he has none and can never have one), but we know perfectly well how to interfere with the development of the entity from which a person will emerge (to use Warren's wording).

If I possess a substance which, if used during the IVF procedure, lowers the IQ of the emerging person to half of what it would have been if the substance was not used, would it then be morally innocuous to use it? According to Warren it must be, because the person which would have emerged, had I not used the substance, is not the same person which emerges now with half the IQ. The two persons in question (the actual and the hypothetical, which would have emerged had I not used my substance) may have the same name and the same appearance, but it is highly implausible that two otherwise identical beings will end up as the same person if one is half as intelligent as the other. No one is therefore harmed, because the person which would have emerged cannot be harmed, and the person who emerges does so only because I used the substance.

Intuitively it seems obvious that great harm is done, even if we set aside the possible harm done to the parents and society. But where do we localise this harm; what is the wrong done and to whom?

Initially I will suggest that the person using this substance inflicts moral harm on himself. Through his actions he deliberately brings it about that a being with less possibility for attaining many of the things which make life valuable develops than could have developed from the same biological entity had he abstained from any action.

Adherence to the Golden Rule is not intended to promote only the good of others, it is in a very real sense intended to promote the good of the person following the rule, and he harms himself if he acts against it.

But apart from the harm he inflicts on himself, could he also inflict harm on the foetus or the embryo, despite Warren's assertions to the contrary? Even if he killed it so that no person would emerge? The answer to this question depends on the answers to two prior questions to which I will now turn, namely: what is the wrong done in killing, and, what is the connection between me and the embryo which started my biological existence?

Why is it wrong to kill somebody? We may follow Tooley and initially try to place the wrongness of killing in the fact that by killing a person we infringe his right to life, a right which is based on his desire for continued existence or his capacity to desire continued existence.

Why is this desire or preference so much more important than all others? It is clear that a person can never have any other desires fulfilled if he is deprived of his life (unless there is an afterlife); and that the importance of the desire for life is based on this fact. But what should we then say of somebody who has the same desires but, because of a psychological peculiarity or conscious choice, no desire for continued life? That is, a being which does not consciously want to have continued existence but which, on the other hand, does not wish to end this existence, and which has all other desires that a 'normal' person has. If the importance of the desire for continued existence is to a significant degree 'parasitic' on the fact that the fulfillment of this desire is a necessary prerequisite for the fulfillment of all other desires, then there is no great moral difference between the being having the desire for life, and the being with similar attributes but without this desire.

This leads to the suggestion that it is far more plausible to locate the core harm in killing not in frustration of a desire to live, but in the fact that the person who is being killed is deprived of the rest of his life.[37]

> The effect of the loss of my biological life is the loss to me of all those activities, projects, experiences, and enjoyments which would otherwise have constituted my future personal life. These activities, projects, experiences, and enjoyments are either valuable for their own sakes or are means to something else that is valuable for its own sake. Some parts of my future are not valued by me now, but will come to be valued by me as I grow older and as my values and capacities change. When I am killed, I am deprived both of what I now value which would have been part of my future personal life, but also what I would come to value. Therefore, when I die, I am deprived of all of the value of my future. Inflicting this loss on me is ultimately what makes killing me wrong.[38]

If it is wrong to deprive me of my future, then it is obviously as wrong to deprive other beings with a future like mine of their future, no matter what species they belong to, and this view is therefore not open to the charge of being 'speciesist'.

If we apply this account of the wrongness of killing to the pre-personal human being, we see that the same core wrong-making characteristic (i.e. the depriving of a future-like-ours) occurs whenever the potential for development into a person is frustrated.

But is this harm being done to somebody, or is Warren right in suggesting a radical discontinuity between the pre-personal biological entity and the later me (i.e. me as a person)? To decide this question it is necessary to consider what kind of sortal 'person' is. Is it a substance sortal describing the essence of a certain entity or a phase sortal describing a certain stage in the life span of an entity?

If we ask the question 'am I (the 30 year old research fellow) the same entity as the four year old child with the same personal register number' we find that both yes and no are fairly good answers. I am obviously not the same in one sense (I don't look, talk or behave (!) in the same way), and still I am the same in another sense, because me/30 and me/4 can be seen as diachronic instances of the same entity, and 'adult' and 'child' as phase sortals describing different stages in the life span of this entity.

The question is now whether or not it would be correct to apply the same reasoning to the sortal 'person'. Initially there seem to be three possible interpretations of the function of this sortal. Either it is a phase sortal and I am not essentially a person, or it is a substance sortal (i.e. I am essentially a person) ranging over the whole life span of the biological entity which is me, or it is a substance sortal referring not to the biological entity but to something which comes into existence at some point in the development of the biological entity.[39]

The first of these options seems the least attractive since, as Warren also points out (see above), if I am essentially anything at all, I am a person, and 'person' ought therefore to be a substance sortal and not a phase sortal.

The third option to a large degree coincides with the position advocated by Warren. I am now essentially a person, but there was a time when the biological entity from which I emerged was not a person, and it was therefore not me. It is fairly uncontroversial that the zygote from which I emerged is diachronically identical with my biological organism, but since I am also separately diachronically identical to myself as a person, this leads, as Carter[40] points out, to the conclusion that the chair in which I am sitting is presently occupied by two distinct and separate entities (i.e. me as a person, and me as a biological organism), which is absurd or at least highly implausible. This conclusion can be resisted if it can be shown that there is no diachronic identity between the zygote from which I emerged and my present biological organism, but this identity seems to be undeniable.

We are therefore left with the second option according to which 'person' is a substance sortal covering the whole of my biological existence, so that I am diachronically identical with the zygote which became me, making it true that I can be glad that I was not aborted. But this does not immediately solve any problems about the moral status of the zygote or later stages of development, unless one accepts the derivation from the Golden Rule. Even though I began to exist when I was conceived, it is fairly obvious that I developed from that point and it is not unreasonable that this should be reflected in my moral status.

Quinn has suggested that some sortals have a two-part extension, covering both the fully realised individual instances and the partly realised individual instances of a given class, and he suggests that we call such sortals 'complex' and distinguish them from 'simple' sortals with only a one-part extension.[41]

If we for instance take the sortal 'house', it covers both actual fully realised houses and houses under construction, and is therefore a complex substance sortal. Such sortals may still have fuzzy borders *vis a vis* other sortals (i.e. when does a hut become a house), but this does not detract from the fact that we can definitely distinguish between a pile of building materials (falling outside the sortal), a house under construction (falling within one of the part-extensions of the sortal), and a completed house (falling within the other part-extension). But wouldn't it then give a better picture of reality to introduce two new simple sortals, 'house under construction' and 'completed house', and give up the complex sortal 'house'? The answer to this question depends upon whether we believe the transition between the two simple sortals to be sharp (i.e. any difficulty in assigning one of the two sortals to an entity is due to the vagueness of the criteria and not due to a gradual transition) or gradual. There are good reasons to believe that the transition is gradual and that the complex sortal is more suitable since, after all, a house under construction is a house of some sort.

If person is a substance sortal applicable to all the stages of the biological development of a person, then it is far more plausible to describe it as a complex sortal, with the two part-extensions 'developing person' and 'actual person', than as a simple sortal with only one extension. There is (as noted above) a clear development in the biological entity classified by the sortal, and this development should be reflected in the structure of the sortal.

The classification of 'person' as a complex substance sortal with the part-extensions mentioned above, can also explain the intuition shared by many people that the wrong done by ending the life of a developing human being varies directly with its developmental stage. For whereas ending the life of a zygote or an early foetus inflicts only the core harm of killing (i.e. the deprivation of a future-like-ours), ending the life of later developmental stages adds more and more wrong-making characteristics as the foetus develops attributes which make it possible to harm it in other ways (e.g. sentience, wants, desires etc.).

But exactly what kind of entities can be correctly classified under the complex substance sortal 'person'? And, more important for the subject of this paper, supposing we know the attributes which make an entity belong to the part-extension 'actual person', which entities do then rightly belong to the part-extension 'developing person'?

The use of the term 'developing' could be taken to indicate a requirement for presently ongoing development towards personhood, but this is not a correct dividing line. To return to the house analogy, a house under construction is still a house under construction even though the work may be temporarily suspended because of adverse weather conditions or industrial action. Likewise, a developing person is still a developing person even though its development is suspended. What is more important as a dividing line is that we classify the entity as a developing *person*. The philosophic and metaphysical rationale behind complex sortals is that they are perfectly suited to describing entities undergoing directional change while preserving their unity as one entity. An entity can therefore be correctly classified only under the first part of the extension as a developing entity if we can adduce reasons to support the claim that, through the directional change, it can develop into an entity classified under the second part of the extension as an actual entity of this specific kind. In this way the criteria for classifying a given entity under a part-extension of a complex sortal as a developing entity, are the same criteria which would make the claim true that the entity has the potential to become the entity which the second part-extension of the complex sortal describes. An entity can therefore be classified under the part-extension 'developing person' of the complex substance sortal 'person' if the entity has the potential to become a person.

5. The Consequences of the Argument From Potential

It is often claimed that the actual consequences of accepting the argument from potential are so bad that the argument fails solely for this reason. These objections are mainly centred on three areas, the first being a putative duty to procreate, the second being the putative duty to actualise the potential in isolated sperm and eggs, and the third being the effects on the moral status of abortion, *in vitro* fertilisation and embryo experimentation.

5.1. A DUTY TO PROCREATE?

If it is wrong to destroy potential persons, and if there is no moral difference between acts and omissions leading to the same result (see below), then there is a moral duty to create potential persons (a duty to procreate), (somewhat in the line of the Biblical injunction: "Be fruitful, and multiply, and replenish the earth..."[42]).

It is claimed that the acceptance of such a duty would logically have to lead to a prohibition of contraception and a prescription of procreation at the maximal possible rate, thereby relegating women to the role of breeding machines. The argument runs as follows: 'if there is a duty to procreate, then the use of contraceptives is wrong and procreation will end up being the primary task of women'.

This argument is seriously flawed because it is predicated on the (hopefully) unsustainable premiss that the duty of procreation will be handled in a completely irrational fashion. (It is further predicated on the premiss that the duty to procreate overrides all other duties, see below.) The duty to procreate can be understood in 3 different ways, and I will submit that the last of these is the most rational, because it, in the long run, leads to the actualisation of most potential.

1. The duty to procreate entails that I and every other person should try to get as many children as we can.
2. The duty to procreate entails that we as a society should try to maximise the number of children in this generation.
3. The duty to procreate entails that we as a society should try to maximise the number of children in the foreseeable future. That is, not only in our generation but in the generations to come.

A society which adhered to the 3rd interpretation of the duty to procreate would certainly not ban contraceptives, and their use would even have to be encouraged in some circumstances.

Our present experience with the ecological crises suggests that to reach the long-term goal of bringing into existence as many people as possible, the appropriate strategy would be to have a slow growing or a stable population. And it would indeed be hard to imagine a society which, without causing permanent ecological damage, could efficiently absorb more than an average of 3 children per fertile woman (with a generation time of 30 years this means a population doubling each 52 years). The production of 3 children per fertile woman would therefore be the absolute upper limit entailed by the duty to procreate, and in societies near to the ecologically possible maximal size the duty would entail procreation at the maintenance rate (approx. 2.1 child per fertile woman) and prohibit further procreation. I might be sexist, but I would not describe women in such a society as breeding machines. If the duty to procreate is not taken to override all other duties, then the 'required' number of children per woman could easily be less, if their prospective quality of life was allowed to enter the calculation.

5.2. THE DUTY TO ACTUALISE ALL POTENTIAL

The second objection mentioned above states that if there is a duty to protect potential life, then this would necessitate that society spend most of its health care resources and indeed most of its budget on prevention of spontaneous abortions in the first trimester and in general on the actualisation of all potential persons.

But there is a hidden premiss underlying this argument, which can be challenged. For the conclusion to be valid it must be agreed that the duty to save life overrides all other societal duties and goals. That is, it must be shown that there is a necessary connection between holding to the validity of the argument from potential and the sanctity of life doctrine. But there is no such necessary connection, although this combination of views is held by many people. It is perfectly possible to agree with Helga Kuhse that the sanctity of life doctrine is internally incoherent and potentially deleterious[43], and still claim that the argument from potential shows that potential persons have a *prima facie* right to life. There are also good empirical grounds for the suspicion that no society truly holds that the duty to save live overrides all other duties. I think it is Joseph Fletcher who has presented the story of the phoenician god Moloch who approaches the head of state of a newly formed African state with the following proposal: 'If you give me 25,000 lives a year, I will give you a brand new road and highway system for your country'. The leader is horrified and answers: 'No, not a single life'. This surprises Moloch, who replies: 'Why not? In America I get 72,000 lives a year'. In modern society many goals are pursued, even though they entail a calculated loss of life.

It must also be remembered that the moral symmetry between acts and omissions with the same consequences hold only if all other things are equal. But in this case all other things are not equal. There are significant differences in the dischargeability of the two duties.

5.3. ABORTION, *IN VITRO* FERTILISATION AND EMBRYO EXPERIMENTATION

The argument from potential establishes only that entities with potential for personhood have a *prima facie* right to life, or that there is a *prima facie* obligation not to deprive them of their life. Even on the most strict interpretation, where this *prima facie* right is taken to be of the same strength as the strength of the right to life possessed by persons, it is not at any stage stronger, and may therefore be set aside in exactly those situations where we would set aside the right of a person. On the derivation of the right to life following from the potential to become a person pursued in part 4 of this paper, the right to life possessed by the potential person is initially weaker than the right to life possessed by an actual person and grows stronger, as the developing person obtains attributes which allow actions towards it to obtain new wrong-making characteristics. It has a serious right to life from the start of its development, because ending its life shares in the core wrong-making characteristic of killing (i.e. depriving of a life-like-ours), but it is a right which can be overridden.

The adoption of the argument from potential does not, therefore, in itself give any absolute guidance as to the permissibility of abortion or embryo experimentation, even though it is possible to derive some broad guidelines. If we follow the strict interpretation, then we are morally allowed to actively end the life of potential persons only in the circumstances where we would be allowed to end the life of actual persons, and abortion on demand and the use of intrauterine devices as a standard method of contraception becomes morally impermissible (although even this is disputed[44]). No plausible moral theory gives me the right to kill other people at my wish. But as long as a strict sanctity of life principle is not applied, abortion to save the mother's life or health could be performed, as could abortions intended to spare the foetus devastating handicap, the limits being determined by the specific interpretation of the right to life.

Concerning embryo experimentation all non-harmful and non-destructive experiments would be morally permissible (if there are no other countervailing moral reasons). Destructive experiments would be morally permissible only in situations where it would be morally permissible to sacrifice persons to gain the same knowledge. The possible number of permissible destructive experiments would therefore be small.

IVF for treatment purposes would be a laudable moral enterprise, because it works to create new persons, but the creation of spare embryos would have to be restricted.

If we follow the interpretation derived in part 4 of this paper, then abortion would be allowed in a wider range of situations where important moral considerations, like serious health risk for the mother, indicated that this would be the most appropriate action.   Abortion on demand or for less important reasons would be morally impermissible, since they would negate any 'seriousness' in the foetus' right to life.

Embryo experimentation would be restricted by similar considerations, as would the production of spare embryos during IVF procedures.

6. Conclusion

The unrestricted classical argument from potential taking the form below is logically valid but false as many examples show.
  1. X has the potential to become Y.
  2. Having the potential to become Y gives the same rights as being Y.
  3. Being Y gives a right to life.
  Therefore
  4. X has a right to life.
But this is not the argument which has been developed in this paper. The argument defended in this paper has a far more restricted scope, and would look something like the following, if put formally:
  1. X is a biological entity with potential for personhood.
  2. The core harm in killing (i.e. the depriving of a life-like-ours) is involved in any killing of an entity with potential for personhood.
  3. This harm is of a sufficient magnitude to ground a *prima facie* right to life.
  Therefore
  4. X has a *prima facie* right to life.
The three premises in this restricted argument are not immediately obvious truths, but have been supported by the following arguments.

First, if X is a biological entity (and especially if X is a pre-personal mammal), then the sentence 'X has a potential P to become Y' can coherently be understood as 'given natural surroundings it is practically possible for X to become Y'. It has been argued that sperm and egg as such do not have potential for personhood, unless they are in a temporal and spatial relationship which gives specific reasons for ascribing potential.

Second, the core harm in killing is not dependent on the actual present presence of consciousness in the entity which is killed, but on the continuity between this entity and the entity which, if not killed, would have experienced a life-like-ours. In the case of biological persons this continuity between the person and the initial biological entity is secured by their diachronic identity, illustrated by the analysis of the complex substance sortal 'person'.

Third, the core harm in killing is the core wrong-making characteristic in the killing of persons, and grounds as such at least a *prima facie* right not to be killed (a *prima facie* right to life). Killing of actual persons contains additional wrong-making characteristics, and is as such more wrong than killing potential persons.

The view which has been defended here differs from the radical view in stating that all potential persons including certain spatio-temporal arrangements of sperm and egg and all embryos, foetuses and infants (excluding those who will never have a life-like-ours, e.g. anencephalics) have a serious *prima facie* right to life, a right which grows stronger as the potential person develops attributes which make new forms of harm possible.

If the moral symmetry principle is accepted[45], then there are grounds for a duty to procreate. But it has been shown that this duty will be far less onerous than is normally supposed.

The conclusions of this paper differ from the traditional exposition of the argument from potential in three major ways. First it asserts that ascriptions of potential cannot be performed solely from properties inherent in the entity in question. Second it accepts that potential for personhood can be ascribed to certain spatio-temporal arrangements of sperm and egg before fertilisation, although it denies a general ascription of potential to sperm and egg. And finally it denies that the right to life possessed by a potential person is the same as the right to life possessed by an actual person, although it is still a serious and not easily overridden *prima facie* right.

This position will therefore please neither side in the 'moral status of the pre-personal human being' debate, and its only impact will presumably be as a suitable object for philosophical target practice, although there are others who defend somewhat similar positions.[46] There are, however, several attractive features of the position which might warrant closer study. First, it is able to explain why abortion for some (frivolous?) reasons is seriously morally wrong, without condemning all abortions which are not performed to save the life of the mother. Second, it is able to explain why pre-personal human beings matter morally, and why some matter more than others, and it is thereby consistent with the common-sense gradualist approach to moral status. And third, it is non-speciesist.

Acknowledgments

This paper contains revised parts of a Masters dissertation submitted to the University of Manchester. In this previous incarnation it was greatly improved by the helpful comments of Professor John Harris.

Notes

1. Engelhardt, H.T., *The Foundations of Bioethics* New York, Oxford University Press, 1986; Glover. J., *Causing Deaths and Saving Lives*, Harmondsworth, Penguin Books, 1977; Harris, J., *The Value of Life* London, Routledge and Kegan Paul, 1985; Kuhse, H. and Singer, P., *Should the Baby Live?* Oxford, Oxford University Press, 1985; Singer, P. and Wells, D., *The Reproduction Revolution* Oxford, Oxford University Press, 1984; Tooley, M., *Abortion and Infanticide* Oxford, Oxford University Press, 1985.

2. Tooley, *op.cit.*, p.99.

3. *Ibid.*, p.101.

4. Kluge, E-H.W., 'Infanticide as the murder of persons' in Kohl, M. (ed.), *Infanticide and the Value of Life* Buffalo, Prometheus Books, 1978, pp.32-45.

5. Stevens, J.C., 'Must the bearer of a right have the concept of that to which he has a right?' *Ethics* 95, 1985, pp.68-74.

6. Nagel, T., *The View From Nowhere* New York, Oxford University Press, 1989.

7. Nathanson, S., 'Nihilism, reason, and the value of life' in Kohl (ed.), *op.cit.*, pp.192-205, p.192.

8. Nagel, *op.cit.*, p.165.

9. Tooley, *op.cit.*, p.166.

10. The following section is inspired by a presentation given by Geoffrey Hunt.

11. Devine, P.E., 'Abortion, contraception, infanticide' *Philosophy* 58, 1983, pp.513-20.

12. Hare, R.M., 'Abortion and the golden rule' *Philosophy and Public Affairs* 4, 1975, pp.201-22.

13. English, J., 'What do grown children owe their parents?' in O'Neill, O. and Ruddick, W. (eds), *Having Children: Philosophical and Legal Reflections on Parenthood* New York, Oxford University Press, 1979, pp.351-356.

14. Sidgwick, H., *The Methods of Ethics* New York, Dover, 1966, p.243.

15. Sommers, C.H., 'Filial morality' *The Journal of Philosophy* 83, 1986, pp.439-56.

16. Sommers, C.H., 'Tooley's immodest proposal' *Hastings Center Report* 15, 1985, pp.39-42, p.41.

17. Hursthouse, R., *Beginning Lives* Oxford, Basil Blackwell, 1987.

18. *Ibid.* and Johnstone, B., 'The moral status of the embryo: two viewpoints' in Walters, W.A.W. and Singer, P. (eds), *Test-Tube Babies* Melbourne, Oxford University Press, 1982.

19. Kottow, M., 'Ethical problems in arguments from potentiality' *Theoretical Medicine* 5, 1984, pp.293-305, p.294.

20. Hursthouse, *op.cit.*

21. At the present stage of technological development the optimal surroundings for a human embryo and foetus are of course often the same as the natural surroundings.

22. Devine, *op.cit.*

23. Singer, P. and Dawson, K., 'IVF technology and the argument from potential' *Philosophy and Public Affairs* 17, 1988, pp.87-104.

24. *Ibid.*

25. Singer and Wells, *op.cit.*, p.91.

26. *Pace* the invention of time travel.

27. Øhrstrøm, P., 'Anselm, Ockham and Leibniz on divine foreknowledge and human freedom' *Erkentniss* 21, 1984, pp.209-22.

28. Zaitchik, A., 'Viability and the morality of abortion' *Philosophy and Public Affairs* 10, 1981, pp.18-26.

29. Quinn, W., 'Abortion: identity and loss' *Philosophy and Public Affairs* 13, 1984, pp.24-54.

30. Singer and Dawson, *op.cit.*, p.94.

31. Feinberg, J., 'Abortion' in Regan, T. (ed.), *Matters of Life and Death* second edition, New York, Random Press, 1986, pp.256-293, p.267. The Stanley Benn quotation is to be found in his 'Abortion, infanticide and respect for persons' in Feinberg, J. (ed.), *The Problem of Abortion* Belmont, Calif., Wadsworth, 1984, pp.135-144, p.143.

32. Harris, *op.cit.*

33. Seedhouse, David, *Health: The Foundations for Achievement* Chichester, John Wiley and sons, 1986, p.74.

34. Hare, *op.cit.*

35. Warren, M.A., 'Do potential people have moral rights?' *Canadian Journal of Philosophy* 7, 1977, pp.275-289, pp.279-280.

36. *Ibid.*, p.280.

37. Devine, *op.cit.*; Marquis, D., 'Why abortion is immoral' *The Journal of Philosophy* 86, 1989, pp.183-202.

38. Marquis, *op.cit.*, pp.189-190.

39. Carter, W.R., 'Do zygotes become people?' *Mind* 91, 1982, pp.77-95.

40. *Ibid.*

41. Quinn, *op.cit.*, p.34.

42. Genesis 2:28.

43. Kuhse, H., *The Sanctity-of-Life Doctrine in Medicine* Oxford, Clarendon Press, 1987.

44. Thomson, J.J., 'A defence of abortion' in Singer, P. (ed.), *Applied Ethics* Oxford, Oxford University Press, 1986, pp.37-56.

45. The question of the status of the moral symmetry principle has not been discussed here, but I think there are reasons for doubting its general applicability.

46. Cf. Fagot-Largeault, A., 'The notion of the potential human being' in Bromham, D.R, Dalton, M. and Jackson, J.C. (eds), *Philosophical Ethics in Reproductive Medicine* Manchester, Manchester University Press, 1990, pp.149-155; and Byrne, P., 'The animation tradition in the light of contemporary philosophy' in Dunstan, G.R. and Seller, M.J. (eds), *The Status of the Human Embryo* London, King's Fund Publishing Office, 1988, pp.86-110.

14. THE IDEA OF BRAIN-BIRTH IN CONNECTION WITH THE MORAL STATUS OF THE EMBRYO AND THE FOETUS

Dr. József Kovács
Semmelweis University of Medicine
Institute of Behavioural Sciences
Department of Bioethics
Budapest POB 370
H-1445, Hungary

The debate about the moral status of the human embryo and the foetus is not new. It has always been part of the abortion debate, since the permissibility of abortion is highly dependent on the moral status of the foetus. The debate over abortion and that over the moral status of human embryos and foetuses, however, are often kept separate, since the abortion debate has philosophically been complicated with questions of womens' rights, their right of self-determination over their bodies, their right to choose, whether they 'lend' their bodies to another human being (the foetus), etc. Since embryo experiments are done *in vitro*, outside the human body, these complications should not concern us in the following discussion. On the other hand, even though embryos *in vitro* cannot be kept alive longer than 7-8 days at present, since we lack the necessary techniques and technology to do so, this situation could change very soon. In theory, it is conceivable that we will be able in the not very distant future to develop a fertilised ovum until viability *in vitro*, in a sort of artificial womb. Then the removal of the mature foetus from the artificial womb would be the equivalent of birth, while turning off the artificial womb of a still immature foetus or embryo will be the equivalent of abortion. In that state of technological development we will need a unified theory of the moral treatment of abortion (early or late) and of embryo experiments. Therefore in the following paper I will discuss the status of the embryo and the foetus as if this artificial womb were already a reality, as if fertilisation could take place *in vitro*, and the human embryo and foetus could be carried to term in a very sophisticated incubator in an artificial womb. Thus I can concentrate my discussion on the status of the embryo and the foetus without having to deal with the complicating issue of womens' right to self-determination. I will ask what is the moral status of human gametes, of the fertilised ovum, of the developing embryo and the foetus, whether this status changes during the process of continuous development, or not, and if it changes, how is this connected with biological facts during this development?

D. Evans (ed.), Conceiving the Embryo, 221–245.
© 1996 *Kluwer Law International. Printed in the Netherlands.*

1. Why the Moral Status of the Embryo is a Sensitive Issue

The abortion debate, and discussion about embryo experiments is emotionally a very sensitive issue everywhere. The cause of this is undoubtedly that the manner in which the question is raised resembles many ominous antecedents in human history. The question is, to what extent human embryos, which belong to the human species from a biological point of view, can be regarded as humans morally. Do we owe them the same moral protection as we owe to our fellow human beings? Formulating the question in this way makes us feel uneasy, since there have been occasions in human history when certain groups of people (e.g. those who had a different skin colour, held different religious views, or belonged to other nationalities) were not regarded morally as fully human. This way of thinking has occurred so often that the suspicion spontaneously arises that regarding the human embryo as not fully human morally is one of the latest forms of discrimination between humans. Those opposing abortion point out how many similarities exist between the old arguments in favour of slavery or racism and the new arguments in favour of abortion.[1] In contemporary debates many compare today's abortion epidemic to a sort of holocaust, referring to how inhumane it is to regard some groups of people as not fully human or as semi-human.

2. The Catholic Doctrine

Early Christianity still shared the view of Aristotle[2], who distinguished three parts of the soul: the vegetative soul, the sensitive soul and the rational soul. According to him, the human embryo at first has only a vegetative soul, like the plants, then later a sensitive soul, like the animals, and finally a rational soul. Thus to kill an embryo which has only a vegetative soul is to destroy a life, but it is not murder. The sign of ensoulment with the rational soul is, according to him, the quickening of the foetus.[3] Although there were theologians (e.g. Tertullian[4] in the third century) who held that the rational soul infused the body from conception, their opinion represented a minority view at that time. Most theologians agreed with Augustine according to whom to kill an embryo after ensoulment is murder, while to kill it before ensoulment is not.[5] In the thirteenth century Thomas Aquinas confirmed this view, since according to him the killing of a foetus before ensoulment is a lesser sin than killing it after ensoulment because the former lacks the rational soul.[6] This tenet was connected with the hylomorphistic conception of man. According to this view the human soul can infuse the body of the embryo only after it has acquired its human body shape and its human organs are already formed, since a human soul cannot infuse a still non-human body.[7] The embryo before ensoulment is living but only in the way a plant or an animal is living. It has vegetative and animal soul but it still lacks human (rational) soul. Today, we would say that the embryo at that stage had reached only the physiological level of existence but still does not exist spiritually, that is, it is not yet a person.

This doctrine of deferred animation was accepted by the Catholic tradition for centuries.[8] In the seventeenth and eighteenth centuries, however, some scientists thought that a totally formed human being could be found already in the sperm, with arms, legs etc. This was the doctrine of preformism, according to which ontogenesis consists of the mere growth of this miniature human body, which already has all the human organs from the very beginning. Under the influence of this doctrine the doctrine of immediate animation began to spread. If a human soul can infuse only a well formed human body, but the embryo is well formed with human body-shape already at conception, then - the argument runs - the soul can infuse the body at conception. Thus, preformism is not contrary to the doctrine of hylomorphism.[9] Starting from the false theory of preformism, the church had already accepted the doctrine of immediate animation in 1708 but did not apply it with full rigour to abortions prior to quickening.[10] In 1854, Pius IXth reaffirmed that animation occured at conception, and in 1869 the distinction between the ensouled and the non-ensouled embryo was officially removed from Canon-Law. From that time Catholic thinking stopped judging early and late abortions differently and began regarding all abortions unambiguously as murder.[11] This is still the dominant view today among contemporary theologians. The minority view, however, is that the Church changed its correct doctrine of deferred animation under the influence of preformism in the eighteenth century. Preformism, however, proved to be false and the contemporary tenet, that of epigenesis, holds that the fertilised ovum is not yet body shaped and the embryo acquires the human body shape only through continuous development and through the differentiation of cells. Given the rejection of preformism the minority view is that the Church should return to the (correct) opinion of Thomas Aquinas as to the distinction between the ensouled and non-ensouled embryo, since this corresponds to the doctrine of hylomorphism which is still held by the Church.[12]

Donceel uses the recent observation that a zygote during the first 14 days of its development can split and develop into two separate individuals, as a counterargument against immediate animation. He notes that this entails that any already infused soul should split as well, which would be a metaphysical absurdity.[13] This theological debate is significant because it is very similar to the contemporary secular debate about when we can speak of a human person during the course of human ontogenesis.

3. Contemporary Views About the Status of the Embryo and the Foetus

In contemporary debates three main positions can be distinguished: the conservative, the liberal, and the moderate views.[14]

According to the conservative view human life begins at conception, so the fertilised ovum (the zygote) is just as human as any of us, and killing it is just as wrong as the killing of an adult human being.

The liberal view holds that a developing foetus acquires human rights only at birth or at the stage when it reaches viability, but before this stage neither the embryo nor the foetus can be regarded as human from a moral point of view, although it is undoubtedly human from a biological point of view.

Both the conservative and the liberal view share the presumption that the moral status of the developing embryo and foetus during the whole process of development is the same. According to the conservative, the developing embryo is just as much human at the time of conception as at the time of birth. The liberals think that the developing foetus is no more human at the time just before birth than at the time of conception. The common element is that neither viewpoint attributes any significance to the development of the embryo and the foetus. According to the conservative killing a zygote is just as wrong as killing a newborn infant, while according to an extreme liberal killing a mature foetus is acceptable in just the same way as killing a zygote. Whereas both these positions ignore the moral significance of development, the moderate position emphasises it. It states that during ontogenesis it is possible to draw a non-arbitrary line after which the developing embryo will be a person with full rights but before which it lacks this status.[15]

4. The Conservative Point of View and Its Criticism

The conservatives think that individual human life begins with conception, therefore to kill a zygote is wrong.

This claim, however, rests on a vague use of the words 'human life'. When we say that it is not permissible to kill a human life then we think of sentient, communicating human beings, who are just as capable of feeling pleasure or pain as we are. In short, we think of persons. To kill human cells, by contrast, is usually not considered wrong, even though these cells, biologically, are also forms of human life. Taking a blood sample, for example, means the destruction of millions of human blood cells, but we do not regard the person taking the blood as a murderer. The fertilised ovum, although it will develop into a human being, cannot be regarded as an actual human being, therefore its destruction is not murder. In the same way, an acorn is not yet an oak-tree, and to crush an acorn is not equivalent to cutting down an oak-tree.[16] The zygote is a potential human being but it is not yet actually a human being. It is rather like the blueprint of a building, the destruction of which is not equivalent to the destruction of an already erected building.[17] The zygote is undoubtedly the beginning of the life of a human being from a biological point of view, but it is still not a human life in the moral sense of the word, i.e. it is not yet a person. Human life has many levels. Human life exists, on the one hand, on the level of cells. In this sense the life of a zygote is a human life, but, by the same token, so is the life of a single sperm or ovum. On the other hand, human life is also the life of an organism, which necessitates the coordinated functioning of the various organs of the organism. The life of a human organism as a whole must be distinguished from the life of the cells, tissues, and even organs of the same organism. It is expedient to call life and death on the cellular level biological life and death, and the life and death of the whole organism personal life and death. Among the many levels of human life (the cell-, tissue-, organ-, and organismic-levels) it is the organismic level which deserves protection. Neither the life of a single cell, nor even the life of a whole organ, is equivalent to the life of an organism, since we cannot say that a human being is alive just because his kidney, transplanted after his death into another person's body, is still living.

To define and determine the beginning of human life we have to face the same difficulties we meet with the definition and determination of the end of life, namely of death. The lessons of the debates about the definition of death, therefore, can help in defining the beginning of life.

The practice of organ transplantation, which began in the sixties, made it necessary to redefine death. As a result of the debate, the brain-death criterion of death emerged, according to which a person can be regarded as dead when all the functions of his entire brain have irreversibly stopped. The brain death criterion has been accepted and used in many countries since that time. It is important to emphasise that the brain-dead person is still alive in a biological sense, since his heart is still beating, his kidneys are functioning, etc. These organs are suitable for transplantation for the very reason that they are still alive. The transplantation of biologically dead organs would be medically senseless. Thus, even though millions of cells are still alive in the body of a brain-dead person, life can be detected only from a minimal biological point of view. Legally and morally he is regarded as already dead because, though his cells, tissues and organs are still living, coordination between the various organs is ended and the functioning of the organism as a whole has stopped. Thus, if a human being in whose body millions of cells are still alive is not considered to be alive from a legal and a moral point of view, even though from a biological point of view there is some human life, then it is consistent to distinguish at the beginning of life, too, the biological beginning of life, which is conception, from the beginning of the life of the person. It could be said that personal life begins later than biological life and comes to an end earlier. Biological life can continue for a short time even after brain-death and it comes to an end only after the death of the last living cell of the organism.[18] Thus, human life, from a biological point of view, begins at conception and comes to an end at the death of the last living cell of the body. (The death of the last living cell of the organism occurs 72-96 hours after the cessation of heartbeat and breathing.) Personal life, however, is shorter than biological life. It begins only weeks after conception and it comes to an end at brain-death. The right to life begins not at the beginning of biological life, but only later, and it ceases to exist not at the end of biological life, but earlier.

The conservative argument against this is that even though the zygote is really nothing other than a single cell, this cell is potentially a thinking human being, it is potentially a person. Thus the zygote must be protected not because of its actual characteristics, not because of what it is now, but because of its future characteristics, because of what it will become. This is the potentiality argument, which plays an important role in conservative positions.

5. The Potentiality Argument

In sum, the conservative answer to the above counterarguments is that killing a blood cell is not murder because it is a cell from which nothing else will develop, and the brain-dead do not deserve protection any longer because they never will develop into thinking human beings. By contrast, this does not hold true for the zyyote because, whatever it is now, it will with a high probability develop into a thinking human being. That is the reason it must be protected more than an 'ordinary' cell.

Two responses are possible to this reasoning. First, if a zygote is only a potential human being it follows that it is not a human being now and will become a human being only if it can develop further for an appropriate period of time. If it is only potentially human it only potentially has human rights.[19] An often cited analogy for this is that the President of the USA in 2010 is now only a potential President, and, as such, he (or she) does not have at present those presidential rights which he or she will have on becoming President.

The other counterargument to the potentiality argument is that it leads too far. That is, if killing a zygote is unacceptable because it prevents it developing into a human being then contraception is also wrong since it impedes a process, conception, the result of which would also lead to the existence of a human being. Thus, a consistent conservative position which rejects the killing of a zygote or an embryo must also reject contraception,[20] since both in the case of early abortion and in the case of contraception the intent of the actors and the result of the act is the same. The aim of contraception is the prevention of conception, in other words it is designed to prevent a developmental process which would lead to the birth of a human being. This aim is attained by the destruction of the two living human cells (the sperm and the ovum) which, without contraception, would unite and develop into a newborn infant. The aim of early abortion is to kill a still non-sentient embryo in order to prevent it developing into a sentient human being. The only difference between the two is that contraception destroys non-sentient gametes while early abortion kills a non-sentient embryo.

The births of all of us could have been prevented in two different ways because, for all of us, the following statements are true. First, we would not have come into the world if we had been aborted when we were embryos. Second, we would not have come into the world if our parents had used a contraceptive in that act of sexual intercourse which resulted in our conception. The result of both acts would have been the same, that is we would not have come into the world, and neither act would have been more painful for us than the other, since embryos are non-sentient just like the gametes. Contraception and early abortion differ from each other only in probabilities. The probability of live birth of an embryo in the 7th week of gestation is about 85%, since 15% of registered pregnancies end in spontaneous abortion. Thus, with the abortion of a 7 week old embryo we destroy a life which would have developed into a newborn infant with 85% probability.[21] In the case of contraception, however, the situation is different. Statistically, about half a year of normal sexual life of a young healthy couple not using contraception results in a pregnancy that leads to the birth of a newborn infant. Taking into account this statistical difference we could say that half a year of normal sexual life with effective contraception is morally equivalent to a single case of early abortion, as both of them impede the birth of a newborn infant who probably would otherwise have come into the world. It is very hard to see any difference between killing a sperm and an ovum just prior to their union (contraception) or killing them after their union (early abortion). Public opinion usually does not feel there to be any moral difference between the type of contraception which involves early abortion (e.g. contraception with an intrauterine device) and contraception with a pessary (where contraception is attained by impeding conception).

Tooley uses the following hypothetical example against the potentiality argument.[22] Let us suppose that a new drug has been developed. Newborn kittens having this injected into their brains would develop into cats having a human brain. These cats would be able to speak, think, and feel in just the same way as any of us and so these creatures would have the same rights as we all have. If this drug already exists then every kitten is potentially a thinking person. Would it be ethically objectionable in this case if the kittens had not been injected with this drug but painlessly killed instead? According to our intuitions it would not be our duty to transform the potentially thinking kittens into actually thinking ones. Tooley's conclusion is that if a being is a potentially thinking person then it is not our duty to help this being to develop into an actually thinking person and that it is morally acceptable to prevent the development of this potentially thinking being into an actually thinking one.

The main problem for the conservative point of view is that if, on the one hand, it regards the zygote as protected because of its actual characteristics then its claim is plainly false, as the zygote as such is only a non-sentient human cell and the destruction of human cells is morally acceptable. But if, on the other hand, it wants to protect the zygote because of its potential to develop into a sentient human being then this is also an argument against contraception since contraception also destroys human cells (gametes) which together could also develop into a sentient human being. This means that if the conservative opinion is right and the embryo must not be killed then contraception is also wrong. Since contraception today is generally accepted and from the point of view of the embryo there is no significant difference between contraception and early abortion then early abortion must also be accepted. In sum, it seems that the traditional religious view, which did not draw a sharp line between early abortion and contraception, can be justified on a secular basis as well.

6. The Liberal Position and Its Criticism

The liberal position can appear in various forms. It can claim that a foetus will become a person only at birth or at viability. I will not discuss these positions here, since they have significance only in the context of the abortion debate and they are related with a womans' right to self-determination. As we are interested in this paper in the moral status of the embryo, or foetus, in themselves, without reference to womens' rights, I will concentrate on another form of the liberal position, namely, on the rationality criterion of personhood.

6.1. THE ABILITY FOR SELF-CONSCIOUSNESS AND RATIONALITY AS A CRITERION OF PERSONHOOD

What forms of life should be protected from a moral point of view? Our first intuitive answer to this question may be that we must protect every human life and only human life. This answer, however, does not seem satisfactory after careful consideration. We must distinguish, for instance, persons from human beings. First of all, if there were other rational, sentient beings in the universe then they also should be protected, irrespective of the fact that they would not belong to the human species. They would be persons, although they would not be human beings. The gods, angels of the various religions, and many mythological figures are persons, although they are not human beings. On the other hand, the brain-dead are biologically living human beings, although they are not persons. Moral protection is due only to persons, irrespective of whether they are human beings or not.[23] If a being is to be given protection simply because it belongs to our species this would be speciesism, morally similar to racism, which, for example, regards person 'A' as more worthy of protection than, say, person 'B', because 'A' belongs to a given race.[24]

If various people on the earth did not belong to the same species they would still be due the same rights because the morally relevant characteristics are ones they all share.

The question is, what characteristics make a being a person, that is what characteristics should this being possess in order to be as much protected as an adult human being? According to the criterion of rationality the person-making characteristics are the abilities for self-consciousness, for use of a language, for rational thinking, and, perhaps, the ability to observe moral rules. These characteristics make it possible for the person to desire the prolongation of her own existence, and this can be an important reason not to kill that being. Since even a newborn infant lacks these characteristics and stands on a lower level as regards self-consciousness and rationality than an adult dog or horse, it would follow that the life of a newborn infant would not deserve as much protection as that of an adult horse or dog.[25]

This radically liberal position, however, can be called into doubt in many ways. For example, the claim that a person must have rationality and self-consciousness, the lack of which means it is not a person and therefore does not have a right to life, seems too strict. Very young children, for example, lack these characteristics from which it would follow that their lives do not deserve protection, which would mean that killing them would not be objectionable. This is so implausible that this criterion must be discarded. The critics of the liberal position correctly point to the fact that rationality, self-consciousness, etc, are necessary conditions for somebody to have moral responsibilities and obligations but are not necessary conditions for a being to have rights.[26] Young children and people with serious mental retardation have rights, even though they lack the level of rationality or self-consciousness which normal adults have.

Thus this criterion, being too strict, is not an acceptable candidate for personhood.

7. The Moderate Positions

According to the moderate view the mistake made by both the liberals and the conservatives is that they do not attach moral significance to the individual development of the embryo or the foetus. That is the reason, according to the conservatives, for which the killing of a zygote or an embryo is just as wrong as the killing of newborn infant; while according to some extreme liberals even the killing of a newborn infant is sometimes acceptable.[27] Both positions are contrary to our intuition which holds that individual development is relevant to the determination of moral status. This is maintained by the moderate position which has many forms.

7.1. THE SENTIENCE CRITERION

In the literature, many think that moral status is given by the existence of sentience. The core of the argument is that a being can have interests only if the being in question is sentient. The primitive form of sentience is the ability to feel pain or pleasure but in its more developed form it includes the ability of the being to set itself an aim, to have aesthetic preferences, values, etc. According to the argument a being can be harmed only if it is sentient, thus we can have moral obligations only to sentient beings.[28] If, for example, somebody saws a table in two this can be an immoral act as regards the owner of the table since it destroys the property of the owner. But this act cannot be immoral as regards the table itself. The table is only a thing, it is not sentient, therefore it cannot have interests. It would be absurd to say that it would be better for the table for it to remain in one piece than to be sawn in half. To saw up a cat, by contrast, would be highly immoral since the cat is a sentient being capable of suffering. Therefore it has an interest in being spared from the infliction of pain upon it.

Thus, we can harm a being only if it is sentient; we can be moral or immoral only towards sentient beings. Sentience, however, has degrees. Beings standing higher on the phylogenetic ladder are more sentient. The most sentient being is undoubtedly man, as intelligence, the ability for rational thinking, creates new possibilities for the perception of the world. A rational being, who is self-conscious and is aware of time, of the past and the future, is more sentient, since it has a richer, a more varied and diversified - in a word, a fuller - existence. It is capable of feeling satisfactions and sufferings which are impossible for a less sentient creature.[29]

From this it follows that non-sentient beings do not have rights and, thus, they do not have any moral status. Only sentient beings can have rights, and they have them in proportion as they are sentient. That is, the more sentient they are, the higher is their moral status. On the top of the ladder of moral status stands man, because of his supreme intelligence and sentience. Since the lack of rationality does not mean lack of sentience animals also have moral status.

Moral problems do not arise in relation to inanimate objects or non-sentient living beings, like plants. It is difficult to determine when sentience appears during phylogenesis since it is theoretically very difficult to construct a method which would show us what an animal perceives from a subjective point of view, how much pain it feels when an injurious stimulus is applied to its body. Since endorphines, which play a role in the human perception of pain and pleasure, have been observed in arthropods, it can be inferred that arthropods have some primitive form of sentience.[30] Vertebrates are certainly sentient, mammals are more sentient than fish, and higher mammals (e.g. primates) are more sentient than mammals lower on the evolutionary scale.

We can make a hierarchy on the basis of sentience both on the level of phylogenesis and on the level of ontogenesis, and this hierarchy would give a measure of those rights due to various living beings. On the level of phylogenesis sentience can be described on a continuum. At one pole of the continuum stand non-sentient beings (those incapable of feeling pain or suffering) and at the other pole stands the most sentient being - man. There is a grey zone on the continuum where sentience develops during the course of phylogenesis. This is somewhere among the invertebrate animals.

The degree of sentience will determine the rights of the living being in question. The more sentient a living being, the more immoral it is to make it suffer or to kill it.[31] This approach is in accordance with our intuitive reactions since most of us find the killing of a dog much worse than tearing off a leaf. We do not accept the killing of primates in experiments as readily as the killing of fish. In other words, our spontaneous thinking reflects our conviction that the more sentient a being, the more right it has not to be caused pain or suffering. This is the reason that sentience creates interests even in animals, which we must protect, and rationality is not a condition of acknowledging these interests.[32]

This course of reasoning can naturally be applied to human ontogenesis as well. At one pole of the continuum of human ontogenesis stands the non-sentient zygote, at the other pole the adult man. However, it is not only the zygote which is non-sentient but also the embryo. (We can call the developing human an embryo until the end of the 10th gestational week. After that point we can call it a foetus.) Since they lack sentience and are unable, therefore, to feel pain or suffering, embryos cannot have interests. To kill the embryo at this stage is therefore an act which has no victim. So, early embryonal development is not the development of an already formed human being, but the development of a zygote into a human being. The organs and body shape which characterise human beings have fully developed only at the end of the embryonal period and the embryo lacks sentience in just the same way as some primitive animals lack it. We do not yet know when exactly sentience of the foetus appears. Its minimal condition, however, is the appearance of those anatomical and physiological structures which make the perception of pain possible. Evidently, sentience does not come into being abruptly but during a gradual process and estimations put its appearance at the 14th gestational week.[33] (Some reflex-like pain reactions can be observed already at the 7th gestational week but these are reflexes only of the spinal cord and they do not represent subjectively 'experienced' pain or suffering.) Many argue that the end of the 14th gestational week would represent the natural boundary onwards from which foetuses already do have rights and deserve protection. There are, however, decisive counter-arguments to this position.

7.2. COUNTER-ARGUMENTS TO THE SENTIENCE CRITERION

The most important counter-argument is that sentience, in the strict sense of the word, does not give a right to life but only to the avoidance of suffering. Accordingly, most contemporary societies condemn the torture of animals but not the killing of animals, so long as it is done painlessly. Its having sentience is a necessary condition for the possibility of torture and thereby may invoke a prohibition of certain treatments of the living being but is not a sufficient reason for not killing it. Painless killing can be bad for a living being only if it has the ability for some kind of self-consciousness, if it can wish to continue its existence. To have this wish it is necessary to have an awareness of one's own possible death. This requires a highly developed brain, which most animals lack. Most animals do not fear death but do fear pain. The ability to fear one's own death is an attribute only of man and possibly of some highly developed mammals. From this it would follow that only those rational beings which could consciously wish to continue their own existence and are capable of fearing death would have a right not to be killed. Most animals are not capable of this and even newborn infants are far below this level. It would follow that they too could be killed quite morally, which is evidently an absurdity. It is a justifiable counter-argument to the sentience criterion that, since the sentience of a newborn infant is much less than that, say, of an adult dog, an adult dog has more right to life than a newborn infant!

A further problem with the sentience criterion is that if a human being's right to life is the function of sentience in its embryonal and foetal period then why is sentience not a determinant of rights after birth? A human adult is evidently more sentient than a newborn infant, or even a small child, in that an adult is more rational. In spite of this contemporary morality and the legal system do not think that an adult has more right to life than a small child.

In sum, if we start from the sentience criterion we cannot account for our basic contemporary values. Another important counter-argument to this criterion is that it is contrary to the widely-held brain-death criterion and with contemporary medical practice. This point justifies a small detour since philosophical and ethical debates about the definition of death help us to a clearer formulation of the moral status of the embryo.

8. The Notion of Whole Brain-Death

For millenia the irreversible cessation of heart-functioning and breathing was considered the most reliable sign of death. In 1967, however, when the first heart transplant was performed, this definiton of death became the subject of intense debate. The human heart which Dr. Barnard implanted into the chest of the patient was a living, beating human heart, so, according to the traditional notion of death, it was explanted from a still living human being. According to the old definition Dr. Barnard saved a patient by killing another one! As a result of the ensuing debate, in 1968, a new criterion of death was born with the Harvard criterion of brain-death.[34] According to this new definition death has come not only to those whose heart function and breathing have irreversibly stopped but also to those whose whole brain is dead, i.e., where all the functions of the entire brain have ceased.

Broadly speaking the brain has two sorts of functions. The first is the coordination of the functioning of the various organs, maintenance of constant body temperature, blood pressure, regular breathing, the neuroendocrin balance, etc. These integrating functions can be put down to the normal functioning of the brain-stem. The brain-stem, phylogenetically, is the most primordial part of the brain and can be found in all vertebrates and very little which is specifically human can be found among its functions. The other brain function is in relation to perception, cognition, thinking, emotions, etc. The final processing of these mental characteristics is put down to the neocortex, i.e., the cortex is the site of some specifically human functions, e.g. human cognition, emotions, rationality, consciousness, etc. According to the whole-brain death criterion the death of a person occurs when the functioning of both the neocortex and the brain-stem irreversibly stops. After brain-death has occured the physiological apparatus of the body ceases to function as an integrated whole and the functions which remain are only the dissociated functions of organs, tissues, and cells. The emphasis of the whole-brain death criterion is not brain function but the function of the organism as a whole. The philosophy behind the whole-brain death criterion, despite its name, is that an organism is living as long as the organism as a whole has an integrated, well coordinated functioning. Loss of this unavoidably occurs after the irreversible cessation of brain-stem functioning.

On the basis of the definition of whole-brain death, death is the cessation of the physiological integration of the body, the end of the coordinated functioning of the organism as a whole. The registration of brain death, therefore, is not important for the death of the brain itself but because it is an infallible sign of the cessation of the integrated functioning of the organism as a whole.[35] In the case of brain-death, all the functions of the brain stop, the patient is ventilated by a respirator but he has spontaneous heart functioning and his other organs (e.g. his kidneys) function too. Today, the brain-dead can he kept biologically alive for days and in some exceptional cases for weeks. After this period biological death irresistibly develops. The few days, however, between brain death and biological death can be used to explant vital organs from the brain dead and to use these organs in organ transplantation programmes.

9. The Notion of Neocortical Death

The various parts of the brain are not equally sensitive to hypoxia. If for any reason the blood supply of the brain is disturbed then the lack of oxygen injures first the brain cells of the neocortex. If medical help is given in time in this case then - since the cells of the brain-stem are less sensitive to hypoxia - the patient becomes irreversibly comatose or gets into a persistent vegetative state (PVS). The latter is one of the most hotly debated issues in contemporary bioethics. Both the irreversibly comatose patient and the patient in a PVS are neocortically dead. The comatose patient is unconscious while the PVS patient is not in a coma. His sleep is interrupted by long, wakeful periods during which his eyes are open and follow moving objects as a reflex action, or he turns his eyes towards the source of a sudden noise. The patient in PVS can grimace and can swallow food or drink put into his mouth. He can wail or shout but he cannot say words. An inexperienced observer would think that these are conscious reactions of the patient. In reality, however, these are not sensible psychological reactions to the environmental stimuli. The PVS patient usually breathes spontaneously so artificial ventilation is not needed, but his survival is possible only with artificial feeding with a nasogastric tube, or with gastrostomy.[36] In this state the patient can survive for years: the longest registered survival is 37 years.[37] Both PVS and irreversibly comatose patients are neocortically dead and both have the central characteristics of this state which are the irreversible cessation of self-consciousness and cognitive functions and the irreversible loss of personality. The neocortically dead do not have emotions, memories, are unable to think, and are even unable to feel pain. Only the brain-stem reflexes remain intact (e.g. yawning, sighing, constriction of the pupils in light, etc).

In the 1970s many philosophers and theologians argued that the irreversible loss of personality, consciousness, and sentience - i.e., neocortical death - is 'real' death. For them, therefore, the whole-brain death criterion is unnecessarily strict since it requires more for the registration of death than just neocortical death: it requires brain-stem death as well. However, the argument runs, the life of the body remaining after neocortical death is human life only in the biological sense of the word and not in a moral sense, as, after neocortical death, everything which is individual and specifically human in a person (his personality, his memories, his emotions, etc.) is irrevocably lost.

The whole-brain conception of death is a vitalistic conception of human life which identifies human life with the integrated functioning of the body as a whole.[38] Proponents of the neocortical brain death conception, by contrast, identify human life with conscious life, and, according to them, human life has to be protected only up to the point where at least a minimal level of sentience or consciousness can be detected. In the absence of these characteristics a body can live but this will no longer be the sort of life we morally regard as valuable since human life differs from animal life mainly in virtue of the neocortical function of the former. We think, communicate, experience our environment and have human emotions with our neocortex, and the irreversible cessation of its functioning means a definite end of everything which was specifically human and individual in us.[39] To illustrate this let us look at the good news, bad news example of Engelhardt.[40]

10. Engelhardt's Example

A neurologist finds that we are suffering an incurable disease which will irreversibly destroy our whole brain. But he has good news as well. Modern medical technology has made it possible to maintain the life of our body despite the death of our brain. In this way our body will be kept alive for the period of a normal life span so our life will not be shortened at all. That person who finds that this good news is not really a comfort, since it is not he who will survive but only his body, already accepts the whole brain conception of death.

The story can be continued so that the bad news is not so bad either since only his neocortex and not his whole brain will be destroyed and the functioning of his brain-stem will continue. Thus, all his psychologically sensible reactions will stop but he will still have spontaneous breathing and the functioning of his body as a whole will remain intact, so it will not be necessary to connect him to a respirator. If someone finds that even this is not a comfort for him he has made the first step toward accepting the neocortical definition of death.

According to the neocortical definition of death 'real death' is neocortical death since it is the personality which we think to be important and its destruction means the real death of a person, while the whole-brain death conception attaches too much significance to the functioning of the most primitive part of the human brain, the functions of which are not specifically human, since it merely integrates the function of the various organs into a coordinated whole.

11. The Opinion of the President's Commission

In 1981 the US Presidential Bioethics Commission was given the task of investigating the debate between proponents of the neocortical death criterion and the whole brain death criterion.[41] The Commission surveying the various positions took sides with the whole brain death criterion again. It brought up many reasons against the neocortical definition of death. First, it pointed out that today it cannot be known with certainty which part of the brain is responsible for human consciousness. The little knowledge we have shows that there is an intimate relationship between the brain-stem, the subcortical structures and the neocortex and it is not known to what extent each plays a role in maintaining human consciousness.[42]

A further argument was that the philosophical debates about the nature and preconditions of human personhood did not lead to a consensus which could be relied upon in deciding such an important issue. When rejecting the neocortical definition of death the Commission attached particular importance to the fact that the neocortical death criterion could mean a radical break from the traditional definition of death, since, according to it, we should regard people as dead who have spontaneous breathing and heart functioning and who could be kept biologically alive by artificial feeding for years.   Although a neocortically dead human is non-sentient, because he breathes and has a spontaneously beating heart he cannot be buried. To stop these functions would require the withdrawal of artificial feeding.   Since this would very slowly lead to biological death more active methods (e.g. stopping heart functioning with a drug) would probably be needed before burial. According to the neocortical definition of death this could not be called active euthanasia since only the heart functioning of an already dead person would be stopped in this case and a corpse, naturally, cannot be killed.[43] For many, however, this would not be an acceptable procedure. We do not have the necessary consensus for acceptance of the neocortical death criterion and this consensus would be needed to introduce such a radical shift in attitude towards death. Therefore the committee took up the cudgels for the whole-brain death criterion.

Proponents of the neocortical death criterion argued that besides the fact that their position would be philosophically correct it would involve serious practical benefits. For example, the irreversibly comatose and PVS patients could be regarded, legally and morally, as dead but they could be kept biologically alive for years. These bodies (naturally with the previous consent of the relatives or the deceased) could be readily available sources of explantable organs for transplant programmes which, today, often stall because of a lack of transplantable organs. These bodies would also be suitable for doing such drug experiments as today can be done only on living volunteers, etc.[44] To take up these opportunities, however, we would have to alter too radically our traditional way of thinking about death. It was primarily this reason which decided the Presidential Commission in favour of the whole-brain definition of death.

12. Some Ethical Consequences of Accepting The Whole Brain Death Criterion of Death

As we have seen, the neocortically dead are legally and morally still living people and must be treated accordingly. A heated bioethical debate is going on as to whether the treatment of persons in PVS or irreversible coma should be stopped, who should decide this question and what the procedural rules for making such a decision should be. It is not necessary to enter into the details of this debate but it must be remarked that even though the neocortically dead are *de jure* still living persons *de facto* they are treated in many cases as if the neocortical death definiton had been accepted. For example, in the USA it often happens that the artificial feeding of a patient in PVS is stopped on the request of the family whereas this would be unacceptable in the case of a patient who is neocortically alive.[45]

13. The Idea of Brain-Birth

Since the conception of brain-death has been widely accepted and applied in medical practice many have used this idea for the determination of the beginning of personal life. According to this argument, if the kind of human life which is to be defended comes to an end at brain-death, that is, earlier than biological death, then that kind of human life begins at brain-birth, later than biological life. We have, then, to make a distinction between biological life and death (on the one hand) and personal life and death (on the other). Individual biological life begins at the time of conception (or, according to the more recent view, on the 14th day after fertilisation) and it comes to an end at the time of the destruction of the last living cell of the body (biological death).

In contrast, personal life, which must be defended morally and legally, begins with the beginning of brain function (brain-birth), and comes to an end with the irreversible cessation of all brain functions (brain-death). So, personal life would be shorter than biological life.

The first elements of this reasoning can be found in the works of some Catholic theologians in the 1960s and 1970s (although still not in this form) who examined the question, When does hominisation of human life take place?[46] They regarded the appearance of the cortical structure of the brain as the decisive step in this process as this forms the biological basis of personal life.

In medical terms this thought arose in 1982 when an American paediatrist, J.M. Goldenring, reformulated this position. According to his approach the human embryo can be regarded as fully human in the moral sense of the word when its brain function can first be registered. According to his reasoning the medical basis for determining whether a particular human being is alive or not has always been to try to register the signs of the functions of some vital organs. For millennia this meant the registration of motion, breathing and heart functioning, and that was the reason that human foetuses for long had been regarded as alive only after quickening and a distinction had been made, morally and legally alike, between abortion prior to quickening and abortion after quickening. Today the determination of death is made by the registration of brain-function. If a foetus has been born the criterion for the determination of death in its case is the same as in any other case: the presence or absence of brain function. (This is only theoretically true, as, in practice, below the age of two months the reliable diagnosis of brain-stem death in infants is rarely possible.)

Thus, if, in the case of a newborn infant, we determine whether it is alive or not by registering its brain activity, why not use this same method to determine whether an intrauterine embryo can already be regarded morally as alive or not? On this basis, the beginning of human life - from a moral point of view - would be the 8th week of gestation as this is the first time when EEG activity can be registered. According to Goldenring a very strict symmetry exists here. We regard an 80 year old, irreversibly comatose, dying patient, kept alive by mechanical ventilation, as alive in so far as he has some kind of minimal EEG activity. Similarly, argues Goldenring, we have to regard an 8 week old embryo as alive for whom the respirator is the placenta of its mother. So, according to Goldenring, human life begins at 8 weeks gestational age and it comes to an end at brain death.[47]

There is an important difference, however, between brain-birth and brain-death, namely, that the brain-dead are definitely dead, while embryos before brain-birth have the potential of brain function. They are actually not human beings morally but they are potentially human beings. This can cause some confusion; but a science-fiction thought-experiment may help elucidate the brain-birth conception.

14. A Thought-Experiment

Let us suppose that a strange disease exists which reverses the direction of the running of an individual's genetic programme. He who has got the disease goes through the inverse of normal human development. So, he grows younger, then becomes a child, and then goes through the stage of infancy. Following this he reaches the intrauterine stage of this regression and it would be necessary to put him into an incubator to keep him alive. (Let us suppose that incubators have been perfected and even embryos can be kept alive in them.) At the end of this regression what is now a foetus would turn into an embryo and the embryo into a zygote. Lastly the zygote would split into a sperm and an ovum which would separately perish and with this the life of the individual in question would definitely come to an end.

When could the individual suffering from this strange disease be regarded as dead? His original personality begins to be destroyed when the person in question reaches the childhood phase in the regression process. Reaching the developmental phase of a newborn infant his personality would come to an end. As the regression continues and the sufferer is in an incubator then at the stage corresponding to the 22nd-24th gestational week of pregnancy the cortex of the individual's brain would stop functioning so he could be regarded as neocortically dead. According to the whole-brain death criterion, however, he can still be regarded as a living human being, his status being equivalent to that of an adult in a persistent vegetative state. Relying on the presently accepted whole-brain death criterion the individual in question can be regarded as dead only when the brain-stem of this regressing individual stops functioning, which is the phase in the disease corresponding to the 8th week of gestation. (Naturally, a different question which might be asked as the disease progressed would be at which phase of the disease we would consider the life of the regressing individual to be no longer valuable and when we would think that the disease had reached the stage at which the state into which the individual had fallen constituted a hurt to the dignity of the former person. This question concerns the phase at which we would cease to have a moral obligation to keep this regressing individual alive, and not, for example, to turn off his incubator. Various answers are possible to this question but from a moral point of view this regressing individual should be considered to be alive as long its brain-stem function can be registered.)

We must see that the embryo regressing in our thought experiment and the normally developing embryo in the uterus differ only in their potentiality. Although their actual state is the same the developing embryo has a potentiality which the regressing embryo lacks. If we do not consider a regressing embryo in the 7th week of gestation to be alive according to the brain-stem death criterion then we cannot regard a normally developing embryo at the 7th week of gestation to be alive either. If we were to value the developing embryo more than the regressing embryo we would do so because of its potentiality. But the potentiality argument leads too far, as we have seen, as it renders contraception morally unacceptable as well.

To elucidate this point let us continue the experimental example. After the time at which the zygote has split into an ovum and a sperm a new drug is invented with the help of which the reversed genetic programme can be turned back to its normal direction. After applying this drug to the gametes and fertilising the ovum (using sperm micro-injection techniques) with the sperm from which it has recently been separated because of the regressing disease, the ontogenesis of the individual in question is started again. The unusual element in this case would be that we know in advance, even before fertilisation, who will develop from the fertilised ovum because the two gametes involved in the fertilisation would be those resulting from the regression of that diseased individual. Would it be permissible in this case not to reunite the two gametes? Those who loved the individual in question would regard failing to reunite these gametes as morally unacceptable because in this case they would know whose fertilisation would be prevented. This thought-experiment suggests that even contraception itself is easily accepted only because we do not know whose conception is prevented by it. If we knew this, then - as in our thought experiment - to prevent the conception of an individual already known to and loved by us would be just as unacceptable for us as to abort it in its embryonal period, attesting again to the moral similarity between contraception and early abortion.

Others do not think that brain-birth occurs so early as Goldenring thinks. The foetus is able to feel pain only after 14 gestational weeks and nothing but a primitive form of cortical activity can be registered at 22-24 gestational weeks.[48] In this way, the debate between the neocortical definition of death and the whole-brain death criterion repeats itself. In line with the two positions on the definition of death we can distinguish, similarly, two positions on the definition of brain-birth.

15. The Brain-Stem Brain-Birth Conception

According to this view if the cessation of brain-stem function is a sufficient condition for regarding somebody as dead at the end of life then an already functioning brain-stem is a sufficient condition for regarding somebody as alive at the beginning of life. This would mean 8 gestational weeks. Before this time the embryo would lack moral status but after this time it would have it. An argument in favour of this position is that it is in accordance with the whole-brain death criterion, it is symmetrical with it and determines the beginning and end of life on the basis of similar criteria.[49]

In sum, the conception of Goldenring would regard brain-birth and brain-death as symmetrical concepts and it would regard embryos from the 8th gestational week onwards as fully human.

Accepting the logic of the brain-birth conception, however, forces us to make a slight modification, the result of which could be called the modified view of the conception of brain-stem birth.

16. The Modified View of Brain-Stem Birth

The emphasis of the whole-brain death criterion is not brain function but the function of the organism as a whole. The philosophy behind the whole-brain death criterion, despite its name, is that an organism is living until the organism as a whole ceases to have integrated, well-coordinated functioning. In adults the functioning brain-stem is a necessary precondition of the coordinated functioning of the various organs. To be able to function in a coordinated way, however, these organs first have to come into being, then they have to develop their particular structures and then they have to show at least a minimal level of functioning. This stage, however, is reached only at the end of the 10th gestational week, which is the end of the embryonic phase of devolopment and marks the beginning of the foetal phase. The reason why the developing human is called an embryo until the end of the 10th gestational week and is then called a foetus is that there exists an important difference between these two developmental stages. The embryonic stage is characterised by the dominance of qualitative changes: this is the stage of organogenesis (the qualitative development of organs) and morphogenesis (the qualitative development of the shape of the human body).[50] By contrast, from the 11th gestational week onwards foetal development is characterised by the dominance of quantitative development. With a measure of simplification we could say that during the embryonal period from a simple cell a new entity comes into being, a human being with human body-shape and human organs; while in the foetal period no new entity comes into existence but rather the growth of an already existing human being dominates.

Now, if the end of human life is the cessation of the integrated functioning of the body as a whole then the beginning of human life is the beginning of the integrated functioning of the already qualitatively formed human organs. With some simplification we could say that the embryonal period is the phase in which a primitive human organism is formed, while the foetal period is the phase in which the growth of an already formed human organism takes place. On this account the embryonal period would be the equivalent of hominisation while the foetal period would be the equivalent of the further growth of an already extant human being.

I think this definition is consistent in spirit with the conception of whole-brain death. It shares the latter's philosophical presuppositions and so it can form the basis of the legal and moral assessment of the status of the embryo and the foetus.

Since the whole brain-death criterion has been criticised it is worth coinsidering the analogue of the neocortical brain-death criterion which would be the neocortical conception of brain-birth.

17. Neocortical Brain-Birth

It can be argued that, rather than the brain-birth conception having to be adjusted to the philosophically problematic whole-brain death criterion, we must create a philosophically correct brain-death definition (that being the criterion of neocortical brain-death) and define the time of brain-birth accordingly. The beginning of neocortical activity can be put between the 22nd and 24th gestational weeks. For reasons of safety we could draw at 20 gestational weeks the line before which we would not acknowledge the moral status of the foetus but after which we would grant it full moral and legal status.[51]

One could even say that at the end of life we must use the accepted whole-brain death criterion and at the beginning of life the neocortical brain-birth criterion. Today this assymetry would not cause any problem since 22 weeks old is the youngest age at which foetuses can be kept alive after birth with the use of sophisticated medical technology. It is not impossible, however, that after some further development, it will be possible to keep alive even, say, 19 week old foetuses born prematurely. In this case, however, the assymetrical definition of brain-death and brain-birth would cause problems. Using the neocortical brain-birth conception, a foetus in its 19th gestational week could be killed (aborted) in the uterus, since it lacks a functioning cortex, while if it were born, it could not be killed outside the uterus, since, in that case, the whole-brain death criterion would be used, and (on that account) everybody is living whose brain-stem is still functioning. It would be strange if one and the same foetus might be regarded as not morally human when in the uterus while being regarded as fully human when outside the uterus. For this reason brain-death and brain-birth are symmetrical concepts and we must define both accordingly. Since the neocortical death criterion invites the previously mentioned problems, leaving as satisfactory only the whole-brain death criterion, I think that the philosophy behind the latter must lie behind the definition of brain-birth as well.

18. Some Conclusions

When we try to define the moral status of the embryo we can make the task easier if we compare it with unambiguous, widely agreed, cases. Such cases are contraception, which is widely accepted, and infanticide, which is unequivocally condemned. The killing of an embryo or a foetus falls somewhere between these two poles and we must determine to which it is nearer.[52] On the basis of the above-mentioned argument we can say that embryos still lack moral status. Thus killing an embryo is nearer to contraception than to infanticide in that it prevents a potential human being becoming an actual one. On the other hand, abortion from the 11th gestational week onwards is nearer, morally, to infanticide, because it destroys a primitive human being.

So, from the 11th gestational week onwards, in other words, from the beginning of the foetal period, killing the foetus is nearer to infanticide. We can distinguish two stages in foetal development in this respect. In the period between the 11th and the 20th gestational weeks the foetus still lacks neocortical functioning. So, killing the foetus in this period is similar to the euthanasia of a neocortically dead adult, from a moral point of view. After the 22nd gestational week, when cortical activity of the foetus is probable, the killing of the foetus must be considered morally and legally alike to infanticide.

(These remarks are not suitable for determining the moral permissibility of late abortion since from them the absolute prohibition of abortion would follow only in the case of the foetus developing in an incubator, in an artificial womb, and not in the body of another human being. Since the woman who carries the foetus to term is herself a person who has rights, the question of abortion from the 10th gestational week onwards can be decided only by weighing the rights of the woman and the foetus.)

Epilogue

We have reached the conclusion that an embryo (being, by definition, younger than 11 gestational weeks) does not have moral status, while a foetus (by definition, older than 10 gestational weeks) has a moral status similar to that of an adult human being. However consistent this view seems to be with the whole-brain death criterion intuitively we still feel some embarrassment. We think, somehow, in the following way: 'If it is morally permissible to kill an embryo then it would have been also permissible to kill me when I was an embryo. This, however, would have been terrible since I love living, I am happy that I was born and I know that if I had been killed when I was an embryo then I would not be alive now and I would never have been born in the future either. Killing me when I was an embryo would have taken away from me the chance of life, which is given only once to everybody. If it were terrible for me not to have been born so that today I would not exist at all then it is also terrible for those future people who are embryos right now. If I accept the Golden Rule, 'do not do unto others that you would not have done unto yourself', then, since I am happy that I was not killed as an embryo, I must hold the same to be valid for everybody else. So, I cannot wish the killing of any present or future embryos'.[53]

This course of reasoning is convincing for us since we cannot imagine ourselves not existing. If we try to conceive that we do not exist we can do it only by way of imagining our existence now and then imagining the cessation of our existence. This is, however, really terrible, since we imagine, in this case, our own death, which is one of the most unbearable thoughts. In reality the killing of the embryo would be bad for the embryo only if it had some kind of consciousness, desires, wishes, etc. The embryo, however, lacks all these characteristics. We simply did not exist mentally, psychologically, in our embryonal period, so we could not have suffered then at all.[54]

Concerning arguments in relation to the Golden Rule, they are just as true for contraception as for the killing of the embryo. If, in the account of the thoughts we have in response to the arguments of this paper, we substitute the word 'killing' by the word 'contraception' in the previous reasoning we get the following: 'If contraception is morally permissible then it would have been permissible also to prevent my conception by contraception. This, however, would have been terrible since I love living, I am happy that I was born and I know that if my conception had been prevented then I would not be living now and I would never be born in the future either. Thus preventing my conception would have taken away from me the chance of life, which is given only once to everybody. If it were terrible for me if I had not been born so that today I would not exist at all, then it is also terrible for those future people whose conception is being prevented right now. If I accept the Golden Rule, 'Do not do unto others what you would not have done unto yourself', then, since I am happy that my parents did not use a contraceptive in that sexual intercourse as a result of which I was conceived, I must hold the same to be valid for everybody else. So, I cannot wish to prevent the conception of anybody else'.

It can be seen that the arguments against killing an embryo can be used against contraception as well. We have come back to our starting point. It is very difficult to argue against killing an embryo (early abortion) and not to argue against contraception as well. As we have already seen, contraception itself is easy to accept only because we do not know whose conception is prevented by it. If we had a wonder video on which we could see what the adult would look like whose conception is prevented right now then we would find contraception much more difficult to accept. The problem is that we are living in a world where contraception is necessary since the Earth is already almost overpopulated. To stop contraception would lead in a very short time to such a demographic explosion in any country, making a hell of the Earth. Contraception is necessary and accepting this we are already on a slippery slope since we cannot consistently argue in favour of contraception but for prohibiting the killing of embryos (early abortion) at the same time.

The above arguments do not solve the problem of embryo experimentation since for this we have to take into account a number of other considerations. But, defining the moral status of the embryo on the basis of the brain-birth criterion can be a good starting point for further discussions.

Acknowledgement

In writing this paper I used some parts of my earlier article in Hungarian ('A müvi abortusz a bioetika szemszögéböl') which was published in Sándor Judit (ed.), *Abortusz és ...* Budapest, Literatura Medica Kft, 1992. I am grateful to the Literatura Medica Ltd. for allowing me to republish these parts from the original Hungarian in English.

Notes

1. Wertheimer, Roger, 'Understanding the abortion argument' in Feinberg, Joel (ed.), *The Problem of Abortion* Second edition, Belmont, California, Wadsworth Publishing Company, 1984, pp.43-57, p.52.

2. Aristotle, *De Anima (On the Soul)* 414b, 415a.

3. See Feen, Richard Harrow, 'Abortion and exposure in ancient Greece: assessing the status of the fetus and the 'newborn' from classical sources' in Bondeson, William B., Engelhardt, H.Tristram, Spicker, Stuart F. and Winship, Daniel H. (eds), *Abortion and the Status of the Fetus* Dordrecht, D. Reidel Publishing Company, 1984, pp.283-300, pp.293-294.

4. Tertullian, *De Anima*, cited in Loewy, Erich H., *Textbook of Medical Ethics* New York, Plenum Publishing Corporation, 1989, p.159.

5. Wertheimer, *op.cit.*, p.52.

6. Aquinas, *Summa Theologica* II-II, Question 64, Article 8.

7. Donceel, Joseph F.S.J., 'A liberal Catholic's view' in Feinberg (ed.), *op.cit.*, pp.15-20, p.15.

8. *Ibid.*, pp.15-16.

9. *Ibid.*, p.16.

10. Loewy, *op.cit.*, p.159.

11. *Ibid.*, p.160.

12. Donceel (1984), *op.cit.*, pp.18-19.

13. *Ibid.*, p.l8.

14. Feinberg, Joel, 'Introduction' in Feinberg (ed.), *op.cit.*, pp.1-8, p.3.

15. Sumner, L.W., 'A third way' in Feinberg, Joel, (ed.), *op.cit.*, pp.71-93, p.73.

16. Thomson, Judith Jarvis, 'A defence of abortion' in Feinberg (ed.), *op.cit.*, pp.173-187, p.173.

17. Puccetti, Roland, 'The life of a person' in Bondeson *et al* (eds), *op.cit.*, pp.169-182, p.173.

18. *Ibid.*, p.171.

19. Engelhardt, H. Tristram, 'Viability and the use of the fetus' in Bondeson *et al* (eds), *op.cit.*, pp.183-208, p.187.

20. *Ibid.*, p.188; Singer, Peter, *Practical Ethics* Cambridge, Cambridge University Press, 1982, p.121.

21. Soupart, Pierre, 'Present and possible future research in the use of human embryos' in Bondeson *et al* (eds), *op.cit.*, pp.67-104, p.79.

22. Tooley, Michael, 'Abortion and infanticide' *Philosophy and Public Affairs* Vol. 2, No. 1, Fall 1972, pp.37-65.

23. Engelhardt, *op.cit.*, p.190.

24. Singer, *op.cit.*, pp.48-71.

25. Tooley, *op.cit.*, pp.50-61.

26. Sumner, *op.cit.*, p.82.

27. Sumner, L.W., 'Abortion' in VanDeVeer, Donald and Regan, Tom (eds), *Health Care Ethics An Introduction* Philadelphia, Temple University Press, 1987, pp.162-183, p.175.

28. Sumner (1984), *op.cit.*, p.83.

29. *Ibid.*

30. *Ibid.*, p.84.

31. *Ibid.*, p.85.

32. *Ibid.*, p.84.

33. Jones, D. Gareth, 'Brain birth and personal identity' *Journal of Medical Ethics* 15, 1989, pp.173-178, p.176.

34. Pernick, Martin S., 'Back from the grave: recurring controversies over defining and diagnosing death in history' in Zaner, Richard M. (ed.), *Death: Beyond Whole-Brain Criteria* Boston, London, Dordrecht, Kluwer Academic Publishers, 1988, pp.17-74, p.17.

35. Zaner, Richard M., 'Introduction' in Zaner (ed.), *op.cit.*, pp.1-14, p.9.

36. Institute of Medical Ethics Working Party on the Ethics of Prolonging Life and Assisting Death, 'Withdrawal of life-support from patients in a persistent vegetative state' *The Lancet* Vol. 337, 12 January 1991, pp.96-98.

37. Smith, David Randolph, 'Legal issues leading to the notion of neocortical death' in Zaner (ed.), *op.cit.*, pp.111-144, p.136, note 12.

38. Engelhardt, H. Tristram, 'Reexamining the definition of death and becoming clearer about what it is to be alive' in Zaner (ed.), *op.cit.*, pp.91-98, p.95.

39. Puccetti, Roland, 'Does anyone survive neocortical death?' in Zaner (ed.), *op.cit.*, pp.75-90, p.85.

40. Engelhardt, *op.cit.*, in Zaner (ed.), *op.cit.*, p.94.

41. President's Commission for the Study of Ethical Problems in Medicine and Biomedical and Behavioural Research, *Defining Death: Medical, Legal and Ethical Issues in the Determination of Death* Washington D.C., Government Printing Office, 1981.

42. Zaner, *op.cit.*, p.4.

43. Smith, *op.cit.*, p.126.

44. *Ibid.*, pp.129-130.

45. *Ibid.*, p.112.

46. Jones, *op.cit.*, p.173.

47. Goldenring, H. John., 'The brain-life theory: towards a consistent biological definition of humanness' *Journal of Medical Ethics* 11, 1985, pp.198-204.

48. Jones, *op.cit.*, p.175.

49. Goldenring, *op.cit.*

50. Moore, L. Keith, *The Developing Human: Clinically Oriented Embryology* fourth edition, Philadelphia and London, W.B. Saunders Company, 1988, p.82.

51. Jones, *op.cit.*, p.175.

52. Sumner (1987), *op.cit.*, p.163.

53. Hare, Richard M., 'Abortion and the golden rule' *Philosophy and Public Affairs* Vol. 4, Spring 1975, pp.201-222.

54. Warren, Mary Anne, 'The abortion issue' in VanDeVeer and Regan (eds), *op.cit.*, pp.184-214, p.197.

PART FOUR

The Legal Status of the Human Foetus

15. THE LEGAL STATUS OF THE HUMAN FOETUS

A Comparative Analysis

Wiesław Lang
Faculty of Law and Administration
Nicolas Copernicus University
Toruń
Poland

Contemporary legal scholars widely agree that from the moment of birth until death the human being is a human person subject to a host of legal rights and obligations. The fully competent adult human being is the paradigm of the human person and the legal subject. With regard to the human foetus however the consensus disappears.[1] In this paper I will try to answer the question: What is the real status of the foetus in contemporary law and jurisprudence?

1.

The human foetus is a living entity that comes into being as the result of the fertilisation (*in vivo* or *in vitro*) of a human egg by human sperm and that develops in the uterus of a woman or is separated from a woman's body but is incapable of surviving and developing ouside the uterus.

This formula includes a miscarried or aborted living but not viable embryo, an embryo produced *in vitro* that has not yet been implanted, as well as a foetus implanted in a genetic or a surrogate mother. The term foetus as defined above will be used to denote both organisms that might be labelled pre-embryos (which label is normally used in reference to the fertilised egg before implantation) and organisms that might be labelled embryos or foetuses. In considerations of legal documents on human reproduction these terms will be used in their original meanings. By the legal status of an entity I mean the standing of this entity in a legal order, defined by legal rules or legal doctrine. A legal system accords implicitly or explicitly legal status to all legally relevant entities. A legally relevant entity is an entity which in virtue of its very existence or actions incurs some legal consequences.

I propose to distinguish the types of legal status of entities based upon the following criteria:

1. The intrinsic legal features of the status.
2. The universality or particularity of the status within a legal order.

D. Evans (ed.), Conceiving the Embryo, 249–268.
© 1996 *Kluwer Law International. Printed in the Netherlands.*

3. The constancy or differentiality of the status.

4. The legal significance of the status in a legal order.

5. The legal source of the status.

The intrinsic legal features criterion. These are the rights of the legally relevant entities and the forms of their legal protection. The entities having at least some rights have in contemporary legal orders the status of legal subjects. Four categories of legal subjects are to be distinguished in contemporary law: full legal subjects, limited legal subjects, conditional legal subjects, and relational legal subjects. Full legal subjects can enjoy all the rights provided by a legal system (on the terms specified by the legal rules). Limited legal subjects can have only some legal rights. Conditional legal subjects can acquire only those rights which become disposable and actionable if the facts defined by law come into existence. These are contingent future rights and a conditional legal subject is a conditional rightholder.[2] A relational legal subject is an entity the subjecthood of which is fully determined by its relation to other subjects. In contemporary legal systems only living persons enjoy the status of full legal subjects. They are persons before law. Foundations, corporations, and associations are the paradigms of limited legal subjects labelled as legal persons. They can enter contracts, have property rights and pay taxes but they cannot marry or vote in elections and they are not endowed with the right to life. The constructions of the limited, conditional or relational legal subjects are extensions of the paradigm concept of a full legal subject (i.e. a living person). The entities to which law refers without according them any rights or duties are the objects of legal regulation. These are the objects requiring special legal protection (like a valuable piece of art) or ordinary objects, protected by law as the objects of property rights of legal subjects (like vehicles or buildings). Both kinds of objects are legal goods, but only in the first case is their intrinsic value the reason for their legal protection.

The Universality or particularity criterion. (1) A general legal status which is a universal status within a legal order (as, for instance, the status of the person before the law). (2) A special legal status which is a particular status with regard to the special features of an entity, special situations in which the entity is involved, the origin of an entity, the stage of its developmment or with regards to various branches of law.

The constancy versus differentiality criterion. The status of an entity is a constant one if it is immutable i.e. independent of the changeable features of the entity or changing situations. Differential legal status is a cluster of various legal standings of an entity which are dependent upon different changing factors but where the ontological identity of the involved entity is assumed to be a legally relevant matter.

The legal significance criterion: fundamental status and marginal status. Fundamental legal status is the universal and constant status in a legal order. The special and differential legal statuses are marginal legal standings. Consequently the status of a conditional, limited or relational legal subject as well as the status of the objects of legal regulations are the marginal statuses within any legal order.

The legal source criterion: primary and secondary legal status. Primary legal status is the status ensuing from legal provisions or regulations. Secondary legal status is the status brought about by actions or performances of legal agents or by other legally relevant facts. The status of a full legal subject is its primary status. The other singled out legal statuses of various legally relevant entitities (which are not living persons) might be their primary or secondary statuses.

Legal subjects may acquire secondary legal standings by their own actions or in virtue of actions of other legal agents or of some natural occurrences. (For instance the status of a debtor, a creditor, of an owner of real property, of a spouse etc.).

In virtue of the facts mentioned above, secondary legal status may be also acquired by the objects of legal regulations (a movable thing may be an object of property, may be sold or pawned etc.)

The bifurcated concept of legal status presented above is nothing unusual in legal doctrines and legal reasoning. "Legal definitions are devices which serve the purpose of an as adequate as possible attainment of certain substantive values and ideals which a given legal rule is supposed to protect. They do not describe an objective reality but form a part of the normative language in which the legally protected values are cast. The specific purpose of any given rule is best captured by describing the special problem that the rule is intended to attack".[3]

2.

The crucial point of my analysis is the status of the legal subject with regards to the status of the foetus. The concepts of legal status and legal subjecthood may be considered on two levels of legal discourse: on a normative and a pragmatic level. From a pure normative point of view every imaginable entity can be accorded the status of a legal subject. So in this respect the legal subjects may be gods, ghosts, animals, trees, the stars, numbers, foetuses, future persons etc. In the normative space of law (considered as an 'ought world') the legal subject is simply an ideal point of ascription of rights, duties and responsibilities.[4] On the pragmatic level of the operation of the legal order and legal communication an entity must meet some practical requirements in order to be treated as a person before the law. In almost all contemporary legal systems these are at least the following minimal requirements: 1. The entity must be identifiable and labelled or named as a discrete, individual object, distinct from its environment. 2. The entity must be amenable to legal procedures, in particular the rules of evidence must be applicable to it. 3. Legal actions or decisions must be taken with regard to the entity, at least through its legal representative. 4. Its legal subjecthood considered in practical terms should consist of the legal capabilities of the entity qualified as a legal subject.[5]

Two types of legal capability are to be distinguished, namely active and passive legal capability. Both are primary and inalienable capabilities. The active capability of a legal subject can be limited or completely annulled only by the decision of a court. Passive capability is a necessary precondition of active capability and can be neither annulled nor limited. So no living person can be deprived of his legal subjecthood nor can get rid of it by his own action. International declarations and covenants of Human Rights proclaim the right of every human person to full legal subjecthood as an inalienable human right. (Art. 19 of the Covenant of Political and Social Rights: "Everyone shall have the right to be a person before law"[6]). Persons lacking active legal capability have the right to be represented as concerns their rights and interests by agents endowed with active legal capability. They act in the name and on behalf of the subjects lacking this capability. The entities which have both passive and active legal capability are legal subjects and legal agents.

The legal standing of the foetus does not differ from the legal standing of a new born or of an incompetent adult person so far as the lack of active legal capability is concerned. Foetuses and newly born children can acquire active legal capability if, after live birth, they attain their majority. A comatose person belongs to the category of beings which, under normal circumstances, would have active legal capability. What makes the difference between them is passive legal capability. A new born child or an incompetent adult (a comatose person) are persons before the law and have unrestricted and unconditional passive legal capability, which implies the full package of personal rights, the right to life included. Foetuses have limited, conditional or relational passive capability. So their primary legal status is a marginal one, whereas the primary legal status of living persons, lacking active legal capability, is their universal and fundamental status within a legal order. Consequently foetuses do not enjoy the right to life or the right to be a person before the law. The primary legal status of a living person is clearly defined and consistent in national legal systems and in public international law. The term 'living person' designates human beings who have been born and are alive. It is quite irrelevant whether they are new borns or adults, competent or incompetent persons. Consider the Universal Declaration of Human Rights which proclaims the principle that "all human beings are born free and equal".[7] In contrast, there is no uniform, universal concept regarding the primary status of the human foetus. Across different legal systems, and even across different branches of law the legal status of the human embryo varies considerably.

The anti-abortionists' campaigns (pro-lifers' movements) have formulated proposals, drafts and demands to accord to the foetus the status of full legal subject. Some constitutions and statutes proclaim the right to life of human beings from conception (Ireland). This rhetoric suggests *prima facie* the recognition of the full legal personhood of the human foetus (from conception) in some legal orders. But it is rather a lipservice which justifies the anti-abortion laws, without changing the real legal status of the human foetus.

Good examples of this type of legal regulation are the statutory provisions of the French law on abortion (1975) and the recent Polish statute on the protection of the human foetus and the terms of the admissibility of abortion (issued in March 1993).[8]

The French and the Polish statutes declare that the law guarantees the protection of every human being from conception. But the provisions of other laws which are in force in these countries, especially the rules of criminal law, civil law, family law, insurance and social security law, administrative law and constitutional law, clearly contradict these statements and declarations.

I will briefly examine the relevant provisions of the aforementioned branches of law in a cross national dimension.

2.1. CRIMINAL LAW CODES

In criminal codes penalising abortion, abortion is labelled an offence against human life. However abortion is not qualified as a privileged crime in relation to murder but simply as a special type of the offence against human life threatened with a milder penalty than the intentional killing of a living person which is labelled the crime of murder. For instance in the draft of the new Polish criminal code the illegal killing of the conceived child is liable to be penalised by imprisonment for up to two years, whereas the murder of a living person is penalised by imprisonment for up to twenty five years or capital punishment. So the criminal provisions penalising abortion do not protect the human foetus on equal terms with living persons. These solutions asssume that the foetus is not a full legal subject otherwise the weaker legal protection of the life of the foetus would violate the equal protection clause, which is a constitutional principle.

The offences against foetuses consisting in killing, injuring or mistreating of the foetus by the pregnant woman or third parties (physicians included) are not penalised on the basis of the provisions concerning these types of crimes against living persons, but rather on the basis of special regulations protecting the foetus as a special subject of legal protection. Consequently these provisions are not fully indicative of the legal status of the foetus. They indicate that the foetus is not protected as a person before the law but rather as a potential human being having a special legal status. But in view of these provisions it is not clear whether the protected being is to be considered a limited legal subject or as a valuable object. The provisions prohibiting the capital punishment of a pregnant woman do not provide a definitive answer to this question either. So they are not sufficient reasons for the acknowledgment of a full legal subjecthood of the foetus.

In the draft of the new Polish Criminal Code the penalty for killing a viable foetus in utero is the same as the penalty for killing a living person (that is both are acts of homicide) where the perpetrator is not the pregnant woman herself. When the pregnant woman ends the life of the foetus, the penalty she bears is less severe and the offence is not homicide but a special offence against human life. So the legal status of a viable foetus depends also on the relationship between the foetus and various actors.

In almost all criminal codes, except the Irish code, the resolution of conflicts of rights and interests between a pregnant woman and her foetus is not based on general rules of necessary self defence and emergency situations but on special regulations concerning abortion or the protection of the human foetus. This is also an indication that the foetus is not assumed to be a full legal subject.

2.2. CIVIL LAW CODES

The provisions of civil law based on the old Roman principle "Nasciturus pro iam nato habetur quod de commodis eius agitur" are often cited in literature as an evidence of the full legal subjecthood of the foetus. The rule providing that the foetus can inherit property if it has been conceived at the moment of the opening of the inheritance and assuming it will be live born, is usually cited as a crucial argument underpinning the view that a foetus is a full legal subject.

But this rule seems to prove the contrary.[9] It is needed simply because a foetus is not a natural person before the law and is not endowed with passive legal capability by the general norms of civil law concerning the legal status of living persons and defining passive legal capability.

When the foetus dies before birth or will be still born his or her pretended legal capability and rights to the inheritance will be considered null (from the beginninmg) as they have never existed. The parents, brothers and sisters of the deceased foetus cannot inherit its property rights, because these were future rights, which become disposable and actionable only in case of the live birth of the foetus. The recently amended Polish civil code states that a foetus has passive legal capability but it acquires property rights and obligations on condition of its live birth. Some jurists contend that limitations of this type concern only property rights and not the personal rights of the foetus following from his legal capability and granted in civil codes.[10] The provisions of these codes specify personal goods protected by civil law. Even if this interpretaion were correct still the scope of the personal rights of the foetus remains unclear and controversial.

The only legal consequence of the above mentioned standpoint would be the power of the legal representative of the foetus to bring a suit against a pregnant woman planning or attempting the performance of illegal abortion or against the physician conspiring with the pregnant woman in carrying into effect her plans (of illegal termination of pregnancy). The purpose of the suit would be to get a court injunction against these actions. There have been no such court injunctions reported to date and the effects of such injunctions could be only symbolic.[11] No legal means can be practically available to enforce court decisions of this type. The legal admissibility of the above mentioned suits would depend not only on a presupposition about the status of the foetus but also, and first of all, on the illegality of abortion. So this procedure will not substantiate the right to life of a foetus.

The provisions of civil law and inheritance law are aimed mostly not at the protection of the rights and interests of the foetus but at the protection of the rights and interests (especially property rights) of living persons. This is true in respect of the rules of inheritance law (considered above) as well as of the rules substantiating actions for prenatal injuries, for wrongful birth and wrongful life. They no more prove the legal subjecthood of the foetus than the preconceptual protection of living persons proves the legal subjecthood of human reproductive cells. They are legally protected as valuable objects. Only an action for the wrongful death of a viable foetus may imply its having some kind of marginal legal subjecthood.

The provisions of civil law relating to the foetus do not prove the full legal subjecthood of the foetus but they might be considered as reasons or arguments for the construction of a limited or conditional subjecthood for the unborn child. However this question remains controversial in legal doctrine.

2.3. INSURANCE AND SOCIAL SECURITY LAWS

The foetus is not eligible for life or health insurance. In some countries social security covers a part of non medically-necessary abortions (in France 75%). If the foetus were a person before law then covering the costs of its killing from social security funds would be impermissible.

2.4. FAMILY LAW

The terms 'conceived child', 'unborn child', 'father or mother of the conceived child' are used in legal codes of family law. But this terminology does not give to the foetus the status of legal subject. The legal concept of parent is limited to the 'parent of a born child'. Adult living persons acquire parental rights and duties only in respect of born children and parental authority relates also to children as living persons. The rights and duties of prospective parents with regards to foetuses, and especially to artificially created pre-embryos, have a different character and are not considered in family law to be parental rights and duties.

The rules of adoption refer only to born children. 'Prenatal adoption' is not (to date) a legally recognised practice. Only the fatherhood of a born child can be denied. The unborn child can be owned by its prospective father but the legal consequences of the owning come after the child's live birth. However the born child can also be owned after his or her death if the deceased child has still living relatives.

The institution of the legal curator of the unborn child provided by family law is also cited as an argument for the legal subjecthood of the foetus (at least in family law). The curator can be instituted in order to protect the future rights of the unborn child. These can be only property rights and not personal rights. So this wardship is aimed at the protection of the interests of living persons but not of the foetus.

2.5. ADMINISTRATIVE LAW

Administrative regulations require obligatory registration and naming of the new born child within a definite time. This requirement has been recognised in the Convention of the Rights of the Child as a right of the born child. The live birth of a child in a hospital must be recorded in the hospital's files. In contemporary legal orders there are no rules requiring the registration of pregnancies; however in almost all countries there are now adminstrative regulations granting pregnant woman special positions or treatments. But the administrative protection of pregnancy has no direct connection with the legal status of the human foetus.

The death of a living person must also officially be notified. The certificate of death must be issued by the hospital or an authorised general practitioner. Dead persons must be buried or cremated.

The legal criteria of live birth and of death are different in various countries but in all countries there are in force some guidelines or regulations on this matter binding on medical and administrative practice. There are no corresponding administrative rules or duties concerning notification or registration of still births. Miscarried or aborted dead foetuses as well as the still born children must not be buried. But the disposal of their bodies depends on the decisions of parents. The bodies may be discarded or used for scientific research. In some legislations they are treated as the bodies of potential human beings.

The conception of a child as a concrete and individual fact has no legal significance in administrative law. Only the visible pregnancy, the birth and the death of a human being are the facts relevant for administrative regulations. The above mentioned administrative procedures and actions do not have a constitutive character as far as civil capability and legal subjecthood of a living person is concerned. They do not constitute a legal subject. A live born child becomes a person before the law even if its birth is not recorded and the child is not officially registered and named. A civil passive legal capacity is independent of administrative procedures as well as of the rules of criminal responsibility for homicide and of legal regulation of abortion.

Administrative regulations are aimed at two objectives: 1) the identification of living persons; 2) the control of information concerning their existence and quantity. The individual identification of living persons as the members of a definite society is a necessary prerequisite for the functioning of a modern state. Foetuses are not covered by these procedures. They are not registered and neither are they named because they are not considered persons before the law. Nor do they figure in the statisitics of the population because they do not belong to the population.

2.6. CONSTITUTIONAL LAW

With the exception of a few constitutions, constitutional provisions do not refer directly to embryos or foetuses and do not define these terms. Neither do they define human beings or human persons though some constitutions grant the right to life of human beings.

The terms 'human person' and 'human being' are open terms. They have a core meaning and a semantic penumbra.[12] The scope of the core meaning of these terms in colloquial language and in legal discourse covers living persons. The foetus (or embryo) is to be found in the semantic penumbra.

There is a widely accepted rule for the interpretation of the statutes that the terms used in ordinary language ought to be understood in their ordinary colloquial meaning and the core meaning of the term must be (at least tentatively) assumed as its proper meaning.

The extension of the core meaning of an open term to the fields of its semantic penumbra is admissable in legal reasoning (a broad interpretation) but needs special justification and underpinning (based on legally relevant reasons). The use of this kind of interpretation in criminal and constitutional law is limited by the leading principles of these branches of law. Consequently the terms 'human being' or 'human person' uttered in constitutional texts must be initially interpreted as terms meaning living persons. The extension of the core meaning of these terms to human embryos and foetuses can be achieved by introducing into constitutional texts appropriate legal definitions of 'human person' or 'human being' or by means of well argued interpretations of these terms (based on commonly accepted rules of legal reasoning).[13]

This position has been clearly confirmed in the decisions and rulings of the supreme courts and constitutional tribunals of many countries anchored in western legal traditions.[14] The U.S. Supreme Court in its famous *Roe vs. Wade* decision ruled that foetuses are not persons before the law, are not American citizens, and do not enjoy the rights granted by the XIVth Amendment. This ruling concerns non viable as well as viable foetuses. In view of *Roe v. Wade* viable foetuses (in the third trimester of pregnancy) can (but must not) be protected by legislation of the states. But they are not persons before the law either.

The constitutional Tribunal of the Federal Republic of Germany ruled in two subsequent desisions that: 1) the constitutional provisions granting all human beings the right to life and the protection of their lives and dignity relate also to implanted foetuses; 2) implanted foetuses are to be protected by law but not on equal terms with living persons (pregnant women); 3) in the case of acute conflicts between the rights of the foetus and the rights of pregnant women (when the life or health of the women is endangered) the rights of pregnant women must prevail; 4) in the situation of conflicts of rights or interests the foetus must have at least some procedural safeguards of its life and bodily integrity.[15]

So the Constitutional Tribunal implicitly acknowledged the implanted foetus as a potential human being deserving of some legal protection, but did not recognise the foetus a person before the law.

One of the most important institutions of constitutional law is citizenship. In no contemporary legal order are foetuses (at any stage of their development) recognised as citizens, although only the U.S. Supreme Court in the *Roe v. Wade* ruling has actually denied (American) citizenship to foetuses. One of the premises for citizenship may be the country of birth, but the country of conception never is. Citizenship is not a necessary condition for legal subjecthood. Persons who have no citizenship are still persons before law. But citizenship is a relevant characteristic of full legal subjecthood.

International conventions accord all living persons a right to citizenship and nationality.

2.7. PUBLIC INTERNATIONAL LAW

Like contemporary domestic constitutions, international declarations and covenants do not refer directly to foetuses. There are only two exceptions. The American Declaration of Human Rights asserts that the right to life "shall be protected by law and, in general, since conception".[16] The preamble of the Convention on the Rights of the Child states, that "the child, because of its physical and intellectual immaturity, requires special care and concern, especially appropriate legal protection before and after birth".[17]

As regards the American Declaration, the Inter American Commission on Human Rights has decided that this provision does not preclude legal abortion.[18] The Convention on the Rights of the Child does not determine the moment from which a human being is to be considered a child. The determination of this moment has been left to the parties to the Convention. The convention states only that the child is a human being up to the age of eighteen years. The Convention formulates the above mentioned right of the child to be registered and named. This is, in the view of the Convention, a right of born children (not of foetuses).

Other international declarations and Conventions on Human Rights proclaim the right to life of human beings but do not define the concept of human being or human person and the scope of the right to life. The rules of the interpretation of these provisions of international covenants are identical with the above mentioned rules of interpretation of the corresponding provisions of the constitutions (formulating the right to life).[19]

The European constitutional tribunals and supreme courts ruled that art. 2. of the European Convention on Human Rights (formulating the right to life) are not applicable to foetuses. The European Commission on Human Rights and The European Tribunal of Human Rights in Strasbourg, interpreting this provision, have not accorded the human foetus the status of person before the law (covered by the wording of art. 2 of the Convention) but have left the scope of the right to life open.[20]

2.8. REPRODUCTIVE LAW

In recent decades a new branch of law has come into being, namely reproductive law.[21] It has grown and developed as a part of medical law. It consists of different kinds of legal regulations directly concerning human reproduction and in particular assisted reproduction, the diagnosis and treatment of embryos and foetuses and embryo research. These are regulations belonging to different levels of the legal order: statutory laws, administrative ordinances, rules and guidelines issued by authoritative medical bodies (soft law) or formulated by international or supranational agencies and organisations.

In Europe the recommendations issued by The Assembly of the Council of Europe and by the supranational organs of the European Union form a major part of developing European reproductive laws.[22] In the majority of European countries assisted reproduction, the treatment of embryos and embryo research are regulated by special statutes. These legal regulations, as well as the recommendations of European transnational organs, refer directly to the legal standing of the human embryo, providing embryos with some forms of legal protection; but they do not accord the embryo full legal subjecthood nor define clearly its legal status. In the following parts of my paper I will consider more closely the provisions of reproductive law.

In some European countries there is no statutory regulation of assisted reproduction and embryo research (Poland, Italy). Some legal provisions concerning these activities are contained in the codes of the criminal law, medical law and medical ethics. The silence of the law on some kinds of human activities does not mean that these activities are beyond the scope of legal control.

From a systemic point of view the silence of the law creates an unspecified space of freedom and privacy protected by law. When assisted reproduction, treatment of embryos or embryo research are activities not regulated by statutes they are still covered by legal protection as legally permitted conduct (on the assumption that everything which is not prohibited is permitted). The provisions of different branches of law are indirectly applicable to these activities. But from the silence of law one can not infer any indications concerning the legal status of the human embryo.

3.

The above presented comparative analysis does not settle definitively the problem of the legal status of the human foetus. The tentative conclusion of the analysis is mainly negative: in contemporary law a foetus is not a legal subject (a person before the law). As regards a positive answer to the question what really is the primary legal status of the human foetus, the analysis suggests it is possible to locate the foetus on the map of legal standings of legally relevant entities. So the foetus has the special and marginal legal status of a limited, conditional or relational subject of law, or of a valuable object protected by law.

In order to grasp the status of the human foetus in all its particulars, four interrelated questions need to be answered. 1) Is the special status of the foetus a constant or differential one? 2) What is the relation between the continuity of life processes and the special status of the foetus? 3) What makes the status of the foetus a special legal standing? 4) What is the relevance of the origin of the foetus and of its location inside or outside a woman's body for its legal status?

3.1. IS THE SPECIAL STATUS OF THE FOETUS A CONSTANT OR A DIFFERENTIAL ONE?

A foetus develops (in a broad sense) from its conception until its delivery and passes through several stages of development. In different phases of gestation a foetus has different legal standings. In most contemporary legal orders the legal status of the foetus is often different before implantation, between implantation and the formation of the active brain (brain birth), between this point and generic or individual viability, and

from the point of viability until birth. In each of these phases the human foetus has a
special and unique legal standing. But through all these stages the foetus remains the
same entity (a living human being) and its biologiocal identity does not change. (For
the sake of simplicity I put aside the problem of individuation.) So, the foetus has in
its foetal (or embryonic) life a differential legal status (through time), which is its
special but primary status.

It may be argued that this development is not unique to foetuses. A living person also
develops during her or his life span from childhood to old-age, passing through different
phases of her or his life and changes to her or his legal status. The legal status of a
newborn is *prima facie* different from the status of the adult and the status of a 14 year
old child is different both from the status of a new born and of an adult human. Also
the legal standings of competent and incompetent persons are seemingly different. So
it may seem that the status of living persons is also differential through time. But there
is a substantial difference between these two types of differential.

What really does change during the life span of a living person is his or her active
legal capability or secondary legal status. As I emphasised earlier, the primary legal
status of a living person, his or her fundamental and basic status as a person before the
law, does not change at all throughout life. This status is acquired at birth and expires
with death. I have now the identical legal status of a full legal subject as I had as a new
born. My passive legal capability has not changed since my birth, even though as an
adult I perform legal actions which change my secondary legal standings. In contrast
the primary status of the foetus (passive legal capability) undergoes changes in different
phases of its foetal life.

3.2. WHAT IS THE RELATION BETWEEN THE CONTINUITY OF LIFE PROCESSES AND THE SPECIAL STATUS OF THE FOETUS?

The special status of the human foetus as contrasted with the universal status of the
living person as a full legal subject seems *prima facie* to challenge the genetic identity
of human beings before and after birth, and the continuity of the process of their
maturation. Passive legal capability captures precisely the genetic identity of a new
born child and an adult person as well as the continuity of the development of a human
being from the birth until the achievement of his or her majority. But differentiation
of the status of the foetus contradicts the continuity of the development of the human
being in its foetal stage and after birth. The above presented contradistinctions of the
legal status between a living person and a foetus, seem to be at odds with the
developmental theory of life processes according to which the development of a human
being from conception to majority is a continuous process. The special and differential
status of the human foetus seems to be incompatible with the indisputable scientific
statement that the foetus and living persons are identical beings as concerns their genetic
endowment.

I will not engage in this paper in philosphical disputes about the continuity and
discontinuity of human life processes. I will look on these problems from the view

point of law as an autopoietic system of social control.

(1) Law needs some classification of human conduct and related phenomena which are the objects of legal regulation or qualification. Legal classifications make possible the answers 'yes' or 'no' to the question of whether a definite entity, conduct or fact belongs to the category of objects singled out as a category of legally relevant matters. The legal classifications and definitions are usually based on empirical data but in many instances they are conventional constructions. For example according to the Convention on the Rights of the Child the child becomes an adult person (and ceases to be a child) when she or he reaches eighteen years of age.[23] This classification of human beings into children and adults is of course conventional (although not arbitrary). Every clear cut classification of human beings based upon the criterion of age contradicts the developmental theory of the continuity of the life processes.

This explanation is also applicable to the special and differential status of the human foetus and related classifications.

The generic viability standard is not more conventional than the age standard of majority. Both standards are in the same degree incompatible with the continuity of the human life process.

(2) Continuity and discontinuity of life processes are relative distinctions related to some features of these processs or to the features of human beings. These are the characteristics considered crucial from a definite point of view. Different regular events occuring in the process of human life may be qualified as points of discontinuity e.g. as points breaking the line of continuous development, From the biological perspective the development of a human being forms a continuum. But in the course of this continous process some very important changes occur, which have paramount importance for the relations between the human being and its social environment.

These changes are usually recognised by law as sufficient reasons for dividing the developmental line of human life into substantially different, subsequent phases. The legal choices of the less or more conventional points of the discontinuity of life processes are determined by the intrinsic features of law as a coercive system of social control, the internal axiology of law and the requirements of legal pragmatics.

3.3. WHAT MAKES THE STATUS OF THE FOETUS A SPECIAL LEGAL STANDING?

The special feature and special situation of an implanted foetus, which makes its legal status special in relation to the status of a living person, is its relationship with the body of pregnant women and with the uterine environment in which it lives.

Pregnancy is a unique biological and social phenomenon. The relation between the pregnant woman and her foetus is different from any kind of relation between living persons. This is true also as regards the relations between a mother and her new born child. In the literature dealing with medical law and medical ethics three concepts of the relation between a pregnant woman and her foetus have been developed[24]:

(1) The foetus is a part of the woman's body like her organs and tissues (a radically

monistic concept).

(2) The foetus is a completely separate being located in the woman's body and the maternal-foetal relation does not differ from the mother-child relation (a radically dualistic concept).

(3) Pregnancy consists in a unique bodily coexistence of two human beings. They are separate beings forming a physical unity of two bodies (a mono-dualistic concept).

The third concept provides the best explanation and justification of the special character of the legal status of the foetus. But an important supplement is needed to make this concept fully adequate to the real position of the foetus in a woman's body. The two beings do not have equal positions. The foetus is dependent upon the pregnant woman's body. It is a kind of parasite on her body, which is the natural environment for the foetus.

The concepts singled out here play an important role in medical law and medical ethics as far as it concerns the diagnosis and treatment of the foetus and clinical experiments *in vivo* with foetuses. In the view of the first concept, the pregnant woman is the patient and the foetus is treated as her organ or tissue. In the view of the second concept the foetus is the patient. His or her legal position as a patient is independent of the position of the pregnant woman. In the view of the third concept the foetus has the status of a quasi patient vitally dependent upon the pregnant woman. His or her rights are limited by the rights of pregnant woman to her bodily integrity. According to the first and the third concept, a pregnant woman always becomes a patient when her foetus is treated.

3.4. WHAT IS THE RELEVANCE OF THE ORIGIN OF THE FOETUS AND OF ITS LOCATION INSIDE OR OUTSIDE A WOMAN'S BODY FOR ITS LEGAL STATUS?

The origin of the foetus and its location inside or outside the woman's body has a significant impact on its primary legal status. The early embryos conceived *in vivo* have before nidation no legal status as individual entities. Their individual existence is simply not noticed and not susceptible to legally relevant observation. Therefore they cannot be legally protected (as individuals). The same is true of naturally conceived and implanted embryos before their existence is conclusively demonstrated (approximately nine days after conception). Before this moment embryos can be legally protected only as a species but not as individuals (the prohibition of production or use of pills preventing the implantation of pre-embryos).

The position of a foetus inside or outside the body of the pregnant woman is relevant to its legal status. Viable miscarried or aborted foetuses become full legal subjects if they meet the local standards defining live birth. Ironically they become persons before the law even if their chances of survival are much less than the chances of a foetus a few days before delivery. This foetus has the status of a limited, conditional or relational legal subject.

In legal documents of major importance, foetuses (and embryos) in all stages of their development are said to be beings deserving respect, presumably as potential human persons.[25] The recommendations of the organs of the European Union as well as the statutes of many European countries impose restrictions and limitations on scientific research and non therapeutic experimentation on foetuses (and embryos). In the legal documents of the European Union and European domestic legislations, non-therapeutic experiments on embryos and destructive embryo research have been made legally admissible only when the statutory conditions and requirements are met.[26] However in all these countries, with exception of the U.K., the production of embryos for research is outlawed.

In some legislations non-therapeutic research and experimentation on embryos are prohibited (Germany, Austria, Denmark, Norway, Portugal, Eire, The Australian States of Victoria and South Australia).[27]

All non-viable foetuses are covered by regulations and medical guidelines limiting commercial turnover of embryos and foetuses. In view of these regulations non-viable foetuses cannot be treated as ordinary commodities or as the objects of ownership. The scale of the application of property rights to foetuses (and embryos) is legally limited. Embryos can be bought and sold only under conditions provided by the relevant statutes.[28] The prospective genetic parents have no property rights to artificially created embryos.[29] These embryos cannot be inherited by the descendants of genetic parents. But in the case of homological *in vitro* fertilisation the genetic father has some say as concerns the implantation if the couple get divorced before the embryo has been implanted.

The above mentioned legal principles and provisions are aimed mainly at the protection of non-viable embryos which come to exist outside women's bodies.[30] But in fact non-viable naturally miscarried or illegally aborted early embryos are of little concern to the law. Early natural miscarriages very often go unnoticed. The expulsions of pre-embryos which have failed to implant are imperceptible, natural and regular processes. The very existence of the expelled pre-embryos is beyond any legal or social control. There are no legal rules imposing on pregnant women positive obligations to naturally miscarried non-viable foetuses or expelled preembryos. In practice only foetuses legally aborted or miscarried in hospitals or clinics are protected against mistreatment in virtue of the above mentioned laws. The life of pre-embryos which do not implant, and of miscarried or aborted non- viable foetuses is not protected by law, since once separated from a woman's body they are doomed to death. The Parliamentary Assembly of the Council of Europe recommends that the embryos expelled in a natural way from the uterus before implantation ought not to be reimplanted in any circumstances.[31] In order to protect these pre-embryos or foetuses against non-therapeutic experimentation the relevant legal regulations allow them to be kept alive only for a definite time.[32]

The legal position of embryos artificially created in the process of *in vitro* fertilisation is more specific and favourable when compared with other categories of embryos, and particularly with the position of naturally conceived embryos which do not implant. Artificially created embryos are recognisable individuals and their existence and life are under full technical control. They have a special and unique legal status different not only from the status of living persons but also from the status of naturally conceived but not implanted and implanted embryos, as well as from the legal standing of aborted or miscarried non-viable foetuses.

The special situation of artificially created pre-embryos (the result of an IVF procedure) consists in their prospects for survival and further development. They are produced in laboratories in order to be implanted into women's wombs. Their chance of implantation is legally granted in many legal regulations concerning assisted reproduction (the prohibition of the production of embryos for research).

However in view of legal regulations now in force (or drafted) artificially created pre-embryos are not accorded the right to implantation. Because octogenesis is forbidden and experiments on embryos are legally limited, pre-embryos which are not implanted must be allowed to die or be killed within a definite period after conception or stored for a definite time.[33] Defective embryos are not allowed to be implanted so they also must die or be killed. Common by-products of IVF are spare embryos, the majority of which must die, and unwanted multiple pregnancies. So in practice the legalisation of IVF entails the legal admissibility of killing artificially created surplus or defective pre-embryos as well as implanted embryos resulting from unwanted multiple pregnancies (the reduction of pregnancies). But some new statutes on assisted reproduction (in Austria, Germany and Switzerland) try indirectly to provide legal protection of the life of the pre-embryos. The provisions of these statutes allow the production in an IVF process only of pre-embryos destined for implantation. The production of spare embryos is forbidden. It is not clearly stated what should be done if the implantation of artificially produced pre-embryos turns out to be practically impossible (if the pre-embryo is defective, the woman dies, or refuses implantation).

The bodily integrity of an artificially created pre-embryo is protected by legal restrictions imposed on scientific research and experimentation on embryos. Restrictions of the commercial use of the artificially created pre-embryo is more articulate and stronger than the prohibitions concerning the commercial use of aborted or miscarried foetuses.

Thus the special legal status of embryos and foetuses in existence outside women's bodies is unclear in legal regulations and controversial in legal doctrine. They are treated within legal regulations as individual human entities but they are considered neither as persons before the law nor as the objects of property rights. They have a transitory legal standing. Legal statutes are more concerned with the protection of the dignity and bodily integrity of these foetuses than with the protection of their lives. Legal protection of artificially created pre-embryos, however limited, is still stronger and more effective than the protection of naturally conceived pre-embryos. In some countries in which early abortions are available, it is almost the case that the request of the pregnant women is stronger then the legal protection of an implanted early embryo (in the first trimester of pregnancy). So the legal position of artificially created pre-embryos is to some extent privileged.

It is ironic that in Germany, where the legal protection of early embryos is stronger than in some other European countries, the Constitutional Tribunal limited the scope of the constitutional protection of the right to life and dignity to living persons and implanted foetuses.[34]

4.

As I have demonstrated in the preceding considerations, the legal status of the foetus is also special and differential in regard to different branches of law. The status of the foetus in civil law is different and to some extent independent of its status in criminal and administrative law. Brain birth and viability are important standards in criminal and medical law (especially as concerns abortion) but they have no relevance in civil law and inheritance law, in which the important criteria are implantation, pregnancy and live birth or the separation of a live foetus from the pregnant woman's body. Only in wrongful death actions does generic viability remain an important issue. In administrative law, live birth and the viability of the miscarried or aborted foetus are of crucial significance. In labour law, pregnancy and live birth are legally relevant facts. In tax law only the live birth of the child is in some legislations the grounds of a legal right to tax reduction (concerning the income of the parents.)

Owing to this differential character of the status of the foetus in a legal system there is no contradiction between the status of the foetus as a conditional and limited subject of law and the statutory provisions legalising abortion.

The relevance of the legal status of the foetus to legal regulations and decisions relating to human reproduction is limited. There are many important legal stances in this field which can be legally and morally justified no matter what legal status the foetus is accorded.

Striking examples of legal settlements for which the status of the foetus is an irrelevant question are the provisions legalising abortion in situations where the pregnancy results from rape or where the health or life of the pregnant woman is endangered[35]; provisions to do with the conditions of availability of assisted reproduction services[36]; provisions concerning surrogate motherhood or access to information about the sperm or egg donor in heterological *in vitro* fertilisation; provisions forbidding octogenesis or cloning of human reproductive cells, prohibiting germ-line therapy or protecting the genetic heritage of mankind. These legal regulations have no relevance to the determination of the legal status of the foetus either. The reasons for these regulations are the rights and interests of pregnant women, the welfare of prospective children, or the interests of future generations.

5.

In my presentation I have been trying to reconstruct the legal status of the foetus in contemporary legal orders. This has been a purely descriptive analysis carried out from a *de lege lata* position. I have not evaluated the existing legal solutions and have not tried to find out and assess critically their rationales. My critical remarks have been focused only on the internal coherence of legal regulations.

This approach is not the only possible one. A critical assessment of the existing laws from a moral, social and political point of view and considerations *de lege ferenda* are crucial tasks of modern jurisprudence and legal philosophy. The discussion of these issues requires a preliminary analysis of the relationships between the moral and legal status of the foetus. But these problems are not the topics of my paper.

Notes

1. See Lang, W., 'The status of human foetus' *Criminal Law Forum. An International Journal* 3 (3), 1992, pp.419-440.

2. This kind of future rights is to be distinguished from the rights of future persons. See Lang, W., 'The concept of rights and the rights of the unborn' in *Challenges to Law at the End of the Twentieth Century* Volume III, Universita degli Studi di Bologna, International Association for Philosophy of Law and Social Philosophy (CIFRID), 1995, pp.111-114, p.113.

3. Sadurski, W., *Moral Pluralism and Legal Neutrality* Dordrecht, Kluwer Academic Publishers, 1992, p.174.

4. Kelsen, H., (trans. Night, M.), *The Pure Theory of Law* Berkeley, University of California Press, 1967.

5. Lang (1992), *op.cit.*

6. United Nations Organisation, 'Covenant of political and social rights' Art. 19, in Newman, F. and Weisbrodt, D. (eds), *Selected International Human Rights Instruments* Cincinnati, Anderson Publishing Corporation, 1990.

7. 'Universal Declaration of Human Rights' Art. 1, in Newman and Weisbrodt *ibid.*

8. France: Law No. 75-17 of 17 January 1975, Art. L 162 reenacted and amended by Law No. 79-124 of December 1979. Poland: Statute on the Protection of Human Foetus and the Conditions of the Admissibility of Abortion, 1 March 1993, Art. 1.

9. Smits, P.W., *The Right to Life of the Unborn Child in International Documents, Decisions and Opinions* The Netherlands, Scholma Druk Beden, 1990, pp.266-272.

10. Hofman, H., *Das Lebensrecht des Nasciturus. Zivilrechtliche Aspekte* (Doctorial thesis presented at the Faculty of Law of Friedrich Wilhelms Universität, Bonn; published privately) 1992, pp.121-130; Smits, *op.cit.*, pp.278-280, and pp.285-288.

11. Hofman, *ibid.*

12. Hart, H.A.L., *The Concept of Law* Oxford, Oxford University Press, 1961, pp.121-137.

13. However, in the United States conferring full legal status on the foetus would be likely to pose serious constitutional problems involving due process and equal protection. See Dworkin, R., 'Unenumerated rights' 59 *University of Chicago Law Review* 381, 1992, pp.400-401.

14. Zielinska, E., 'Dopuszczalność przerywania ciąży w orzecznictwie sadow konstytucyjnych' (The admissibility of abortion in the decisions of constitutional courts) *Państwo i Prawo* (Monthly Review *State and Law*) No. 3, 1988, pp.19-30.

15. Weigend, E. and Zielinska, E., 'Dopuszczalność przerywania ciąży w świetle orzeczenia niemieckiego Trybunału Konstytucyjnego' (The admissibility of abortion in view of the ruling of the German Constitutional Tribunal) *Państwo i Prawo* (Monthly Review *State and Law*) No. 4, 1993, pp.71-76.

16. Organisation of American States, 'American Convention on Human Rights' Art. 1, in Newman and Weisbrodt *op.cit.*

17. *The Convention on the Rights of the Child* (United Nations Treaties Series) New York, United Nations Organisation, 1989.

18. Case 21441 Am. Am. C.H.B. OEA ser. (v) 11 54 doc. 9 rev. 1981.

19. See Art. 31 of the *Convention of Vienna on Law of Treaties* (United Nations Treaties Series) New York, United Nations Organisation, 1961.

20. Gronowska, B., 'Problem aborcji w świetle międzynarodowych praw człowieka' (The problem of abortion in view of international standards of the protection of human rights) *Państwo i Prawo* (Monthly Review *State and Law*) No. 8, 1993, pp.67-75.

21. See Cohen, S. and Taub, N. (eds), *Reproductive Laws for the 1990s* Clifton, New Jersey, Humana Press, 1989.

22. Recommendations of the Assembly of the Council of Europe 1046 (1986), 1100 (1989), 934 (1982), Strasbourg, Council of Europe.

23. Article 1, *The Convention on the Rights of the Child op.cit.*.

24. Weigend and Zielinska *op.cit.* Compare: Gallacher, J., 'Foetus as patient', and Fleishman, A.R., 'Commentary: Foetus as patient' in Cohen and Taub, *op.cit.*, pp.185-236, pp.239-248.

25. Committee of Inquiry into Human Fertilisation and Embryology *Report* (The Warnock Report) London, Her Majesty's Stationary Office, 1984, paragraphs 11.15, 11.16, 11.17, pp.62-63, Recommendation of the Assembly of the Council of Europe 1046 (1986) *op.cit.* paragraph 10.

26. Warnock Report (Committee of Inquiry *op.cit.*) paragraphs 11.18, 13.10, 13.11, and 13.12, and 'List of Recommendations' D 42-50; Recommendation of the Assembly of the Council of Europe 1046 (1986) *op.cit.*; paragraphs 3(1), 8, 11(1)(c), and 12, U.K. *Human Fertilisation and Embryology Act 1990* in Morgan, D. and Lee, Robert G., *Blackstones Guide to the Human Fertilisation and Embryology Act 1990* London, Blackstone Press Limited, 1991, pp.190-194.

27. Cf. Morgan and Lee (eds.), *op.cit.*, pp.85-88.

28. Cf. Warnock Report (Committee of Inquiry *op.cit.*) paragraphs 10.11, and 13.13, and M. Safian, *Prawo wobec ingerencji w naturę ludzkiej prokreacji* (Law in the face of the intervention in the nature of human procreation) Warsaw, Uniwersytet Warszawski, 1990, pp.392-397.

29. Safian, *ibid.*

30. This is clearly stated in the U.K. *Human Fertilisation and Embryology Act 1990* (in Morgan and Lee *op.cit.*) paragraphs 1 and 3. The provisions of the Warnock Report (Committee of Inquiry, *op.cit.*) and the Recommendations of the Assembly of the Council of Europe (*op.cit.*) are formulated in general terms as applicable to all kinds of foetuses, implanted and not-implanted, viable and non-viable, gestating in the wombs of women or existing outside women's bodies.

31. The Recommendation of the Assembly of the Council of Europe 1100 (1989), *op.cit.*, Annexe B7.

32. The Warnock Report recommends "that no live human embryo derived from *in vitro* fertilisation, whether frozen or unfrozen, may be kept alive, if not transferred to a woman, beyond fourteen days after fertilisation, nor may be used as a research subject beyond fourteen days after fertilisation. This fourteen day period does not include any time during which the embryo may have been frozen" Committee of Inquiry, *op.cit.*, paragraph 11.22. pp.66. The *Human Fertilisation and Embryology Act 1990* (U.K.) states, that "a licence cannot authorise keeping or using an embryo after the appearance of the primitive streak" Morgan and Lee *op.cit.* paragraph 3(3)(a).

33. Warnock Report (Committee of Inquiry *op.cit.*) paragraphs 10.10 and 10.11; U.K. *Human Fertilisation and Embryology Act 1990* (Morgan and Lee *op.cit.*) 14(5) and 14(6).

34. Weigend and Zielinska, *op.cit.*

35. See Thomson, J.J., 'A defence of abortion' in Singer, P. (ed.), *Applied Ethics* Oxford, Oxford University Press, 1986, pp.37-56.

36. U.K. *Human Fertilisation and Embryology Act* (Morgan and Lee, *op.cit.*) paragraph 13(5).

16. LEGAL STATUS OF THE HUMAN EMBRYO

Overview of the Hungarian Regulation

Judit Sándor J.D. LLM
Central European University
Budapest College
Hungary

1. Introduction

In an age of tremendous bio-technological challenges, medical law, or health care law[1] is very often considered an unlimited and flexible tool for providing justification for biomedical science. The content of legal rules - according to this practical view - depends entirely on political decisions and the level of biotechnology. Nevertheless there exists another but often forgotten competing theory which can be formulated in the following way: there are some general legal norms which are fundamentally unchanging, and in order to adapt them to the new circumstances, judges and legislators must simply find a way for these legal norms to preserve their original content. On this view, which one might call the 'interpretative' view, the question of how to regulate assisted procreation is connected to the concepts of personality, human life, motherhood and rights itself.

In applying the latter 'interpretative' view to the constitutional and civil law protection of persons, we may find that we are not without legal sources in the regulation of assisted procreation. There are principles which can be adopted in this new, often controversial, area of medical law. Here are some examples:

(1) The human person is inviolable.

(2) No one may cause harm to the person of another without his consent.

(3) *Inter vivos* disposal of a part of a human body is in the gift of the person unless it is a regenerative body part.

(4) The child's best interests in every decision concerning it must be an important and perhaps determining factor.

(5) Everyone has the right to respect for his private and family life.

In the legal responses to the new technologies, legislators often seem to forget about this concept of 'legal reconstruction' which, before any innovative legal responses are suggested, might attempt to interpret existing legal principles in the new context. I am aware how complex the legal approach towards assisted procreation is; it involves the very diverse approaches of philosophy and medicine, and economic constraints. Although I feel it is necessary to provide comprehensive regulation in respect of the

269

D. Evans (ed.), Conceiving the Embryo, 269–275.
© 1996 *Kluwer Law International. Printed in the Netherlands.*

new biomedical technologies, in order to give some order to the complex social and legal problems which they generate, I recommend first looking at the steps and principles which the relevant legal fields - constitutional law, criminal law, civil law, medical law - have already provided for the related area of human rights protection.

2. The Status of the Human Embryo Under Hungarian Law

Legal questions related to assisted procreation are strongly influenced by the concept and moral status of potential persons. The extent to which the law recognises rights attributed to potential persons and so provides protection to the foetus, determines whether methods of assisted reproduction will be excluded, permitted or restricted by the law. However, we have to mention here that legislators and scholars have focussed their attention on the *in utero* and not *ex utero* status of foetuses. This is due in part to the fact that whilst at the moment there are seven *in vitro* centres in Hungary, there is still no embryo research.

Since the nineteenth century, only very few changes have occurred in the legal concept of the foetus in Hungary. The law still applies the suspense condition of live birth which consolidates certain legal obligations from the moment of conception. If the suspense condition fails, the obligation is deemed never to have existed. Under this concept, the *nasciturus* or *conceptus* is still not a legal person. Still the law recognises that after the live birth, the neonate will be a person under the law and the law therefore ensures and preserves certain rights for it. *"Nasciturus pro jam nato habetur, si de ejus commodis agitur."* Protection of the potential rights and interests of the unborn child is usually ensured by the appointment of a proxy.[2] Appointment is mandatory if the rights of the natural parents and the foetus are in conflict. But this legal protection is generally limited to conflicts over property rights, and the legal protections afforded in that area have not (yet) been seen as appropriate in potential conflicts of interests which may arise in abortion and in the various conflicts of rights and interests which may arise in the hard cases of *in vitro* fertilisation and surrogacy agreements.

The other heritage of the law is that, since the Roman law *praesumptio iuris et de iure* the foetus is considered to have been conceived between the 180th and 300th day before the delivery.

Even in the 19th century, Hungarian criminal law provided different levels of protection to foetuses, small children and other persons. The offences of 'homicide', 'child killing', 'termination of pregnancy' and 'child leaving' were separate crimes. Under these criminal provisions, a different level of criminal protection was applied to illegitimate children, foetuses and persons.[3] Under article 284 of the Criminal Code of 1878 when the mother killed her own illegitimate child during or soon after the delivery, she was sentenced to up to 5 years imprisonment, while the sentence for homicide was 10-15 years of imprisonment. To leave a child alone in an isolated place where the chances of his or her survival was very low was a different crime under article 287(1) (today it would be accounted merciless killing), and so also was it when a woman left a child in a place where the child could receive help from someone else (article 287(2)).[4]

The other obvious source for analysing the legal status of the embryo is the constitutional concept of right to life. Constitutions carefully avoid defining potential or prenatal life. As a result, it is very difficult to derive any generally accepted and legally sound answer to the question of the status of the embryo from them. The American constitutional approach applies the rights and limits of a zone of privacy - as conceived in the Fourth Amendment[5] - and equal protection under the Fourteenth Amendment[6] to conceptualise the status of a foetus. The Supreme Court's position can be summarised by the following statement: decisions which affect marriage and childbirth are so intimate, and personal, and so much connected to the development of the personality, that individuals must be allowed to control decisions about them.

This concept can be identified in cases related to contraception[7], the elimination of discrimination against illegitimate children, decriminalisation of consensual homosexual relationships and oral sex etc. However, as Ronald Dworkin points out, the decision on abortion involves even more private questions since it includes not only a woman's connection towards the others but also the use of her own body.[8]

When the Hungarian Constitutional Court has faced the problems of individual privacy in general, it has usually applied a form of balancing test between a right to life and human dignity. "In the Hungarian Republic everyone has an inherent right to life and human dignity from which no one shall be deprived." (Constitution 54 (1)) This general protection of the personality, in the interpretation of the Hungarian Constitutional Court[9], is a subsidiary provision when there is no concrete special provision for the given violation of personal autonomy.

The Hungarian Constitution does not establish a rank order between these rights, nor does it specify justifications for limitations on these rights. Therefore basic rights and obligations are ensured for and imposed on 'everyone'. Since the current national and international laws and conventions use the words 'human beings', 'persons' and 'everyone', they have become legal synonyms and 'human being' has become a legal normative conception.[10] Although the constitution does not provide a definition of persons, it is clearly defined in the Hungarian Civil Code. Under the Hungarian Civil Code (Article 9) only individuals born alive are considered persons under the law. However, as has already been indicated, foetuses possess certain legal rights in case of live birth from the moment of conception.

Although the Hungarian Act on the Protection of Foetal Life represents generally a liberal approach towards abortion, there are still several Articles where some more or less implicit guarantees serving as protection of the foetus's life are implemented.

At the end of 1991 the Hungarian Constitutional Court issued a decision on the regulations 76/1988 (XI.3.) and 25/1988 (XII.15.) SZEM r. which were based upon the Health Act (1972. evi II.tv) and dealt with the termination of pregnancy. The Court did not examine or resolve the substantive question of whether the regulations on abortion were unconstitutional. Instead the Court found these laws unconstitutional for procedural reasons. The Court stated clearly that the two regulations violate Article 8

(2) of the Hungarian Constitution which requires that all the basic human rights should be regulated by Parliamentary Act. However, instead of declaring the challenged regulations immediately unconstitutional, the Constitutional Court provided a period of one year for Parliament to pass new regulations. It should be mentioned here that the Hungarian Constitutional Court has an extremely broad jurisdiction. Complaints with which it can deal are not limited to those contesting the constitutionality of existing laws and administrative regulations, but extend even to allegations of negligence against the legislature for not having passed a law, if the absence of such a law creates an unconstitutional situation. If the Constitutional Court concludes that lawmakers should have passed such a law, parliament is given a limited period of time in which it has to pass the required legislation. That was the case with the abortion law since there was no regulation at the Parliamentary level (except the short clause in the health Act).

After long months of public debate, the Parliament passed the new Act at the end of 1992. The Act shows signs of compromise between the restrictive and liberal views on the availability of abortion.

As the title of 1992: LXXIX Act shows, the lawmakers intended to issue a law on the protection of the foetus's life. However, due to the political compromises, and notwithstanding different restrictions, abortions remain generally available under the new Act.

As the preamble states, the Act is based on two different principles: (1), on the one hand, that prenatal life enjoys respect and protection from the moment of conception, and abortion cannot be considered a method of contraception; and (2) that, on the other hand, there is a parental right to family planning though the preamble also emphasises that this right involves the duty to protect the foetus' life.

Articles 2-4 deal with several means of protecting the foetus, such as education about family planning, free medical care for pregnant mothers, and financial support for pregnant women.

Articles 5-13 regulate the conditions and procedures for performing abortions. The Act regulates the availability of abortion based upon different time limits. These time limits and regulations are the following.

1. An abortion may be performed up to the twelfth week of pregnancy if:
   a) there is a grievous threat to the mother's health;
   b) the foetus is suffering a probable grievous handicap or injury in the judgement of medical science;
   c) pregnancy is the result of a criminal act;
   d) there is a grievous crisis in the mother's life.

2. An abortion may be performed up to the eighteenth week of pregnancy if:
   a) the pregnant woman is incompetent (Hungarian law distinguishes three categories of competence based on age and mental state);
   b) if the pregnant woman did not recognise that she was pregnant for reasons outside her control, such as medical misdiagnosis, or the failure of any health institute or other authority to act as required by the law.

3. An abortion may be performed up to the twentieth week of pregnancy, or, if a

diagnostic procedure has been postponed, up to the twenty-fourth week, if the probability of genetic or teratological damage/defect is greater than 50%.

4. A pregnancy may be terminated at any time:

    a) if there is a grievous medical threat to the mother's life; or

    b) if the foetus has such a grievous malformation that the child physically could not lead a normal life.

There are, also, some procedural requirements where non-medical reasons for abortion are considered. If there is no medical reason for the termination of pregnancy, an abortion may still be performed upon the written request of the mother. The pregnant woman shall personally deliver her written request, together with the medical evidence of pregnancy to a staffmember of the Family Protection Service (F.P.S.).

Under Article 9(1) of the Act, women with restricted mental capacity may request an abortion only together with the consent of their guardian, natural or otherwise. For those who are not competent, only the guardian can request the abortion.

The member of the staff of F.P.S., respecting the human dignity of the pregnant woman, and preferably in the presence of the father of the foetus, is expected to provide information to the pregnant woman about: a) the laws about the termination of pregnancy; b) possibilities of material and other support for maternity care provided by the State and non-governmental organisations; c) institutions and organisations that may provide material and moral support for mothers; d) possibilities of adoption; e) methods of abortion; f) institutions where abortions are performed; and g) contraceptive methods (in order to avoid future unwanted pregnancies). The information should be given in a personalised way.

After giving this information, the F.P.S. staff member will fill in the request form. Within 8 days the pregnant woman should go to the chosen health institute (one mutually agreed upon by both the woman and the staff member). Should the woman fail to go within 8 days, the request form required for the abortion is no longer valid. Abortions may not be performed until three days after the date upon which the request form was filled out.

If the doctor of the health care institute recognises that the pregnancy is not within the time-limit fixed by the law or that performing the abortion would threaten the pregnant woman's life, he may refuse to perform the abortion. The pregnant woman must then be informed about the possibility of requesting and obtaining a second opinion.

In cancelling the specifically enumerated bases for abortion (being a lone parent, lacking a flat, being aged above 35, having more than two children already etc.) in the previous law (161988 (XII.15.) SZEM r.), and introducing a general category of 'grievous crisis', the Act radically changed the conditions under which abortion may be obtained. Article 12 (6) of the Act defines a 'grievous crisis' as a state that causes either a physical or a mental crisis or socially impossible conditions and, for these reasons, threatens the foetus' life. The previous system of enumeration was subject to much criticism because it was discriminatory and provided easier access to abortion for the poor and young couples who had no accommodation. However in the application of the definition of 'grievous crisis', the current Act presents other difficult questions.

The definition of 'grievous crisis' is itself ambiguous since it is not clear whether it is intended mainly to protect women in crisis or the foetus's life.

The procedure for providing information before the termination of pregnancy raises other difficult questions. Although the Act stresses that the staff member of the F.P.S. cannot change the woman's decision, the system of 'request for abortion' furthers the stated legislative intent of the Act - to protect the foetus's well-being. Thus the Act tries to achieve a balance between a restrictive and a permissive system in such a way as to preserve the availability of abortion despite the Act's implicit position that abortion is an evil.

Other restrictions can be imposed on the requests of patients for abortion in order to ensure the freedom of conscience of medical doctors. Many laws therefore not only implicitly but also explicitly ensure that doctors who do not want to perform certain medical interventions because of their religion or conscience cannot be forced to do them. It follows from the legality of a doctors' free conscience that the law should provide guarantees for those doctors who do not want to perform abortion that they will not be obliged to perform abortion when it is socially indicated. On the other hand it appears to prescribe to doctors the obligation to perform abortions where there is a medical emergency, without regards to the conscience of the medical doctor.

However our question still remains unanswered: do we have to create a different status for the *ex utero* embryo, with special respect to the custody of the frozen embryo, or do we simply have to apply to the *ex utero* embryo the status of the *in utero* embryo. Since we have still not developed an independent status for the *ex utero* embryo, the legal protection of the foetus is strongly related to the abortion laws of a given country.

3. Conclusions

The legal status of the human embryo in different legal fields does provide a useful contribution in the process of thinking about and drafting a European Model Law on medically assisted procreation. Nevertheless there are major reasons why the legal status of the human embryo, which is mainly based on suspense legal capacity and the *praesumptio iuris et de iure* conception of Roman law, cannot fully resolve the possible legal debates on new reproductive techniques. While the Roman law approach was designed to resolve property and hereditary law debates in case of the death of the father or the foetus, access to assisted procreation has brought fundamentally new ethical issues into legal scholarship. These include the concept of motherhood and family, the allocation of resources, and the right to personal identity. The other relevant legal stream, developed mainly through abortion decisions, is also a limited tool since, in the abortion debate, the major conflict of rights occurs between the state's interest in protecting human life and the woman's right to self-determination, while in the case of assisted procreation, the conflict of rights and interests are more complex.

Notes

1. Health care law is often considered a synonym for medical law. However one can make a distinction between them by construing medical law as a discipline dealing with the issues of jurisprudence raised by medicine and biotechnology, and health care law as consisting of mainly administrative legal norms regulating access to health care services, health insurance and regulation (e.g., licencing) of a health care system, etc.

2. 1877: XX. t.-c. article 30., 1894: XVI. t.-c. article 128.

3. Angyal, Pál, *Magyar Buntetojog Tankonyve* Budapest, 1943, pp.112-113.

4. *Ibid.*

5. "The right of the people to be secure in their persons, houses, papers, and effects against unreasonable searches and seizures, shall not be violated, and no warrants shall be issued, but upon probable cause, supported by Oath or affirmation, and particularly describing the place to be searched and the persons or things to be seized."

6. Section 1: " ... No state shall make or enforce any law which shall abridge the privileges or immunities of citizens of the United States; nor shall any State deprive any person of life, liberty, or property, without due process of law; nor deny to any person within its jurisdiction the equal protection of the laws."

7. See: *Griswold v. Connecticut* 381 U.S. 479 (1965).

8. Dworkin, R., 'The Great Abortion Case' *New York Review of Books* 29 June 1989, p.51.

9. The Constitutional Court decision of 8/1990 (IV.23.) AB h. and also 64/1991 (XII.17.) AB h. in *Magyar Kozlony* (the Hungarian official legal gazette) 139, 1991, p.2811.

10. Decision 64/1991 of the Hungarian Constitutional Court in *Magyar Kozlony op.cit.* p.2815.

17. THE LEGAL STATUS OF THE EMBRYO IN POLAND

Prof. dr hab. Eleonora Zielińska
Faculty of Law and Administration
Warsaw University
Poland

The legal status of the embryo in Poland changed significantly in 1993. Prior to that time, Polish law did not include any general provisions dealing with the legal status of the embryo or the foetus. Instead Polish civil law stated, in Art.8 of the Civil Code (C.C.) that every person enjoys legal status from the moment of birth.

However Polish legislation did provide fragmentary regulations directly concerning the unborn child. Section 2 of articles 927 and 972 C.C. give the unborn rights of inheritance and legacy if it was conceived before the testator's death and was born alive. Articles 75 and 77 of the Tutelary and Family Code (T.F.C) state that the unborn child can be legally recognised by its father if it has already been conceived. According to article 182 of the T.F.C. a conceived, yet still unborn, child may be assigned a guardian if it is necessary for the protection of its future rights. The guardianship ceases to be effective at the moment of the child's birth.

From 1952 the Supreme Court handed down a series of rulings guaranteeing protection of the conceived child's interests with regard to events taking place during its foetal stage. Characteristic of these rulings was that they were not based on provisions which clearly regulated the *nasciturus* status, since such provisions were lacking, but resulted from an interpretation of provisions concerning the general liability for torts and an application of analogies to the existing fragmentary regulations.[1]

In addition to these Supreme Court rulings, liberal abortion provisions were in force from 27th April 1956, which allowed termination of pregnancy by physician for medical, legal and social indications. The last, in practice, meant abortion on request for pregnant women in the first three months of pregnancy.

The criminal provisions of the Penal Code (art. 153 and 154) had prohibited forced abortion and abortion committed in violation of the law only. Among those commenting on the criminal law the opinion prevailed that the object of protection in those penal provisions was the life and health of the woman rather than the life of the foetus.

This, then, was the legal position with relation to the human embryo which was so significantly changed by the law of 7th January 1993 on family planning, protection of human foetuses and the conditions under which termination of pregnancy is possible (referred to hereafter as the anti-abortion law).

This law repeals the liberal Law of 27th April 1956 mentioned above, and amends

D. Evans (ed.), Conceiving the Embryo, 277–279.
© *1996 Kluwer Law International. Printed in the Netherlands.*

certain other items of legislation.

According to the first article of the anti-abortion law "every human being shall have an inherent right to life as from the moment of his conception" and "the life and health of the child shall be placed under the protection of the law as from the moment of its conception". The anti-abortion law amended, in addition, article 8 of the C.C., which stated that every person has a restricted legal capacity from the moment of birth, by the insertion of a new subsection 2 reading as follows:

> A conceived child shall likewise enjoy legal capacity: it shall acquire the same rights and duties as regards financial obligations in so far as it is born alive.

It also introduced a new provision into art. 446 of the C.C. (art. 446.1) confirming a principle already recognised in many Supreme Court rulings that "after its birth, a child may seek compensation for damage which he underwent prior to his birth".

Very important changes were introduced by the above mentioned law into the Penal Code (P.C.).

First of all, a new article 23b P.C. was added to the general provision of art. 23 P.C. (providing for the conditions of admissible risk in case of economic, technical or medical experiments) according to which "the conceived child may not be subject to any procedures other than those intended to protect its life and health, or its mother's life or health, other than the procedures referred to in subsection 2".

According to this subsection

> prenatal diagnosis that does not significantly increase the risk of abortion shall be authorised in cases where: 1) the conceived child belongs to a family manifesting a genetic burden, 2) it is assumed that a genetic condition may be cured or that it is possible to remedy the condition or to limit its effects at the foetal stage, 3) a presumption exists that the foetus presents a serious defect.

The new article 23b P.C., in spite of its unclear wording, contains therefore an explicit ban on non-therapeutic ('scientific') experiments on a human embryo or foetus. However since it remains by its nature *lex imperfecta* (because it does not provide any sanction for the mere violation of the prohibition without resulting damage), it constitutes a somewhat symbolic protection,

It is worth mentioning that the law in its final form does not specify any kind of prohibited experiments on human embryos, though in its earlier drafts some kinds of genetic engineering (such as cloning, and creating hybrids or chimeras) had been specifically enumerated.

Second, the anti-abortion law substitutes for previous provisions of the P.C. dealing with illegal interruption of pregnancy the offence of "causing the death of a conceived child" as a specific form of homicide (art.149a P.C.). It introduced also a hitherto unknown type of offence: "causing physical injury to a conceived child or the destabilisation of the health of a conceived child in such a way as to endanger its life" as a specific kind of illegal act (art. 156a P.C.).

In comparison with previous regulations the above mentioned provisions extended significantly the scope and intensity of legal protection of the foetus during pregnancy by means of the criminal law. They can also be interpreted as encompassing penal protection for a foetus *ex utero* as well, however opposing opinions have also been expressed on this point. The point at which this intensive legal protection of a foetus begins is still an object of controversy. The law does not precisely define when, for its purposes, conception occurs. Moreover, speaking about the 'moment of conception' in the context of human conception is at odds with the biological fact that fertilisation is a process rather than a single event.

The term used within the anti-abortion act - 'conceived child' - gives some support to view that legal protection of the embryo begins some days after fertilisation, e.g. after individuation has occurred (when it is already known whether embryo will develop as one individual or twins). This means that the moment, some days after the zygote implants in the uterus (that is, about 14 days after fertilisation) might be considered legally relevant.

If such an interpretation is broadly accepted, the anti-abortion law will not necessarily have negative repercussions for *in vitro* fertilisation.

Note

1. Compare: Dybowski, T., 'The legal status of the conceived child' in Safian, M. (ed.), *Medicine, Ethics and Law - Canadian-Polish Perspectives* Montreal, 1991, pp.295-296.

PART FIVE

Human Embryo Research

18. WHAT DEVELOPMENTS OF HUMAN EMBRYO RESEARCH WOULD BE PHILOSOPHICALLY CHALLENGING?

Alex Mauron
Fondation Louis Jeantet de Médecine
C.P. 277, CH-1211 Genève 17
Switzerland

1. Preamble

Whether it is ethical to experiment on early human embryos is a contentious question in Europe today. It is one of several bioethical issues that stand in the way of a European consensus on bioethics. This lack of agreement obviously reflects deep-seated divergences in assessing the ethical standing of the early embryo. But it also reflects differences in the way the political debate and the law-making process of various countries have either sought a minimum procedural consensus, or allowed one particular moral conviction to prevail.

The possibility of research on early human embryos arose from the development of *in vitro* fertilisation (IVF) and the existence of 'spare' embryos. These embryos result from the fertilisation process but cannot actually be transferred to the patient, either because one aims at limiting the risk of multiple pregnancies, or because transferrable embryos are selected on the basis of criteria that are more or less predictive of normal development and/or on the basis of genetic tests (preimplantation diagnosis) or because they are left over when treatment is completed. Over and above the 'spare' ones, embryos created specifically for research purposes can be used; to my knowledge, this is possible only in the U.K.

Embryo research is often classified as either *therapeutic* (undertaken in order to benefit specifically the very embryo on which it is performed) or *non-therapeutic* (not designed to benefit this specific embryo). Another distinction that seems more to the point in ethical terms is between *invasive* and *non-invasive* research. Whatever its purpose, embryo research is non-invasive whenever it is compatible with the ensuing transfer of the embryo to a patient. This can include various observational investigations and also non-destructive biochemical analyses such as metabolic measurements or the identification of substances secreted by the embryo into the culture medium. Invasive research is defined as incompatible with further use of the embryo for transfer and further development in the patient's womb. Invasive embryo research is opposed by those moral traditions which assert that (morally relevant) personhood starts at 'conception'[1], or more broadly, by those who believe the early embryo to be the locus of considerable moral stakes, even if they are not quite as high as those

283

D. Evans (ed.), Conceiving the Embryo, 283–296.
© 1996 Alex Mauron. Printed in the Netherlands.

invested in persons in the ordinary sense. Conversely, moral traditions that either link moral standing to properties that early embryos do not possess (such as psychological states) or who query the grounding of moral standing in purely ontological considerations will generally be much more open to this kind of research.

This is not intended to be an exhaustive report on the very latest news from the science-front.   In the field of human embryo experimentation, U.K. human embryologists are in the best position to discuss recent progress since the U.K. is the only European country in which such research is both permitted and flourishing due to a pre-existing, strong research tradition in the field of mammalian developmental biology.[2] Therefore, rather than a complete review of recent progress in human embryology, I will limit myself to the question asked in the title and try to focus preferentially on areas of current or foreseeable progress that would seem to be philosophically interesting, either because they raise novel philosophical questions about the standing of the human embryo, or provide unusual or striking illustrations of old quandaries.   Other philosophical issues, such as the concerns for justice raised in matters of access/rationing of infertility services will be left aside, even if they are arguably just as important, or even more so.

The objectives of research on early human embryos (or pre-embryos, or preimplantation embryos) can be classified as follows (allowing for the usual grey zone present in these sorts of classifications):
- to advance basic knowledge on the early growth and development of human embryos, and to use early human embryos as model-systems to investigate various biomedical questions (here is an example of the latter: a blastocyst 'invades' the uterine lining and this process has long been seen as a model for studying the molecular basis of the invasive properties of metastatic cancer cells);
- to improve reproductive services with a view to furthering the understanding and diagnosis of infertility and increasing the success rate of various procedures, especially IVF; also to develop genetic diagnostic techniques that are closely linked to IVF, such as preimplantation diagnosis; and to advance other aspects of reproductive medicine such as novel contraceptive strategies.

I will examine these areas in turn.

2. Human Embryo Research For Basic Knowledge

In the foreseeable future, human embryo research will probably play a modest role in advancing basic, general biomedical science. In the last decade, we have gathered infinitely more basic information about vertebrate development, including human development, from studying *drosophila* (the fruit-fly) than from human embryo research. Of course this is already changing. The time has come to cash in the benefits of our investment in drosophila (and a few other lowly beasts) by transferring concepts and molecular tools to mammalian embryology. But even so, it is still the case that much of what is interesting in human early development can be discovered by studying other mammalian species. This is not, of course, to deny that there are features of human embryogenesis that are unique to *homo sapiens*. In fact, one of the earliest results from human embryo research is the finding of Braude *et al* that, in human embryonic development, it is at the 4-8 cell stage that embryonic genome activation occurs. This means that at this point, the dependence on maternal messenger RNA ceases and transcription and translation of the newly-formed embryonic genome takes over[3], which is much later than in mouse development. (In fact, it seems that in the mouse zygote transcriptional differences between the male and female pronuclei may be observed[4], which means that unlike the human egg, the mouse zygote has a genetic identity of its own very early on, if one interprets 'genetic identity' in terms of patterns of gene expression.)

Nevertheless, for the most part, conceptual breakthroughs as well as broad generalisable knowledge are likely to come from experiments with other species, with human experiments filling in details here and there. A partial exception may be the establishment and study of human embryonic stem cells (ES-cells) in culture. This was started in the mouse in the seventies and initiated a very fruitful line of investigation into the determinants of early cell differentiation and development.[5] How is the initial totipotency of blastomeres progressively restricted? What is the identity of the progenitor cells of various tissues and what are the molecules (growth factors) that guide them along specific pathways of cell differentiation? Mouse studies will go a long way towards answering such questions, yet one may soon want to fill in the human-specific details, given the kind of differences between human and mouse early development that have already been ascertained and the wish to establish the relevance of such findings to human pathology. Establishing human ES-cells in culture has proven difficult because methods that are successful in one species are not readily transposable to another.[6] Nevertheless, the successful isolation of human inner mass cells and their subsequent culture for a limited time has recently been reported.[7] This first step on the path towards human ES-cell cultures will certainly revive this particular line of research, with implications for several aspects of basic and applied biology, including gene therapy. On a more conceptual level, the existence of established human ES-cells will force us to rethink the very fuzzy notion of totipotentiality. It may become more obvious that a cell can be 'totipotent', in the sense of having the ability to turn into any one of the body's cell types given the right conditions, without being 'totipotent', in the sense of being able to give rise to a complete human being upon further development. Let us call these two concepts of totipotentiality T_c and T_i (respectively for 'cellular' and 'individual'). We would want to say that an established ES-cell growing as a uniform monolayer in a Petri-dish has retained T_c but lost T_i, while a native inner mass cell sitting in its original blastocyst has both. But do these potentialities T_c and T_i actually 'inhere' in these cells as definable biological properties? Perhaps so; but then again it could well be that we have reached here the limits of potentiality thinking in biology. What is clear is that the conflation of the two meanings of totipotentiality is a mistake, one that runs through a great deal of bioethical and even legal discourse.[8]

Culturing ES-cells will use pre-implantation embryos only, but may shed light also on biological processes that occur after implantation, thus bypassing to some extent the 14-day limit for human embryo experimentation that seems solidly established even in the most permissive countries. Finally, ES-cell cultures may be the first step towards the admittedly far-fetched goal of growing transplantable human tissue in vitro. This would be the scientifically (and ethically) sounder version of the journalistic nightmare of growing for oneself a twin to be used for 'spare-parts'.[9] Again, this is highly speculative, but may still be on this side of science-fiction.

Another factor to consider is the logistics of human embryo research and the fact that most of it is done in laboratories attached to clinical reproductive medicine units. The logistics are such that whatever human early embryos are available will be used mostly to advance practical solutions in reproductive medicine and that more basic questions will be lower on the list of priorities. This is likely to remain so, unless one were to embark on the creation of human embryos specifically for research, and on a grand scale at that. This seems rather unlikely and may be considered ethically problematic, even if one does not entertain particular ontological beliefs about human pre-embryos: at least, proponents of the production of embryos solely for research purposes should show that it can be done without serious disadvantages to the women involved. (This raises a little-discussed problem, namely the conflict of interests that pits the wish of the physician/researcher to have as many spare embryos as possible against the medical interest of women not to undergo ovarian hyperstimulation.) To summarise, and again insisting that I have no moral axe to grind with human embryo research per se, one cannot help thinking that the sweeping arguments in which human embryo experimentation is sometimes touted as an essential prerequisite for many crucial biomedical advances are a bit disingenuous. Human embryo research must probably stand or fall on its merits for applied purposes such as the diagnosis, management and correction of infertility, genetic diagnosis on early embryos and contraceptive research. More generally speaking, human embryo research will mostly be aimed at discovering the specifically human details of early development whose knowledge is required for the various practical purposes of reproductive medicine.

3. Human Embryo Research in the Context of Reproductive Services

In basic research, much can be achieved by using non-human models and when it comes to addressing specifically human experimental subjects or human-derived material, scientists are often merely filling the gaps in existing knowledge. Human-specific data or parameters obviously exist in basic biomedical science, but they are like icebergs floating in an ocean of knowledge that is valid for many species. This is inherently much less the case in clinical or other applied research, such as is needed to perfect reproductive technologies or new contraceptive methods. Validating a medical method or technology in humans is an essential step before it can be implemented in patients at large. As one moves from general basic knowledge to the applied goals of relieving infertility or controlling fertility, many biological details of human reproductive processes come to the fore and must be specifically understood on the basis of human studies. (For a thorough review of the present state and prospects of IVF, see Winston and Handyside.[10])

Most of the current experimental use of human embryos has the character of applied research aimed either at improving the IVF methodology, or at perfecting genetic diagnostics on pre-embryos (pre-implantation diagnosis). Various improvements in embryo culture conditions have allowed normal in vitro development to the blastocyst stage to be obtained, although IVF with embryo transfer at that stage still has low rates of success. The ability to postpone transfer to later stages is likely to have an impact in several directions. For instance, it allows detailed study of chromosomal abnormalities in the very first stages of development. Moreover, the fact that the first few divisions of the embryo happen in observable conditions makes it possible to define predictive criteria for choosing which embryos are most likely to develop normally and should therefore be transferred. Furthermore, freezing embryos at the 8-cell stage has advantages over cryoconservation of earlier ones. Finally, cultured blastocysts produce various chemical signals such as hCG (human chorionic gonadotropin) and as yet ill-defined implantation factors whose discovery would potentially advance many areas of reproductive medicine. As mentioned already, this latter objective of embryo research does not necessarily need invasive procedures (i.e. procedures that 'use up' spare embryos), since one can also analyse the culture fluid of embryos destined to be transferred to patients.

Another lively area of IVF research concerns male-factor infertility. Various micromanipulation techniques have been devised to bring sperm directly in contact with the oocyte. These include *partial zona dissection*, whereby an opening is created in the zona pellucida to allow sperm entry from the fertilisation medium; *sub-zonal sperm insertion*, the microinjection of sperm cells into the perivitelline space; and finally *intracytoplasmic sperm injection (ICSI)*, in which sperm is injected directly into the cytoplasm of the oocyte.[11] ICSI seems to be the most promising technique.[12] On the positive side, this development may bring some change to our overall ethical framework for assisted conception services by lessening their dependence on heterologous procedures. However it may also raise new ethical problems. For instance, some males whose sterility is of hereditary etiology could conceivably father children who might be sterile themselves. Inheriting sterility from your father is an intriguing situation that requires further reflection. More generally, the question whether injected oocytes may have been damaged in ways that are not immediately obvious must be considered. Practitioners will answer that the whole field of IVF has always been based on the assumption that damaged embryos are selected out at later stages (implantation, pregnancy), so that damage to early embryos is an 'all or nothing' matter: either the embryo is intact and results in a normal birth or it is damaged and is unable to implant or is aborted early on. This argument has been largely validated for standard IVF. However one could argue that this built-in safety net is being stretched quite a bit further in the ICSI procedure. For one thing, the quasi-Darwinian logic that underpins this argument is undermined to some extent in ICSI, where the 'winner-takes-all' competition between spermatozoa occuring in normal fertilisation is abolished. In fact, ICSI can be used with sperm cells microsurgically aspirated from the epididymis, so that other mechanisms required for conventional fertilisation are by-passed.[13] It is true that preliminary outcome data for children born by ICSI reported by the media show little basis for concern[14], but long-range genetic problems cannot be excluded at this stage. This illustrates a recurring worry about IVF research in general, which proceeds with relatively little preliminary animal experimentation and in which - some would claim - future children are in effect used as research subjects.

3.1. PREIMPLANTATION DIAGNOSIS

Matters are different in the case of preimplantation diagnosis, which has sometimes been seen as controversial.   Preimplantation diagnosis is implemented to detect chromosomal abnormalities or single-gene defects in embryos, and to select normal embryos for transfer. Sexing of embryos is also possible, with a view to avoiding male offspring in couples who are at-risk of transmitting an X-linked recessive condition and when a more precise gene-specific test is not available. Sex selection for non-medical reasons is generally regarded as unethical.

Preimplantation diagnosis usually involves a biopsy of one or more cells of an early embryo (morula or blastocyst) and has been made possible by revolutionary advances in our ability to make genetic analyses using the DNA of single cells. Technically, preimplantation diagnosis has benefitted a great deal from the improvement of various DNA-specific detection techniques such as 'chromosome painting' (FISH, fluorescence in-situ hybridisation), and PCR (polymerase chain reaction) analysis, the latter having become far more reliable than in its early days. Nevertheless, there are still problems that may be more substantial than mere technical obstacles. Misdiagnoses have been reported[15], that may be due to recombination and/or genetic anomalies not previously accounted for.   As a result, preimplantation diagnosis is still to be regarded as an experimental procedure.

On the ethical side, practitioners of preimplantation diagnosis have generally defended the practice as an alternative to prenatal diagnosis using amniocentesis or chorionic villus sampling combined with elective abortion (therapeutic abortion), claiming it to be superior both in terms of psycho-social acceptability as well as ethics. Indeed, in a case of an unfavourable diagnostic result preimplantation diagnosis involves the termination of an earlier form of prenatal life than abortion.   On a developmental view of the embryo's ethical standing, this argument is not without merit. However it may be rather too theoretical, if one places it in the proper context, i.e. considering the actual moral traditions that are competing in today's ethical supermarket. Therapeutic abortion for severe disease or handicaps of the offspring enjoys a large consensus in most European societies, while the dissenting minority which strongly opposes not just abortion on demand but therapeutic abortion as well is likely *also* to take a dim view of reproductive technologies generally. After all, being against abortion, and IVF, and artificial insemination with donor, and any 'unnatural' interferences with divine life-giving processes: that is the moral package-deal most visible in the public moral arena for those who dissent from the liberal majority view. We must not confuse the variety of thinkable argumentative strategies in academic ethical debate and the actual, socially effective clusters of moral opinions. The latter are far fewer in number. Therefore - and unless they have very special ethical motives - women who have reasons to undergo prenatal genetic testing will not (and ought not) necessarily to accept that they should undergo a difficult, invasive, low-success procedure such as IVF plus preimplantation diagnosis in a situation where they could just as well become pregnant in the traditional way and take in their stride the possibility of therapeutic abortion. Finally, in the real world of limited health-care budgets and of rationing, hidden or overt, the fate of preimplantation diagnosis is linked to the fate of IVF itself. Its perceived priority in most societies will be far lower than many common types of prenatal diagnoses based on amniocentesis, chorionic villus sampling, analyses of foetal blood or, increasingly, of foetal cells taken from the mother's bloodstream.

3.2. CRYOPRESERVATION

Cryopreservation of embryos in liquid nitrogen in the presence of a cryoprotectant substance (such as dimethyl sulfoxide) is a common procedure. One technical development that would have rather important philosophical consequences is the possibility of freezing unfertilised oocytes. For those who disapprove of IVF on metaphysical grounds having to do with the personhood of early embryos, the consequences will be quite puzzling. This is especially the case for conservatives who rely entirely on the zygote-as-person thesis (according to which an embryo is to be treated as a person from the time of fertilisation) to reject most reproductive technologies and especially IVF. Since there would no longer be any spare embryos but only spare oocytes, which no one considers to be persons, they will suddenly be left with nothing to disapprove of. And yet the biting irony is that this particular technical change - if and when it occurs - will not change the broader social, economic, cultural and existential dilemmas raised by IVF.

Oocyte freezing would also take the sting out of some of the ethical dilemmas linked to oocyte donation. Winston and Handyside[16] note that "surplus eggs donated by superovulated infertile IVF patients could be held until treatment was completed by a confirmed pregnancy". This would avoid the painful quandary arising when an oocyte recipient gets pregnant whereas the donor herself fails to achieve a pregnancy.

At this point, even if no decisive breakthrough is presently in sight, it seems possible that oocyte freezing will eventually become a viable alternative to freezing embryos. However, the technical problems of oocyte cryopreservation are substantial and considerable care will have to be devoted to the issue of chromosome abnormalities, which may occur more often in cryopreserved oocytes than in similarly preserved fertilised eggs.[17] Furthermore, it would be odd for a liberal-pluralist society to steer the further development of IVF in a direction that entails concrete risks to future persons (the risk of bearing children with chromosomal abnormalities) in order to avert purely 'metaphysical' risks (the risk of violating the presumed rights of zygote-persons) that cannot be substantiated by recourse to secular arguments alone.[18] Furthermore, oocyte cryoconservation might open up possibilities that are themselves ethically problematic (see paragraph 3.3).

   Some European countries have tried to steer the conservative course of allowing the fertilisation of only such oocytes as can be returned to the woman in a particular treatment cycle and/or prohibiting cryoconservation of embryos. This was a major victory for the conservative camp in the IVF debate as it incorporates into law the idea that embryos must not be treated instrumentally - and therefore can be said to enjoy some human rights - at the earliest stages of development. However, the defenders of this position may have painted themselves into a tight corner, because they now owe the rest of us a clear definition of what exactly constitutes a (protectable) human embryo, in other words they have to define at what precise stage of the fertilisation process they believe an embryo to be entitled to moral and legal protection. But they have to do it in a way that is principled and intellectually compelling in a secular context - and that is where things get tricky. In Germany, IVF practitioners have switched to freezing zygotes before the male and female pronuclei fuse since the law defines the (protectable) embryo as arising at pronuclear fusion.[19] This view is defensible but only within a very particularistic philosophical tradition. This is not the place to examine the issue fully[20] but in short, the biological essentialism of the neo-scholastic view currently articulated by the more conservative Catholic theologians points to the formation of a new genomic unit (the diploid genome of the zygote) as the start of a new being. It basically reinterprets the medieval concept of *forma* in terms of the new genetic unity arising from the fusion of the male and female haploid genomes present in the gametes and in the pronuclei.[21] This emphasis on the 'newness' and 'oneness' of the zygote after the formation of the diploid genome, i.e. after pronuclear fusion, makes it impossible to move the crucial point back to a previous stage[22], while it is less clear how far forward one can move it. A. Suarez, a prolific writer committed to this philosophical tradition admits as much and proposes the completion of the first cleavage as the crucial point.[23] In fact, if one were to use as an ontological benchmark the *expression* of a new genome rather than its mere presence, then one could move the start of a new being to the 4-8 cell stage (see paragraph 2), while still fully adhering to neo-scholastic concepts and still discounting the well-known problem of monozygotic twins (of which even some Thomist thinkers such as N. Ford[24] have admitted that it is deadly for this whole conceptual framework). Therefore, even if one were to accept their own strongest metaphysical terms - again insisting that there is nothing rationally compelling in this choice - the conservatives fail to make an argument against IVF and against cryopreservation of zygotes unless they have recourse to a rather different argumentative strategy that involves the 'natural' unity of sex and procreation. But that line of thinking has even less credibility in a secular arena, especially since the discussion on chemical contraception in the late sixties.

Cryopreservation at the two-pronuclei stage is much safer than the freezing of unfertilised oocytes, so that IVF supported by cryconservation could go on in countries that disallow cryopreservation at later stages, albeit with some important handicaps. Other methods that do not involve culturing embryos such as GIFT (gamete intra-fallopian transfer), ZIFT (zygote intra-fallopian transfer) and PROST (pronuclear oocyte and sperm transfer) cannot be objected to solely on the zygote-as-person view.

3.3. RESEARCH ON FOETAL OOCYTES

Another question that is not completely novel but had received little attention until recently is the research use of oocytes harvested from aborted foetuses.[25] This question has gained some currency from the sucess of another promising field of IVF-related research: the maturation of immature oocytes in vitro. It opens up the possibility of doing IVF by recovering immature oocytes obtained from unstimulated ovaries, followed by in vitro maturation. This procedure would bypass the need for hormonal stimulation of patients. This is an important piece of medical progress for women entering IVF programs but at the same time, it opens up the rather disturbing prospect of being able to 'mine' the ovary of one young woman for hundreds of oocytes to be used in oocyte donation.[26] From there, it is a small conceptual step to consider studying the maturation of foetal oogonia (oogonia are precursor cells to oocytes). If such cells are used to address basic questions of developmental biology, this could probably be accommodated within the existing ethical framework regarding the use in research of foetal material. However, it would be quite another story if such foetal oogonia could ever be used in infertility treatment after in vitro maturation in the way that donated oocytes from adult women are. Individuals resulting from this kind of IVF would face the rather odd prospect of having a living grand-mother, but no (biological) mother except an aborted foetus. Psychoanalysts will have a field day! Another consequence is that this use of foetal tissue could endanger the ethical consensus on another important area of foetal research, *viz.* the use of foetal material for transplants. This is an area of clinical investigation that holds much promise[27], especially the grafting of foetal mesencephalic neuronal cells into the brains of Parkinson patients. The basic ethical premise adopted in many countries is that there should be a separation between the woman providing the aborted foetus and the recipient of the graft. This ethical framework clearly does not work if one construes oocytes obtained from aborted foetuses as representing transplant material, since 'donor' and 'recipient' are necessarily related in this case. In brief, there seems to be a rather good *prima facie* case for prohibiting the use of foetal eggs in IVF. This is the position taken by the U.K. Human Fertilisation and Embryology Authority (HFEA), which has issued a ban on the use of foetal oogonia in infertility treatment. Research using such immature oocytes or foetal ovarian tissue is permitted.[28]

4. Human Embryo Research For Novel Contraceptives

It is important to remember that assisted reproduction technologies are not the only medical innovations that raise questions about the human embryo. Contraception is another major field in which human embryo research has promising prospects. For many years now, ideas about immunological contraception involving early embryonic antigens have been discussed, without many concrete results, but that situation may simply be a reflection of the fallow state of contraception research generally. In the last two decades, the political and commercial obstacles to innovative contraception have been rather formidable. However, some observers believe the end of the tunnel is in sight and we may soon see novel immunological approaches to contraception that could make good use of the enormous progress of immunology in the last twenty years and which would entail the use of human pre-embryos as research material at some point. Also pre-embryos could become research material indirectly: experiments with immunological reagents preventing fertilisation would lead to the 'inadvertent' creation of pre-embryos to the extent that the experiment is not fully successful, i.e. that the antibody preparation does not fully prevent fertilisation.

Finally, research in the 'black box' of tubal factors and implantation factors, that are important in embryo transport to, and implantion in, the uterus would sit in the grey zone between basic and applied research. That such factors may be important is suggested by the 50-60% of natural conceptions that end in pre-clinical 'abortion' and which may not be attributable in their entirety to embryonic abnormalities. A better understanding of tubal transport and implantation could shed new light on idiopathic forms of infertility as well as provide the biological basis for novel contraceptive strategies.

Whether or not embryo research will prove important in contraception research, it is still likely that the cluster of issues including post-coital contraception, long-term or vaccinal contraception, contragestion/medical abortion (using mifepristone and prostaglandin) will provide a major focus for societal debate on the status of the early human embryo. This is both because in several countries (for instance the U.S.A. and Germany) the abortion debate has never really quieted down after the crucial turning-point of the seventies. In addition, novel birth-control technologies will increasingly address the early embryo/foetus (contragestion) and may also effect major changes in the social psychology of abortion, mostly because early abortion could become more private.

5. Conclusion

Within the foreseeable future, human embryo research is likely to play a rather modest role in advancing very basic general biomedical knowledge. Of course, it is the very nature of scientific breakthroughs to be improbable in the sense of somehow defying prediction. My point is simply that it would be incorrect to predict, by extrapolating from present trends, that human embryo research will solve many basic problems in biomedical science. When defending human embryo research in the public arena, one should avoid overselling it, lest one create overblown expectations that could eventually backfire.

Applied human embryo research will probably be an important asset for reproductive medicine in its effort to understand the etiology and pathogenesis of infertility, in improving reproductive technologies and in devising new methods of fertility control. This raises the problem of assessing the consequences of prohibiting human embryo research, since several European countries seem now to take that direction. As often happens with inappropriate policies, the criminalisation of human embryo research and restrictive regulation of IVF and of cryoconservation of embryos will not show their deleterious effects immediately. They will not make IVF completely impossible, as the attempts of German practitioners to adjust to this situation show. However, in the longer run, it is unlikely that reproductive technologies can progress without recourse to human embryo research. This means that practitioners in prohibitionist countries will have to rely on results obtained elsewhere, without taking responsibility for the way in which the results were obtained. In other words, they will involuntarily be thrust into a morally mediocre position. Politicians who want to claim the moral high ground by prohibiting embryo research should think again and become aware that their position is not devoid of a certain hypocrisy. In addition, if there is one topic in which bioethics has acquired a great deal of experience, it is the regulation of human experimentation. Therefore, is it not better to authorise human embryo research and to control it as such, rather than drive it into a semi-clandestine status where some of it may well still go on under the guise of clinical trial-and-error?

The idea that the human embryo embodies considerable moral worth - if not downright personhood - from the time of conception is a major inspiration of restrictive attitudes towards embryo research. Proponents of this view often claim it to be consonant with commonsense intuition: 'the zygote I was is the very person I am'. But whatever superficial appeal this view may have disappears when one gets drawn into hair-splitting distinctions (paragraph 3.2) as to the exact moment when a protectable embryo arises. Various proposals conflict: sperm entry, syngamy, first cleavage, initiation of embryonic gene expression at the 4-8 cell stage. One finds oneself in the realm of semi-arbitrary choices, of 'probable' opinion (in the casuistic sense). In short, one rediscovers the kind of relativistic uncertainty that the personhood-at-conception thesis was supposed to do away with. Defenders of this thesis cannot dismiss these controversies as moot, because if they want to challenge the techniques of IVF practitioners, they must give them principled answers. Thus IVF and its attending conceptual problems act as a kind of moral microscope, that brings in focus the fuzziness of the personhood-at-conception view and may well contribute to undermine it.

Finally, one should probably not view the issues of the embryo's ethical standing in relation only to IVF. Novel fertility control methods, especially contragestion, will contribute decisively to reviving these issues in public debate and this can be expected to undermine further the conservative position.

Acknowledgements

Stimulating discussions and information received from Prof. Aldo Campana, Dr. Knut Ruyter, Dr. Denny Sakkas, Dr. Jean-Marie Thévoz, Prof. Jean-Dominique Vassalli, Prof. Pierre Vassalli are gratefully acknowledged. Opinions expressed in this paper are purely personal.

Notes

1. This position is usually associated with the pronouncements of the Catholic magisterium. Of course, I am aware that the latter never authoritatively asserts that the embryo is a person from the time of fertilisation. It merely says that it should be treated like one, often under the *tutiorist* assumption that this is the safe thing to do in view of the philosophical uncertainties surrounding the early embryo's status. However, it does suggest the personhood-at-conception thesis as a philosophically preferred or most plausible interpretation and lets its conservative exponents defend it, especially since issuing the *Donum Vitae* document in 1987.

2. A good summary of early research on human pre-embryos can be found in: Singer, P., Kuhse, H., Buckle, S., Dawson, K. and Kasimba, P. (eds), *Embryo Experimentation* Cambridge, Cambridge University Press, 1990; see particularly Trounson, A., 'Why do research on human pre-embryos?' pp.14-25.

3. Braude, P., Bolton, V. and Moore, S., 'Human gene expression first occurs between the four- and eight-cell stage of preimplantation development' *Nature* 332, 1988, pp.459-461.

4. Ram, P.T. and Schultz, R.M., 'Reporter gene expression in G2 of the 1-cell mouse embryo' *Developmental Biology* 156, 1993, pp.552-556.

5. Cf. Evans, M.J., 'Establishment in culture of pluripotential cells from mouse embryos' *Nature* 292, 1981, pp.154-156; and Martin, G.R., 'Isolation of a pluripotent cell line from early mouse embryos cultured in medium conditioned by teratocarcinoma stem cells' *Proceedings of the National Academy of Sciences of the U.S.A.* 78, 1981, pp.7634-7638.

6. Notarianni, E., Laurie, S., Moor, R.M. and Evans, M.J., 'Maintenance and differentiation in culture of pluripotential embryonic cell lines from pig blastocysts' *Journal of Reproduction and Fertility* Suppl. 41, 1990, pp.51-56.

7. Bongso, A., Fong, C.Y., Ng, S.C. and Ratnam, S., 'Isolation and culture of inner mass cells from human blastocysts' *Human Reproduction* 9, 1994, pp.2110-2117.

8. For instance the German Embryo Protection Law uses a set of definitions that are unworkable in this respect (Embryonemschutzgesetz s. 8).

9. A fear revived by the human embryo 'cloning' experiments of Hall and Stillman (*Science* 262, 1993, pp.652-653). For a conceptual distinction between these 'induced-twinning' experiments and cloning as usually understood (non-sexual reproduction of a pre-existing individual), see Mauron, A., 'Le clonage humain: la montagne accouche d'une souris' *Médecine et Hygiène* 51, 1993, p.2612.

10. Winston, R.M.L. and Handyside, A.H., 'New challenges in human *in vitro* fertilisation' *Science* 260, 1993, pp.932-936.

11. Palermo, G., Joris, H., Devroey, P. and van Steirteghem, A.C., 'Pregnancies after intracytoplasmic injection of single spermatozoon into an oocyte' *The Lancet* 340, 1992, pp.17-18.

12. Van Steirteghem, A.C., Liu, J., Jorris, H., Nagy, Z., Janssenswillen, C., Tournaye, H., Derde, M.-P., Van Assche, E. and Devroey, P., 'Higher success rate by intracytoplasmic sperm injection than by subzonal insemination. Report of a second series of 300 consecutive treatment cycles' *Human Reproduction* 8, 1993, pp.1055-1059.

13. Silber, S.J., Nagy, Z., Liu, J., Godoy, H., Devroey, P. and Van Steirteghem, A.C., 'Conventional *in-vitro* fertilization versus intracytoplasmic sperm injection for patients requiring microsurgical sperm aspiration' *Human Reproduction* 9, 1994, pp.1705-1709.

14. Nau, J.Y., 'Selon les résultats d'une équipe belge: La microinjection de spermatozoïdes se révèle peu nocive' *Le Monde* 3-4 July 1994, p.8.

15. Cf. Handyside, A.H. and Delhanty, J.D.A., 'Cleavage stage biopsy of human embryos and diagnosis of X-linked recessive disease' in Edwards, R.G. (ed.), *Preimplantation Diagnosis of Human Genetic Disease* Cambridge, Cambridge University Press, 1993, pp.239-270; and Verlinsky, Y., Rechitsky, S., Evsikov, S., White, M., Cieslak, J., Lifchez, A., Valle, J., Moise, J. and Strom, C.M., 'Preconception and preimplantation diagnosis for cystic fibrosis' *Prenatal Diagnosis* 12, 1992, pp.103-110.

16. Winston and Handyside, *op.cit.*, p.934.

17. The reason is that in humans, mature oocytes are arrested at metaphase II of meiosis. The metaphase plate is a fragile structure that can be damaged by the freezing process, leading to aneuploidy.

18. Engelhardt, T.H., 'Personhood, moral strangers, and the evil of abortion: the painful experience of post-modernity' *Journal of Medicine and Philosophy* 18, 1993, pp.419-421.

19. Embryonemschutzgesetz s. 8.1.

20. The misunderstandings between biological, metaphysical-descriptive and normative levels of discourse are examined in Mauron, A., 'The human embryo and the relativity of biological individuality' in this volume.

21. See for instance, Malherbe, J.-F., 'Les équivoques du moindre mal' *Ethique (Rennes)* No. 2, 1991, pp.79-85.

22. Given the 'personalist' polemic of many theologians of this school against a supposed dualism of their opponents (see for instance Crosby, J.F., 'The personhood of the human embryo' *Journal of Medicine and Philosophy* 18, 1993, pp.399-417) and their insistence on ontological oneness as the basis for defining the

zygote as person, they cannot move the origin of the new person to an earlier time, when there are still two genomes rather than one.

23. Suarez, A., 'Ist der Mensch eine Person in jedem Zeitpunkt seines Lebens?' *Schweizerische Aertztezeitung* 70 (49), 1993, pp.2084-2087.

24. Ford, N., *When Did I Begin?* Cambridge, Cambridge University Press, 1988.

25. Dickson, D., 'Use of fetal eggs in research to be debated' *Nature* 364, 1993, p.372.

26. Winston and Handyside, *op.cit.*

27. Bianchi, D.W., 'A revived opportunity for fetal research' *Nature* 363, 1993, p.12.

28. Human Fertilisation and Embryology Authority, *Donated Ovarian Tissue in Embryo Research and Assisted Conception* 1994, report available from HFEA, 30 Artillery Lane, London, E1 7LS.

19. THE HUMAN EMBRYO AND RESEARCH

Panagiota Dalla-Vorgia
Department of Hygiene and Epidemiology
University of Athens Medical School
Greece

1. Introduction

The presentation which follows is based on two reports[1] of a Working Party of the European Union on Human Embryos and Research (HER) of which the writer was a member. This working group was set up following the recommendations of a Ministerial meeting on Ethical Issues in Human Embryology and Genome Research held in Kronberg, Germany on 9-10 March 1990. The Working Group started meeting in 1991 and has so far presented two reports. The first one concerns the pre-implantation embryo and the second the post-implantation embryo and the foetus. The Working Group did not formulate guidelines but rather reviewed the present situation in Europe in relation to the status of the embryo, research on embryos, etc.

The main conclusion of the Working Group was that there is no consensus on the status of the embryo within Europe. There are two main views prevailing:

One view is that from the moment of fertilisation there is a new human life, and that the identity, integrity and life of every embryo must be protected from this very earliest stage.

Others take the view that the moment of penetration of the egg by the sperm does not have this special significance. It is not until the primitive streak appears that one is able to identify a potential human being (or beings). Many pre-implantation embryos perish naturally at this stage. While an embryo merits special respect because of its human origin, any rights and protections later accorded to a live-born child are acquired progressively as the stages of pre-natal development advance.[2]

In relation to this second view, one should note that, as Dr. McLaren in her report to the Council of Europe puts it, up to the eight or sixteen cell stage (three days of development) all of the cells are believed to be equivalent to one another and they are potentially able to contribute to any part of the future embryo or extra-embryonic membranes.[3]

D. Evans (ed.), Conceiving the Embryo, 297–301.
© 1996 *Kluwer Law International. Printed in the Netherlands.*

2. Pre-Implantation Embryos

A survey of the legislation of member states on human embryo research and related matters showed that a variety of approaches has been adopted by various states, and this reflects their differing views on the status of the embryo. These approaches are:

(i) all non-therapeutic research on pre-implantation embryos is prohibited. Research is only permitted if the intention is therapeutic and the embryo is replaced

(ii) non-therapeutic research is permitted but regulated (and usually includes some prohibitions).

However, in other countries the discussion is continuing so that:

(iii) no formal political or legal decision has been taken but, in the absence of directly relevant laws, regulation may be through recommendations by ethical committees or "codes of practice" promulgated by professional bodies and without legal force.[4]

It is worth noting that states in which non-therapeutic research on pre-implantation embryos is prohibited, therapeutic procedures - in some cases not yet fully tested - may be allowed so long as the procedure is intended for the benefit of the particular embryo, there is a chance of success, and the embryo is to be replaced in the uterus. On the other hand, states that allow non-therapeutic research on pre-implantation embryos tend not to allow a new putatively therapeutic procedure if it has not been adequately tested on animal embryos first and human embryos afterwards.

The main goals of research on pre-implantation embryos, although not always permitted even in states which permit such research are: advancing the treatment of infertility, developing methods for the preservation of viable pre-implantation embryos, and developing safer and more effective methods of contraception.

It is generally agreed that when research on embryos is permitted it should not be carried out after the primitive streak appears, that is to say 14 days after fertilisation. Also, the embryo is not to be replaced in the uterus unless it can be assumed that there has been no deleterious effect on the embryo from the research.

Genetic modification of normal pre-implantation embryos is clearly not allowed, and is considered ethically unacceptable because it might result in the alteration of the genetic material of future generations. Any such manipulation in the present state of knowledge is not acceptable.

There is general agreement in all member states that informed consent of the donors should always be obtained and that all proposed research on pre-implantation embryos should be examined by bodies which are able to assess not only the scientific but also the ethical and legal dimensions of the research project.

In the light of this review of the current situation within Europe, it is worth reflecting on the relevant articles of the Report of the Council of Europe on Human Artificial Procreation.[5]   In section VII of this report 'Acts and procedures carried out on embryos' all acts and procedures on embryos *in vitro* which are not intended for thier benefit or are not observational studies which do no harm to the embryo are prohibited (Principle 17.1) as is the obtaining (by fertilisation or lavage) of embryos specifically for research purposes (Principle 16).   However, Principle 17.2 recognises that some states may allow procedures other than is mentioned and allowed in 17.1.   In these cases, such research is allowed where it has a preventive, diagnostic or therapeutic purposes for serious diseases of embryos and, in addition, the purpose cannot be achieved by any other method (Principle 17.2.a); where no embryo which has gone beyond the 14 day developmental stage[6] is used (17.2.b); where the consent of the couple and of any donors of gametes has been obtained (17.2.c); and where "a properly constituted multidisciplinary ethical committee has given its approval" (17.2.d). Splitting of cells of an embryo should be allowed only for the purpose of diagnosing "a serious illness or anomaly in the future child", and again only if the embyo used has not yet reached the 14 day developmental stage, if the consent of couple and any gamete donors has been given, and if the multidisciplinary ethics committee has approved (17.3).   Also in the same section of the Council of Europe report, it is stated that if an embryo has undergone any act or procedure other than those allowed, it should not be implanted (Principle 18); and by Principle 19 no embryo which has resulted from *in vitro* fertilisation (IVF) should undergo any experimentation once it has been implanted *in utero*.

3. The Post-Implantation Embryo and Foetus

As far as the post-implantation embryo and foetus are concerned, the report found that there is also a wide range of attitudes among member states towards embryonic and foetal research, as well as to uses of foetal material for research, diagnosis or transplantation.[7]

Interventions with therapeutic intent and diagnostic procedures such as ultrasound visualisation, are allowed in all member states.   Somatic cell gene therapy, a technique that offers great promise and may be ethically acceptable, still may not be carried out *in utero*.   Germ line gene therapy is generally agreed to be ethically unacceptable in the present state of knowledge.

Non-invasive studies, e.g. ultrasound visualisation by high resolution, may be carried out on intact foetuses.   In some member states more experimental interventions may be undertaken, once the decision to terminate a pregnancy has been taken, e.g. methods of foetal reduction.

In states where uses of foetal tissue for research, diagnosis or transplantation are not prohibited, foetal material may be obtained from abortions, spontaneous or induced or ectopic pregnancies or even still births.

Scientific research on foetal material may be carried out for various reasons, e.g. the study of human development, cancer research, vaccines, therapy of certain diseases, such as Parkinson's disease. Foetal material can also be used for diagnosis of a defect in a particular embryo or for diagnostic procedures in non-foetal disease, e.g. the diagnosis of viral disease by the use of cell lines. Therapy based on the use of foetal cells could be of help to patients suffering from Parkinson's disease, insulin-dependent diabetes, and others. Needless to say there are many conditions when the above mentioned procedures are allowed.

Research on embryos, foetuses, or foetal tissue should be subject to ethical review by bodies which are able to assess not only the scientific dimensions of the project but also the legal and ethical ones. One consideration urged on such committees might be whether the scientific objectives of the proposed research could be achieved "by some other, less problematic, means or without protracted delay" in which case research on foetal material should not be undertaken.[8]

Always, where the use of foetal material is in question, the informed consent of the pregnant woman should be obtained; and generally speaking this should be on condition that the decision to terminate the pregnancy has been taken in advance (that is, for reasons wholly unconnected with the research or interventions in question). However, it is acknowledged that it may be felt acceptable to generate, terminate or prolong a pregnancy in order to produce material for transplantation, diagnosis or research, "where this is the express wish of the woman, and there is a specific medical indication".[9]

A number of other ethical ground rules are put forward concerning those who may wish to research foetal material, the woman who is potentially the supplier of the material, and those with responsibility for her clinical management. The management of the woman's pregnancy should not be influenced by considerations pertaining to the use of foetal material; no financial or other inducements may be offered "to the pregnant woman or to any person who is in a position to influence her decisions" to obtain foetal material for research; those who carry out a termination or who determine the death of a foetus should not be the same as those who are to use the foetal material for research; and "every effort should be made to ensure that pressure is not put on the pregnant woman to abort in order to provide foetal material".[10]

In addition, and looking ahead, the report considers that the development of the ability to transplant foetal gonads "would pose ethical problems which will deserve particular attention".[11]

4. Conclusion

Human embryo research is one of the most controversial issues in medical ethics. This is due to the fact that opinions on the moral status of the embryo differ among people according to their religious and cultural background. Differences exist not only between countries but also among people in the same country. On the jurisprudential side, the legal status of the embryo is also unclear, and the question of to what extent, if at all, the right to life of the unborn child is protected by Article 2 of the European Covention on Human Rights is still an open one. The differences which exist are of such a nature that, even if it were desirable to eliminate them, it is not possible to do so.

In the mean time, science advances rapidly, and its progress is difficult to prevent; and in particular, research on embryos is under way, shows promise, and will be extremely hard to stop. Human embryos can be said to have some level of moral status, being at the least a potential human being deserving of respect and protection as such, and so we are enjoined to take care. Where research on human embryos is to be permitted it must be strictly regulated. This means that only absolutely necessary research should be allowed, under clearly defined and specific conditions, and with the approval of a multidisciplinary Ethics Committee.

Notes

1. Cf. European Commission, Directorate General XII, Science, Research and Development, European Community Working Group on Human Embryos and Research (HER), *Research on Bioethics* Luxembourg, Office for Official Publications of the European Communities, 1995.

2. *Ibid.*, p.5.

3. McLaren, A., *Report on the Use of Human Foetal, Embryonic and Pre-Embryonic Material for Diagnostic, Therapeutic, Scientific, Industrial and Commericial Purposes* (an information document prepared for the Council of Europe) revised March 1990, p.9; cf. also McLaren, A., 'Research on the human conceptus and its regulation in Britain today' *Journal of the Royal Society of Medicine* 33, 1990, pp.209-213.

4. European Commission, *op.cit.*, p.6.

5. Council of Europe's *Ad Hoc* Committee of Experts on Progress in the Biomedical Sciences, 'Report on human artificial procreation' in Rogers, A. and Durant de Bousingen, D. (eds), *Bioethics in Europe* Strasbourg, Council of Europe Press, 1995, pp.359-366.

6. By '14 day developmental stage' is intended the appearance of the primitive streak (also known as individuation). The time period '14 days' here does not include any time spent cryopreserved (Council of Europe *Ad Hoc* Committee, *op.cit.*, Principle 17.2.b).

7. European Commission, *op.cit.*, p.20.

8. *Ibid.*

9. *Ibid.*

10. *Ibid.*

11. *Ibid.*

20. THE REGULATION OF EMBRYO RESEARCH UNDER THE HUMAN FERTILISATION AND EMBRYOLOGY ACT OF 1990

Arlene Judith Klotzko, J.D.
Research Fellow in Medical Law and Ethics
The London Hospital Medical College
England
Research Fellow
The Center for Bioethics and Health Law
Utrecht University
The Netherlands

You cannot put genies back into bottles. You can, however, try to make sure that the genies do not go around granting any old wish. You can give the genies some rules.[1]

Introduction

Ian Kennedy, the distinguished President of The Centre of Medical Law and Ethics at Kings College, London, expressed this sense of caution in the face of rapid biomedical advances in the context of an examination of the moral status of embryos, three years before the Human Fertilisation and Embryology Act (hereinafter the HFE Act) came into effect in the UK on 1 August 1991. This paper will assess the degree to which the HFE Act has defined the legal status of the embryo and given the genies effective tools for the regulation of embryo research in the United Kingdom.

1. The Common Law and Civil Law Families

Before I go on to a detailed examination of the legislation, I would like to situate it in the family of law in which it resides - the common law family. Britain and Ireland are the only members of the European Union that belong to this legal family - a family that is fundamentally different from its civil law counterparts. While I will speak of the common law as a family, there are, of course, differences among the various family members, such as England and the United States. When I am specific, my frame of reference will be English common law. When I speak of the civil law, it will be with reference to the so-called Romano-Germanic family.

In the common law, the expression of the legal rule is found in judicial decisions. Statutes, or enacted law, have a role, but it is subsidiary. Within the common law are

D. Evans (ed.), Conceiving the Embryo, 303–314.
© *1996 Kluwer Law International. Printed in the Netherlands.*

judicial decisions that relate to actions by one private party against another. This body of court decisions - including decisions that interpret relevant statutes - is called civil law.

When I speak of the civil law family, however, I am not referring to individual legal actions by one private party against another. I am referring to countries with a systematic, complete, and coherent body of enacted law that regulates the relations between private parties. The legal system in civil law countries then is not cast in the judicial mode of thought. The perfect form of law is seen as a statute, not a court case, and the perfect form of a statute is a coherent and systematic code.[2]

My discussion of the common law family will cover three main areas: First, the disadvantages and shortcomings that the primary mode of law creation, judge-made law, may hold out in the area of regulation and control of biomedical advances; second, the role of a statute in a common law system; and third, the effect that the tendency of 20th century common law to be increasingly pragmatic might have had on the design of the HFE Act.

The model of the common law is judge-made law. Its legal rule is one which will provide the solution to an existing dispute or trial, rather than a general rule of conduct for the future. It is, then, far less abstract than the typical legal rule of the Romano-Germanic family. Historically, the immediate preoccupation of the common law has been to re-establish peace rather than to articulate a moral basis for the social order."[3]

Legal rules in civil law are not left to the judge to enunciate at the level of his individual decision. The legal rule is the product of reflection founded on not just judicial practice, but also considerations of justice, morality, policy and consonance with the system. This concept of the legal rule is the fundamental basis of codification. A code would be no more than a mere compilation if one were to see a legal rule in every judicial decision and only at the level of such decisions.

Thus, according to the Romano-Germanic notion, a code should not attempt to provide rules that are immediately applicable to every conceivable concrete case, but rather it should embody an organised system of general rules from which a solution for any given problem may be easily deduced by as simple a process as possible.[4]

While in common law systems, judicial decisions are primary, in the Romano-Germanic civil law family enacted law is preferred.[5] Judicial decisions arise within a legal framework established by legislation. It is the task of legislators to create this framework. Thus, the scope of judicial law making is different and the situation is exactly the reverse of that in the common law system.[6]

What are the disadvantages for a system which makes judge-made law the standard, when it is confronted by the new and morally complex issues presented by biomedical technology? I view the common law as operating under five considerable disadvantages.

The lack of antecedent certainty.

Civil lawyers are shocked at the common lawyer's view that the law is what has been decided or what can be predicted with assurance will be decided by the Courts. They think of law as existing quite apart from the courts and before the courts can have a chance of settling it in a doubtful case.[7]

The retrospective nature of the common law. Judges usually rule on the legality - or lack thereof - of events that have already transpired.

Its reactive - as opposed to proactive - character. Judges must wait for a plaintiff to bring a case, and then take the parties and the issues as they present themselves.

The ad hoc and unsystematic character of the common law. Thus, large and important gaps may exist in the law because cases on those issues were never brought before a court.

The fact-specific nature of common law decisions.

> The English legal rule is capable of providing the solution to a dispute immediately, but the rule cannot be understood and its significance cannot be measured unless one knows all the facts of the case in which it was enunciated. The continental legal rule, linked to moral theology rather than to procedure, is enunciated by the *doctrine* or the legislators and designed to direct the conduct of citizens in a range of cases without any reference necessarily to a particular dispute.[8]

There is also another factor that - while not intrinsic to the common law - has increasingly characterised it for the last century. P.S. Atiyah has discerned

> a profound shift away from the belief in the hortatory function of the law [the desire to encourage behaviour of a positive or affirmative kind], a shift from principles to pragmatism, a shift from the desire to lay down rules for future application to the desire to do justice according to the particular circumstances of the case. In the language of Mill, the law has become increasingly concerned to patch up the consequences of wrongdoing after it has been committed rather than to prevent it.[9]

In a civil law system, every attempt must be made to keep the law ahead of the facts. The common law, on the other hand, has nothing to say about really new and unfamiliar facts or combinations of facts. Common law must be made by the judges when the problems arise, and are brought before them in an actual case.[10]

Thus, when rules must be laid down for future application, the common law system turns to statutes. But are they viewed, as they are in civil law systems, as the "best means of enunciating the rules needed at a time when the complexity of social relations demands that precision and clarity be paramount?"[11]

Common law statutes are not seen as embodying within themselves clear direction. Rather, they are viewed as "somewhat abnormal in character...and legislative provisions...are not fully assimilated into the English legal system until they have been taken up and affirmed - and sometimes even deformed - by the courts in the course of the *normal* working process of the common law".[12]

English statutory provisions are drafted to be as concrete and specific as possible; in contrast to the legislative practice of the Romano-Germanic systems, they avoid the use of general and comprehensive expressions.[13]   But what of statutes that address developments, as in assisted conception technology, that transform the social order? Such legislation is

> often able to articulate only the leading principles, establish standards of behaviour and to delegate considerable discretionary powers to administrative bodies and those called upon to control them. Thus, they vary from the statutory norm in the common law family.
>
>   In this context, statutory interpretation could be carried out in ways other than the traditional manner and, in effect, in a way that is reminiscent of European continental techniques. This is achieved by limiting the scope of the control that the courts - alone empowered to pronounce upon the law - exercise over the decisions of bodies handling quasi-judicial disputes, rather than by creating a new concept of the legal rule requiring new principles of interpretation.[14]

As I go on to discuss the specifics of the HFE Act, I would like to keep two main points in mind.   These are, first, the description of the mode of drafting and the functions of statutes that deal with transformations of the social order; and, second, Atiyah's theory that the common law - in its judicial as well as statutory manifestations - has evolved from an earlier emphasis on principles to its current emphasis on pragmatism.

In short, does the HFE Act represent a kind of triumph of pragmatism over principle?

2. The HFE Act

2.1. THE BACKGROUND

In July 1982, the Committee of Inquiry into Human Fertilisation and Embryology (the Warnock Committee) was formed. Its mandate was to examine the social, ethical, and legal implications of recent and potential developments in the field of human assisted reproduction. The Committee reported to the Government in June, 1984.[15] Among its recommendations was a proposal to permit research on embryos for up to fourteen days after fertilisation. Another document, a white paper published in November, 1987, entitled *Human Fertilisation and Embryology: A Framework for Legislation*[16], have been described as "well-meaning attempts to secure an impossible consensus".[17]

There was a delay in implementing the recommendations of the Warnock Report. And during the period between the issuance of that Report and the effective date of the HFE Act, IVF treatment and embryo experimentation were conducted in the United Kingdom. The point at which such research should ethically be terminated was a matter to be decided by the individual researcher.[18]

In order to fill the regulatory gap, in 1985, The Medical Research Council and the Royal College of Obstetricians and Gynaecologists agreed to set up a Voluntary Licensing Authority to monitor and license IVF treatment and embryo research. In 1989, in "a heavy hint to the Government", the authority changed its name to the Interim Licensing Authority. At no time did this organisation possess any legal powers.[19]

2.2. THE FRAMEWORK

On 29 Nov 1989, The Human Fertilisation and Embryology bill was introduced in the House of Lords. It received Royal Assent on 1 November 1990, and the Human Fertilisation and Embryology Authority - an entity created by the new legislation - replaced the Interim Licensing Authority. The Act deals with two fundamental moral issues - the status of the embryo and the status of infertility - issues on which there was no social consensus. (There was general agreement in Parliament that embryo research should be regulated and made subject to the criminal law. That consensus broke down, however, with respect to the question of what types of embryo research should be banned.)

The relative weights of the competing views on underlying issues of moral principle were left to be determined within the regulatory structure of the Human Fertilisation and Embryology Authority, a body that was established by section 5 of the Act. Few issues of principle have been resolved by the creation of the Authority. The Act merely establishes an institutional framework within which compromises can be worked out. Answers to questions of principle have not been provided by Parliament. Instead, their resolution has been entrusted to "a relatively autonomous group of the great and the good".[20] These private persons have the power to determine what embryo research and infertility treatment will be allowed to take place. The Government has reserved a number of powers to circumscribe the discretion of the Authority. The boundaries of the power to licence may be contracted and expanded by regulations (section 45). An annual report, detailing past and projected activities, is required to be submitted to the Secretary of State (section 7). The reports are to be submitted to Parliament by the Minister.[21]

Although the Act does create a system of checks and balances, many of the normative principles to be applied have not been established by law or through democratic discussion.

The HFE Act divides activities involving human embryos and gametes into three categories. These are, first, those, such as cloning, that are illegal and cannot be licensed; second, those, such as embryo research, that are illegal unless carried out with a licence; third, those, such as artificial insemination by husband, that are not within the ambit of the Act and are, therefore, lawful without a licence.[22] Section 25 of the Act requires the Authority to maintain a Code of Practice as guidance for proper conduct of the activities performed under licence.

The details of the licensing procedures are set out in sections 9, 10, and 16-22 of the Act. Licences may not be granted combining treatment and research. They are granted for a maximum of 5 years for storage and 3 years for research; research licences must be granted for a specific project for one or more of the purposes set forth in Schedule 2, para.3.[23]

The regulatory reach of the Act is much greater with respect to embryos than gametes. The Act regulates the creation, use, and storage of embryos, *ex utero*, whether for treatment or research purposes. However, only if donated gametes are involved is their use regulated. *In vitro* fertilisation usually requires the creation of several embryos through drug-induced super-ovulation. Those not implanted - the spare embryos - are frozen, pending future need. The maximum storage period for embryos under the Act is five years (section 14(4)(5)). The Act requires that embryos that are left at the end of the statutory period be allowed to perish (section 14(1)(c)).

Margaret Brazier has identified two crucial ground rules of the Act.[24] Section 12(c) prohibits payment for gametes or embryos unless authorised by directions from the HFEA. Schedule 3, para. 3 mandates the full and informed consent that is required for IVF treatment, the storage of gametes or embryos, and the donation of gametes. The HFE Act requires that a prospective patient or donor be given a suitable opportunity to receive counselling about the implications of the proposed procedures.

Schedule 3, para. 2 deals with consent for the use of an embryo. One or more of the following purposes must be specified: use by the person giving consent or by that person and another specified person together; use in providing treatment to persons not including the one giving consent; use for research. Thus, any spare embryos that remain after IVF has been completed cannot be used for research unless the couple has specified - in advance - that research would be an acceptable purpose.[25] Sections 4.1 through 4.5 of the Code of Practice spell out the information that is required to be given to clients and donors.

Embryos that are specifically created for research often have as their source eggs from women who have agreed to undergo sterilisation. The fully informed consent of such women is, of course, crucial as they will have to take drugs to induce super-ovulation (and thus be exposed to the attendant risks involved), and they will derive no benefit from the procedures.

2.3. PROHIBITIONS IN CONNECTION WITH EMBRYOS

Activities proscribed under the HFE Act are set forth in section 3 (about embryos) and section 4 (about gametes). Those related to embryos are as follows:

Prohibitions in connection with embryos:

3.-(1) No person shall
   (a) bring about the creation of an embryo, or
   (b) keep or use an embryo,
except in pursuance of a licence.
(2) No person shall place in a woman -
   (a) a live embryo other than a human embryo, or
   (b) any live gametes other than human gametes.
(3) A licence cannot authorise -
   (a) keeping or using an embryo after the appearance of the primitive streak,
   (b) placing an embryo in any animal,
   (c) keeping or using an embryo in any circumstances in which regulations prohibit
      its keeping or use, or
   (d) replacing a nucleus of a cell or an embryo with a nucleus taken from a cell of
      any person, embryo or subsequent development of an embryo.
(4) For the purposes of subsection (3)(a) above, the primitive streak is to be taken
    to have appeared in any embryo not later than the end of the period of 14 days,
    beginning with the day when the gametes are mixed, not counting any time
    during which the embryo is stored.

The HFE Act allows research on human embryos only if the HFEA has licensed the research project. What is permissible is circumscribed by two provisions in schedule 3: 3(3)(a) and 3(4) which, when read together, limit the power to grant licences for research to projects involving embryos which have not yet developed a primitive streak. Section 3(4) irrebuttably presumes that this develops no later than 14 days after the gametes are mixed.[26]

Because there was no social consensus on embryo research, the bill had a somewhat odd Parliamentary history. When it was introduced into the House of Lords as a Government bill, it had alternative versions of a crucial clause concerning research on human embryos. The original text of section 11 contained both an absolute prohibition on research and a provision allowing licensing.[27]

[A] It will be a criminal offence to carry out any procedures on a human embryo other than those aimed at preparing the embryo for transfer to the uterus of a woman: or those carried out to ascertain the suitability of that embryo for the intended transfer.

[B] Except as a part of a project specifically licenced by the Statutory Licensing Authority, it will be a criminal offence to carry out any procedures on a human embryo other than those aimed at preparing the embryo for transfer to the uterus of a woman: or those carried out to ascertain the suitability of that embryo for the intended transfer.

Option A would have narrowly circumscribed permissible embryo research. The intent of this option was to prohibit embryo experimentation while limiting any resulting damage to the IVF programme. This provision would not have prohibited the storage of embryos or the creation of spare embryos in the context of IVF super-ovulation procedures.

It would have allowed pre-implantation diagnosis to ascertain the suitability of the embryo for transplantation, as well as the destruction of surplus embryos.[28] Most importantly, this option would have fitted into the traditional conception of the physician's duty - acting in the best interests of the patient. The procedures to be allowed were all calculated to create a pregnancy.

Option B was far different. The moral calculus now included society's interests and not just those of the prospective parents. This marked a clear move from the domain of clinical ethics to that of research ethics. And, as Daniel Callahan has noted, the task of establishing moral proportionality between the claims of the research and the status of the embryo is a problematic one.[29] It is the essence of option B that has become law.

During the Parliamentary debate on the HFE Bill, there were attempts in both the House of Lords and the House of Commons to limit research to involve only the spare embryos created during the provision of IVF treatment. In the House of Lords, an amendment which would have criminalised any other type of research, was defeated by 214 votes to 80.

> Lord Bridge, opposing the amendment, argued that the 'moral scrupulosity' which distinguishes between the propriety of research upon a spare embryo and ... research upon a specifically created embryo 'may be an admirable subject of debate in the senior common room but it has no place at all in the dock of the Old Bailey'.[30]

Although English law has given legal voice to the moral principle of double effect in the context of end-of-life decision making, this amendment was voted down. Thus, the deliberate creation of embryos for allowable research purposes is permitted under English law, until the development of the primitive streak.

2.4. PERMISSIBLE AIMS OF EMBRYO RESEARCH

Schedule 2 para. 3(2) mandates that each research protocol be shown to relate broadly to one of the existing categories of research aims (see below); schedule 2 para. 3(6) requires that all research be necessary to achieve the purposes of the research.

The permissible research aims are as follows:

(a) promoting advances in the treatment of infertility (para.3(2)(a));

(b) increasing knowledge about the causes of congenital disease (para.3(2)(d)); an amendment seeking to limit this to life-threatening or severely disabling conditions was withdrawn;

(c) increasing knowledge about the causes of miscarriage (para.3(2)(c);

(d) developing more effective techniques of contraception (para.3(2)(d); an amendment condemning this as frivolous was defeated;

(e) developing methods for detecting the presence of gene or chromosome abnormalities in embryos before implantation (para.3(2)(e);

(f) more generally for the purpose of increasing knowledge about the creation and development of embryos and enabling such knowledge to be applied (para.3(3)).[31]

2.5. THE PRIMITIVE STREAK

As stated above, the scope of permissible embryo research is circumscribed by two provisions in schedule 3, 3(3)(a) and 3(4), which limit the power to licence embryo research to projects involving embryos which have not yet developed a primitive streak. The point of demarcation is clear. This is an example of a so-called bright line rule - the kind of rule favoured by the law. The appearance of the primitive streak as an end point for embyro experimentation has been used in other countries as well. Its significance lies in the impossibility of identifying before it appears which cells will develop in which ways; the cells are 'pluripotential' and 'totipotential'.[32] Only after the primitive streak appears can we discuss an individual, specific human life.[33]

What is the usefulness of this scientific fact in moral and legal analysis? As noted in the dissent to the Warnock Report, the determination as to what constitutes "[t]he beginning of a person is not a question of fact but a decision made in the light of moral principles".[34] Speaking of the scientific significance of the primitive streak, Lord Kennet said that it may be true, but wondered if it was morally important.[35] Margaret Brazier has characterised the 'verdict' on the moral status of the embryo as 'not proven'.[36] This description seems to have a factual cast to it, but moral status cannot be a fact.

And what does the law do with scientific facts and pseudo-moral facts? The HFEA accepts the scientific fact of the primitive streak as a bright line rule; the Interim Licensing Authority - the nonstatutory predecessor of the HFEA - did as well. For reasons of public policy, one must draw the line somewhere, and this seemed to be as good a place as any other.

But such legal lines do not settle moral disagreements; although they may offer legal certainty, they are often found to be inadequate from a moral point of view. The American abortion decision, *Roe v. Wade*[37], regulates abortion based upon the viability of the foetus - another scientific fact. More than twenty years later, the moral controversy still rages.

2.6. THE LEGAL STATUS OF EMBRYOS

Under the HFE Act, the embryo is given the status of neither a chattel nor a person.[38] In Britain, control of gametes and embryos is vested in the providers of the genetic material. This is accomplished through an elaborate scheme of consents. Schedule 3 requires that a gamete provider must, at the time the gametes are procured, indicate in a written consent the permissible use or uses for those gametes.

The gametes or any resulting embryos may be used in accordance only with those consents as subsequently varied under the HFE Act section 12(c) and schedule 3. The control amounts to dispositional authority over the embryo. This policy effectively prevents a situation that arose in an American case, *Davis v. Davis*[39], in which a divorcing couple disagreed as to the fate of several frozen embryos; the wife was given custody. In Britain, each gamete donor is, in effect, given a veto over what may be done with the embryo.

2.7. REMEDIES

What happens if the licence holder fails to comply with the consents or fails to allow the embryos to perish? What is the legal remedy? Recourse to contract law is a possibility, but only if treatment or storage is provided outside of the National Health Service, unless payment is made for these services within the NHS.[40]

Section 17 of the Act imposes a statutory duty upon the licence holder to comply with the conditions of the licence. Therefore, a failure to comply with the provisions of schedule 3, or with the duty to allow the embryos to perish might give rise to a private right of action.[41]

Conclusion

The HFE Act creates a highly elaborated framework governing the morally contentious practice of embryo research. It is virtually a law without norms - or at least a law with very few. Instead the HFE Authority is created and empowered as a pragmatic means of facilitating medical advances. There is no real attempt at a principled approach to the vindication of patient rights.[42] Such an interpretation is consistent with Atiyah's description of the pragmatic cast of contemporary common law.

Acknowledgement

The author wishes to express her gratitude to Radu Popa, of the library of The New York University School of Law, and to Margaret Davino, Vice President and General Counsel, Saint Vincent's Hospital and Medical Center, for their assistance.

Notes

1. Kennedy, Ian, *Treat Me Right: Essays in Medical Law and Ethics* New York, Oxford University Press, 1988, p.119.

2. Lawson, F.H., *A Common Lawyer Looks at the Civil Law* University of Michigan School of Law, 1953, p.80.

3. David, Rene and Brierley, John E.C., *Major Legal Systems in the World Today: An Introduction to the Comparative Study of Law* third edition, London, Stevens and Sons, 1985, p.24.

4. *Ibid.*, pp.95-6.

5. *Ibid.*, p.108.

6. *Ibid.*, p.136.

7. Lawson, *op.cit.*, pp.80-81.

8. David and Brierley, *op.cit.*, p.359.

9. Atiyah, P.S., *From Principles to Pragmatism: An Inaugural Lecture delivered before the University of Oxford on 17 February 1978* Oxford, Clarendon Press, 1978.

10. Lawson, *op.cit.*, p.79.

11. David and Brierley, *op.cit.*, p.108.

12. *Ibid.*, pp.361-2.

13. *Ibid.*, pp.351-2.

14. *Ibid.*, pp.361-2.

15. Cmnd 9314 (1984).

16. Cm. 259 (1987).

17. Brazier, Margaret, *Medicine, Patients and the Law* 2nd edition, London, Penguin books, 1992, p.269.

18. Morgan, Derek and Lee, Robert G., *Blackstone's Guide to the Human Fertilisation and Embryology Act of 1990: Abortion and Embryo Research the New Law* London, Blackstone Press Ltd, 1991, p.81.

19. Brazier, *op.cit.*, p.261.

20. Montgomery, Jonathan, 'Rights, restraints and pragmatism: the Human Fertilisation and Embryology Act 1990' 54 *Modern Law Review* 1991, pp.524-34, pp. 528-9.

21. *Ibid.*, p.527.

22. Kennedy, Ian and Grubb, Andrew, *Medical Law: Text and Materials* London, Butterworths, 1994, p.769.

23. *Ibid.*, p.777.

24. Brazier, *op.cit.*, pp.273-4.

25. *Ibid.*, p.272.

26. Kennedy and Grubb, *op.cit.*, p.771.

27. Montgomery, *op.cit.*, p.524.

28. Brazier, Margaret, 'The challenge for parliament: a critique of the White Paper on Human Fertilisation and Embryology' in Dyson, A. and Harris, J. (eds), *Experiments on Embryos* London, Routledge, 1989, pp.127-129.

29. Callahan, Daniel, 'The puzzle of profound respect' *Hastings Center Report* 25 (1), 1995, pp.39-40.

30. House of Lords, Official Report, 6 March 1990, col. 1072, cited in Morgan and Lee, *op.cit.*, pp.76-77.

31. *Ibid.*, pp.84-5.

32. *Ibid.*, p.73.

33. *Ibid.*, p.74 (quoting Evans, Donald, *Making and Taking Life* then unpublished, and now appearing in 'Pro-attitudes to pre-embryos' in this volume).

34. Morgan and Lee, *op.cit.*, p.77.

35. House of Lords debate, quoted in *ibid.*, p.77.

36. Brazier (1992), *op.cit.*, p.297.

37. *Roe v. Wade* 410 US 113 (1973)

38. Morgan and Lee, *op.cit.*, p.31.

39. *Davis v. Davis* unreported No. E-14496, 21 September 1989.

40. Kennedy and Grubb, *op.cit.*, pp.798-9.

41. See Montgomery, *op.cit.*, p.524.

42. *Ibid.*, pp.528-9.

21. PROCURING GAMETES FOR RESEARCH AND THERAPY

Donald Evans
Centre for Philosophy and Health care
University of Wales, Swansea
Singleton Park
Swansea
Wales

In the United Kingdom the Human Fertilisation and Embryology Authority (HFEA) has statutory responsibility for regulating practice in the areas of assisted procreation and research on human embryos. As such it has an almost unique responsibility in the United Kingdom for ethical review of both clinical research and practice in a given field. It is therefore interesting to ask whether it has a useful role to play in resolving some pressing practical and ethical problems which have arisen in both of these areas, *viz.* the lack of supply of gametes (notably oocytes) for both therapeutic and research purposes, the question of the selling and buying of gametes and, finally, the inequality which exists between male and female donors in terms of recompense made for donation of gametes. If the answer is yes then we might have an interesting precedent created for the kind of practical control of practice called for in the suggestion of practical closures to moral disagreements concerning the status of the earliest stages of human life referred to earlier.[1]

1. Practical and Ethical Problems in the Procurement of Donor Gametes

1.1. PROBLEM 1: THE SHORTAGE OF DONATED GAMETES

Let us first consider the question of the shortage of oocytes which reveals itself in the waiting lists of couples needing assisted procreation services due to the inability of the female partner to produce oocytes. As a result of such lists the chances of successful therapy for couples is severely reduced during the prolonged waiting period and some who might have benefitted from such services are denied therapy altogether. In addition, less than desirable solutions to the infertility of some couples will be adopted as in the case sanctioned by the HFEA where the oocyte of a white donor was employed due to the inability of practitioners to procure an oocyte from a black donor.[2] Two of the questions posed at a discussion meeting convened by the HFEA[3] were: How could the levels of donation be improved to meet this shortfall? and Should the HFEA or some other body be responsible for a promotional programme of procurement? I made

315

D. Evans (ed.), Conceiving the Embryo, 315–322.
© 1996 *Donald Evans. Printed in the Netherlands.*

a proposal to that meeting which I shall present here in more detail.

It is fairly clear from published research[4] that the withdrawal of financial inducement to donors would, at least in the short term, seriously threaten the supply of sperm, the gametes which currently present the least problems in terms of supply. The investment of the further time and resources necessary to increase substantially the supply of oocytes on a voluntary basis, or in return for infertility services or hysterectomies would be prohibitive as increased effort in these directions would be subject to the law of diminishing returns. As these avenues offer a small return for the investment already made by treatment centres the realistic hopes of marked improvement of supply seem to lie elsewhere. It is fairly clear that a financial inducement to donors, using the male donor programme as a comparator, offers the most likely solution to the problem. This probable gain is noted even by opponents of payments for gametes.[5]

But this solution raises the other two problems listed above, *viz.* the ethical problems of the differential treatment of male and female donors in terms of financial rewards and the negative responses to the suggestion of the buying and selling of gametes.

1.2. PROBLEM 2: THE DIFFERENTIAL TREATMENT OF MALE AND FEMALE DONORS

The resort to financial inducements to female donors of gametes would not create a differential between male and female donors out of nothing. In fact such a differential already exists and, as currently practised it is one which is impossible to justify. On average a male donor is paid, subject to various controls, about £15 per donation. If a clinic takes two donations per week for a five month period this amounts to an inducement of about £600. Female donors are paid nothing for donation though some of them are offered payments in kind in the form of medical treatments which they need. This differential treatment is especially problematic as the physical and social invasiveness of the techniques necessary to farm female gametes is vastly greater than that experienced by male donors. In addition there is a real measurable physical risk involved in donating oocytes which could have grave repercussions on the health of the donor and her family which has no parallel in sperm donation.

The differential which already exists also demonstrates that gamete donation as currently practised already involves the controversial activity of buying and selling gametes. Part of the payment made to sperm donors is witheld for a sixth month period after the last donation, the incubation period of the AIDS virus, to facilitate screening for HIV. Only when the provided sperm is cleared as acceptable for use in assisted procreation therapy is full payment made for the donations. This is tantamount to a payment for the gametes in question for if those provided do not meet the advertised standards of the goods promised by the donor then payment is witheld.

1.3. PROBLEM 3: BUYING AND SELLING GAMETES

In some countries, including the United Kingdom, the proposal to buy gametes is met with considerable resistance. Indeed the HFEA has made it clear that it is reluctant to permit payments for gametes. The HFE Act (Section 12(e)) states that "no money or other benefit shall be given or received in respect of any supply of gametes or embryos unless authorised by Directions". The Authority issued its Direction in 1991 allowing the kinds of payments listed above. It made it clear at the time that this was a compromise designed to minimise disruption to current treatment services and to control any new payment system. However it then gave notice that its intention was to allow these payments for the supply of gametes for a few years only and that it would then wish to phase them out.

It might be claimed that the Direction asserts that payments are for the supply of gametes and not for the gametes themselves. That is, they are inconvenience payments for the procedures necessary for their supply rather than for the goods supplied. This would constitute a somewhat unnatural reading of the Direction however and the way in which the Direction is executed most certainly places another interpretation upon it as shown above. As the Authority has permitted the practice described above then it can be fairly concluded that it has condoned, until now, the buying and selling of gametes, though not at any price.

Now that the few years are up the question arises as to whether the buying and selling should be allowed to continue. Without raising the ethical question of whether donated gametes should be harvested and used for assisted procreation services at all, an ethical issue already dealt with in the public sphere by the HFE Act in terms of which the Authority has to regulate practice, we can still properly ask whether payment for such is ethically justified and whether the HFE Authority should continue to permit it. It is a difficult question which provokes rival camps to present arguments concerning the nature of persons, slavery (the selling of people), commodification of people (manufacturing people), the body as property and so on on the one hand and the freedom of people to make independent choices, the relief of suffering, the greatest happiness of the greatest number and so on on the other hand.[6] If the HFEA awaits the resolution of these arguments before restricting or expanding the practice of payment for gametes then it will wait forever.

What then should the HFEA do, if anything in the face of this impasse?

2. A Proposed Response

2.1. THE ANALOGY WITH HEALTHY VOLUNTEERS

I think that the regulatory authority could do much to address all three problems and that it is ideally placed so to do. It could best address each of them by the adoption of a method of compensation already worked out in some detail in another area of medical activity. I have in mind the recruitment of healthy volunteers in clinical trials. These people offer the use of their bodies and body products (such as numerous blood samples) for the purpose of furthering medical knowledge with a view to benefitting others. They stand to gain no medical benefit from their involvement in the procedures in question and are expected to take no more than minimal risk. Though there are some important differences between their activity and that of providers of gametes, in that the status of the gamete and its relation to the provider is somewhat more complex, the similarities are striking. The provider of the gametes stands to gain no medical advantage from his or her involvement in the procedure and ultimately the point of the provision is to attempt to provide a benefit to others. Clinical research using healthy volunteers would almost certainly come to an abrupt halt if financial arrangements were not made with the volunteers and important developments in medicine and improvements in the welfare of future patients would be jeopardised. There is clear evidence that a similar fate awaits assisted conception services if adequate financial considerations are not introduced.

Though the recruitment of healthy volunteers and the ethical review of research trials is not controlled by statutory authority a system of self-regulation has developed which is highly commendable. It does not pretend to avoid the offering of financial inducements to candidates for trials. However it does seek to produce firm controls over those payments so as to protect the subjects from undue pressure to engage in activities which are not in their best interests. For example payment is not calculated according to risk. Neither does it relate to the success or otherwise of the trial. It is based purely on the inconvenience endured by the subject in the course of the research. The payment is calculated on a tariff basis where maximum payments for various procedures and activities are laid down. For example in one such tariff £2 is paid for each venepuncture, £60 for each twenty four hour stay in an observation unit, £15 per visit to the unit plus all expenses, and so on. In this way all volunteers are treated equally though they are paid greatly varying sums of money depending on the length of the trial and its complexity all of which affect the number of procedures and activities in which the volunteers are engaged. Monies are paid in full at the end of the trials to all subjects who have complied with the conditions of the trial. Those who have been withdrawn are paid for the procedures undergone up to withdrawal and those who voluntarily withdraw at any point are paid *pro rata* at the discretion of the researchers depending on their reasons for withdrawal. The Association of Clinical Research Contractors endeavours to keep the tariffs of member research organisations roughly in line so that rogue units will not exert improper pressures on certain population groups such as the unemployed to engage in something they would rather not do. Thus though the sum of £600 for a trial will certainly induce an unemployed father to put up with the inconvenience of involvement in a trial the manner in which the sum is calculated acts as a protection for that man against undue exploitation.

A similar tariff could be devised for the providers of gametes for use in research or in therapeutic services. Payment would be according to numbers of visits made to the unit, numbers of procedures undergone of varying degrees of invasiveness such as the taking of super-ovulatory drugs, the extraction under anaesthetic of oocytes and so on. The HFEA would be an ideal body to impose such a tariff on all assisted conception units and centres of research. Conformity to the tariff could be made a condition of licensing. The tariff could be made public so that justice would always be seen to be done. The inconvenience allowances need not exceed the scale of those currently offered as payments. How would the adoption of such a scheme meet the problems outlined above?

2.2. PROBLEM 1: THE SHORTAGE OF GAMETES

We have noted that in order to maintain the supply of provider sperm it is generally agreed that the withdrawal of financial considerations would prove to be disastrous. Given that the total sums of money involved would remain much the same as at present the tariff system would not constitute a threat to the service but it would remove the appearance of making payments for sperm. I shall say more about this in the next section.

With respect to the supply of oocytes the present system of recompense to current providers would be greatly improved. Instead of offering medical services of which the provider stands in need allowances would be offered for procedures and activities undergone in the provision of gametes which would doubtless amount to sums with which the provider could, if she wished, purchase such medical services given that the character of the procedures in which she must engage are so intrusive both physically and socially. This would avoid the appearance of blackmail which the offer of much needed medical services in lieu of donation of oocytes unfortunately provokes. In addition it would offer precisely the same incentive to large numbers of women who do not stand in need of such services but who would, for this kind of consideration, be prepared to put up with the inconvenience involved. The same degree of counselling would apply as at present enabling a responsible decision on the part of the provider. It would not be unacceptably coercive for payments would always be capped by the maxima laid down by the HFEA. It would be surprising if, given the much wider field of women for whom such payments would consitute a considerable benefit, such a system did not markedly improve the rates of provision of oocytes.

2.3. PROBLEM 2: THE DIFFERENTIAL TREATMENT OF MALE AND FEMALE PROVIDERS

Given the invasiveness and complexity of the procurement of oocytes and the limits imposed on the number of offspring produced from one provider's gametes it is inevitable that female donors will receive financial allowances in excess of those received by male providers. This differential is not unjust in any sense however as it is based on a tariff system where payments for like inconveniences are recompensed at the same rate as between male and female providers.

The tariff system does remove the present injustice of denial of financial recompense to oocyte providers whilst it is a standard provision for male providers. Such a revision of practice may render much of the burgeoning discussion of gender differences in respect to attitudes to assisted reproduction less important in relation to gamete procurement than they are currently thought to be.[7] The tariff scheme makes room for those seeking no financial return and those desirous of a modest financial return to engage in the important activity of gamete provision whatever their gender. Such gender differentiations become unimportant from the point of view of establishing motives for provision. Indeed these would not really be the business of the clinicians or recipients involved in assisted procreation services, even if it was possible to divine them accurately, which it rarely is.

2.4. PROBLEM 3: THE PROBLEM OF BUYING AND SELLING GAMETES

In some countries there is no such regulation of the procurement of gametes and private advertisements for oocytes often appear in public newspapers. For example *The Times* (8/2/95) reported that the following advert appeared in the Yale and Columbia University student newspapers:

> Donor sought: empathetic, intelligent, healthy, attractive (preferably dark-haired Jewish) woman 21-28.

for which a payment of $2000 and a free physical examination was offered.
  The report also mentioned a similar advert which appeared in a newspaper at Wellesley College:

> Caucasian woman in 21-32 age range, preferably over 5'6" tall. One week in New York + $5000 for an egg. Photograph required.

The Direction of the HFEA already makes this kind of activity difficult though not impossible in that no-one can offer infertility services without a licence from it as the regulating authority. It has been argued that exchange of money for gametes compromises the altruistic character of donation and that by definition donors cannot receive money.[8] This is little more than a semantic problem. If the sources of gametes were called *providers* then the group could include donors and others. That money changes hands for the provision does not necessarily impugn the morality of the provision. No-one can be expected to be generous though generosity is a quality we admire when we find it in people. Consequently we might admire someone who for no financial consideration provides oocytes for use in assisted conception services for others more than we would someone who makes such provision for a financial consideration. This does not, however, rule out the possibility of our admiring the latter provider, for altruism may vary in degree and a person's motives may well be mixed. Indeed it is usually the case as saints are few and far between. It hardly seems to be the business of the regulatory authority to become an inspector of people's motives and a protector of their saintliness. In any case even where there was no particular concern to ease the suffering of others and the provision was made purely for the financial consideration we may not admire the act but we need not condemn it simply because it has that character. After all people constantly do things for financial considerations when their heart is not in those activities. They are not seeking admiration but neither are they thus deserving of condemnation. So long as such people are protected against harms and injustice it is surely a matter for them to decide whether they engage in work of various kinds or whether they provide gametes or not.

Such protection against harms and injustices would be built in to the tariff system outlined above. Further, the system would not rule out the possibility of the donation of gametes in that the tariff payments would not have to be accepted by the provider. What the tariff system clearly removes is the activity of buying and selling gametes as the possibility does not even arise given that providers would be paid not for the gametes produced but for the inconvenience suffered in the provision. This can be best illustrated by contrasting the scheme with the current method of paying sperm donors. In that scheme a proportion of their payment is witheld until such time as the provided sperm is cleared for use in therapy. I have argued above that this makes the payment a payment for the gametes. On the tariff system the payment would be made in full for the inconveniences endured in the provision and not for the provided gametes. This would have the effect of increasing slightly the cost of procuring useful male gametes from male providers but maybe these increases could be cut by more careful screening of providers at the recruitment stage.

In the case of female providers the position would be similar. For example a woman who undergoes the drug regime, who complies with all the observation requirements, who is anaesthetised, who undergoes invasive procedures to extract follicles and so on will be paid for each of those procedures and not for the number of follicles extracted. Indeed at each stage of the process she will be due the inconvenience allowances earned to that point whether or not she is able to go on to successfully provide useful gametes. Thus she will in no sense be selling oocytes to the clinic.

3. Conclusion

Thus whilst it may not be agreed that it is the business of a regulatory authority to take responsibility for promoting the activity it regulates the HFEA could do both providers of gametes and the assisted procreation services a favour by means of a fresh Directive regarding payments to providers. They could at one and the same time resolve the injustices that exist in the differential treatment of male and female providers, protect providers against harms and injustices arising from undue pressure to provide and encourage a considerable increase in the numbers of female providers by the one measure of adopting a tariff type payment system such as has been well tried in facilitating clinical research and protecting healthy volunteers who are the subjects of that research.

322   Donald Evans

Acknowledgement

This paper first appeared as a guest editorial in the *Journal of Medical Ethics* 21, October 1995, pp.1-4.

Notes

1. See Evans, D., 'Pro-attitudes to pre-embryos' in this volume.

2. *The Independent* 2 January 1994.

3. HFEA discussion meeting, St. Anne's College, Oxford, June 1st 1995.

4. See, for example, Cook, R. and Golombok, S., 'A survey of semen donation: phase II - the view of donors' *Human Reproduction* Vol. 10, No. 4, 1995, pp.951-959.

5. See Shenfield, F. and Steele, S.J., 'Why gamete donors should not be paid' *Human Reproduction* Vol. 10, No. 2, 1995, pp.253-255.

6. Cf. for example, John Harris, *Wonderwoman and Superman: The Ethics of Biotechnology* Chapter 6, Oxford, Oxford University Press, 1993; and Shenfield and Steele, *ibid.*, p.253.

7. See, for example, Cook and Golombok, *op.cit.*, Haimes, Erica, 'Issues of gender in gamete donation' *Social Science and Medicine* Vol 36, No. 1, 1993, pp.85-93, and Schover, L.R., Rothmann, S.A. and Collins, R.L., 'The personality and motivation of semen donors: a comparison with oocyte donors' *Human Reproduction* 7, 1992, pp. 575-579.

8. See Shenfield and Steele, *op.cit.*

PART SIX

Legislation Concerning Human Embryology

22. LEGAL CONSENSUS AND DIVERGENCE IN EUROPE IN THE AREA OF HUMAN EMBRYOLOGY - ROOM FOR HARMONISATION?

Associate Professor of Law Linda Nielsen, Dr. juris,
Faculty of Law, The University of Copenhagen
Denmark
Member of the Danish Council of Ethics

1. Introduction, Purpose and Legislative Approaches

1.1. INTRODUCTION AND PURPOSE

In this essay legal issues involved in the area of human embryology are analysed and the predominant legal views in various European countries are compared, to see whether some kind of consensus is possible. For this purpose the existing legislation in Europe is outlined.[1] To a certain extent existing practice described by national experts is also included.

The need for such analysis is initiated by the fact that there is legal - and ethical - dispute throughout Europe as to what should or should not be allowed in the practice of reproductive medicine and human embryology. Many of the countries in Europe have either enacted or are in the process of drafting legislation to govern the activities of medical practioners and researchers. The result is that we have serious incompatibilities between laws of member states on matters such as assisted conception and embryo research.

There is a broad choice between aiming, on the one hand, at a uniform minimum threshold of law and regulation - thus emphasising individual freedom of choice - and, on the other hand, at a uniform maximum coverage of law and regulation - thus emphasising societal protection of embryonic life and future generations.

In the following the different legislative approaches are described and the areas of consensus and divergence on the different topics within embryo research are outlined together with some indications of what might constitute the reasons for the differences. Some remarks are made about the advantages and disadvantages of trying to reach consensus and finally some concluding remarks regarding the analysis are made.

The survey includes *the UK, Germany, France, Austria, Spain, Italy, Greece, Norway, the Netherlands, Poland, Hungary, Sweden* and *Denmark*. The description is by no means exhaustive but suggests how and why some countries have a 'restrictive' attitude towards the area of embryo research, whereas other countries hold a more 'permissive' attitude.

D. Evans (ed.), Conceiving the Embryo, 325–338.
© 1996 *Kluwer Law International. Printed in the Netherlands.*

1.2. DIFFERENT LEGISLATIVE APPROACHES

Although the questions that arise with respect to law, medicine and bioethics are similar all over the world, there are differences of a philosophical, economic, social, political and religious nature which have led to different regulations. The legal solutions regarding these questions may be characterised as a) the prohibitive approach, b) the cautious regulatory approach, c) the liberal regulatory approach, and d) the laissez-faire approach. A number of examples may illustrate this:

1.2.1. *The Prohibitive Approach*

In *Germany* the attitude towards use of the embryo has been restrictive, centered almost entirely on penal provisions but without forming part of the Criminal Law. The Embryo Protection Act[2] prohibits a) fertilisation other than for purposes of pregnancy, b) the fertilisation of a human egg cell for any purpose other than to start a pregnancy in the woman who produced the egg, c) the fertilisation of more eggs than may be necessary for transfer in one cycle, d) undertaking a genuine embryo transfer, or extraction of an embryo from a woman's uterus for any other purpose than to keep it alive.

In *Austria* a range of prohibitions in relation to both assisted conception services and embryo research was enacted in 1992. Destructive embryo research is prohibited, and any interference with the germ cell line is prohibited. *In vitro* embryos may not be used for purposes other than medically assisted reproduction. Embryo donation is prohibited. Storage may not exceed one year after which any stored embryos or gametes must be allowed to perish.[3]

1.2.2. *The Cautious Regulatory Approach*

In *Denmark* donation of fertilised human eggs is prohibited according to the 1992 Act.[4] It is permissible to cryopreserve human eggs, but according to administrative regulations only for a maximum of one year and aiming at treatment and research only within Denmark. Embryo research is allowed up to 14 days on certain conditions (see below). A new bill on assisted procreation is expected to be presented in the 1995-6 session of the Danish Parliament. The 1992 Act also laid down prohibitions concerning experiments intended to make possible a) cloning (creating genetically identical human individuals), b) the creation of human individuals by fusion of genetically different embryos or parts of embryos prior to implantation (nucleus substitution), c) the creation of living human individuals who will be hybrids with a genome containing constituent parts of other species (cross species fertilisation) and d) development of a human individual in the uterus of a different species.

In *Sweden* embryo research is forbidden if it takes place later than 2 weeks after fertilisation. In addition, the research must not have the intention of developing methods of creating genetic effects which can be hereditary. A fertilised egg which has been subject to research must be destroyed without delay after the expiration of the 2 weeks. Freezing of surplus embryos is allowed for up to one year only with the couple's consent.[5] However, the National Board of Health may allow a more prolonged timespan if there are 'marked reasons' for it. If a fertilised egg has been subject to research, the egg must not be introduced into a woman's body.

In *Norway* only establishments which are authorised to carry out artificial fertilisation may freeze or store sperm or fertilised eggs. The latter may be utilised only for implantation in women and may not be stored for more than three years.[6] Embryo research is not allowed.

In *France* new legislation was enacted in 1994.[7] According to this legislation, while donation of embryos is possible, no payment whatsoever may be made to the couple giving the embryo. A human embryo may not be conceived or used for commercial or industrial purposes. The creation of human embryos *in vitro* for study, research, or experiments is forbidden. Any experiment on an embryo is forbidden. Exceptionally both members of the couple may permit studies to be carried out on their embryos. These studies must have a therapeutic purpose and may not impair the embryo.

1.2.3. *The Liberal Regulatory Approach*

In the *UK* the attitude towards embryo research has been more liberal.[8] The Human Fertilisation and Embryology Act of 1990 (HFE Act) deals *inter alia* with the keeping of human embryos outside the body, embryo research and a number of prohibitions regarding genetic engineering. A statutory agency charged with a wide range of responsibilities - the Human Fertilisation and Embryology Authority (HFEA) - licenses clinics which undertake the storage of gametes and embryos and research on human embryos.

In *Spain* legislation concerning assisted reproduction and embryonic human life has been made to a certain extent. The 1988 legislation regulates the donation and utilisation of embryos and foetuses, their cells, tissues and organs. Insemination of human ova for any purpose other than human procreation is expressly prohibited. Other prohibitions are inferred from existing legal provisions, e.g. donation of gametes and pre-embryos for commercial or money-making purposes. There are detailed regulations on research and experimentation with pre-embryos. The last is expressly forbidden, either in the womb or in the fallopian tubes.

1.2.4. *The Laissez-faire Approach*

In *Italy* the legal approach towards the use of embryos is omissive. Italy has not yet produced any statute regarding the issues related to artificial fertilisation, treatment of human gametes, human embryos etc., although proposals have been made.

Greece is another example of a country adopting the laissez-faire approach with almost no regulation, though Law 2071/1992 provides for the establishment and function of Units for Artificial Fertilisation and authorises this regulation by a Presidential Decree.

2. Areas of Consensus and Divergence - the Different Topics

The following description is based on the different legislations and reports from national experts regarding existing practice. Not all of the countries are mentioned, when the national attitudes towards the different topics are outlined, but the survey presents a picture of the basic areas of consensus and divergence within the countries.

2.1. STORAGE OF EMBRYOS AND GAMETES

2.1.1. *Limitation on Embryonic Life*

In most countries there are certain limitations on embryonic life, normally 14 days.

2.1.2. *Time Limits of Storage*

In a number of countries there are time limits on cryopreservation of fertilised eggs, but the time limits differ. In *Denmark* and *Austria* the time limit is one year, in *Norway* it is 3 years, and in *France* and *Spain* 5 years. In *Spain* pre-embryos from couples who have made use of infertility services may after 2 years remain at the Centre's disposal if unused by the couple. They may be used for donation or research.

2.1.3. *Other Questions*

In *Greece* it has been proposed that storage of gametes in the Unit for future personal use should be permitted on the condition that the donor is asked to give precise guidance concerning the future of his/her gametes in case of death or disappearance. Moreover, it has been proposed that the surplus preembryos which are not replaced in the uterus are not destroyed, but kept for future use of the couple.

In *Austria* legislation restricts the ability of couples in an assisted treatment programme to direct what may be done with their gametes. While they may be stored in accordance with certain regulations gametes and embryos may not be returned to their genitors nor to any other person other than for specified treatment.

In *Denmark* the cryopreserved embryos must be destroyed in the case of divorce between the parties or the death of a spouse/cohabitant. Stored embryos cannot be taken out of Denmark.

In *France* every year each member of the couple must confirm his/her will to keep the embryos stored. One member is sufficient to decide to discontinue the storage but only the two together could give the embryos to another couple or accept that the embryos be used for research purposes. Research protocols should be executed only after due authorisation and consultation with the National Commission of Reproductive Medicine and Biology. Commercial and industrial use of embryos is prohibited. Penal sanctions ensure that these provisions are respected.

2.2. EMBRYO RESEARCH

2.2.1. *Prohibitions*

Normally some kinds of genetic engineering are forbidden. In *Germany, Denmark, Austria* and the *UK* cloning and blending of animals and human beings is punishable. Hybrids and chimeras are forbidden.

2.2.2. *Experimentation on Human Embryos*

In *Germany* research on foetuses is punishable. It is expressly stated in the legislation that extracorporeal development for other purposes than to keep the embryo alive is prohibited. In *Austria* destructive embryo research is forbidden, and any interference with the germ line cell is prohibited. *In vitro* embryos may not be used for purposes other than medically assisted reproduction and hence may be examined and treated only in so far as it is necessary in accordance with clinical practice.

In *Denmark* research on living, human individuals, human gametes which are intended for use in fertilisation, fertilised human eggs and preembryos or embryos should be reported to ethical committees. The 1992 Act sanctions embryo research but this must have the purpose of improving the techniques of IVF with a view to promoting pregnancy. Removing and fertilising eggs or embryos for any other purposes is prohibited.

In *France* an embryo may be conceived *in vitro* only within the context and for the purposes of medically assisted procreation. The creation of human embryos *in vitro* for research is forbidden. Exceptionally both members of the couple may permit studies to be carried out on their embryos. These studies must have a medical purpose and may not impair the embryos.

2.3. OTHER QUESTIONS

2.3.1. *Sex Selection*

In *Germany* the choice of a particular sex is prohibited unless specific sex dependent grave diseases justify it. In *Norway* a similar prohibition has been enacted.

2.3.2. *No Commercialisation*

In *Germany* it is expressly stated in the legislation that the sale and purchase of an embryo is prohibited. A similar prohibition can be found in a number of other countries, e.g. *France* and *Spain*, while in yet others, in *Scandinavia* for instance, the non-commercialisation principle forms part of an underlying principle in these areas of health care, whether embraced by specific legislation or not.

2.3.3. *Gene Therapy*

Germ line gene therapy is prohibited in the legislation of the *UK*, *France*, *Norway*, *Sweden*, *Germany* and *Austria*. In Norway the danger of altering the human species has been emphasised in the explanatory memorandum.[9] The danger of eugenics has been recognised as important in Austria and France. In, for example, *Italy* and *Greece*, there is no regulation of gene therapy.

Somatic gene therapy has also come under legislation enacted in a number of countries where the focus has been either on limiting serious diseases or establishing procedures of approval. In *Norway*, for instance, the legislation makes future use of somatic gene therapy conditional on aiming at the treatment of serious disease; and each new treatment has to be approved by the Social Department. In *Austria* somatic gene therapy is covered by detailed regulation. It may be carried out only when in keeping with the current state of science and technology and only for the purposes of therapy or prevention of serious disease in humans or in order to establish appropriate procedures within the framework of a clinical trial.

3. Basic Areas of Convergence and Divergence

The primary areas of *convergence* concerning the embryo are found in the normal or widespread occurence of:
a. non-commercialisation principles
b. time limits on the maintenance of embryonic life
c. time limits on cryopreservation
d. prohibitions concerning cloning, hybrids, chimeras and the like, where embryo research is allowed.

The areas of *divergence*, where disagreement or national difference is more pronounced, are mainly centered on the following aspects:
a. donation of human embryos and eggs
b. conservation of human embryos and eggs
c. experimentation on human embryos

The area of *consensus* is widespread, but the same goes for the area of divergence. Some of the differences are fundamental, especially as the status of the embryo is of great concern here; a matter not likely to be agreed upon between the different countries. Thus, the possibility of a comprehensive policy, or of consensus in legislation encompassing all of the problems related to fertility, infertility and the human embryo, in the different countries within the EU may never be forthcoming in this area. It may also be questioned whether such comprehensive consensus and legislation is desirable. To investigate these questions further, some indications of the cultural, social, economic and religious reasons behind the current position in the various countries is necessary.

4. Possible Reasons for the Areas of Convergence and Divergence

In the following some indications of what constitutes the main similarities and differences in culture and regulation between the EU countries are pointed out. The purpose is to present only some snapshots of cultural concepts and behaviour in these countries, to begin to evaluate the possibilities of making common regulations embracing countries of very different cultural backgrounds. Further elaboration and corrections are necessary, but even small contributions to an understanding of the cultural differences seem worthwhile.

4.1. SIMILARITIES - BASIC HUMAN VALUES

The basic human values concerning
- protection of life,
- autonomy,
- human dignity,
- protection of human rights, including the right to found a family,
- abandoning eugenics and discrimination
are common in the countries surveyed.

These similarities tend to make some harmonisation and perhaps common regulation a realistic possibility. The possibilities of achieving consensus on a European level are reflected in e.g. the European Convention on Human Rights and the difficulties are reflected in the problems connected with the drafting of a Bioethics convention.[10]

4.2. DIFFERENCES - RELIGION, PUBLIC DEBATE, EXTENT OF REGULATION

4.2.1. *Religion*

Differences in religion must be respected. Problems in this respect may concern e.g. the status of the human embryo. However, the effect of the differences in religion is not - as one might expect - that Italy has the strongest rules concerning biotechnology, genetics and life. On the contrary, in this field this country has no statutory regulation. It may seem that attempts to introduce rules on these issues have been frustrated because of the (formal or informal) opposition of the Catholic party and the Catholic Church. These may consider any attempts at regulation a slippery slope leading to the appropriation by the State of matters that are properly the business of the church.[11]

A few examples may be illustrative:

In *Denmark, Sweden, Holland, Belgium* and the *UK* it is probably fair to say that religion for many people plays a minor role in their everyday life, but that christian thinking, and the moral values derived therefrom to a very high degree affects the way of living and of thinking as a fundamental part of their cultural inheritance.

Italy is the only country within the EU with a Catholic party as a majority party: in other countries, there are no Catholic parties as such or, if they do exist, their composition is more complex than in Italy (for instance, *Germany*). Nevertheless, there are no specific legal rules concerning the limits of the research and development of new technologies, the priority of public investments, or the protection from dangerous or uncontrolled implementation of genetic technologies by private institutions in Italy. This lack of regulation[12] has a twofold perverse effect: a) Public institutions (hospitals, health services, etc.) either do not offer any assistance, or, if they do, they often act at the risk of the doctors or the patients, without any protection of their respective rights; b) lacking any type of criminal as well as civil regulation, private health institutions are free to offer any type of intervention. This means that a highly speculative activity on the free market is now flourishing which is both extremely expensive and dangerous for women and for the newborn.[13]

4.2.2. *Public Debate and Openness*

The importance of public debate and openness in these sensitive areas must be noted. If the legislation is to be effective it must be felt as norm-setting and preferably reflect the State as a friend rather than a 'big brother watching you'. Knowledge and openness are preconditions both of such a norm-setting and educational function, and if the consent of the public to legislation is to play an important role.

Again a few examples may be illustrative:

In *Denmark*, *Norway*, *Sweden*, *Holland*, *France* and the *UK* the public debate is widespread and extended. This must be seen in connection with people as very well informed populations. In the mass media there are lots of programmes including discussions, and one task of the Councils of Ethics is to create a debate amongst the population concerning ethical questions related to the life sciences.

In some of the countries in *Southern Europe*, the public debate is generally not as widespread and the State has no tradition of encouraging information and debate to the same extent about either ethical or medical issues.

4.2.3. *Women's Movements*

Women's movements are strong in some of the countries, e.g. the Scandinavian ones, and they have to a large extent been quite hostile towards the expansion of technologies concerning assisted human reproduction and genetic screening.

4.2.4. *Intensity and Extent of Regulation*

The differences concerning the intensity and extent of regulation must be taken into consideration. In the area of personal affairs and the area of health the difference does not seem overwhelming. There seems to be reluctance in most of the countries to legislate in the health area, and especially in the area of reproduction, which is seen as a private sphere. Nevertheless, legislation is now being enacted in these countries; but its extent and forms differ very much. One such contrast is between the very wide-ranging *French* legislation (on the one hand) and the *Italian* laissez-faire approach (on the other). Different legal and medical traditions are also of importance in this respect. For example, in the *UK* tradition professional guidelines are predominantly important, whereas the *Scandinavian* and *French* traditions lay much emphasis on substantial law as well.

5. Is Consensus Desirable? Some Pros and Cons

5.1. WHAT CAN WE LEARN FROM THE PAST? (INTERNATIONAL PRIVATE LAW)

From the history of the origin of the Hague Conference[14], one can tell that the first Hague Conventions were built on the principle of nationality as the cornerstone of both public and private international law. The concept of nationality was seen as distinctly cosmopolitical. The world was seen as a community of nations, each with its own culture and legal traditions. It was precisely because the legal diversity was valued that clear limits were seen as to the possibilities of unifying the various private laws of the world. Certainly, the possibilities for unification of fundamental rules of universal justice were recognised - nowadays we would call them human rights. But a complete unification of substantive private law was seen as an illusion.

This was true in particular for the laws relating to personal status, family and succession. Unification of law in these areas was seen not only as an illusion but also as undesirable, because it would curtail human freedom. The principle of nationality was thought to ensure that a person would retain a sphere of freedom when he travelled abroad - and this was in turn thought to be his destiny and mission, since he is born a cosmopolitical being. Hence the utility of concluding multilateral conventions on the conflicts of laws which, provided they are based on the principle of nationality, will ensure personal freedom of the citizens of Contracting States when they travel around.

Another approach taken was more pragmatic. The emphasis was on putting an end to any legal uncertainty, resulting from that variety of laws, which was prejudicial to individual interests. Later one of the recurrent features of the Hague Conventions is the use of the concept of habitual residence by which a person living in Countries other than that of his or her birth could claim some of the rights given to citizens of those Countries. Additionally, one of the important innovations of the last 20 years has been the introduction of a limited form of party autonomy in family law as a result of which the parties may decide on certain aspects of juridiction and choice-of-law by agreement.

The experience from the United Nations Convention on the Rights of the Child and the draft Bioethics Convention[15] seems to be that consensus can be obtained as long as the Conventions are centred on broad principles. However, as can be seen e.g. from the difficulties of the EU regulation on the protection of individuals with regard to the processing of personal data and on the protection of biotechnological inventions (patents), achieving consensus over specific rights and duties is often problematic.

5.2. ARGUMENTS AGAINST CONSENSUS AND INTERNATIONAL POLICY-MAKING IN HUMAN EMBRYOLOGY

a. When considering the content of international regulation, consensus carries the risk of 'harmonisation downwards', where the regulation is based on the lowest common denominator.
b. Moreover, international instruments or international regulation may have difficulties in taking the local culture into account; may be too difficult to change in this unstable area; and may lack precision.
c. Finally, comprehensive EU regulation would face serious problems in stating the fulcrum of bioethical balance: Which is the position to which the plural system should be magnetised - towards a more restrictive or a more liberal approach? What institutional structures are necessary to articulate and effect the determinants of public choice?

From this point of view it is probably not feasible to produce a detailed set of guidelines to which all nations within Europe could subscribe. The differences of culture in their legal systems seem to make this too difficult.

5.3. ARGUMENTS FOR CONSENSUS AND INTERNATIONAL POLICY-MAKING

a. International regulation or policy may enlarge the protection, for example, of human dignity or the (unborn) child. Moral pluralism may carry the risk of underestimating the danger of embryo research to the concept of human dignity.
b. International regulation or policy-making would promote transnational equality.
c. Consensus is the only way of setting tangible limits which are likely to be followed broadly. The need for regulation and policymaking may be seen as a way of securing democracy in the bioethics field.

Justice Michael Kirby has made this observation about the dangers of the law failing to keep up with science:

> My chief point is a simple one. Science and technology are advancing rapidly. If democracy is to be more than a myth and a shibboleth in the age of mature science and technology and more than a triannual visit to a polling booth, we need a new institutional response. Otherwise we must simply resign ourselves to being taken where the scientists and the technologists' imagination leads. That path may involve nothing less than the demise of the rule of law as we know it. It is for our society to decide whether there is an alternative or whether the dilemmas posed by modern science and technology, particularly in the field of bioethics, are just too painful, technical, complicated, sensitive and controversial for our institutions of government.[15]

5.4. THE ROLE OF LAW AND INTERNATIONAL POLICYMAKING

Regulation may happen through informal or formal law. Either way, if law is seen as necessary or appropriate, regulation may have both different functions, and different levels.

5.4.1. *Functions of Regulation*[16]

A norm-setting function. This involves declaring certain values and interests as worth protection against any infringement (e.g. of human dignity). This function is based on the vision that law may be educational - a way of implementing ethics.

A protective function. This involves balancing the protected values, including human dignity, against other interests, providing sanctions for abuses and minimising risks to (perhaps) human embryos.

A regulative or declarative function. This entails securing clarity and certainty in handling controversial areas of bioethics, ensuring that the persons involved know what is acceptable and what is not acceptable so they can act accordingly. An example is the prohibition of research on any embryo after the development of the primitive streak.

5.4.2. *Levels of Regulation*

Object of protection: individual or society at large? This level includes the choice between pluralism and universalism. The trend in western culture has for a number of years been pluralism and individualisation, which tends to embrace ethics, too. This has lead to moral pluralism via individual autonomy administered by informed consent. A wish to obtain national and international solidarity and to protect human dignity may speak in favour of universal solutions.

Timing: ex post facto, current or anticipatory? This includes the dilemma of opting for the risks of a slippery slope versus opting for exaggerated legislation. Moreover, there may be worries as to the factual possibilities of control.

Location: clinic, Council of Ethics, government, international body? Professional control at clinics may ensure the quality of medical treatment, and independent Ethics Councils take into account broader ethical considerations. Problems of international private law may call for international instruments.

Form: prohibition, permission, criminalisation. The urgent need for flexibility in this area may make formal legislation less adequate. Thus procedural measures may be sufficient in a number of areas concerning research on embryos, whereas commercialisation (for example) may be penalised. It is imperative that the legislation secures consequence, predictability and equity.

5.5. KEY ISSUES IN HARMONISATION

It would be a valuable gain to secure:
* the protection of human dignity, the (unborn) child-to-be, and the patient;
* the self-determination of the various countries in respecting differences of a cultural, philosophical, social, economic, religious and political nature;
* freedom of research, freedom of contract and free movements between EU countries;
* the efficiency of medical care;

One solution is to accept that there is no need for absolute uniformity, but a need to try to establish broad, basic areas of harmonisation. We can perhaps profitably aim for international agreement on broad principles to guide the development and use of embryo research and to give legal content to the moral concept of human dignity and protection of the (unborn) child.[17]

International measures may serve as safeguards *per se* and may serve as a basis for national measures protecting the values described above.

6. Conclusion

In my opinion the area of human embryology calls for national legislative measures and should also concern the international community.

This conclusion is based on the fact that the wide-ranging consequences of the new possibilities are a matter of concern for society as such. It is also imperative to ensure that this sensitive area becomes part of the democratic process which will secure openness as to the use of the new biotechnologies and a broad debate and consensus in the area. This should also secure a public acceptance of the use of the new biotechnologies. Finally legislation may be necessary in certain areas to protect weak groups including the child-to-be and future generations. To a certain extent I think it advisable to declare a moratorium in certain areas until we are sure that any solution is well debated and widely acceptable.

These arguments, in my opinion, override the arguments stressing the barriers restrictions may set up to research in biotechnology. I also think they override the advantages of self-regulation between professional groups.

In my opinion the international regulations or guidelines should be based on very broad principles, accepting that national differences be accepted in a large number of areas. *Nationally* the areas of legislation might include provisions on embryo storage, donation and research. These topics should be dealt with according to the local culture, legal traditions and medical practices of the respective countries.

Internationally it might be thought advisable to make provisions on broader themes connected with embryonic life, e.g. a non-commercialisation principle, limitation on embryonic life, prohibition of cloning, hybrids, chimeras and the like, and maybe some provisions on the cryopreservation period. Such topics are partly dealt with by the draft bioethics convention, but others are not.

It is important to stress that, despite the importance of scientific autonomy and the freedom to research, the nature and consequences of the new reproductive technologies make public intervention necessary in some areas - nationally and internationally. However, this intervention cannot free each individual from taking responsibility for choices made regarding research. We need responsibility from the individual, the different countries and the international community, for the sake of our children.

Notes

1. A comparison between Scandinavia, England and Austria and an analysis of different approaches to a number of topics are included in Morgan, Derek and Nielsen, Linda, 'Prisoners of progress or hostages to fortune?' *The Journal of Law, Medicine and Ethics* 21 (1), 1993, pp.30-42.

2. Embryo Protection Act (Embryonenschutzgesetz) of 13 December 1990.

3. Act No. 275 of 14 May 1992 on Procreative Medicine.

4. In a court decision it has been established that donation of a human egg, and subsequently fertilising it with semen from a donor cannot lead to criminal sanctions.

5. Act No. 711 of June 1988 on Fertilisation Outside the Human Body.

6. Act of 14 June 1994 on Medical Use of Biotechnology. Cf. the Norwegian Bill with explanatory memorandum, nr. 37, 1993-94, on the Medical Use of Biotechnology, and the report this Bill is based on, Report No. 25 (1992-93): *Biotechnology in Relation to Human Beings*.

7. Law No. 94-654, 29 July 1994, on the Donation and Use of Elements and Products of the Human Body, Medically Assisted Procreation, and Prenatal Diagnosis.

8. The Human Fertilisation and Embryology Act 1990.

9. Act of 14 June 1994 on Medical Use of Biotechnology with explanatory memorandum, nr. 37, 1993-94.

10. Council of Europe, *Draft Convention for the Protection of Human Rights and Dignity of the Human Being with Regard to the Application of Biology and Medicine: Bioethics Convention and Explanatory Report* Dir/jur (94) 2, Strasbourg, Directorate of Legal Affairs, 1994.

11. The following analysis is partly based on Nielsen, Linda and Nespor, Stefano, *Genetic Test, Screening and Use of Genetic Data by Public Authorities in Criminal Justice, Social Security and Alien and Foreigners Acts* Copenhagen, The Danish Centre for Human Rights, 1994.

12. During the legislative period which ended in 1992, there were 100 bills concerning the regulation of the Reproductive Technology, not one of which has been passed into law; cf. *ibid.* p.37.

13. *Ibid.*

14. van Loon, Hans, 'The Hague Conference - its origins, organisation and achievements' *Svensk Juristtidning* 1993/4, pp.293-315.

15. *Op. cit.*

16. Kirby, M., *Reform the Law* Oxford, Oxford University Press, 1983, pp.238-239.

17. Eser, Albin, 'Legal aspects of bioethics' in *Europe and Bioethics. Proceedings of the First Symposium of the Council of Europe on Bioethics* Strasbourg, Council of Europe Press, 1985, pp.41-42.

18. In the course of the reflections of the European Commission research project Fertility, Infertility and the Human Embryo, a preference for a uniform minimum threshold of law and regulation has emerged.

23. THE EMBRYO IN FRENCH LEGISLATION

Christian Byk
Associate Professor of Law
University of Poitiers
France

1. Rules for Harvesting

1.1. GAMETES

Sperm and oocyte donations are permitted (art L673-1 Public Health Code) under the general conditions applying to the donation of human organs, cells and tissues (Ch.II, Title I, Book I of the Civil Code; Ch.I and II, Title I, Book I of the Public Health Code) but only by donors living as heterosexual couples and having children (art 673-2 PHC). In addition minors and incapacitated persons cannot be donors (art L672-5 PHC). Consequently foetuses are implicitly excluded as a source of donated oocytes.

The consent of the donor and his/her companion is required and can be withdrawn before insemination or embryo transfer (art L673-2 PHC).

Harvesting can be performed only by non profit making health institutions authorised for this purpose by the Minister of Health and subject to compliance with specific regulations regarding safety and storage conditions of gametes (art L673-5 PHC).

1.2. EMBRYOS

Exceptionally, a couple for which an embryo has been procreated can consent to the 'adoption' of this embryo by another couple for whom a medically assisted conception with gamete donation is not possible. This shall be authorised by a Court (art L152-4 and 5 PHC).

The institutions licensed to harvest gametes can serve medical practice by storing the embryo and performing the transfer (art L673-5 PHC).

The practitioner has no right to accept payment for individual items of service in the course of this practice. However, the institution will be paid a standard charge determined by the Ministry of Health.

D. Evans (ed.), Conceiving the Embryo, 339–341.
© 1996 *Kluwer Law International. Printed in the Netherlands.*

2. Use of Gametes and Embryos

2.1. GAMETES

Gamete donation is only for medically assisted reproduction (art L673-1 PHC) and donation involving both sperms and oocytes is not legal. One of the gametes must come from a member of the couple seeking medically assisted conception (art L152-3 PHC). Furthermore, the use of donated gametes is permitted only when it is not possible to use the gametes of the couple (art L152-6 PHC).

2.2. EMBRYOS

Embryos *in vitro* shall be created only for medically assisted reproduction (art L152-3) but a couple can decide that embryos can be stored and used within 5 years for this purpose. Exceptionally (see 1.2 above) a couple, or the surviving member of a couple, can consent to the 'adoption' of the embryo by another couple (art L152-4 and 5 PHC).

As a result of these acts, embryos cannot be conceived or used for industrial purposes (art L152-7 PHC). The procreation of *in vitro* embryos for study, research or experimentation is also prohibited. Experimentation on embryos is clearly prohibited but, exceptionally, the couple can consent to studies on embryos. Such studies should have a medical objective and their carrying out is subject to the agreement of the National Commission of Biology, Reproductive Medicine and Prenatal Diagnosis (art L152-8 PHC).

However, the law does not explain the difference between an experiment and a study. Further regulations are still expected to clarify this important distinction. They will probably take into account the invasive aspect of acts performed on embryos.

3. Commercial Transactions

As neither the human body as a whole nor any part of it can be subject to property rights (art 161 of the Civil Code) any commercial transaction involving gametes or embryos is prohibited and would be void.

Therefore no payment can be made for obtaining gametes or embryos (art L665-13 PHC); physicians cannot be paid for each individual intervention they perform (art L673-5 PHC); and advertising is prohibited (art L665-12 PHC). Health institutions are, however, paid, according to a tariff decided by the Minister of Health, for their different activities (harvesting gametes, treating couples, storing gametes and embryos, and performing insemination or embryo transfer).

4. Rights of Use (Widows and Divorcees)

Law 94-654 of 29 July 1994 (related to donation and use of human body parts and products, medically assisted procreation and prenatal diagnosis) prescribes the criteria of access to medically assisted technologies. They are accessible only to heterosexual couples facing a medical diagnosis of infertility or a particularly serious disease that could be transmitted to the offspring. The husband and wife must both be alive at the time of the insemination or at the time of the embryo transfer. Both partners should be of reproductive age. Finally they should have been married or prove that they have been cohabiting for at least two years (art L152-2).

Given these criteria, it is clear that widows and divorcees cannot have access to reproductive technologies. However, a widow can consent to the adoption of her embryo by another couple (art L152-4 PHC).

5. Storage Regulations and Decisions

Storage, as has been mentioned above, can be practised only in licensed non profit making institutions (art L673-5 HPC). Regarding the storage of embryos, a couple can decide to store embryos for the completion of their parental project within a five year timespan. They will be consulted each year to find out if they want to go on with their parental project (art L152-3 PHC).

Administrative regulation is expected to define the obligations of licensed institutions regarding storage, and in particular the time limits for storage. The 94-654 Act, however, does not say explicitly what should happen to embryos after the five year storage period, except in one case: that of the embryos which already exist at the date of enactment of the law. If they have been stored for 5 years and if it is not possible to have them 'adopted' by another couple, storage can then be ended (art 9 of the law). But as the law is due to be reviewed by Parliament after 5 years, the legislators have certainly preferred not to tangle yet with this difficult issue.

24. THE USE OF GAMETES AND ZYGOTES IN GERMAN LAW

Prof. Dr. Drs. h.c. Erwin Deutsch
Faculty of Law
University of Göttingen
Germany

1 Introduction

The German law on the use of gametes and zygotes has more than one source. The one statute directly regulating these matters is the Embryonenschutzgesetz (Embryo Protection Act) of 1990 (ESchG).[1] The Act is a criminal law, making punishable a given number of techniques of artificial reproduction, protecting the embryo from commercial exploitation and experimentation and prohibiting the creation of hybrids and chimeras.

In addition to the ESchG there is the German Medical Association's *Model Code of Professional Ethics* (MBO)[2] which, since 1985, has dealt with physician's rights and duties connected with reproductive medicine. This code is suppletmented by guidelines of the German Federal Medical Council (the BAeK *Guidelines*)[3] for the practice of gamete intrafallopian transfer (GIFT), *in vitro* fertilisation (IVF) and embryo transfer (ET) as therapeutic methods against human sterility.

According to sec. 8 of ESchG an embryo is: a fertilised, viable human cell from the time of fusion of the nuclei; it is also any totipotent cell taken from an embryo (sec. 8 ESchG). Even the blastodermic site is comprehensively defined: all cells which from the fertilised oocyte lead directly in one cell line to the sperm-cell and oocyte of the human being who stems from them. Pursuant to this definition of an embryo, the ESchG does not deal with gametes but with zygotes. The use of gametes might, however, be affected by a law (currently in draft) on commercial trade with organs.[4] Owing to the wide definition of organs in sec. 1, an organ is any natural part of the body, irrespective of whether it is reproducible or not. Though the main application of this law will be to organs like the heart, kidney or liver, reproducible cells like sperm and ova will also be covered by the statute. However, in so far as the trade in gametes is non-profit oriented there will be no conflicts with this statute.

2. Rules for Harvesting

There are no specific rules for harvesting gametes. It is the constitutional individual's right (art. 2 sub. 1 German Constitution) to self determination that guarantees the

D. Evans (ed.), Conceiving the Embryo, 343–346.
© 1996 *Kluwer Law International. Printed in the Netherlands.*

unrestricted harvesting of genetic material belonging to one's self at one's own discretion. For any harvesting of gametes informed consent is necessary. The number of gametes which may be harvested is not limited.

3. Uses Allowed

Sec. 1 sub. I nos. 1-6 ESchG declares the following abusive uses of reproductive technologies to be prohibited and punishable: (a) the transfer of an unfertilised, extraneous oocyte into a woman's uterus, (b) the artificial insemination of an oocyte for any purpose other than to create a pregnancy, (c) the transfer of more than three embryos during the same cycle, (d) insemination through intratubary gametic transfer more than three oocytes, (e) the insemination of more oocytes than can be transferred to the woman over the course of one cycle, and (f) the undertaking of a genuine embryo transfer, or extraction of an embryo from a woman's uterus for any other purpose than to keep it alive. By the same token, the artificial transfer of a human sperm-cell into a human oocyte for any purpose other than inducing pregnancy is punishable. In particular, research with human embryos is now prohibited, because an oocyte must not be fertilised for any other purpose other than to induce the woman whose oocyte is fertilised to become pregnant (sec. 1 sub. 1 no. 2 ESchG).

The gametes can be used for the fertilisation of no more than three oocytes during the same cycle, sec. 1 sub. 1 no. 3-5 and 4.1 BAeK *Guidelines*. It is up to the physician to choose the oocytes to be fertilised.

4. The Identity of Gametes

In contrast to many other countries the anonymity of the semen donor is considered unconstitutional. In 1989, the German Constitutional Court, in a case involving a child's right to void a determination of affiliation, decided that a child in principle has the right to know who his or her father and mother are.[5] The court held this to be part of a person's right to privacy, which is guaranteed in art. 2 sub. 1 and art. 1 sub. 1 of the German Constitution, and is a result of the very close connection between the execution of one's right to self-determination, that is one's right to determine one's own individuality, on the one hand, and information about the factors constituting this individuality, on the other hand. Constitutionally, this is not, however, an absolute right but rather one that is granted only within the framework of the constitutional regulations.[6] The legislator can thus limit this right through regulations insofar as such limits are not formulated for unconstitutional purposes and under the totality of the circumstances this is a proportionate regulation. One constitutionally valid limitation of the child's right to know who his or her true father and mother are, is to maintain a peaceful relationship in the social (adoptive) family.[7] This constitutional background means that anonymous donation or semen cocktails are prohibited. A promise to the donor to keep his identity a secret is void.

5. Commercial Transactions

The essence of embryo protection is contained in secs. 2 to 4 ESchG. There it is expressly stated that the sale and the purchase of an embryo as well its extracorporeal development for other purposes than to keep it alive is prohibited. Sec. 4.4 BAeK *Guidelines* contains a similar prohibition of any commercial transaction. This in effect makes the carrying of a child to full term a part of our legal order sanctioned by criminal law; any undertaking for a different purpose is prohibited. Also prohibited is the choice of a particular sex unless Duchenne's muscular dystrophy or another, similarly grave, sex-linked genetic disease justifies the choosing of a particular sex.

6. Research Uses, Uses in Treatment and Prohibitions

Any research which leads to the death of the embryo is strictly forbidden (sec. 2 ESchG). Sec. 6 ESchG states that it is also prohibited to use a human embryo's, a foetus's, a person's or a deceased person's genetic material artificially to create an embryo with identical genetic material. The creation of twins, which may happen naturally and is not considered to be an anomaly, is prohibited in this context for the protection of man's singularity and dignity.

Any creation of hybrids and chimeras of different human embryos or of a human being and an animal is prohibited under punishment of up to five years in prison (sec. 7 ESchG). In this context, too, human dignity ranks higher than scientific research. Consequently, the fertilisation of an animal oocyte with human sperm for the purpose of creating a differentiable embryo, is also punishable.

Similar to the ESchG, sec. 1 sub. 5 of the MBO does generally not allow diagnostic treatment of embryos before transfer. Sec. 3 ESchG allows treatment in case of sex linked hereditary diseases.

7. Rights of Use

Sec. 4 sub. 1 no. 3 ESchG prohibits post-mortem insemination, but the female who is inseminated is exempt from punishment. This regulation is based on the best interests of the child.[8] It is not the purpose of reproductive medicine to preserve the ability to procreate children under all circumstances. By German Law a child procreated after the death of his father is not his heir (sec. 1923 sub. 2 BGB).

8. Storage Regulation and Destruction

In contrast to the ESchG, the BAeK *Guidelines* contain a regulation on cryopreservation. Sec. 4.2 expressly allows cryoconservation of fertilised, viable human cells before the time of fusion of the nuclei. It is for this reason that the conservation of gametes is not restricted. On the other hand, the storage of embryos is allowed for medical reasons only.

Recently the German Supreme Court handed down a judgement concerning damages for the destruction of stored sperm.[9] The plaintiff, who suffered from cancer, knew that necessary surgery would lead to his infertility. To retain his ability to procreate children he had his sperm stored by the defendant using cryopreservation techniques. Two years later the plaintiff refused the defendant's request (made as a result of storage capacity problems) to end storage. Despite this refusal the sperm was destroyed without the plaintiff's consent. According to the Court, the plaintiff was entitled to claim damages in tort for the destruction of his gametes on the basis of an invasion of his personal privacy.

Notes

1. Embryonenschutzgesetz Bundesgesetzblatt 1990 I: 2746.

2. German Medical Association, 'Model Code of Professional Ethics' *Deutsches Aerzteblatt* Vol. 91, 1994, pp.B-39.

3. German Federal Medical Council, 'Guidelines' *Deutsches Aerzteblatt* Vol. 91, 1994, pp.B-44.

4. See Deutsch, E., 'Criminal prohibitions on commercial organ transactions' *Zeitschrift fuer Rechtspolitik* Vol. 27, 1994, pp.179-181.

5. Bundesverfassungsgericht, *Neue Juristische Wochenschrift* 1989, p.891.

6. Coester-Waltjen, D., 'Artificial procreation and civil law' *Zeitschrift fuer das gesamte Familienrecht* Vol. 39, 1992, pp.369-373.

7. *Ibid.*, p.373.

8. Keller, R., Günther, H.-L. and Kaiser, P., *Commentary on ESchG* Stuttgart, 1992, p.227.

9. Entscheidungen des Bundesgerichtshofes in Zivilsachen Vol. 124, p.52. See Taupitz, J. 'Tort law of human body' *Neue Juristische Wochenschrift* 1995, pp.745-752.

25. SPANISH LEGISLATION ON USES OF GAMETES AND ZYGOTES (PRE-EMBRYOS)

Jaime Vidal Martínez
Profesor Titular de Derecho Civil
Departamento de Derecho Civil
Universitat de València
Spain

1. Background

At the end of 1988, two Acts were published in Spain: on Assisted Reproduction Techniques (ARTA) and the Donation and Utilisation of Embryos and Foetuses, their cells, tissues and organs (Acts 35 and 42, 22 November and 28 December 1988). They established detailed regulations on the subjects, which have been, however, for seven years in need of subsequent statutory development.[1] The aforementioned Acts were the object of an Appeal before the Constitutional Court in 1989 and that Appeal is still pending resolution (at the end of 1995).

2. Rules for Harvesting

Semen (not ova) and pre-embryos resulting from IVF can be cryopreserved for a five years (maximum) period in authorised Centres. After two years have passed, the gametes and pre-embryos (defined as human embryos prior to the 14th day after conception) which were not donated but originate from couples who have used the infertility services, and which remain unused by them will remain at the Centre's disposal (as a sort of property, to be used, for example, for research, if not viable, or for donation, if viable) (art. 11-4, ARTA).

3. Uses Allowed

Research on gametes (semen, oocytes) is authorised but not their subsequent use for the purposes of reproduction (art. 14). Among permitted uses are the *hamster test* to evaluate the fertilisation capacity of human sperm. This experiment must be stopped at the two cells-division stage. Other cases of the fusion of human and animal gametes might also be authorised (art. 14-4, ARTA).

Research on pre-embryos is authorised within certain limits (until the fourteenth day,

D. Evans (ed.), Conceiving the Embryo, 347–349.
© 1996 *Kluwer Law International. Printed in the Netherlands.*

where they are non-viable, as long as consent (for example of the biological father) is forthcoming and the institution is authorised to carry out research, according to well-detailed but ambiguous regulation (arts. 15, 16 and 17 ARTA).

4. Commercial Transactions

Neither the donation of gametes or of pre-embryos should have financial or commercial purposes according to ARTA. Trading with pre-embryos or their cells is regarded as an offence serious enough to provoke disciplinary penalties (arts. 5-3 and 20-2.B.e).

5. Research Uses and Prohibitions

With research uses, there is both complex regulation and a number of explicit and implicit prohibitions, which appear in the fact that a diversity of activities are regarded as very serious offences. These are: fertilising ova for purposes other than procreation, obtaining human pre-embryos by uterine washing, the utilisation of pre-embryos for cosmetic and industrial purposes, cloning, parthenogenesis, making choices of sex or carrying out genetic manipulation for other than therapeutic purposes, attempting to produce hybrids or chimera (art. 20-2.B, ARTA).

6. Uses in Treatment and Prohibitions

It seems that in IVF practice, three pre-embryos are transferred and the remaining are kept frozen. The increasing use of microinjection could render unnecessary or at least reduce the need for donated gametes. It also seems that most donors do not assume any responsibility for the remaining frozen embryos, once the assisted reproduction needs of a couple are met.

7. Rights of Use

A judge on one occasion ordered the Valèncian Infertility Institute not to make use of some frozen embryos originating from a married couple that was about to separate.

The donation of gametes and pre-embryos is reversible where the donor needs them for him or her self in order to overcome his or her own infertility, as long as they are available and the donor is willing to meet the costs (art. 5-2, ARTA). It seems to be the case, based on art. 11-4, ARTA, that, once two years have passed, and allowing for this possible exception, gametes and pre-embryos will remain at the Bank's disposal for a five year period.

8. Storage Regulations and Destruction

From arts. 11-1 and 11-4, ARTA, it can be inferred that after five years the stored gametes and pre-embryos must be either used or destroyed, given that cryopreservation will be no longer authorised.

Note

1. The forthcoming enactment of two decrees-law has now been announced by the media (*El País* (Madrid) 7 November 1995). These concern the requirements for the authorisation of ART Centres, protocols of donors and users, and registers of donors and of preembryos.

INDEX OF NAMES

INDEX OF SUBJECTS